Unlimited action

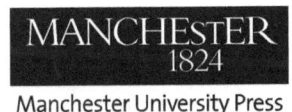
Manchester University Press

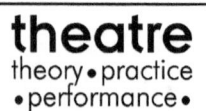

theatre
theory • practice
• performance •

series editors
MARIA M. DELGADO
MAGGIE B. GALE
PETER LICHTENFELS

advisory board
Michael Billington, Sandra Hebron, Mark Ravenhill, Janelle Reinelt, Peter Sellars, Joanne Tompkins

This series will offer a space for those people who practise theatre to have a dialogue with those who think and write about it.

The series has a flexible format that refocuses the analysis and documentation of performance. It provides, presents and represents material which is written by those who make or create performance history, and offers access to theatre documents, different methodologies and approaches to the art of making theatre.

The books in the series are aimed at students, scholars, practitioners and theatre-visiting readers. They encourage reassessments of periods, companies and figures in twentieth-century and twenty-first-century theatre history, and provoke and take up discussions of cultural strategies and legacies that recognise the heterogeneity of performance studies.

also available

Directing scenes and senses: The thinking of Regie
PETER M. BOENISCH

The Paris Jigsaw: Internationalism and the city's stages
DAVID BRADBY AND MARIA M. DELGADO (EDS)

Theatre in crisis? Performance manifestos for a new century
MARIA M. DELGADO AND CARIDAD SVICH (EDS)

World stages, local audiences: Essays on performance, place, and politics
PETER DICKINSON

Performing presence: Between the live and the simulated
GABRIELLA GIANNACHI AND NICK KAYE

Performance in a time of terror: Critical mimesis and the age of uncertainty
JENNY HUGHES

South African performance and the archive of memory
YVETTE HUTCHISON

Jean Genet and the politics of theatre: Spaces of revolution
CARL LAVERY

After '89: Polish theatre and the political
BRYCE LEASE

Not magic but work: An ethnographic account of a rehearsal process
GAY MCAULEY

'Love me or kill me': Sarah Kane and the theatre of extremes
GRAHAM SAUNDERS

Trans-global readings: Crossing theatrical boundaries
CARIDAD SVICH

Negotiating cultures: Eugenio Barba and the intercultural debate
IAN WATSON (ED.)

Unlimited action

The performance of extremity in the 1970s

DOMINIC JOHNSON

Manchester University Press

The right of Dominic Johnson to be identified as the author of this work has been asserted by him in accordance with the Copyright, Designs and Patents Act 1988.

Published by Manchester University Press
Altrincham Street, Manchester M1 7JA

www.manchesteruniversitypress.co.uk

British Library Cataloguing-in-Publication Data
A catalogue record for this book is available from the British Library

ISBN 978 0 7190 9160 5   hardback
ISBN 978 1 5261 3551 3   paperback

First published 2019

The publisher has no responsibility for the persistence or accuracy of URLs for any external or third-party internet websites referred to in this book, and does not guarantee that any content on such websites is, or will remain, accurate or appropriate.

Typeset by Servis Filmsetting Ltd, Stockport, Cheshire

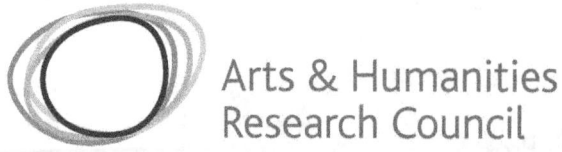

For Brian Routh, aka Harry Kipper (9 March 1948–3 August 2018)

CONTENTS

List of figures   *page* viii
Acknowledgements   xi

Introduction: Performance – action – extremity   1

1   The preferred ordeal   30
2   A criminal touch   62
3   The dirtying intention   90
4   Impossible things   124
5   The art of sabotage   155

Conclusion: Reckless people   188

References   206
Index   214

FIGURES

0.1   Ana Mendieta, *Moffitt Building Piece* (1973), 35 mm colour slide,
           document of performance © The Estate of Ana Mendieta Collection,
           LLC. Courtesy Galerie Lelong, New York   *page 2*
1.1–1.5   Kerry Trengove, *An Eight Day Passage*, photographs from a
           durational performance, The Acme Gallery, London, 25 October to
           1 November 1977. Courtesy Acme, Acme Archive   31–42
1.6   Kerry Trengove, *Solo*, photograph from a durational performance,
           The Acme Gallery, London, 17–30 June 1979. Courtesy Acme, Acme
           Archive   59
2.1–2.2   Ulay, *There is a Criminal Touch to Art* (1976), film stills from the
           Berlin Action, Gelatin silver print, 20 × 25 cm, series of 18 works ©
           Ulay. Courtesy of the artist   65–69
2.3   Carl Spitzweg, *The Poor Poet* (*Der arme Poete*) (1839) © bpk/
           Nationalgalerie, SMB/Jörg P. Anders. Used with permission 79
2.4   Ulay, *Soliloquy* (1974), from the series *Renais sense*, Polaroid type
           107, 8.5 × 10.8 cm © Ulay. Courtesy of the artist   85
2.5   Ulay, *GEN.E.T.RATION ULTIMA RATIO* (1972), Polaroid type 107,
           10.8 × 8.5 cm © Ulay. Courtesy of the artist   87
3.1   COUM Transmissions, *Omissions* (1975), performance, Kiel,
           Germany. Courtesy of Genesis BREYER P-ORRIDGE and Invisible-
           Exports, New York   93
3.2   Genesis P-Orridge, *Untitled* (*Time Transfixed*), postcard with
           collaged elements sent to 'Ted Glass', 27 November 1975 © Genesis
           BREYER P-ORRIDGE. Courtesy of the artist and Invisible-Exports,
           New York   103

3.3   COUM Transmissions, *Mail Action* (1976), documentation of solo
        action by Genesis P-Orridge, Highbury Corner Magistrates Court,
        London. Photographs by Barbara Reise © Genesis BREYER
        P-ORRIDGE. Courtesy of the artist and Invisible-Exports, New
        York. *The group includes Genesis P-Orridge (top centre), Ian
        Breakwell, Richard Cork, Colin Naylor, David Offenbach and Pauline
        Smith.*   109

3.4   Cosey Fanni Tutti, *Tessa from Sunderland, Park Lane, Issue 12*
        (1975–76), Magazine Action. Colour print on paper. Courtesy the
        artist and Cabinet, London   117

3.5   Genesis P-Orridge, *Untitled (Thee Reel Mee)*, postcard with collaged
        elements sent to Barbara Reise, 28 October 1976 © Genesis BREYER
        P-ORRIDGE. Courtesy of the artist and Invisible-Exports, New York   119

4.1   Anne Bean, *Imposters* (1971), action with Natasha Lawrence and
        Malcolm Jones, London. Photograph by Martin von Haselberg.
        Courtesy of Anne Bean   126

4.2   Anne Bean, *Digging a Hole in Water* (1973), Essex University.
        Photograph by Martin von Haselberg. Courtesy of Anne Bean   127

4.3   Anne Bean, *Ghost of a Shadow, Shadow of a Ghost* (1972), Reading
        University. Photograph by Graham Challifour. Courtesy of Anne
        Bean   134

4.4   Anne Bean, *Low Flying Aircraft* (1980), with Paul Burwell, Vanguard
        Gallery, Los Angeles. Photograph by Charles Hill. Courtesy of Anne
        Bean   137

4.5   Anne Bean, Paul Burwell and Paul McCarthy, *Two Ps and a Bean*
        (1983), Bow, London. Photograph by Linda Frye Burnham. Courtesy
        of Anne Bean   151

5.1   The Kipper Kids, untitled performance, Vanguard Gallery, Los
        Angeles, 1978. Photograph by Dorothy L. Hailey © The Kipper Kids.
        Courtesy of Martin von Haselberg   157

5.2   The Kipper Kids, untitled performance, Saletta Gramsci, Pistoia,
        Italy, 1980. Photograph by Dorothy L. Hailey © The Kipper Kids.
        Courtesy of Martin von Haselberg   159

5.3   The Kipper Kids, untitled performance, Whisky a Go Go, Los
        Angeles, 1978. Photograph by Dorothy L. Hailey © The Kipper Kids.
        Courtesy of Martin von Haselberg   161

5.4   The Kipper Kids, untitled performance, Los Angeles Institute of
        Contemporary Art (LAICA), Los Angeles, 1974 © The Kipper Kids.
        Courtesy of Martin von Haselberg   168

5.5   The Kipper Kids, *Up Yer Bum With a Bengal Lancer* (1976),
        production photograph for video-performance © The Kipper Kids.
        Courtesy of Martin von Haselberg   180

5.6   The Kipper Kids, *K. O. Kippers* (1988), dir. by Miroslav Janek,

Cinemax, production photograph on set © The Kipper Kids.
Courtesy of Martin von Haselberg   184

6.1   Stephen Cripps, *Cripps at the Acme: Drawings & Performances*,
       photograph of Stephen Cripps performing, 9–17 May 1980. Courtesy
       Acme, Acme Archive   189

6.2   Stephen Cripps, *Cripps at the Acme: Performances*, photograph of
       Stephen Cripps after a performance, 1–5 June 1981. Courtesy Acme,
       Acme Archive   191

6.3   Anne Bean, Paul Burwell and Paul McCarthy, *Two Ps and a Bean*
       (1983), Bow, London. Photograph by Linda Frye Burnham. Courtesy
       of Anne Bean   197

6.4   Stephen Cripps, untitled action with Paul Burwell, Museum of
       Modern Art Oxford, 1979. Photograph by Michael Heindorff.
       Stephen Cripps Archive © The Family of Stephen Cripps, Courtesy
       of Leeds Museums and Galleries (Henry Moore Institute Archive)   200

6.5   Stephen Cripps, *Notes on a Dance for Jets and Helicopters* (c.1978–
       82), ink drawing on paper with collaged elements. Stephen Cripps
       Archive © The Family of Stephen Cripps, Courtesy of Leeds
       Museums and Galleries (Henry Moore Institute Archive)   202

6.6   Stephen Cripps (*Missile*) *Organ* (c.1978–82), ink drawing with
       collaged elements on card. Stephen Cripps Archive © The Family of
       Stephen Cripps, Courtesy of Leeds Museums and Galleries (Henry
       Moore Institute Archive)   203

ACKNOWLEDGEMENTS

The last was an object to be destroyed. At its launch in 2015, my book – an oral history of performance art – was tied to helium-filled balloons by Anne Bean, who stripped pages from its core and sang cutups from its words. After some minutes, the balloons lifted the book beyond her reach, allowing the exalted tatters of my authorship to nestle in the eaves of the chapel that accommodated its launching. A year later, the book fell into the hands of Ulay, who soaked and froze it, then prised open its glacial mass with the heat of his concentration and of his fingers, finally to open the bifurcated fossil on its broken spine: fortuitously, even spookily, on a spread that displayed Ulay himself, photographed in the act of stealing a painting.

If Anne Bean exposed my book's internal dream to be a parody of transcendence, Ulay's action staged the immobilising of practical knowledge – the halting or chilling effect of intellectual capture – that history (this history) sometimes must engender. The most sympathetic of approaches – the loving will to knowledge, the spirit of its pursuit and the care of its conduct – is a thing to be forever revisited, they seemed to declare; it must be held up to anomalous acts of scrutiny or otherwise contested, even destroyed. It was a rare pleasure to see artists respond to scholarship, *as one leveraged it open and the other set it free*. Their performances were object lessons in the continuous work of critical disputation that we might turn upon ourselves as writers, as artists or as readers. In writing the present book, I hope I have paid attention to their instruction.

The process of writing *Unlimited Action* began with a question about hardship and was turned on its head by endurance, friendship, death, generosity and good fortune. I am profoundly grateful to the artists I interviewed or corresponded with and who opened, variously, their homes, studios or archives to me: Anne Bean, Genesis BREYER P-ORRIDGE, Brian Routh and Martin von Haselberg (the Kipper Kids) and Ulay.

Generous funding from the Arts and Humanities Research Council (AHRC) in the form of a two-year Early Career Fellowship (2014–16) allowed me relief from teaching and administration in the Department of Drama at Queen Mary University of London and provided resources to undertake primary research and public engagement activities that pushed this writing forward.

I have benefited from the support and encouragement of current and former colleagues at Queen Mary and the friendly yet tough shepherding of ideas that its research culture fosters. I am especially grateful to Julia Bardsley, Shane Boyle, Maria Delgado, Jen Harvie, Eirini Kartsaki, Aoife Monks, Martin O'Brien, Daniel Oliver, Catherine Silverstone and Lois Weaver – and additionally, my collaborators in the Sexual Cultures Research Group, especially Nadia Atia and Sam McBean.

This book found an ideal home in the series 'Theatre: Theory – Practice – Performance' at Manchester University Press. I offer my deepest gratitude to series editors Maria Delgado, Maggie Gale and Peter Lichtenfels. I also thank Matthew Frost and his colleagues at Manchester University Press for their support.

In 2015, I was provided with space and time to think and write for three months as a Visiting Scholar at QueerLab, University of California Riverside, thanks to an invitation and support from Jennifer Doyle. While there, I shared early parts of the introduction at *Overstimulated: The Limits of Performance*, an AHRC-funded event Jennifer and I co-convened at Human Resources, Los Angeles, on Valentine's Day 2015. The speakers – Nao Bustamante, Cassils, Jennifer Doyle, Zackary Drucker, Amelia Jones and Sheree Rose – and the keynote performance by La Congelada de Uva (Rocío Boliver) and Thibault Delférière blew much of my thinking out of all reasonable proportion and I am indebted to them all for their extremity. I returned to the USA in 2016 as Global Visiting Scholar in the Center for the Study of Gender and Sexuality at New York University, which afforded me three further months and additional resources to finish a first full draft. I am grateful to Ann Pellegrini and Tavia Nyong'o for extending their invitation.

The AHRC afforded me two postdoctoral research assistants. I thank Harriet Curtis and Eleanor Roberts for the meticulous support they provided.

Three institutional archives were especially crucial to this research. I thank, first, the Live Art Development Agency for its Study Room (a singular archive for performance and live art in the UK and Europe) and its co-directors Lois Keidan and C. J. Mitchell for their consistent encouragement and friendship; second, the Acme Gallery Archive at Acme, London, where Arantxa Echarte and Jonathan Harvey gave me privileged access to materials relating to Kerry Trengove and Stephen Cripps; and third, the Stephen Cripps Archive at the Henry Moore Institute, Leeds, where Claire Mayoh, Lisa LeFeuvre and Jon Wood were supportive and kind. I am grateful to the staff at: Tate Archives, British Library, and Foyle Reading Room at Whitechapel Gallery, London; National Review of Live Art Video Archive, University of Bristol; Fales Library, New York University; and Getty Research Library, Los Angeles. I also thank William Raban for generously sharing his archival film materials.

The development of several chapters benefited from comments and questions by audiences at research seminars and lectures I presented at: University of York; University of Essex; Roski School of Art and Design, University of Southern

California (Los Angeles); Edinburgh College of Art; MU Eindhoven; School of the Art Institute of Chicago; Henry Moore Institute (Leeds); Wellcome Collection (London); Aksioma Project Space (Ljubljana); De Montfort University (Leicester); Cooper Gallery (Dundee); Sotheby's (London); Royal Academy (London); and Royal College of Art (London). For their invitations I thank Jo Applin, Amy Tobin, Catherine Spencer, Jason Edwards, Matt Lodder, Amelia Jones, Fiona Anderson and Glyn Davis, Cassils, David Getsy, Sandra Reimann, Sally Rose, Janez Janša, Paisid Aramphongphan, Sophia Yadong Hao, Pierre Saurisse, Eliza Bonham Carter and Nigel Rolfe.

An earlier, shorter version of Chapter 3 is published as 'File Under COUM: Art on Trial in Genesis P-Orridge's *Mail Action*' in *London Art Worlds: Mobile, Contingent, and Ephemeral Networks, 1960–1980*, ed. by Jo Applin, Catherine Spencer and Amy Tobin (University Park: Pennsylvania State University Press, 2018), pp. 183–99. Revised excerpts from the conclusion are published as 'A Pyrotechnics of the Mind: The Performances of Stephen Cripps in Context' in *Stephen Cripps: Performance Machines*, ed. by Sandra Beate Reimann, exh. cat., Museum Tinguely, Basel (Vienna: Verlag für Moderne Kunst), pp. 33–8.

Conversations with critical friends helped me to experiment in my approach and to hone my thinking around extremity – and my writing about performance more broadly: in particular I offer and reiterate my heartfelt thanks and affection to Oreet Ashery, Ron Athey, Franko B, Gavin Butt, Cassils, Jennifer Doyle, David Getsy, Amelia Jones, Lois Keidan, Slava Mogutin, Martin O'Brien, Kira O'Reilly and Manuel Vason.

Finally, thanks and love to Seb Castle, for his kindness and his cuteness.

Introduction: Performance – action – extremity

A deluge of blood seeps to the street beneath her whitewashed door. Incidental viewers stop to look at, ostentatiously avoid or miss it altogether. Flowing outwards, the blood's viscous wetness soaks the worn taupe of her welcome mat in a coagulating puddle, leaching in six or more mounting rivulets of gore to encroach upon the blankness of the pavement and the day. It is a slender slice of awfulness, this scene: compulsive and unexplained, as in a world of dream. The main gush of blood looks livid red, the rest a russet brown.

The performance at hand is *Moffitt Building Piece* (1973) by the Cuban-American artist Ana Mendieta. It was undertaken in front of the battered entrance to her home in Iowa City and filmed on a single Super-8 reel and captured on slides by the artist secreted in a car parked across from the spectacle (**Figure 0.1**). Mendieta's action was one in a series in which she explored the culture of sexual violence against women, prompted by the rape and murder of a fellow student earlier the same year. Mendieta sourced animal blood and mingled it with scraps of meat so as to stage a deceptively simple but devastating piece in which an unsuspecting series of viewers would fall upon a scene of apparent misadventure or crisis (it would be unclear to viewers if the fluid was blood – and if it was human blood) prompting their own micro-performances of astonishment, bewilderment or obliviousness.

The active source of the torrent remains obscured and inexorable, enabling the scene's spectacular strangeness and a political aspect of its experience. As Julia Bryan-Wilson writes of the action, Mendieta 'created a situation that unfolded unpredictably over time, in which the bodies [of passers by] were visibly marked by gender, age, race and class' on account of the way we might read a relation between their appearances, their identities and their performed reactions – even if the unmarked body that represents the source of the bloody irrigation remains 'unknown and unknowable' to the

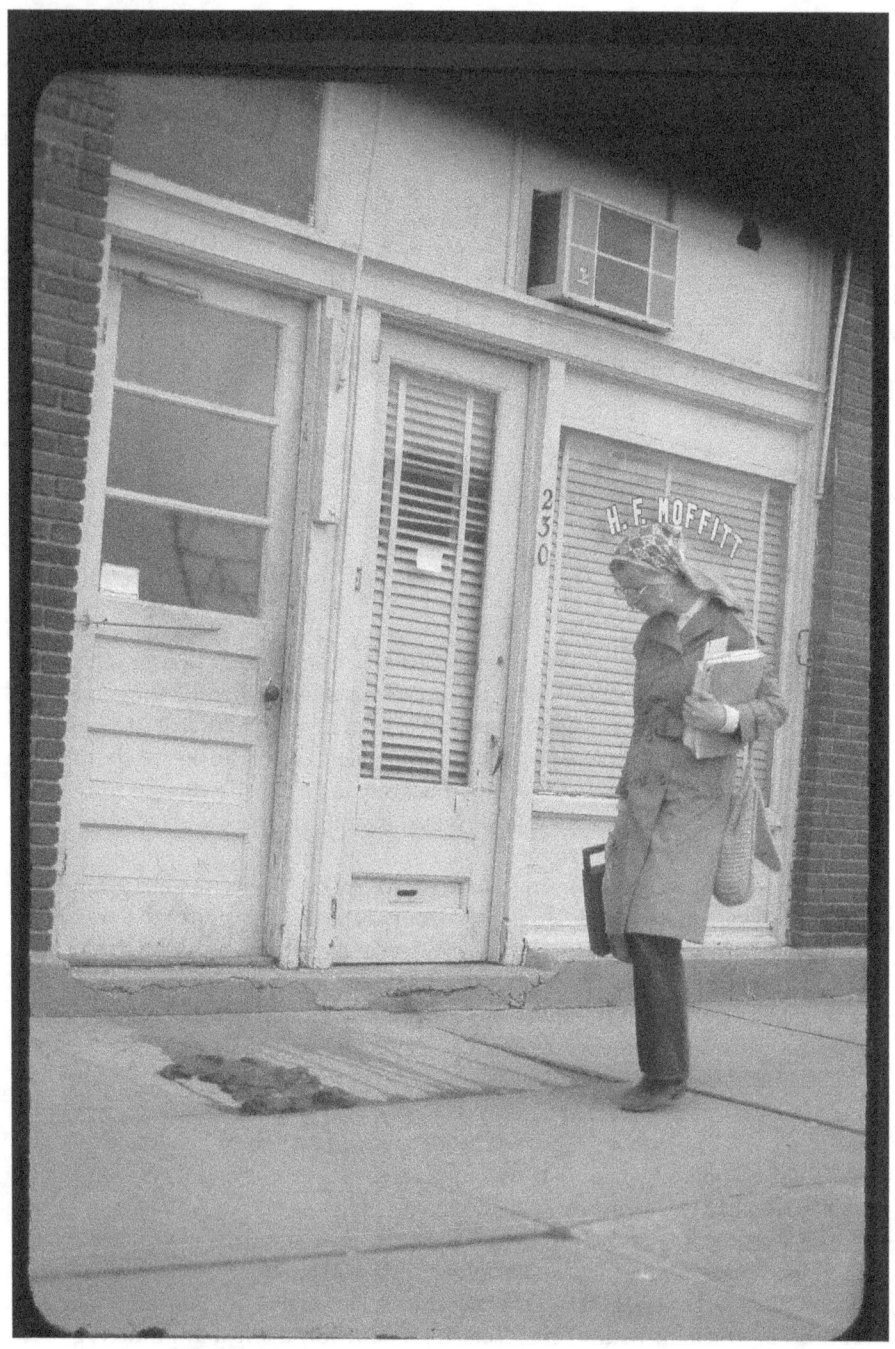

0.1 Ana Mendieta, *Moffitt Building Piece* (1973), 35 mm colour slide, document of performance © The Estate of Ana Mendieta Collection, LLC, courtesy Galerie Lelong, New York

witnesses (Bryan-Wilson 2014: 27). The action is a minor epic of interpersonal disaster for which there is no clear victim or perpetrator. Freighted neither by a performer nor an audience according to conventional expectations of each term, the performance is built around a visual sign that makes meaning in unexplained (but explicable) ways. In the context of Mendieta's other works, *Moffitt Building Piece* asks how the singularity of blood (a woman's blood, Latinx blood) burdens the field of vision. Across her performances, she imagines a fuller range of incidental abandonments, from normal filth to fantastical excrescences: say, of garbage, dust, fire, blood, bones or a corpse (of human or of bird); the street, a home or a field becomes a crime scene, a grave, a site of spontaneous combustion or a makeshift altar for a humble mess of flowers.

In *Moffitt Building Piece*, Mendieta uses a modest tactic – a prank or stunt of sorts (but one that is no lark) – to pose a series of nuanced ethical questions: Who may notice the blood, even investigate its source? With how reduced a palette and with how distilled an action might a performance create a visceral relation or a lasting impact? With what effects might the incidental viewer, suddenly a witness, ignore (or indeed seek to intervene in) whatever crimes might appear to be occurring behind closed doors? The poet Claudia Rankine writes tellingly of the experience of public invisibility, witnessing the way this clashes with intimate scenes of racialised and sexualised insult or affray: 'Each moment is like this – before it can be known, categorized as similar to another thing and dismissed, it has to be experienced, it has to be seen' (Rankine 2015: 9). The spectacle at hand demands itself to be seen, experienced and properly known – even, paradoxically, when some refuse to look.

Many do not see the bloodshed at their feet. Some pause hard to look at this slender pageantry of another's distress – and then walk on. Others keep strolling but look back. Few stop. Some peer up at the window above, perhaps to check for the sound or sight of commotion that one might report or else to manifest the home more evidently as a house of horror. One woman pokes the clotting viscera with her umbrella. Another, carrying books, walks haphazardly through the mounting carnage at Mendieta's doorstop, bloodying her shoes but oblivious to the scene.

In the 1970s, performance artists devised actions, whether simple or convoluted, which privileged or prioritised the contingent materiality of the body of the performer – and, inevitably perhaps, the bodies of her, his or their audiences. Artists did so, as Mendieta's action suggests, through performed images that brought suffering, survival, agency, pleasure or desire to the fore of our awareness, staging activities that foreground how we think and feel about or engage with history, with others and with our surroundings. Performance art did not originate in the 1970s: an authoritative genealogy by RoseLee Goldberg reads it as emerging circuitously from the European avant-garde experiments of Futurism, Bauhaus, Surrealism and Dada in the early twentieth century (Goldberg 1979: 9–78). Yet the 1970s are significant for the trenchant ways artists revivified performance art's forms to animate the ways we interact with (to confirm, challenge, pleasure or injure) the bodies of others and inhabit and transform the spaces of our world. In doing so, performance artists depended on a multiple articulation to histories of fine art and experimental theatre, as well as to other genealogies: rethinking, refining or rejecting the tendencies or values they identified in sculpture, painting, plays, Happenings, dance, poetry, music or sound. The relation of performance art to theatre, in particular – as continuation or repudiation – is hotly contested: perhaps a kind of unresolvable and reluctant relation of indebtedness. The artist and critic Scott Burton notes as much in a short essay of 1970, where the link between performance art and theatre depends upon their distinctive inhabitations of the audience's time and attention. Works of performance art are:

> categorizable as 'theatre' [to the extent that] they can only be experienced in extension, as processes or sequences in time, and they control the audience's length and rate of exposure (the opposite is true of reading a book or looking at a painting). But these works . . . are unlike traditional dramatic art because they exist explicitly in the same, actual time as that of the viewer instead of offering fictive times and places. They are not illusionistic but literalist theatre pieces. (Burton 2012: 222–3)

In occupying and exposing time and attention in this way and by opposing historical conventions of theatrical time and place, performance artists subjected their bodies to duration, repetition, pain, injury, sociality or duress; to actions undertaken frequently without regard for the traditional demonstration of skill, technique or training (in contrast to the virtuosic use of performance in, say, theatre, music or dance); and to activities that appropriated modes of being and doing that seem to belong to 'non-art' domains of practice, like work, play, love, sport, vaudeville or crime.

In their apparent exceptionality, many signature performance actions of the 1970s might to contemporary eyes look gratuitous, odd, illegible or unwarranted. This novelty or difficulty inherent to performance art was (and still is) partly the point: the anomalous body practices that artists pursued would enable them to depart from the orthodoxies that clung (and cling) to institutional and other traditions of art-making, criticism and reception; and such practices also exposed or exploded the social checks placed on bodily comportment and daily performances of identity and selfhood. Existing at a limit – of art or the social, of bodily integrity and comfort – extremity is written into existing accounts of what performance art is and does. For example, Edward Scheer writes that 'performance art provokes [a] crisis of representation as part of its core aesthetic', as 'by presenting the body (usually of the artist) as the central motif of the artwork, the representational frame of the work is disturbed, its referentiality is disordered by the forceful engagement of the work with the presence of the artist' (Scheer 2010: 219).

Karen Gonzalez Rice addresses this function in her study of the 'prophetic' power of endurance art. 'In the face of physical and psychic extremity', she writes, the performance artist 'simultaneously embodies ethos and pathos, death and survival, vulnerability and discipline, victimhood and heroic agency' (Gonzalez Rice 2016: 4). For Gonzalez Rice, performance actions are legible as 'both pathology *and* art' and both 'respond to trauma *and* constitute ethical relations' (*ibid.*, emphasis in original), suggesting that a performance, in its extremity, may vacillate on a series of highly volatile distinctions: between the acceptable and the unacceptable, truth and fiction, stigmatisation and apologia, reckless activity and anomalous strategy – or, finally, between the stuff of art and the praxis of an irredeemably precarious life.

This apparent excess or eccentricity – this art's *extremity* – has been significant despite or because of the aesthetic revolutions that emerged or intensified in vigour in the 1960s; indeed, performance art both drew from and heightened the aesthetic challenges posed by conceptual art, do-it-yourself art, Happenings and experimental film – all forms for which performance was in fact typical, fundamental or exemplary. An imperative of performance art – to identify and overcome the limits of form – complemented and extended the historical priority of much advanced art after modernism *tout court*. As John Roberts writes, modernism accepted or realised 'art as a historical category that logically cannot be submitted to limits or norms, outside, that is, of the *negation* of the negation of negation'; after modernism and in a more intensified manner in the 'post-conceptual' terrain of art after the 1960s, 'to make art is at the same time to *define* art, to subject it to a process of self-scrutiny on the basis of art's historically and socially constructed norms' (Roberts 2015: 11, emphasis in original). Yet performance art in the 1970s is not simply camouflaged against a general backdrop of mutual and sustained excess. It stands out as a repertoire of its own particular extremity, despite the superlative nature of its moment.

The central problem of *Unlimited Action* is to attribute a kind of troubled legibility to performance's extremity, while opening up a scope for less well-known works whose historical marginality is also crucially at play. If extremity assumes a limit, what might we make of the borders, gaps or ruptures between art and its purported outsides? How are the distinctions between the aesthetic and the extra- or anti-aesthetic staged, upheld or transgressed in works of art and in our critical encounters? How do we historicise and theorise the works and practices that subsist as and beyond a limit of the aesthetic? What is at stake in celebrating works of art for their extremity (which is always relative), their difference (which is surmountable) or their novelty (which can be neutralised by repetition or acceptance)? How does one attend to the event's apparent luxation from time in its excessiveness, its dislocation from the past as a singularity, without pretending it assumes the same inverse grandeur as real atrocity, whose limits must exceed those of the paradigmatically consensual space of art, however unsurpassable, strange or destitute the latter might sometimes appear? Performances such as the ones foregrounded throughout this book, beginning with Mendieta's *Moffitt Building Piece*, stage their own social extremity, as painful, isolated, dangerous or anomalous actions and as facts of life. They tend to lack, reject or annihilate the formal properties that often seem to signal an activity or object's proper status as art. As such, the performances will often seem to relegate themselves to the purported outside of art. Yet the discourse of art may overcome, contain or at least make nonsensical the contention of art's specificity or the apparently insurmountable difference or distance between itself and something else. When a work of art appears to be exceptional or inassimilable, has a limit been crossed – or was it less a boundary than a yet-unseen path to be taken?

Unlimited Action undertakes a counterhistory, depicting a series of encounters between acts of performance and the limits against which they brace. I account for actions whose makers often struggled – or patently refused – to acknowledge the status of their works straightforwardly as works of art; and others still whose performances were denied such a status by others or were barred or deterred from being made at all. Moreover, I discuss actions that have generally slipped below or beyond the purview of the critical and scholarly establishments of art in the 1970s. How, then, might a broader history be constituted for performance art and proximate media, bigger than or beyond the ones given in previous accounts, from the late 1960s onwards? The project of what I call *the performance of extremity* – and of the thinking and writing it might give rise to – enables or requires an excessive route of imaginative action, then feels out the borders and boundaries of the possible and the impossible. By learning what is more than enough, in part to suggest what may be known (in itself, and as *enough*), the performance of extremity endeavours to engage, anatomise and finally overcome one's limits as a maker, viewer or critic.

The horizon of performance art in the 1970s includes actions presented for live audiences (often small, intimate or invited ones), as well as 'stealth' interventions with incidental audiences. It also includes private or intimate performances to camera, whose audiences only ever accessed the event by still or moving images. Its histories also includes works that exist only in hearsay or otherwise as heavily obscured, embellished anecdotes, either because the conditions under which they were made preclude documentation or authentication or because their mythic quality is written into the very idea of the performance. Throughout, difficulty, singularity or anomaly produces or sustains a work's own critical legend. For example, the suggestive power of a work such as Chris Burden's *747* (1973) capitalises on this self-mythologising aspect of performance art. A photograph by Terry McConnell seems to confirm the facticity of the performance – in tandem with the artist's written statement, the photograph authenticates the narrative that Burden shot bullets at an overhead aircraft with a pistol – but the image only evidences that Burden held a handgun aloft and aimed it at the Boeing as it passed through the frame. Either way, the idea of the performance works its provocative magic, staging the profound risks that accompany art's seemingly final (but serial) breaks with form. In *747*, the threat of criminal damage, mass death and personal ignominy ground the formal challenge that confirms the action as a performance, despite the lack of a live audience, a stable object or the facticity of his claims. Uncertainty, notoriety and doubt form part of such a work's existential charm.

Burden is perhaps the best-known performance artist to have worked with endurance, ordeal or self-directed hardship in the 1970s. A kind of notoriety was conferred upon or claimed by the artist when he was shot in the arm with a rifle (*Shoot*, 1971); threatened his own death by electrocution (*Doorway to Heaven*, 1973); invited an audience to force thumbtacks into his skin (*Back to You*, 1974); crucified on a car bonnet (*Trans-Fixed*, 1974); or kicked to fall down a concrete stairwell (*Kunst Kick*, 1974), among other actions. (The brevity with which I describe these performances can only compound their excessiveness, their internal sense of desperation or apparent gratuitousness.) As Donald Kuspit writes, Burden's 'early self-torturing performances were unusually foolhardy – more extreme than the typical avant-garde risk-taking' associated with avant-gardism and artistic experimentation (Kuspit 1988: 37).

Over a short but intensive period of activity between 1971 and 1975 (though he continued to perform until 1984), Burden presented now-classic performance actions that typically put him in situations of physical risk, heralded the threat of injury or death, activated the audience as participants by implicating them inside difficult events and prompted other conditions of indeterminacy, laying a ground for the performance of extremity. If Burden's actions – like those of many other artists in the period – lend themselves to disapprobation, misapprehension, hyperbole or caricature, they pushed art to a certain limit, particularly by exposing the agency of his audience, curators or passers-by and their implicit complicity in his own physical (sometimes potentially mortal) endangerment.

Burden's exemplarity was reluctant, at least retrospectively: by the 1980s, he would begin to distance himself from the causative power of his earlier landmark works as an apologist of sorts for the broader excesses of the performance of extremity. Yet Burden's actions were among the most visible – and remain the best remembered and most efficiently contained – in a vast repertoire of instances of performance art that redefined the limits of art in the 1970s. The extreme aspect of such work is overwhelmed in its writing by the alien or unnamed situations one is cast into – *cast* as in *thrown*, but also in its theatrical sense of being induced to play a role, dressed in fraught styles of witnessing, doing and showing. The performance of extremity, then, involves acts of physical, emotional or conceptual excess – extremes of too much or not enough – to an extent that harasses the artist, us and the category of art; yet, crucially, in its resistant or elusive character, the performance of extremity also invites the means to dislodge the narrative already established of performance art in a given context.

Extremity is a promiscuous or tendentious word. It vacillates in its attribution to performance or art and pulls into its orbit a whole host of other significations. Extremity might broadly suggest violence, pornography, criminality, misanthropy, danger, recklessness, eccentricity or obscurantism and a host of other variously taboo, undesirable or repulsive spheres of activity or feeling. Outside of art it recalls the apparently wanton risks associated with extreme sports, like free-fall parachuting, parkour, bare knuckle fist-fighting or white water rafting, where a feat's gratuitousness, sublimity and pleasure are self-legitimising for the practitioner; the newly forged legal concept of extreme pornography, which in Britain criminalises – and thus expels from the aesthetic realm – the representation of violent and non-consensual actions, but also demonises marginal sexual practices that are non-violent (like female ejaculation, watersports or fisting); or extreme body modification, in which physical pressure, strenuous training and time (or do-it-yourself surgery) fashion new holes or alien contours in human flesh or move bones and cartilage into unexpected silhouettes; or else extremity recalls extravagances of feeling, association, irrational belief or action, including religious or political extremism, militancy or fanaticism, typified in the narcissistic bravado of radical ascetics, suicide-bombing, self-immolation or Yukio Mishima's *Seppuku*. Extremity reminds me, too, of the extremities of the body, of fingers, toes or genitals – the pieces of oneself that interpenetrate with other bodies and objects in the sensible world, often sensually or painfully, when they slip inside or get succoured, snagged, sliced or severed by autonomous things outside ourselves, are licked or fondled, caught in machinery or trapped in doors. The performance of extremity engages and eclipses the sensationalism of these preceding associations, but tightens the promise of performance art by posing the question of how post-war art – typified, historically, by postmodernism and its aftermaths – provoked the expansion or hopeful dissolution of the category of art itself.

Action

For Frazer Ward, canonical works of performance art in the 1970s – Burden's *Shoot* in which he was shot, Vito Acconci's *Seedbed* (1972) where he concealed himself masturbating beneath a ramp, and Marina Abramović's *Rhythm 0* (1974) in which she offered herself as a sacrificial object to the ultimately violent whims of her audience – may represent 'the result of a logic of escalating extremity at work within avant-garde circles' in contemporary art and thus became (he writes with some caveats) 'icons of the 1970s heyday of experimental and frequently confrontational performance art' (Ward 2012: 2). The precedence of injurious, risky or indecent activities in these and other iconic works is not gratuitous but signals, for Ward, 'the physical and/or psychological extremity and intensity' that typified experimentation in art in the 1970s (2012: 2). He explains that the new possibilities, however surprising or distasteful to some, were prompted or enabled by earlier transformations in the social milieu of the 1960s. These included artistic or aesthetic possibilities, notably for him the way minimalism commanded the viewer as an active component in the completion or activation of the work, such that the sobriety of minimalist sculpture enabled or invited a more potently embodied inhabitation of the newly activated milieu of art. The new uses of escalating extremity in art were also prompted, Ward suggests, by far-reaching social transformations, including new relations between public/private, inside/outside, as information moves more freely in and out of homes and institutions in unprecedented ways; the experience of art was remade as 'both public and embodied' in a context of new technologies of commerce and communications and of progressive but sometimes frightening reorganisations of the politics of the intimate and the personal sphere, including the politics of identity (2012: 6–8).

The subsequent transformations in art and performance were necessarily frightening to the old guard, prompting charges that the emperor wasn't wearing any clothes, the clowns were now running the circus and the barbarians were at the gates. The art historian and philologist Thomas McEvilley notes that after the late 1950s, the category of art became 'virtually unrecognizable to those who had thought it was theirs', namely, to academic artists, gallerists and critics. He continues, 'art activity flowed into the darkness beyond its traditional boundaries and explored areas that were previously as unmapped and mysterious as the other side of the moon' (McEvilley 2005: 233). Artists embraced the 'dark side' in both senses, as the hidden (or occulted) aspects of the semantic category of art, as well as the nihilistic, creepy or Dionysian underside of life. Specifically, McEvilley argues, performance art dragged the expanded or exploded category of art into a face-to-face encounter with physical, psychological and interpersonal extremity, often by reminding us of 'the awkward embarrassments of living in a body' (2005: 217). These provocations are germane to the emotional, physiological or sentimental – even, at times, seemingly metaphysical – limits encountered in *Unlimited Action*.

In performance art of the 1970s, I privilege a specific – though perhaps nebulous – model of performance, namely the *action*. 'Action' became a keyword for art after the publication of Harold Rosenberg's influential essay 'Mobile, Theatrical, Active' in *Art in America* in 1964. In the same moment that Ward identifies as a crucible of sorts for subsequent practices in performance, Rosenberg observed the emergence of new modes of painting and sculpture that were 'striving to become something different than pictures on the wall or forms quietly standing in the corner of a room', suggesting, rather, new kinds of images and objects with 'an unmistakable impulse to erupt into the life around them' (Rosenberg 1966: 259). The mobile, theatrical, active art Rosenberg witnessed in its emergence in the 1960s innovated by way of an 'active art' and an 'artist-actor', two surprising and simultaneous novelties that require that art 'is not merely shown', but 'puts on a show and solicits audience participation' (1966: 260). To complete itself as a temporal, spatial and deictic form, artists subsequently placed the performing body – living, breathing, shitting, pissing, suffering, loving, dying – at the core of art marking, displacing painting and sculpture as ends to point far outside the conventional limits of art's substantive objecthood, in acts of desublimation that often entailed (as McEvilley identified) seemingly negative, nihilistic or destructive effects.

The new 'art as action' drew upon contingent experiments in a new sensorium of art, including Happenings, street theatre, expanded cinema, protest performances and new dance, adding grist to the mill of the conservative antipathy towards art's newly vaunted theatricality, ephemerality and aesthetic strangeness. In painting's move towards showing itself as labour (especially in action painting) and the wholesale renovation of activity that it licensed, art undertook a formative turn to action, with '*doing* replacing *making*' (Rosenberg 1966: 272, emphasis in original) in a critical move that would arguably find its feet in the 1970s, with the emergence of endurance art, ordeal art and hardship art – or, in a word, the vital realisation of performance as singular *action*. In the catalogue for his landmark exhibition *Out of Actions: Between Performance and the Object, 1949–1979*, Paul Schimmel defines action-based performance art in terms of 'an overriding preoccupation with the temporality of the act', giving rise to variously explosive, joyous, dangerous or destructive permutations of 'the execution of performative actions whose primary goal was the process of creation rather than the production of objects' (Schimmel 1998: 17). While remaining in dialogue with the traditions of fine art and of theatre, then, calling a work an 'action' signals a performance that subscribes to all or some of the following characteristics: singularity or unrepeatability; non-virtuosity; unrehearsed or unrehearsable activity; the activation of audiences in visceral or affective terms; an emphasis on the brute materiality of the body; extended or anticlimactic durations; social engagement in terms of the rejection of meanings in favour of the production of an effect; an emphasis on process over product; and a refusal of the commodity form in the creation of a work. An action could be actively solicitous, antagonistic or aggressive, novel or strange, funny or frightening, dangerous, thrilling, reckless,

provocative, exceptional or obscure; such affects are provoked in an action's undertaking as in its myth's retellings.

The performance of extremity

Not least as audiences, we are often intimately aware of our own contingent and evolv-
ing limits – be they physiological, emotional, ethical or moral. We may feel squeamish
before the creation of a wound in performance or cringe at the sight or smell of blood;
we may be struck shy by sexual acts or intimate overtures or become overextended
emotionally amid bloodless but exhaustingly sustained performances of endurance.
In any such instance, how does one deal with having been urged towards or even past
a certain limit? We might close our eyes or turn our face away, feel angry or offended
or bored, fall asleep, fall fainting on the floor, intervene in the performance or simply
leave. No such response is categorically separate from the function of the work – even
if our affective involvement sometimes feels like a distraction from, an insult to, or an
overdetermining factor in our reading. Anomalously, the perception of a performed
image is translated into a physiological response: our sweaty palms, flushes and
blushes, increased heartbeat, fainting, vomiting, fight or flight. What meanings are
foreclosed or produced in such reactions? By imposing or upholding a certain limit,
we say something in unconscious or pre-verbal terms: *this is too much, you've gone too
far; that is unacceptable, I've had enough.*

Along with works by, say, Ana Mendieta and Chris Burden, introduced thus
far, the history of performance art discloses many performances that may strike one
as extreme in the terms so far suggested. Some of these performances have already
breached the horizon of historical legibility – of legitimacy, even. A history of the
performance of extremity in the 1970s might include Carolee Schneemann, naked and
daubed in paint, reading a poem about oppression from a strip of paper she unravels
from her vagina, in *Interior Scroll* (1975); or William Pope.L preparing seemingly to
set himself ablaze at the doorway to a commercial gallery, using cheap fortified wine
as fuel in *Thunderbird Immolation* (1978); or Ulay and Marina Abramović's *Relation
Works* (1976–79), in which they variously ran naked towards and into each other
(*Relation in Space*, 1976), ran into walls (*Interruption in Space*, 1977), screamed into
the other's open mouth until their voices were lost (*AAA-AAA*, 1978), slapped one
another rhythmically (*Light/Dark*, 1977) or drove in interminable circles in a van
(*Relation in Movement*, 1977), each over durations that rendered a simple action
excruciating for the artists – and, perhaps, for some spectators, unfathomable. The
central problem of this book is to attribute a kind of troubled legibility to performance's extremity, specifically by opening up a scope for less well-known works
whose historical marginality is crucially at play and to think through the particular
challenges such works pose. This attempt does not negate or overcome the established
histories and theories of difficult or challenging performance art, but works in concert
with them.

Where performance art was violent, upsetting, erotic or otherwise overwhelming, its extremity was typically received in the service of a political, formal and/ or social function. For Amelia Jones and Kathy O'Dell, in their definitive accounts, performance artists in the 1960s and 1970s achieved such ends by revealing or exploiting our assumptions about how we engage with art, with the world or with others, challenging the ethical and cultural assumptions we make about the conventional, proper or inevitable shapes such engagement must take (Jones 1998; O'Dell, 1998). Yet regardless of its putative utility, the cumulative effect of all this formal, conceptual or emotional difficulty – sometimes, even, brutality – can make performance art of the 1970s seem uniformly transgressive or affronting to the viewer. In a benevolent exaggeration, written as a foil to her account of apparently more measured and effective practices in the present, Catherine Wood writes that 'performance art [in the 1970s] was angry . . . and its signature traits were naked bodies, self-harm [*sic*] and extreme duration' (Wood 2016: 54); performance artists, she concludes, sought 'to express their interior angst' (2016: 57). Inevitably, this was never uniformly the case. Such a reading pathologises artists or draws too clear a line between intention or biography and the effects of a particular work; it also suggests uniformities across individual works and different artists' practices that are open to critique.

Anxious refusals of the farthest reaches of performance art in the 1970s forget that extremity works in both directions, in terms of the upper and lower limits of concepts and practices – here, specifically, of art and aesthetics. In my definition, extremity stages or dramatises the challenge to push art to its limits, in actions that smack of being *too much*, as well as *not enough*. For example, in their extremity, performance artists in the 1970s sometimes appropriated or invented a single action, as a kind of experiment in form, either in a short, discrete exercise or as a life-altering commitment. Where the effects of taking an extreme stand could be painful, it could also be playful; either strategy could be bluntly formal or frightening, muscular or fleeting. In *Drawing a Line as Far as I can Reach* (1972), Tom Marioni followed the terms of his title, scraping a graphite mark on the floor to the wall and up as high as possible, creating a simple, perpendicular gradient. The extremity of such an action relies on pushing the acceptability of what may count as art – or as a critical question about art – to a kind of breaking point, not by urging the body towards disaster or suffering, but by depleting the substance of art to towards a lower limit, risking negligibility, inconsequentiality or insignificance in the process as a thrilling kind of negative potentiality.

Performance art history is studded with such acts of negative potentiality. For example, in *Catalysis I* (1971), Adrian Piper (in her own account) 'saturated a set of clothing in a mixture of vinegar, eggs, milk and cod liver oil for a week, then wore them on the D train during evening rush hour, then while browsing in [a] bookstore on Saturday night' (Lippard 1972: 76). So doing, she may incite more dramatic overtures of racist and misogynistic disdain than her body would otherwise trigger in more muted fashions. Of the *Catalysis* series, Piper states, 'One thing I don't do, is say: "I'm doing a piece," because somehow that puts me back into the situation I am trying to avoid . . . There is very little that separates what I'm doing from quirky personal activity' (Lippard 1972: 78). We might ask how the artist's practice and speculative discourse refuses to illustrate or be tied down by prohibitive definitions of art's work or by demands for its proper intellectual labour.

In a formally similar feat of formidable, negated slightness, Bas Jan Ader fell out of a tree into a canal (*Broken Fall (Organic)*, 1971); and, in a related piece, he fell off a vaulted roof, landing in a bush and losing a shoe in the process (*Fall 1*, 1970). If Marioni, Piper, Ader and others distilled performance to an essential, formal and seemingly banal activity and rendered such banality spectacular – what Alexander Dumbadze describes (specifically of Ader) as 'ordinary occurrences that abruptly become highly unusual experiences' (2013: 23) – contemporary performance artists also pushed the task-based project of performance to its polar extreme. In *One Year Performance (Cage Piece)* (1978–79), the first in a series of five breathtakingly excessive one-year performances, the Taiwanese-American artist Tehching Hsieh imprisoned himself in an 11 × 9 ft steel cage, for a full, uninterrupted year. At the commencement of the action on 30 September 1978, he certified, 'I shall NOT converse, read, write, listen to the radio or watch television, until I unseal myself on September 29, 1979' (Hsieh in Heathfield 2009: 66, emphasis in original). Whereas Marioni, Piper or Ader did substantially little over a slice of time, Hsieh does nothing for a duration so monstrously long that his action's sustained lack of activity makes his endurance devastating. In their discontinuous exemplarity, such artists or their works seemed to demonstrate too much or not enough commitment, pungency or feeling; they were pointedly too threatening or vastly too frivolous, too profound or too negated in their investments in what art might do, tell or mean.

In works by Marioni, Ader, Piper and Hsieh, with wildly differing intensities, we see the performance artist enact what performance theorist Adrian Heathfield calls a 'lifework' or 'existence art' (2009: 11) – an 'absolute conception of art and life as simultaneous processes' that seeks both to strip art of its transcendence and to bulk up the day-to-day remarkability of life, with effects that are banal, funny, profound or terrifying (2009: 55). Blurring art and life, Hsieh in particular submits so violently to the logic of his performance (as well as to subsequent one-year performances) that he exempts himself from a full life: the discipline of art as a rule for living makes a year of his life sound barely survivable. Ader, too, aimed at a long-term performance with relevant effects: on 9 July 1975, he set sail across the Atlantic in a pocket cruiser, in a durational work set to last up to 90 days, *In Search of the Miraculous*; in contrast to the frivolity of his candid falls, he was lost at sea and died during the course of the action. Too little slips and slides to the mortal superlativity of too much. Extremity works its violations of the norms of behaviour in multiple and unpredictable directions. Such non-compliance with expectations of what art might do, the question of how far one might go and the stakes of such limit-acts together enable the backbone of this book.

The performance of extremity – as too much or not enough – thus asks us to reconsider the style and substance of living, of bodies, identity or relationality and the tasks and habits that make these concepts readable or recognisable as art or its others. The problem, that is, goes beyond us asking if the activity is, conclusively, an artefact belonging properly to art or to life. As Anne Wagner notes, the attempt to interrogate and perhaps violate the limits of the discursive category of art prompts a series of questions concerning the function and interdependency of knowledge, distinction, difference, power and communication. By instigating situations of 'communicative breakdown', Wagner writes, art in the 1960s and 1970s could ask:

> How, if at all, can art remake the ruling order? Can that order be forced to appear? What sorts of freedom do humans possess? Do we mean what we say? Can art trump speech? Can it change or erase what people perceive? How else might it reshape, even interrupt the given patterns of life? (Wagner 2016: 20)

The perennial question of how and with what effects one might blur the boundary between art and life – here, becoming exemplary, unsurpassed, a historical or formal cynosure – exceeds the issue of whether or not the constitutive action belongs to or operates discretely in and upon one or the other domain. Wagner reminds us to take seriously the charges behind superficially strange or desperate actions: the dream of deconditioning the self; of devising new shapes for social or communal relations; of extending the political and affective ranges of the body; and of remaking the horizon of sensory perception.

Performance artists in the 1970s oftentimes exemplified this questioning practice through the use of a singular action, repeated or sustained. For example, Vito Acconci bit himself repeatedly and made prints from his indented skin (*Trademarks*, 1974), manifesting his body as the raw materials of art, as both canvas and technological rudiment, to the exclusion of investments in the body's pain, struggle or angst. In a more pungently abject imagining, Stuart Brisley lay in a bath of black water for two hours per day for two weeks, in a room filled with rotting meat and offal, 'like a victim of some disgusting, unexplained murder', as one critic put it (Cork 2003: 181), as a disturbing deliberation on struggle, dehumanisation and death (*And For Today ... Nothing*, 1972). Tightening the political acuity of performance art even further, Alastair MacLennan walked through war-torn Belfast, wearing a large target and a plastic sheet – focusing the crosshairs of sectarian violence upon his own anonymous person – and repeated the action daily for a whole month (*Target*, 1977). In *Three Day Blindfold/How to Become a Guru* (1974), Linda Montano used a profoundly delimited range of materials and actions to 'interrupt the given patterns of life' (to borrow Wagner's phrase); she blindfolded herself and relied on assistance from her silent companion, Pauline Oliveros, for three uninterrupted days, staging one's capacity to choose incapacity as an imposition on another's will to care or love. Each action asks questions about consciousness, embodiment, process, form and political or personal transformation, specifically through actions that appear *extreme*: that is to say, through actions that seem injurious, dangerous, vulnerable or unnecessary; whose duration seems unendurable or transformative – or too much like an undoing; and whose identity as art seems to beg the question of its own viability or verisimilitude (its lack of resemblance to prior landmarks or lauded practices of art making).

Feelings, desires, expectations and fantasy clearly influence or condition our critical encounter with art – and particularly so with the performance of extremity.

As Jennifer Doyle has argued, works of performance that seem to invoke excessive responses from audiences may be difficult or demanding, but the turn to emotion or affect functions not as a means of narcissistic escape or (mere) self-indulgence, but as an instrument of counterintuitive social engagement: such work appears 'stubbornly unfundable, uncollectable, and impossible to curate for fear of offending politicians and donors' (Doyle 2013: 15); it 'feels emotionally sincere or real' and 'produces a dense field of affect around it even as it seems to dismantle the mechanisms through which emotion is produced and consumed' (2013: xi). Nevertheless, Doyle notes, to the extent that such works seem to require a sympathetic, complex or ardent labour of critical response, a performance that pushes a viewer to her or his limits may just as likely produce violent or stigmatising responses. For example, work that is 'shaped by a comingling of narrative, feelings, and politics . . . can appear to some critics as naïve and propagandistic', prompting active attacks or passive refusals; for Doyle, each response 'reflects a critical limit, and not a limit to the work itself' (2013: 21). Doyle is not calling for a criticism without limits but, rather, she invites the writer to admit the limits – of taste, comfort, vocation and so on – against which one's writing strains, so to revel in the pleasures and pains of such recognition. Doyle suggests the conscientious transgression through writing of a limit in oneself, now desublimated by the spectacle of another's performance.

The approach towards a perceived limit may make one's extension into the corporeal and conceptual world around us feel less safe, but performance teaches us that such experiences of extremity also enliven us or give us *permission to become more than what one is or feels one is allowed to be.* Such an approach involves, perhaps, the recognition of our social, political, subjective and interpersonal precariousness, prompting an attempt at the repudiation of the limits that give us pause (or worse, that threaten to oppress, arrest, traumatise, demoralise or destroy us). Griselda Pollock argues that the way difficult or upsetting art does its work depends upon the formal situation of trauma itself as 'irrepresentable', 'transmissible' and 'belated': that is, trauma undergirds both pedestrian and singular experience, not as personal pathology or hermeneutic origin but as that which cannot be known or shown; and despite its ineffability, such experience returns to us in 'after-images' and 'after-affects' whose difficult materiality might provoke, for the politically acute and patient viewer, a formative, 'culturally transitive', *transformative* experience (Pollock 2013: 4–11). This accompanies the works of art Pollock studies, namely, works that directly confront the historical realities of suffering. Her feminist approach also allows us to think more carefully about the possibilities for engagement that are opened up in any work that greets us like 'a surprise attack', foiling the vigilance of our psychic defences or that otherwise shocks or knocks our stability off course (2013: 47). Art, for Pollock, remains agonistic, passionate and confrontational: culture is not so volatile and we are not so vulnerable that neither it, nor I nor you can take the psychic pressure it subjects us to. If this orientation seems, by turns, destructive, masochistic, antagonistic, wishful or naïve, it may as likely involve a playful act of creativity, a perverse fantasy or a reversal of fortunes. The difficulty entailed in the performance of extremity models a leap of faith over the constraining boundaries one encounters, in the world, in oneself or in art.

Unlimited action?

The performance of extremity, both singularly and cumulatively, attempts to dissolve or buckle the strictures of the category of art, hybridising it with the limits of life itself. Such attempts are never final or triumphal – even if a whiff of heroism, catharsis, romanticism or the *rite de passage* may accompany the rhetoric of the limit. The categories of art or life are never fully and finally broken open, dissolved or intermingled, but demand serial unpicking, thresholding, ritual affronts, re-wilding and increasingly innovative interventions, in order first to broach and then to ballast the destabilisation of the limits of the particular semantic category under attack. 'This is a mode of willing', McEvilley writes, 'which is absolutely creative in the sense that it assumes that it is reasonable to do anything at all with life; all options are open and none is more meaningful or meaningless than any other' (2005: 249). McEvilley's point refuses or complicates the pervasive criticism that performances of physical, psychic or ontological difficulty tend regressively to recuperate agonistic or expressionistic conceptions of art and meaning, including modernist assumptions about the transcendent capacity of painful, difficult or sincere thought and action.

I do not believe that the performance of extremity can demolish the category of art or obliterate with any finality the borders between art and life. Neither do I wish to recuperate the triumphalism or transcendence of scenes of seeming mastery. I argue that the spectral power of the limit will work according to its promise: labouring in *the spirit of the limit*, artists have been succoured by the ambition or will to violate the sanctity of forms, to bid valediction to orthodox values or to invent oneself anew by forcing a hairline fracture in the way of things.

The 'unlimited action' invoked in this book's title, then, is a challenge and a myth: a totemic ideal rather than an objective thing to be delineated, claimed and studied. For the excremental philosopher Georges Bataille, a limit is imposed specifically to be surpassed or violated: 'There exists no prohibition that cannot be transgressed. Often the transgression is permitted, often it is even prescribed' (Bataille 1986: 63). Translated to aesthetics, Bataille's philosophical contention would mean that the discursive construction of the phenomenon of art installs within itself a series of limits – conventions about what art is or does and taboos against foreign modes of being or doing – but that the practice of art 'prescribes' or necessitates transgression as a means of enabling its own future. Bataille's conception of the limit-experience and its social and cultural force are given their best elucidation in his late treatise *Erotism* (first published in 1957), which explores the way extreme experiences – of ecstasy, cruelty, violence, violation, sacrifice, taboo and mysticism – are *erotic*, in the specific sense that eroticism consists of 'assenting to life up to the point of death' (1986: 11). Bataille's is a world of scandalous limits, a frightening plateau of taboos and transgressions, punctuated by totems that have been erected to ward the subject from intolerable desires: for murder, ritual orgy, cannibalism, degradation, profanation, voodoo. These limits become all the more seductive, he suggests, according to the force of their proscriptive function.

Bataille writes that within a given discourse 'licence' is always given for certain permissible transgressions, generally under tight and contingent circumstances. During the course of such licensed transgression, however, 'unlimited urges towards violence may break forth': the freedom to exceed a convention produces wild possibilities of disturbance that cannot be contained. Such acts of 'unlimited transgression' Bataille terms 'sacrilege' (1986: 65–6). To apply Bataille's theory to the performance of extremity, opportunities for excess are given or authorised by the discourse of art, perhaps to enable its own risk-oriented evolution; but at these and other limits, artists may go above and beyond the implicit terms of art's fearful yet permissible transgressions, with riotous, reckless, fearsome or baffling effects that the discourse of art might fail to integrate into its vulnerable or overextended whole. Is there such a phenomenon, then, as a work without limits? What would such an act of aesthetic sacrilege look like? Where would one find such a space to create, in which one's agency is not enabled and/or curtailed by a palimpsest of limits: material or financial impositions, including poverty; by networks of power, including the law, censorship in tacit or explicit forms and the imposition of institutional regulations and policies; the limits of one's ability, access or freedom; or the self-imposed limitations of catering to imagined audiences, including the frequently (or supposedly) squeamish, unadventurous, expectant and preoccupied constituencies of museum- and gallery-goers?

Certain transgressions may be activated – and regulatory impositions may be avoided – by moving one's work into the streets or other public spaces or by presenting unauthorised or stealth performances, summoning (or eluding or overcoming) the strong arm of the law as an eventuality of one's performance of social maverickhood or cultural invulnerability. Yet, does such a strategy free an artist from the bounds of a particular discourse, history or form? The art historian Pamela Lee queries the validity of any terrain of cognition that might be deemed immune to, or cauterised from, art – and the 'art world' – by way of the problem of globalisation and aesthetics. Lee questions the contention that 'one could lay claim to a space beyond [art's] imperial reach by wandering just far enough afield' and critiques the 'naïve' argument that 'outside' the traditional domain of artistic practice and reception, there may be 'the fabled Archimedean point from which to survey the workings of the art world as they take place down below' (Lee 2012: 2). For Lee, art is a domain without formal or categorical limits, just as culture extends itself to encroach upon everything that global capitalism can touch, remake and claim. Yet other limits remain to appertain, as disclosed in the persistent shocks instigated by the perpetually renewed 'contemporary'. As Bataille notes, '[t]ransgression outside well defined limits is rare' (1986: 71). Even the imagination, as a space of apparent freedom, is subject to limits originating inside or outside it, despite its own regenerative and subversive potentials: its purported purity is alloyed with cheaper metals, which is to say the fantasy of a free imagination may be truncated by power, conscience, superego, self-preservation or self-sabotage. After Bataille, limits may be loosened or periodically camouflaged, but their restrictive effect is never fully or finally overwhelmed and neutralised.

Perhaps there may be no performance without limits – no unlimited action, as such. To the charge, in an interview, 'You went over the limits' – specifically, of human capacity or endurance – the performance artist Ulay replies: 'No. If I had gone over my limits, I'd be dead. The question is: who creates these limits' (Jelinek and Kalan 2016: 15). The strategic, antagonistic, irreverent, licentious performance will always find a limit (the final limit, for Ulay, the iconoclast, being one's finitude). Where there is a limit, one might identify the vested interest: to paraphrase Ulay, who – or what – creates and sustains a limit? What mortal or metaphysical threat is kindled in the attempt to surpass it?

The allure of lawlessness and of the limits to the fantasy of our own triumphant subjectivity has a credible philosophical history. A formidable precedent is Friedrich Nietzsche's dictum: 'Nothing is true, everything is permitted', written in 1887 (Nietzsche 2008: 126). It was borrowed from an apocryphal text by the Persian mystic Hassan-i-Sabbáh, the 'Old Man of the Mountain' and subsequently taken up by the experimental writers (and iconoclasts) William S. Burroughs and Brion Gysin, whose countercultural influence reached a fever pitch in the 1960s and 1970s. For Nietzsche – and for Burroughs and Gysin – such a statement proclaims the contingency of moral, ethical, political and social mores and modes of conduct. Truth itself, as an operating principle that might guide our ways of thinking and being – in life or in the specialised domain of art – is shown to be an invented category of knowledge. Anticipating Bataille's theorisation of the proscriptions and prescriptions that constitute human capacities for desiring action, Nietzsche imagines the very concept of truth and, with its converse, fiction (or, in a similarly denuded dyad, reality and unreality) as a limit forced on human thought and individual potential, produced and instrumentalised by a vested interest.

In the twentieth century, in Bataille's wake, the logic of the limit was valorised by thinkers associated with post-structuralism, including Michel Foucault, whose writings were often concerned with the limits to discourse; and Jacques Derrida, who studied the limits to language and to philosophy itself. For Foucault, in *The Archaeology of Knowledge*, published in French in 1969, to rethink the nature of discursive formations by uncovering their formative rules may reconstitute the practice of history and the nature of knowledge itself: the historian is 'forced to advance beyond familiar territory, far from the certainties to which one is accustomed, towards an as yet uncharted land and unforeseeable conclusion[s]', suggesting the obliterations of prior limits to what can be studied or known, leaving 'a blank, indifferent space, lacking in both interiority and promise' – for Foucault a useful potentiality, even if it sounds like a daunting one (Foucault 2003: 42–3).

First published in French in 1972, Derrida's *Margins of Philosophy* opens with a consideration of limits by asking how 'a discourse that has *called itself* philosophy . . . has always, including its own, meant to say [or stage] its limit' (Derrida 1982: x, emphasis in original). Having included its limits within its own conceptual scope and attempted to render these limits intelligible to itself, philosophy has 'recognized, conceived, posited, declined the limit according to all possible modes; and therefore by the same token, in order better to dispose of the limit, has transgressed it' (1982: x). Derrida seeks to reassert the ineffable, constitutive unfamiliarity of a limit and its beyond, to estrange properly the outside of discourse and stage the means by which 'the limit, obliquely, by surprise, always reserve[s] one more blow for philosophical knowledge' (1982: xi). For Derrida, a discourse lays claim to its content and interiorises its limits according to two key operations of 'appropriating mastery': first, it establishes and maintains a *hierarchy* of objects and forms of knowledge, to subordinate its materials to its own discursive jurisdiction; and second, it practices *envelopment*, as a synecdochic variation on containment: 'the whole is implied, in the speculative mode of reflection and expression, in each part', such that no part is authorised to speak or be spoken of *properly* outside the domain of the whole of the discourse (1982: xix–xx). In a discourse, no thing remains categorically impertinent or incorrigible, as the newly discovered object or idea at the margin may be appropriated, classified, subjected to a hierarchy or enveloped within its own recalibrated epistemic spread.

My own use of signature performances as examples or as illustrations threatens to do the work of recuperating or extending the 'epistemic spread' that I claim they otherwise seek to undermine. Such is the price – at least, the risk – of a scholarly practice of historical recovery. To abandon the work to historical forgetting and to lay claim to an apologetic silence would serve to honour the incidental resistance of the action in its time and place of performance. Yet such an orientation would ignore the function of the document and revoke the work's future-oriented capacity to vacillate on the margin and call into question the identity and function of a given discourse: here, of art or, more specialised still, of performance art. In its vacillation and the paradoxes of its retelling, a performance asks us to see which 'texts' – history and politics broadly conceived and the immanent tasks of activism, vigilance and sociality – lay beyond the territorialisations of a professional or disciplinary field; it calls on us to pose a narration that might scupper the dominance of our inherited knowledges. As Derrida asks, 'How to conceive what is outside a text? That which is more or less than a text's *own, proper* margin?' (1982: 25, emphasis in original). Property or propriety are contestable and remind us of the need to lay claim to one's contingent subject position as a writer or witness, not least in the task of deciding what is a limit and which action can be claimed to invoke or vacillate upon it. John Tagg engages in detail with a similar question, namely the extent to which a scholar might be required to 'know their place': in art history, Tagg argues, despite a series of urgent political reformulations of the discipline in the 1970s and 1980s 'there never was . . . a place, outside the continual production, exclusion and elision of positions for speaking, within a discursive and institutional regime whose conditions of existence, limits and effects have to be gauged and regauged from perspectives which cannot claim privileged exterior vantage points' (Tagg 1987: 100). By putting into question the relation between art and its purported outsides and by highlighting the extreme position the historian may find oneself occupying, Tagg suggests an urgent call to risk abjection in one's vocation, precisely by means of losing one's place in the face of the artists, objects or actions one attends to.

Does it hurt?

A key imperative of *Unlimited Action* is to pose a counterhistory to the narrative givens concerning performance art in the 1970s. In particular, works involving physical self-injury – in direct service of or as a side-effect in performance art in the 1970s – have been variously celebrated, canonised and stigmatised. For example, in VALIE EXPORT's film-performance, *Remote . . . Remote . . .* (1973), she meticulously carved away the cuticles from her fingers using a carpet knife. Separating the flesh from her fingernails, pushing the knife gruesomely into the nail bed to draw blood, EXPORT intermittently bathed her tattered meat in a bowl of milk held between her knees, where we see the blood dissipate from her fingers into the milk's corrupting whiteness. Accompanied by an ominous, clanking percussive sound, the effect of watching the video document of EXPORT's performance is harrowing and strangely compelling. Sitting with the film, in a screening and later on my laptop, I am moved by the experience of watching: I wince, narrow my eyes with concentration and concern and feel vaguely nauseous. In a public showing of the film at *(Re)Presenting Performance*, Guggenheim Museum, New York in 2005, EXPORT sits elegant, unfazed and perhaps confronting in her demeanour on the stage in front of the screen, while collectively we sweat and groan and shift in our seats. The colossal close-ups of the blade and her bloodied hands loom large and images of her fingers in the milk or nibbled in her mouth dwarf the interruption posed by our discomfited noises or by others' intermittent walkouts. We don't quite *read* the document – much less enjoy it – as much as we experience it, subsequently perhaps to process or reorder our embodied responses, to come to terms (in the moment or in studied or traumatic reflection) with her boldness or brutality, and our not-quite-consensual subjection to it in the scene.

The means by which injurious performance may prompt (or overwhelm) our critical encounter with it has been a frequent question for performance studies. Marina Abramović's physically arduous performances are exemplars of the use of self-injury in the 1970s and a frequent conduit for scholarly discussions of agency, active witness and consent (see Goldberg 1979; Iles 1988; O'Dell 1998; McEvilley 2010). In one such work, *Lips of Thomas* (aka *Thomas Lips*) (1975), Abramović ate large quantities of honey, lashed herself bloody and carved a large Star of David into her abdomen with a razor blade, prompting her audience to storm the performance space and bring an abrupt end to the performance. For Erika Fischer-Lichte, *Lips of Thomas* posed conceptual problems for its live audience, not by the strength of its symbols or allusions, but by its 'transformative potential' to overhaul or wreak havoc to received ways of reading, understanding and valuing performance – as demonstrated by the audience's mass refusal of the full promise of it completion. By transforming her audience into actors, or active co-authors, Abramović prompts an ethical crisis, for the viewer must choose either to consent to, or to revoke, the shape of the encounter, which otherwise subjects the audience to the perverse authority of the artist (Fischer-Lichte 2008: 12–13). Fischer-Lichte notes that there are indeed signs and symbols in Abramović's performance (honey, the cross, the star, flagellation and so on), but these are 'incommensurable with the event of the performance' because one's ability to read these literary functions of the production of meaning is overwhelmed by the visceral experience of the event (2008: 16). As with the experience of EXPORT's *Remote . . . Remote . . .* there is no distanced, passive orientation to take up, no space from which to give a detached response. In the extremity of each artist's action – variously cutting, flogging, freezing or otherwise overwhelming her body – and the exceptional demands placed upon the audience, Fischer-Lichte argues that 'the materiality of her actions dominate[s] their semiotic attributes' (2008: 16–18), precisely because pain, injury and consent cannot be assimilated into the conventions that otherwise govern spectatorship in theatre, art or performance art.

A common claim made by artists is that performance under duress allows her or him to master pain or to access a state of being beyond pain, paradoxically by way of the spectacle of self-directed injury. A core example is Stelarc, who rationalised his performances – beginning in 1976 with a series of suspensions from hooks inserted into his skin (attached to wooden structures, cranes or the interiors of buildings) – as a means of breaking loose from the bounds of embodiment, towards a posthuman condition in which he claims 'the body is obsolete' (Farnell 1999: 140). In tandem with such rationales, in performance art of the 1970s wounding is often deployed persua-sively as a corporeal practice of mark making and as a technique for representing or manifesting the body as raw material – as when, in *Sentimental Action* (1973), Gina Pane inserts a row of thorns into her forearm and slashes the palm of her hand with a razor blade to create a bloody flower atop a punctured stalk of flesh. Such practices may never be fully formal, as the wound is too loaded to float free from its social and cultural significations. Moreover, the critical effort to separate the wounding or duress from feeling as an audience member or reader – to treat the body of another as pure matter, object or meat – is riven with anxieties about a chain of politically disastrous histories of embodiment, including of torture, assault, abuse, slavery or war.

Cognisant of the semiotic trouble promised by injury, duress or endurance in art, by the end of the 1970s and beyond, critics and scholars sought to narrate and theorise a history of physical extremity in performance. A new rhetoric for doing so was provided by the term 'hardship art', as coined by the critic Jill Johnston in *Art in America*. Published in 1984, Johnston's essay 'Hardship Art' analysed *Art/Life: One Year Performance* (1983–84), a performance by Tehching Hsieh and Linda Montano in which the artists were bound at the waist by an 8-ft rope, for a whole calendar year. While Johnston does not elaborate directly upon her usage (and probable coinage) of the term, 'hardship art' described the production of a conflicted situation of social togetherness and isolation in the performance, as a trigger for psychological insights with political ramifications (Johnston 1984: 176–9). As a *rite de passage* of sorts for Hsieh and Montano, the difficulty of the so-called 'Rope Piece' was compounded by the formal absence of an object of study (how might a historian study the whole?) and by Johnston's necessary abjuring of the critical detachment supposedly required of critics of art.

Subsequently, scholars have continued to explore new and existing terminologies to address the frequently confounding effects of the use of injury, pain or duress in performance. In *Unmarked*, for example, Peggy Phelan notes that 'a genre of per-formance art called "hardship art" or "ordeal art" attempts to invoke a distinction between presence and representation by using the singular body as a metonymy for the apparently non-reciprocal experience of pain' (Phelan 1993: 152). For Phelan, anticipating aspects of Fischer-Lichte's argument, pain's intrinsic refusal of com-munication provokes theoretical questions about documentation, mediation and immediacy, presentation, representation and reproduction: 'ordeal' points to a particularity – or, more precisely, a limit – of her argument that performance art distinctively 'uses the performer's body to pose a question about the inability [of language or writing] to secure the relation between subjectivity and the body *per se*' in the anomalous acts that make up its history and which leave traces in archives (1993: 150–1). Rather than simply contributing another coinage to a repertoire of unwanted designations, I propose the term 'the performance of extremity' to gather and analyse extraordinary actions that strain against the common knowledge of art's limits, specifically through performance, while refusing or avoiding the interpellation of such works as governed by emotional, psychological or other modalities of pain and suffering that are unavoidable when the author privileges the definitive operations of hardship and ordeal. Extremity must remain wild: it cannot be codified as a genre, genus or style; it must not be schematised as a new orthodoxy in a series of past subversive gestures that have been reiterated, contained and overcome.

The scenes historicised in *Unlimited Action* sometimes involve physical hardship or ordeal – in, for example, Kerry Trengove's act of durational manual labour; Ulay's appropriation of tattooing and surgery; incidental works by COUM Transmissions and Anne Bean involving bloodletting or similar bodily practices; or the Kipper Kids' madcap adventures in self-boxing. Yet, in their selection and mapping I also seek to expand the concept of extremity to include acts that endanger artists, institutions or audiences in more varied terms, though still in altercations with the law or social decorum, thus posing the limits to form, sensibility, sense or art itself. This move away from physical hardship is not a moralistic strategy – a polite turning from the perceived prevalence of wounding in performance art of the 1970s – but, rather, performs a critical attempt to situate such tactics within a broader range of formally, conceptually and politically suggestive means by which artists strove towards extremity to stretch the bounds of aesthetic possibility. These begin with the lower limits of extremity (in the performances of Marioni, Piper and Ader) and include a further range of novel interruptions to the category of art in the 1970s. The critical shift away from the valorised (though stigmatised) shapes of extremity – as established by the work of, say, Abramović, EXPORT, Stelarc or Pane–, takes on its starkest expression in the final two chapters. Here, the work of Anne Bean and the Kipper Kids does not allow or enable a mere expansion or refinement of the accepted horizon of difficult performance art in the 1970s, but seems to sit particularly askew alongside better-known precedents (neither seems to elucidate the other). Extreme actions require anomalous models of witness, which may return a wilder array of practices to the scope of one's critical awareness: to repurpose, perhaps, the extremity *of* extremity.

That which was

The performance of extremity stages the identification – and perhaps the overcoming – of the formal limits of bodies, material conditions, institutions, moral or political assumptions or the law, *in and as* the practice of art. If art's limits, like the limits of

Georges Bataille's 'human spirit', run from the 'voluptuous' to the 'ascetic' (1986: 7) – from too much to not enough beauty, pleasure or sense – how might these and other limits be seen, tracked, known or figured, in art and subsequently by writing? By what procedures and assaults, in which time and place and with what consequences might such an undoing of performance and of art stage itself? A basic challenge here, then, is to specify precisely *how* and *with what effects* such disturbances, disorderings, over-extensions or reconstitutions of representation and form took place in and through performance art in the 1970s. My strategy here is to do so not through re-readings of arguably canonical works – the flashpoints registered thus far – but by way of a series of actions (and associated practices) that have been less visible in the existing histories of performance art.

The core case studies that ballast this book's writing –works by Kerry Trengove, Ulay, COUM Transmissions, Anne Bean, the Kipper Kids and Stephen Cripps – demonstrate the politics of form: the inevitability by which the formal choices an artist makes will always incite a series of political and affective eventualities, particu-larly when read through the frame of the conceptually fraught division between art and life. As a history, the book is not a survey but a series of connected scenes that I pose as exemplary. Each chapter focuses on a case study, namely, a single artist or group active in the 1970s. I focus predominantly on performances that took place in the United Kingdom and Europe, but also take in works that toured to the United States or were made there or elsewhere, to set the scene for a given analysis. This geo-graphical scope is more accidental that deliberate: I have been guided by methodo-logical commitments to explore practices for which archives of differing natures may be accessible, conducting interviews with living artists where possible and addressing practices that have been under-acknowledged by others (to date, arguably, American artists in the broader milieu of performance art's histories have received relatively more attention – that is, generally while still remaining marginalised). Being fluent only in the English language precludes me from archival research in many non-Anglophone nations.

I focus on single works in various cases, but not exclusively, for the shape of some artists' practices precludes this methodology. Where I do privilege a single work, I endeavour nevertheless to ground it in context with other performances, including some by the same artist, to acknowledge that individual practices of subterfuge do not exist in or emerge from a vacuum. Documentary traces for many of these case studies in the period are scattered. Reconstructing the works entails a historiographical exer-cise of patching together archival traces and inquiries into the ways historical veracity about an event is both enabled and foreclosed by the stories the archive is equipped to divulge, including those sought first-hand from surviving artists.

If the past contains everything that has happened and is untold and uncontain-able, history is an intellectual and discursive operation that takes place only in the present. This distinction between narrative orders is complemented or enabled by the archive, which, as historian Carolyn Steedman notes, is discussed frequently (but inaccurately) as a metaphor or analogy for history itself or for human memory or the unconscious (Steedman 2001: 68). However, for Steedman, the archive is a specific kind of repository, a passive (though symbolically loaded) storage system governed in its accumulation of documents neither by logic nor comprehensiveness. Things end up in archives by compulsion as well as by accident: although they may later be subjected to logic (to systems of sorting and classification) and to critique (as supports for nationalistic and colonial imperatives), 'as stuff', Steedman explains, 'it just sits there until it is read, and used, and narrativised. In the Archive, you cannot be shocked at its exclusions, its emptinesses, at what is *not* catalogued' (*ibid.*, emphasis in original). While we can take issue with history, as a narrative that emerges from the application of established methods and personal agency to the things sitting in archives, such umbrage does not suit our orientation to the archive or its documents, whose 'condition of being deflects outrage', Steedman argues (*ibid.*). The genealogy I construct in the present – a series of links, lineages, prioritisations and exclusions – sifts through the traces of the past, as found in various archives (paper ones, predominantly), to provoke provisional and sometimes fantastical scenes of history, subject to each event or artist's own inevitable exposure or recovery, like a revelation of an uncertain fate.

My efforts to seek out and narrate performances of extremity are also indebted to a methodological tradition of questioning the politics of scholarship and of extending its conventions and its limits. Specifically, the 1970s saw the emergence of a period of remarkable change in discursive understandings of the politics of art and of aesthetics, characterised by the full emergence of feminist, anti-racist and Marxist scholarship. As Janet Wolff has written, in the 1970s the sociological (or social) critique of art and aesthetics took hold in academic art history, the effects of which were to question the types of work that art history takes as its objects of study, revealing the traditions of selection and their criteria to be arbitrary, and destabilising the distinctions between art and proximate fields of cultural production (Wolff 1993: 14). By the end of the decade, art and the practices of reading had been revolutionised by questions of identity, exclusion, representation, the linguistic function of the sign and other issues emerging from critical theory and identity politics. *Unlimited Action* engages with the spirit of such advances – namely, to extend the reach of performance in art's (and theatre's) histories and to explore the effects of the extended or reconstituted scope of its relevance. That said, the relative lack of gender balance in this book's major case studies and my failure to decolonise and internationalise the history of performance art in the 1970s give me pause.

Unlimited Action poses the long 1970s as the scene of the performance of extremity at its most vital. I do not propose a cultural history of the period, but notable aspects of the 1970s emerge via key political events, scenes of economic transformation and specific instances of censorship and the social climate of culture war, protest, esoteric sensibilities, counterculture, music and so on. The development across chapters is not chronologically scripted, but thematic, narrative, intuitive in its ordering of significant scenes and innovations. As a whole, I take the decade as a fairly loose scope, exploring works that belong, rather, to the 'long 1970s' (Bennett 2009: 516); that is, some key works take place as early as 1969, while others bleed into the early 1980s. The development of practices and styles, the curious plays of cause and effect and the construction or collapse of strategies of making and living do not fit well the neat and artificial boundaries of the turns of calendar decades.

The performance of extremity, as explored here, is interwoven into the backdrop of political, social and cultural events that constitute the discursive frame of 1970s. The novelist and firebrand cultural critic Gary Indiana recalled the polarising of affect around the 1970s in terms of its combination of dissolute thrills (borne on the back of the 1960s) and a tendency towards fiasco:

> Can you even remember the urgency we felt in the '60s . . . to move human society in the direction of life against death? It was all on the verge of really happening, the so-called transvaluation of all values, apocalyptic changes in the social order, a polymorphically perverse, orgasmic version of the Rapture – [until in the 1970s] violence pulled it totally down the toilet. (Indiana 2014: 34–5)

For Indiana, by the end of the 1960s, American hopes for the good life of counter-cultural revolution and sexual and intellectual emancipation had been swept down the drain and into the sea. The culture of possibility signalled by the 1960s is notion-ally recorded as vanquished by the shame or horror of: the assassinations of Martin Luther King, Jr and Senator Bobby Kennedy in 1968; the massacres in California committed by Charles Manson's death cult in 1969 and their highly mediatised trials in 1971; and the killing of a fan by Hells Angels at a Rolling Stones gig at Altamont Free Concert in 1969. Such flashpoint events are all North American occurrences; as horrible and spirit-rending as they were, their power to act as symbols for global paradigm shifts suggests America's cultural imperialism, whereby its occurrences are mythicised and naturalised for their power to create or destroy universal narratives of culture, epistemology or ontology. That said, the British Socialist politician Tony Benn continued or echoed Indiana's depiction of a downward trajectory across the 1960s into the 1970s, focusing specifically (and in more staid terms) on the situation in Great Britain and Northern Ireland. For Benn, the end of the 1970s 'marked the end of the consensus, based on full employment and the welfare state', which had been accepted as a matter of principle in British politics and social consciousness after the Second World War; the consensus around social justice, he suggested, had been bolstered by the post-war economic security that peaked in the late 1950s on the back of rearmament, pressure from the International Monetary Fund and the European Economic Community, oil price increases and the reconstruction of world trade, resulting in 'the birth of a new liberal capitalism that could promise plenty for all' (Benn 1979: 19).

By the late 1960s and into the 1970s, this economic stability was in tatters, resulting in major local skirmishes – strikes, walk-outs, work-ins – and national catastrophes, including the Three-Day Week of 1974, at the tail-end of Edward Heath's Conservative government and prompted by a recession on the back of the international oil crisis of 1973. The 1970s in Britain and Northern Ireland were a time of political and economic insecurity, with the election of three one-term gov-ernments over the course of the decade (Conservatives in 1970, Labour in 1974 and a Conservative return to power in 1979). Financial insecurity, mass unemployment, a fever pitch of social anxieties around immigration and broad manifestations of civil unrest colluded to make the 1970s the most turbulent decade of the twentieth century after the end of the Second World War. Liberal capitalism – or neoliberalism – was consolidated forcefully after the defeat of Labour in 1979 by Margaret Thatcher's Conservative government and her emphasis on monetarism, privatisation, authoritarianism and the dismantling of both consensus politics and the prior sanctity of the welfare state.

If the 1970s were politically and economically volatile in both the United States and UK, the decade also sustained and monumentalised the last gasps of liberal freedom in cultural phenomena from David Bowie to disco, punk to funk. The utopian possibilities they represented were enervated by neoliberal capitalism from around 1979 and dealt a seemingly final deathblow by the simultaneous emergence of the global AIDS pandemic early in the 1980s. The cultural theorist Mark Fisher observes that neoliberal capitalism participated in 'a transnational restructuring of the economy' in the 1970s: 'The shift into so-called Post-Fordism – with globalisation, ubiquitous computerisation and the casualization of labour – resulted in a complete transformation in the way that work and leisure were organised', he writes, with repercussions that are now pervasive, introjected and irreversible (Fisher 2014: 8–9). The end of the 1970s thus signified what he terms 'a threshold moment . . . when a whole world (social democratic, Fordist, industrial) became obsolete, and the contours of a new world (neoliberal, conformist, informatic) began to show themselves' (2014: 50). Elsewhere, Fisher names this emergent cultural logic in which we are entrenched as 'capitalist realism', denoting a new historical sensibility seemingly without past or future, in which values and practices commonly held separate from bureau-administrative, regulatory and commercial imperatives have been subjected to ironic distancing and a generalised structure of disavowal, namely, a 'massive desacralization': 'beliefs have collapsed at the level of ritual and symbolic elaboration, and all that is left is the consumer-spectator, trudging through the ruins and the relics' (Fisher 2009: 4–6).

Fisher's characterisation of the 1970s suggests why the decade demands renewed attention. The chapters in *Unlimited Action* historicise performance art in a series of fairly promiscuous historical and national contexts in the 1970s, including the British miners' strikes, national guilt in post-war Germany, apartheid in South Africa, countercultural mysticism and occult turns, radical pedagogy, and legal and moral rulings about pornography and indecency. Fisher's own solution to the banalisation of history is elusive but consoling and prompts a rationale for this book's ambitions; he writes, '[t]he most powerful forms of desire are precisely cravings for the strange, the unexpected, the weird. These can only be supplied by artists . . . who are prepared to give people something different from that which already satisfies them; [namely] by those . . . prepared to take a certain kind of risk' (2009: 76). My attention to archives of performance art in the 1970s – to a history of the performance of extremity – is sustained in spirit by Fisher's call, as evidenced in his own desiring investments in postpunk and related subcultural and 'popular modernist' attachments in the 1970s (2014: 23). The spirit of that call, in the necromantic countenance of this book, emboldened me to seek out a certain strangeness in the traces of the 1970s, a probable anomaly in how we know things have been done, as if before a fall. Such strangeness is not lost entirely but can be sustained imaginatively in the present, if we find the means with which to endure and sustain the ghosts of the past.

That which is to come

The performances discussed so far push at the limits of our collective understanding of what art can or might do. Yet *Unlimited Action* is categorically *not* a history of the 'most extreme' examples of performance or of art.[1] The rhetoric of extremity risks camouflaging or celebrating how artists sometimes cement their own aesthetic and historical priority; this procedure is most notable, perhaps, in Marina Abramović's *Seven Easy Pieces* (2005), which harnessed the authorising power of the Solomon R. Guggenheim Museum, New York to reassert the extremity – and scaffold the iconicity – of the work of Vito Acconci, Joseph Beuys, Bruce Nauman, Gina Pane and Abramović herself. Her re-performances licensed a number of extreme performances as representatives of the period in which they were first performed. For art historian Mechtild Widrich, *Seven Easy Pieces* performs a 'distillation of reception and memory' by which 'Abramović proposed a new, more self-consciously canonical status for the performances she staged', thus 'canonizing' and 'monumentalizing' (and perhaps taming) provocative works of performance (Widrich 2014: 33). A historio-graphical project on Abramović's part, *Seven Easy Pieces* affirms a received historical narrative, while confirming herself as a pioneer to stake a claim to her own extremity and virtuosity. The five reclaimed pieces plus her own *Lips of Thomas* are extreme: conceptually speaking in their notoriety and formal excessiveness; and more plainly in the physical difficulty of performing (and watching) them over extended dura-tions. Yet each is rendered 'easy' (perhaps only facetiously) by Abramović's seasoned mastery of the form of performance art.

The accounts to come, then, struggle to avoid conferring the triumphalism and mastery that arguably accompanied Abramović's project of recovery. The scenes that populate this book's milieu include artists who have variously appropriated grand larceny, a trial for indecency, sustained acts of manual labour, anomalous strategies including sabotage, pranks and stunts and other arguably 'normal occurrences' of life (normal, that is, even if vilified) by recasting and reframing such activities as the sub-stance of performance. The performance of extremity characterised in my case studies appears necessarily to avoid institutional licence, approval or condescension.

Chapter 1 explores a gruelling performance by Kerry Trengove, in which the artist was walled into a gallery and subsequently dug his way out, by hand, over the course of eight days. I argue that Trengove's performance of extremity undermines the institu-tion of art and broaches new ways of thinking about the politics of endurance in per-formance. The brute force of *An Eight Day Passage* (1977) enables the extension of the performance into new formal imperatives for art, giving rise to dialogical, pedagogical and political opportunities for the performance of extremity. In Chapter 2, I turn to Ulay's action in *There is a Criminal Touch to Art* (1976) and argue that by stealing one

---

1 Journalists regularly publish such lists, often as click-bait responses to newsworthy performances. For an example, in response to Pyotr Pavlensky's activist performances, see Jonathan Jones (2013); his examples from the 1970s include works by Ader, Abramović, Burden, Acconci and Hermann Nitsch.

of Germany's national treasures – a priceless nineteenth-century painting – Ulay seeks to irritate his German-ness and provoke politically nuanced understandings of the limits of art and performance, of what counts as art or crime and of how these border-crossings might work upon national identity, selfhood and self-knowledge. In Chapter 3, I investigate the provocative performance actions of COUM Transmissions, focus-ing on the *Mail Action* (1976), a performance that appropriated a trial against Genesis P-Orridge (COUM's ringleader) for indecency; and the subsequent media scandal over COUM's exhibition *Prostitution* (1976) at the Institute of Contemporary Arts, London, prompted in great part by Cosey Fanni Tutti's documentation of stealth performances, among other provocations. Based on interviews and correspondence with P-Orridge and primary research in institutional archives, I ask how these two events harassed the distinctions between art, crime and pornography and refigured the attendant themes of censorship, punishment, indecency, decorum and culture war.

Chapter 4 looks beyond singular, central works by focusing on Anne Bean's practice of 'life art', exploring how and with what effects she constructs a continuum between works and between art and life, in the context of historically specific ques-tions about counterculture, occultation, 'wakefulness' and eccentricity. Doing so prompts a kind of theoretical or conceptual excess, urging the historian to think in unfamiliar ways and to depend upon alien figures of thought, in a practice of attend-ance that brings art to bear upon occultation and the occult to bear upon the vibrant materialities staged by the object in performance. Whereas previous chapters enable me to seek out the limits of a particular action, Bean's work in its totality provokes a limit-experience in the methodological practices of research and writing, partly because her performances have existed at the limit of intelligibility and visibility.

In the final chapter, I study the performances of the Kipper Kids, a duo of perfor-mance artists with a shared persona named Harry Kipper. If Ulay's extremity aggra-vated his own sense of national identity, for the Kipper Kids subjectivity itself comes under attack, through the dismissal of individual identity and, more robustly, perhaps, through an anti-aesthetic pursuit: namely, of a strategy of self-sabotage – represented by the ultraviolence of self-boxing – where violence, confusion and antagonism are exploited to avoid the burdens of success, singular works or a career. The sensibil-ity of senseless unravelling in the performances of the Kipper Kids pulls together the assaults on form elaborated in the preceding examples of the performance of extremity and tugs the reader back to the scene of self-injury otherwise so redolent in performance art of the 1970s, which this book seeks to contextualise. The conclusion introduces a final example – the pyrotechnic performances of Stephen Cripps – as a lens through which to highlight, in relative brief, two additional themes of the previ-ous chapters, namely, the limit-experiences of recklessness and impossibility.

There is a tension throughout the case studies: in articulating the conceptual and political reach of each work, prompted by the historical and material conditions of production and reception, one may run the risk of disarming the action at hand, defanging the brute power, strategic invisibility or muscular unintelligibility of the performance (what feels like its peerless-ness, its immediacy or its radicality). I think this is no risk at all. There is no cost (beyond a loss of sensationalism). I am not so wedded to the shock or pain or madness of these actions, to your pain or to my joy.

Strange lives and incorrigible habits

In 'Extremes', a short chapter of his book *Violence and Splendor*, the philosopher Alphonso Lingis sketches – without commentary – the topic of extremity via examples drawn from his far-flung travels and the experiences of limits opened up concomitantly in his phenomenal horizon. He finds extremity manifested in scenes of ontological vastitude: the 'selflessness [and] voluptuous pleasure' experienced in dancing; the 'oceanic experience' of being at sea; the mirthless solitude of being sick; a paranormal healing experience where 'cosmic splendor vaporized your misery'; social ostracism where 'nobody talks to you, even greets you anymore'; the strange lives and incorrigible habits of animals; Patagonia (Lingis 2011: 5–6). In a later chapter, Lingis writes again of extraordinary, surprisingly tenable situations of extremity: of trusting in surgeons, sky falling, walking the vast dioramas of the Mongolian desert or infection with bubonic plague (2011: 13–14). All these instances signify extremity in their difference to, or exceeding of, the averages and means of daily life, in the inherent risk that such experiences harbour and manifest or the sublimity of their scale, each of whose degrees of excess can never imaginatively be surmounted or conceptually held, even if the experiences themselves may be undertaken or survived.

At the other end of the scale of extremity, Lingis considers the radically miniature, through his example of the visually inaccessible ecosystems that live in 'a wonderland of minute lichens and microplants' encountered in wild adventures, constituting '[w]hole tundras you were about to crush with your foot' (2011: 17). He continues,

> The radius across which you move each day, whose vistas your eyes scan, is one stratum of fractal layouts and ecosystems just under and also just beyond what your naked eyes can see. In them there are no objectives you can want to reach and acquire, no things to detach and refashion with tools and stamp with the spirit, make yours and annex to your identity, will, and status. (2011: 17)

Lingis's carnal phenomenology reminds us of the pure wonder of looking awry at the world: the freedom and terror of seeking out that which is too big or too small for the ordinary scales and styles of being, existing at a limit of experience or perception. Notwithstanding the beauty of his writing, Lingis's powers of observation are profound: his understanding of what constitutes extremity stages that which in its sublimity obliterates our security and suspends our comfort; but he also venerates that agent whose diminutive ontological power or autonomy we ourselves annihilate when it finds itself underfoot. The miniature ecologies 'just under and also just beyond what your naked eyes can see' disclose the vulnerable entities, living systems, histories and flows that exist at a beleaguered and precarious level of extremity in the world of sensible phenomena, because they cannot be secure in their selfhood, longevity or sanctuary (2011: 17). They are too small, too unimportant in their seeming, but not too negligible to be known or cared for. Superlatives work in both directions, then, for the performance of extremity can seem too much to bear, but, as significantly, may also look too little, be not enough or appear too far removed from visibility and cognition for us to feel we could adapt our perceptual styles and methods to greet them.

Looking inwards, as it were, for extreme signs – for motifs of one's own attraction to excess – I may think less of sublime panoramas and animal weirdness, than to the attempt to obliterate and recast the given image of oneself through, say, tattooing and body modification of cosmetic or monstrous proportion; or possession by urges sexual, sadomasochistic or too deep in romance; supernatural and corporeal modes of horror; the extreme disquiet of bad feelings, like shame, regret, paranoia, embarrassment or guilt (so vast they might swallow me whole); of bleeding on command; or suicidal ideation. These problems are, typically, not those of contemporary art or of traditional aesthetics. Such conceptual drifts dovetail with Lingis's turn to the microbial worlds of flora (and, closer to home, to unfamiliar and precarious styles of doing, making and living) because each extreme to which one is drawn might command a new methodological focus on what commonly exceeds or undercuts the intelligible horizon of the aesthetic (or, for him, the philosophical – in whose own ecology aesthetics lives as a species of thought).

That is, we do not see the world at our feet, including the scope of practices that might be admitted and celebrated as the extension and intensification of the history of art or performance art (rather than as the distinct or discrete terrain of the history of life). Our technologies of vision and comprehension are not appropriately precocious or capaciously attuned. The performance of extremity asks, precisely, for sensorial and intellectual recalibration, as anticipated by Lingis's perceptual drift to unmapped or uncomfortable spaces of the anthropocene. The scenes of performance in *Unlimited Action* tend to toe the line, either delicately or rambunctiously, between the heretical and the humble, between militancy and a more subdued endurance. In each of its directions and however varied and unique, the performance of extremity signals a determination to exist without comfort or resolution in one's own chosen place – to make a singular home for oneself – even if it means setting the house on fire.

1

The preferred ordeal

On the morning of the 25th October 1977 I shall be incarcerated within the confines of a concrete cell and the entrance sealed behind me. [W]ith only the basic essentials for life support and limited external contact via a microphone, my task within the eight day duration of this work will be to attempt to free myself from the isolation of these chosen limits of time and space. This will necessitate the intense activity of creating a passage from the cell, beneath the foundations of the Gallery structure, which will demand both a physical and mental extension of my present state. A journey into the unknown. (Kerry Trengove, press release for *An Eight Day Passage*)

But the struggle to be more fully human has already begun in the authentic struggle to transform the situation. (Paulo Freire, *Pedagogy of the Oppressed*)

The half-imagined clank of a steel pickaxe on stone sets the scene for an encounter with extremity. The year is 1977. A tunnel takes its shape through human toil. It is autumn. The performance artist's statement of intent marks out the extremity of his own action: he will enact a feat of physical and psychological endurance by digging through concrete, brick and mortar, with the bare provisions required to survive the ordeal, across an injurious duration. It seems a kind of crossing of the Rubicon, in the name of art or of its revived and newly politicised spirit, by way of eight days of muscular transit through time and space, with the privations of the flesh that will accompany the passage. The performance is a challenge – a journey into the unknown – that cannot be revoked once commenced. Yet, moreover, the artist's discursive and formal frames for the performance signal its broader implications, its attack of sorts on the state of art and of the social, or upon the politics of life. How may a tunnel speak? What might be achieved by the action of tunnelling that enables one's own safe passage? If endurance-based performance might suggest the triumph of masculine subjectivity over a formidable (and usually pointless) task, how else might we read such an action? I argue that the performance of extremity in question appropriates and recasts a kind of manual labour in order to elaborate the priority of experience – and one, at that, in service of social connection and commentary – over art as a process of aesthetic and commercial production, refashioning performance on the cusp of art and life. How, so doing, does the artist – or the action – occur at a limit? What is at risk in the struggle and in the attendant endeavour *to transform the situation*? According to what principle may one tell the digger from the dig?

An unrepeatable performance by the British artist Kerry Trengove, *An Eight Day Passage* (1977) took place at the Acme Gallery, London, at 43 Shelton Street, Covent Garden. From 25 October to 1 November 1977, the gallery remained open 24 hours a day for the uninterrupted eight-day action (**Figure 1.1**). In its pursuit of a task-based

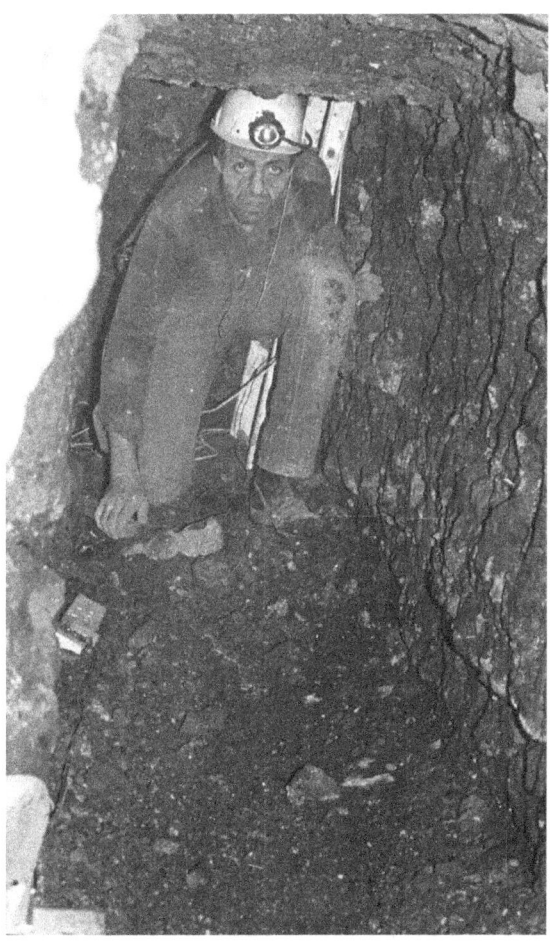

1.1 Kerry Trengove, *An Eight Day Passage*, photographs from a durational performance, The Acme Gallery, London, 25 October to 1 November 1977

activity over an alien duration, the *Passage* is an exemplary performance art action of the 1970s. It captured the imagination of contemporary audiences, local and national broadcast media and typifies a certain strand of performance art in the decade. In its duration and the intensity of its task at hand, Trengove's extremity belongs to a compelling context of classic endurance performances, such as: Kim Jones's *Wilshire Boulevard Walk* (28 January and 4 February 1976), in which he walked as 'Mudman', caked in clay and cluttered with homemade sculptures, from sunrise to sunset across Los Angeles' 25 km arterial highway and again from sunset to sunrise; or William Pope.L's *Times Square Crawl* (1978), the first of thirty urban crawls he has performed to date, in which he seeks to 'crawl to remember' the experiences of those for whom horizontality is not a choice but a fact of their destitution, from poverty, penury and placelessness (English 2007: 266); or Linda Montano's *Handcuff* (1973) with Tom Marioni, in which the two artists were handcuffed together for three days, perhaps to relearn how intimacy and interdependency work *in extremis*.

There are a small number of critical writings on Trengove's work from the 1970s, though he otherwise seems mostly forgotten. His work is largely not exhibited, with the exception of the inclusion of two images from the *Passage* in Paul Schimmel's landmark exhibition *Out of Actions: Between Performance and the Object, 1949–1979* (Museum of Contemporary Art, Los Angeles, 1998). Published writings include a few detailed obituaries and essays published after his death on 4 September 1991, aged 45, from cancer of the tongue and throat. In an obituary, the art historian Michael Archer confirmed the significance of Trengove's work, writing that in the context of performance art in London in the 1970s, the extremity of the *Passage* 'epitomised that period' (Archer 1991: 25). Returning the *Passage* to the light of day revives Trengove in his prescience, to foreground the relevance of his call to actualise, as he put it, '[t]hat moment in art when one is beyond reason, when instinct liberates from puritan suspicion, when vision and velocity are one' (Trengove 1985). This work of recovery also re-establishes what Moss Madden called Trengove's 'reputation as an artistic brinksman' (Madden 1991: 12), which has since been undermined or neglected. Referring to the mid-1960s, Madden writes that Trengove's brinksmanship was inaugurated in his 'first attempt at performance art . . . during his early days at Falmouth Art School': in an action for which he was convicted of vandalism, Trengove 'took a diamond ring and walked through Falmouth's main street, scoring a line on the windows of the shops as he passed' (*ibid.*). Yet he was celebrated best for a series of long durational performances in the late 1970s and early 1980s, the *Passage* being the most iconic; after turning to sculpture and drawing around 1983, he fell into obscurity, devoting most of his energies to teaching, as well as fighting to survive several years of debilitating terminal illness.

Trengove published a series of statements to accompany the *Passage*, which were reproduced in a press release and advertisements for the performance and invoked in some of its extensive press coverage. A short statement by the artist is set out in broken lines like a poem:

The act, time, or right of passing.
Movement from one place to another.
A journey, a voyage, entrance or exit,

a corridor, an encounter,
an incident.[1]

The action of digging a hole for eight days – and his means of accounting for his project in verse – recalls both formally and politically Bertolt Brecht's socialist redefinition of enduring acts of work as critical gestures:

Canalising a river
Grafting a fruit tree
Educating a person
Transforming a state
These are instances of fruitful criticism
And at the same time
Instances of Art. (Brecht 1987: 308–9)

Trengove liked to recite this passage: an obituary by John Roberts notes as much and reproduces the lines (Roberts 1991: 24). The poem was read in full at Trengove's funeral in Sheffield in 1991 (alongside readings from Apollinaire, Van Gogh, Lao Tzu and Trengove's own writings) and published in the accompanying Order of Service.[2] The lines are the second and final stanza from *On the Critical Attitude*, Brecht's poetic statement on the necessary rearming of criticism so as to entertain a more strident approach towards the dominant social order. As his first stanza concludes, 'Give criticism arms / And states can be demolished by it' (1987: 309).

Written around 1938, Brecht's verse was published in 1963 (and translated into English in 1965) as one of *The Messingkauf Poems* (or *Buying Brass Poems*), a sequence of 38 texts that reflected on his aesthetic theories concerning the theatre. In an appendix, Brecht summarised his overarching imperative: 'the question is whether it is at all possible to make the representation of real-life incidents the task of art, and thereby to make the spectator's critical attitude towards those real-life incidents compatible with art' – a challenge, he adds, that depends upon a transformation of 'the nature of the interaction between stage and auditorium' (Brecht 2014: 122). For Trengove, the questioning imperative holds, although he approaches the problem of a critically invested spectatorship from outside the theatrical apparatus, replacing the stage with the problem of the gallery and substituting the phenomenon of the individual spectator with dialogic environments in situ. Through Brecht – and more profoundly through the then-emergent writings of the Brazilian decolonial activist Paulo Freire – Trengove would create politically insightful performances that twinned ordeal or endurance with a new dialogical aesthetic, by prioritising, framing or extending 'real-life incidents' (such as digging, surviving and conversing). As such he also opposed the incipient market for the commodities that had begun to accompany performance art in the decade.

---

1 Press release for Kerry Trengove, *An Eight Day Passage* (1977), Acme Gallery Archive, Acme, London, Box 3, Hanging File, Folder: 'Kerry Trengove, *Eight Day Passage* and *Solo*'. Subsequent references are given in the text as 'Trengove, Press release'.
2 Order of Service, 1991, Acme Gallery Archive, Acme, London, Box 3, Hanging File, Folder: 'Obituary and Other Material'.

On the same press release as his staggered poem of intent, Trengove published a more substantial discursive commentary (under the heading 'The Activity'):

> *Passage* is essentially about the necessity and methodology of the act of creativity. [It asks] how a series of individuals, mostly unknown to each other, have each perceived, imagined, and believed in creating, an alternative future, committing their lives to making that future occur. This *shared belief in the conscious extension of their own limits* has been strengthened by persisting situations of extreme personal or social duress, which also divides them into two groups, those whose beliefs lead them to undertake severe experiences of their own free will, and those whose beliefs have had to be maintained through periods of excessive involuntary constraint. (Trengove, Press release; emphasis added)

Trengove is referring to a specific series of individuals, namely, former political detainees (contacted through Amnesty International) and professional athletes, whom he interviewed towards the action. He inserts his own labour into this series, by playing extracts from taped interviews with 30 detainees and 30 sportsmen, on a loop throughout the eight days of the *Passage*, to provide a discrete context for the activities in the upper and lower galleries (Pooley 1977). The artist Rose Garrard (his wife at the time of the action) recalls that she edited the tapes into the performance loop as 'Kerry found it too upsetting to listen to [the recordings] again' (Garrard 2010), suggesting the gravitas of the content of the memories recounted by the detainees. The tapes are no longer extant, but a reporter noted that one interview narrated an Argentinian political prisoner's ordeal of being 'kept for 40 days with his head in a canvas sack'; another speaker, a South African detainee, told of the horror of being held in solitary confinement for three years (Pooley 1977). The subjective difficulty of listening to the detainees' stories of war, atrocity and torture would have framed, complemented and exacerbated the physical exertion and personal privation required by Trengove in the eight-day action – and arguably, though differently, for his audience. The interviews with sportspeople introduced the issue of consent, reminding audiences of the con-stitutive difference in Trengove's relation to the detainees' harrowing accounts of suf-fering, namely, the fact of the artist's agency in contriving and undertaking the scene of endurance.

Trengove refers directly to the experiences of a promiscuous selection of cat-egories of persons who undergo what he calls 'the conscious extension of their own limits', including both physical and psychological, self-determined and causal limits, in the course of their durational subjection to 'severe experiences' (Trengove, Press release). He might as well, though, be writing directly about artists such as himself, as suggested by the introductory statement concerning 'the necessity and methodology of the act of creativity' (*ibid.*). He implies the labour of voluntary training and invol-untary detainment and connects this (at least implicitly) to the voluntary privations experienced in durational performance.

Despite – or precisely on account of – their palpable strangeness, difficulty and self-directed violence, Trengove's signature actions investigated his own profound concerns about how art might enact a politics of the self or otherwise inform the central ethical and existential questions of how to live and how to act. As the art historian John Roberts writes, '[w]hat concerned [Trengove] was "what was it to be fully human?" given the *limits* currently set on human emancipation. The pursuit of extreme or constraining experiences was therefore what had to be passed through to deny these limits' (Roberts 1992, emphasis in original), suggesting an immanent relation between intuitive difficulty – what Trengove calls the 'moment' (of action or location) 'beyond reason' – and the rupture of oppressive limits, be they political, ethical or aesthetic (Trengove 1985).

Approaching the *Passage*

Relics of the *Passage* exist today in the form of a number of photographs, short videos and archival documents. A more substantial archive for the performance – and, more emphatically, for the rest of Trengove's work – is missing, because Trengove instructed that his archive be destroyed after his death (his first wife, Rose Garrard confirms he was 'self-destructive to the end'); Trengove's wish was carried out by his widow, Alison McLeod (now Radovanović), who burnt the work and scattered its ashes alongside those of her late husband in Falmouth Bay in 1992 (Garrard 2010). Radovanović confirms that the archive was destroyed in its entirety with the exception of a small number of sketchbooks or 'highly cryptic aides de memoires rather than pictorial, analytical and/or descriptive' (email to the author, 12 September 2015). Fortunately, a further cache of images and videos of two of Trengove's key actions of the 1970s survive in the Acme Gallery archive.

An Eight Day Passage began at 9 a.m. on 25 October 1977, with Trengove being bricked into a section of the lower gallery. A number of printed images show the cell behind which he was imprisoned: a neat, secure structure of breezeblock and mortar, creating a cavity of around 10 × 15 ft in size, enclosed from floor to ceiling. The walls are solid, apart from a hole the size of one missing block, which acts as a viewing (and documentation) portal to the action inside it (**Figure 1.2**). The aperture afforded a view of Trengove's working progress during the day or the artist resting or sleeping on his bunk if gallery-goers visited late at night. The walls are those of a prison cell, tomb or ziggurat. The tunnel is a catafalque. Inside the walled structure, Trengove lived among basic provisions, including rations of meal replacements and water, an extractor fan and a chemical toilet; and his building materials: a stack of timber boards for lining and supporting the passage, a ladder and a system with a pulley, ropes and a canvas bag for moving soil and concrete. 'Safety', Garrard recalls, however, 'was never a priority with Kerry' (Garrard 2010). In the event, aspects of Trengove's planning and research gave way, as he abandoned the use of timber supports, perhaps to quicken the completion of the action to fit the projected eight-day duration – or as a symptom of masculine abandon.

The relational structure of the *Passage* was essential to Trengove's design, here as for other performances. In the upper galleries, Trengove installed a monitor showing

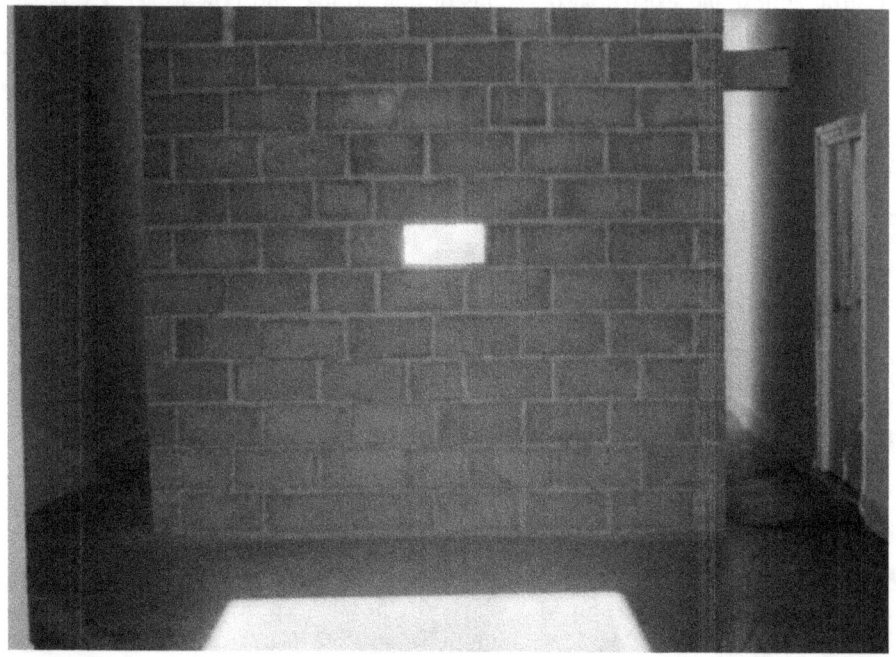

1.2 Kerry Trengove, *An Eight Day Passage*, photographs from a durational performance, The Acme Gallery, London, 25 October to 1 November 1977

closed circuit footage of the tunnel and his progress; facing it, a leather office chair and a microphone on a stand, with a two-way sound system connected to a red telephone in Trengove's cell; four neon light corners surround the set-up in a sculptural manner (**Figure 1.3**). Slides show him working in the lower galleries inside his concrete bunker. A video camera stands inside the bunker on a tripod. Other images show gallery visitors seated in the leather chair in the upper galleries and speaking to Trengove through the microphone; or they huddle round, standing or seated on the floor, watching the monitor. A short untitled video complements these slides, showing audience members interacting with Trengove in a serious, inquisitive or jovial manner.

The digging of the tunnel would begin with Trengove drilling a 3-ft square hole into the gallery floor, 3½ feet down through the deep foundations of the gallery (the top 18 inches consisted of concrete) and a sharp bend would allow him to dig a long straight route to emerge in the gallery's front basement, eight days later, about 20 gruelling feet from his point of origin. Trengove prepared by consulting experts on building works, nutrition and physical training. He used a small pneumatic drill, a shovel and a pick. As Trengove began to dig, he would fill the cell with displaced earth. The cell was designed to be as small as possible while facilitating the dig; as it filled with rubble, he would be forced to live further into the tunnel. Photographs taken inside the hole show a rough but remarkably uniform rectangular cavity,

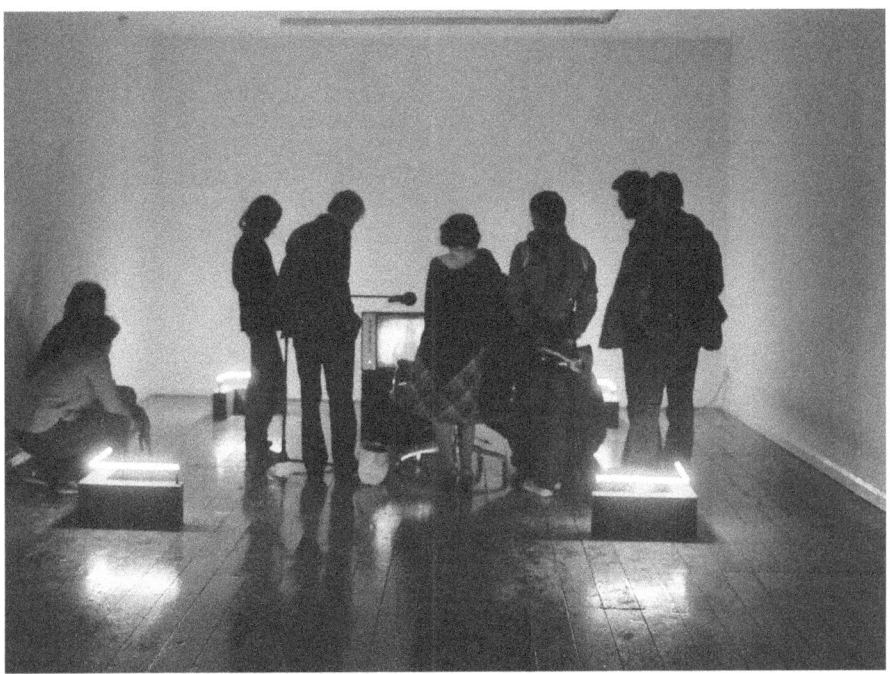

1.3 Kerry Trengove, *An Eight Day Passage*, photographs from a durational performance, The Acme Gallery, London, 25 October to 1 November 1977

pockmarked at the sides and dirty on the floor with debris. The tunnel is high enough for Trengove to crouch or crawl through – probably 4 feet high and 3 feet wide – with a tight, rougher exit point (through which the photographs were taken). A photograph taken at the conclusion of the eight days of digging shows Trengove emerging from the hole, at an exit point in the basement of 43 Shelton Street (**Figure 1.4**). He wears dark overalls, a white builder's helmet with a mounted torch, a layer of dirt covering his hands, arms and face. He screws up his features and bears his teeth as he rubs his face with the butt of his hand, bringing his body forward by bearing his weight on his elbows.

At least two videotapes are extant from the action. The unedited archival tapes, identified as *Bunker Roll 1* and *2*, include stretches of video filmed from the television monitor installed in the upper galleries, which relayed the progress in the holding area and tunnel below. The first, silent video shows Trengove in his work clothes, helmet and miner's torch; he stands in the tunnel up to his chest and talks to the camera (without sound) as he manipulates a large jagged piece of debris free of the tunnel. The shot changes to the viewing aperture in the breezeblock wall, through which we can see shadowy movements. The remaining footage shows Trengove on his bunk: after talking on the red telephone, he removes his helmet, places a tin bowl on his lap, spoons white protein powder from a large tub of Complan and mixes it with water. Taking a mouthful, he grimaces lightly and shakes his head. He pops a

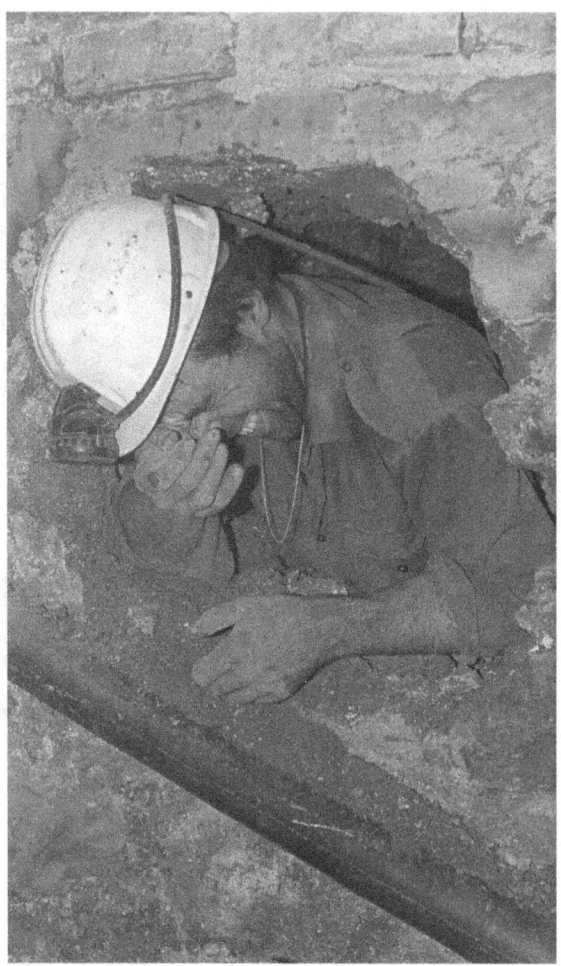

1.4 Kerry Trengove, *An Eight Day Passage*, photographs from a durational performance,
The Acme Gallery, London, 25 October to 1 November 1977

vitamin pill in his mouth and washes it down with his protein soup. He writes in his
journal, fixes a piece of equipment and beds down to sleep.

The second *Bunker Roll* tape has sound and shows an audience gathered round
the upstairs monitor, talking into the microphone, watching Trengove's progress or
viewing the exhibited materials. It shows a vitrine containing a 'key' or legend explaining the contents of each space; we also hear a muffled voice from Trengove's taped
interviews. The reception area of the gallery contains information on sloped viewing
banks and large posters mounted on the walls alongside accumulated press cuttings.
The same roll shows Trengove emerge from the tunnel into the basement. This would
later be reported as occurring at 8.25 p.m. on 1 November 1977, some eight days and
11 hours after the commencement of the performance (in total an astonishing 203

uninterrupted hours). We see the black expanse of the wall lit by cameras flashes, and hear the hard repetitive sound of Trengove's pneumatic drill breaking through from the other side of the remaining partition of cement or stone. The camera pans to show the congregated audience: spectators, well wishers, press cameramen and a number of children.

The artist's emergence from the wall is performed as a media event: it is very much staged for the press, and embellished (or constrained) by its requirements. Trengove hovers in the hole for several minutes: posing, altering his position, looking to the side, rubbing his face, as the cameras flash to catch the image. It is stage-managed for the press cameramen's documentation, to be reproduced in local and national newspapers. 'Give us that smile, again', they holler, to which Trengove consents, prompting giggles from the audience. 'You did it, Trengove!' someone calls out. Another reaches forward to shake the artist's hand. A woman leans in for an affectionate peck. Trengove remains lodged in the hole in the wall throughout the extended photo shoot. A cameraman asks him to turn off his miner's torch. He switches it off. Another says, 'leave it on'. He switches it on. He's offered a bottle of champagne and a cigarette. He accepts the bottle, holds it by the neck and swigs to the audience's cheerful ovation. The atmosphere is profoundly jovial, ceremonial in a banterly fashion. He is asked to drink again for a photograph and the cameras flash to capture the celebratory moment. 'Can I come out now?' he asks. 'I want to get out', he says calmly, matter-of-factly. He backs into the tunnel, then exits into the basement. The passage is complete.

After exiting the tunnel and the melee, Trengove stands in the ground-floor reception area of the Acme Gallery, still drinking from the champagne bottle. He is subdued. He must be exhausted. He talks to Reuters on a telephone. 'Hello?' Pause. 'Super. Absolutely super', he says, in an articulate, quietly spoken voice. He explains his surprise at sleeping well, despite the lights being on throughout the seven nights. He talks about his senses. 'Hardly aware of smell at all down there', he says, also noting the sound of the interview tapes, which he could always hear recounting stories of torture, persecution, duress and exertion. His sense of taste was curtailed too, he tells the journalist; what little flavours he encountered were 'obnoxious'. He pauses while being asked an inaudible question. 'Beer!' he replies, then laughs, showing his teeth and the pink of his gums.

Trengove talks to Reuters about time, 'chronological time, time by watch' and how the sense of it becomes distorted when measured in space or by the distance one has tunnelled: 'I'm very spatially conscious, you know, being primarily a sculptor.' He recalls children talking to him during the week and their gifts of flowers and grapes when he emerged. He talks about trust, about isolation as a ritual experience in other cultures and giving up smoking during the course of the tunnelling action. Pause. 'I want something to eat! Something solid. A nice big steak.' Pause. 'A nice cuddle.' Laughter. He now drinks a pint of beer while talking. Whatever the unheard question, his answer is strident: 'No, no. I am a filthy, dirty, stinking, smiling mass.'

The human mole

The *Passage* was covered assiduously in the national print press and received serious as well as vacuous critical attention in its pages. The 1970s were significant for performance art in Britain not least for the enthusiasm and hostility with which broadcast media and, by extension, popular audiences, engaged with its novelties and perceived excesses. As Neil Mulholland argues, in the 1970s artists were frequently presented by the press as charlatans, with the effect that 'a plethora of new offending "modern" artworks were met with the press's contempt on the grounds they spoke in the profane language of unsanctioned materials, events or processes' (Mulholland 2003: 6). In the case of COUM Transmissions' *Prostitution* at the ICA in 1976 (discussed in Chapter 3), this was stigmatising in tone and effect and fulfilled conservative imperatives on the part of the media and the state. On different terms, other contemporary performance art actions were ridiculed by the press as stunt-like or trivial, such as that of Ddart Performance Group (Ray Richards, Dennis de Groot and Tony Emerson) who received £395 from the Arts Council to perform *Circular Walk* (1976), a performance lasting one week, in which the men walked single-file in a 150–mile circle through East Anglia, attached at the head by a 10–ft yellow pole, stopping at pubs along the way to perform invented rituals. Richards described the work as 'a transient piece of sculpture' and the performance-poet Adrian Henri called it 'pure and beautiful' (Walker 1999: 79–80); yet, Richards notes, the work was dismissed in its subjection to 'a terrible distortion of the facts', by being mocked in newspaper cartoons and as the subject of parliamentary questions about the misuse of public funds (Walker 1999: 80–2). One of these disapproving critic, Fyfe Robertson dismissed Ddart's work on BBC television, ridiculing it a symptom of the critical foible of 'treating with owlish seriousness way-out crap as art' (Editorial 1977h: 4). Yet Trengove's example shows that public and popular attention in the period was not exclusively a derisory affair. A year after *Prostitution* and *Circular Walk*, print press, television and radio journalists (especially the BBC World Service and Capital Radio) followed the *Passage* across its eight-day duration with a mix of fascination, bemusement and care.

The press coverage began with a number of calmly provocative 'fluff' pieces. In *Time Out*, for example, Sarah Kent announced the performance as 'a Colditz style escape bid', with reference to the popular prison-break series of the same name, then recently aired on British television (Kent 1977). *Miss London* magazine reports that Trengove 'suffers from claustrophobia [and] he hopes to rid himself of it en route', adding that 'anyone who finds this explanation obscure can go and chat to Kerry at any time, day or night', granting a flattening psychological imperative to the work, while gesturing to the novelty of its dialogical form (Editorial 1977g). In London's *Evening News*, Helen Minsky likened the action to 'something out of an Edgar Allan Poe story', suggesting her bafflement at the artist choosing to subject himself to an unwarranted 'nightmare'. Trengove contradicts this aspect directly: 'It may seem macabre,' he tells her, 'but it isn't' (Minsky 1977a). In the popular music magazine, the *NME*, rock journalist Jamie Mandelkau gently mocked Trengove, suggesting that after the performance the cell could be repurposed as 'a gallery for midgets'; more usefully, he also recounted some of Trengove's practical discoveries, from the surprise of 'four feet of hard London rubble' instead of the soft clay he planned for, to finding 'medieval' brick foundations, 'clay pipes', 'jawbones', 'a horse's tooth' and other subterranean revelations (Mandelkau 1977).

The first significant article on the action appeared on 24 October 1977 in the *Evening Standard*, then a respectable venue for art criticism. Leana Pooley's article shows that on the eve of the dig, the majority of the concrete cell had been constructed: a photograph shows a large ragged hole, through which Trengove is clearly visible inside the structure, seated on the floor behind a large breezeblock. Pooley explains the facts of the preparation and plan for the *Passage* and notes that this 'curious exercise in claustrophobia [is] costing Trengove most of his earnings teaching sculpture over the past 10 months', adding that he has trained physically (running and bodybuilding) for two months (Pooley 1977). The information on the cost indicates that Trengove himself substantially financed the project and that no external funding was provided, perhaps thus mitigating a potentially unforgiving angle on the part of journalists (the fact of public subsidy was the key alibi for attacks on COUM Transmissions and Ddart in 1976). Journalistic indignation is shelved in favour of a rational tone and a 'human interest' approach, hence the *Standard*'s mildly sensational title describing Trengove as 'buried alive' (*ibid.*). Pooley attends to the political imperatives of Trengove's action, citing the artist as saying: 'Sportsmen have creative freedom to extend themselves as far mentally and physically as they can. Political detainees, on the other hand, have had that essential human right taken away from them. What I am going to try to do is recreate those two states . . . to gain something of their experience' (Trengove in *ibid.*). The article suggests a means to think Trengove's self-imposed endurance without pathologising him (his endurance is no wackier than that of sportspeople) and confirms a political context from which to read his endurance, in a continuum with the limits of those who have no control over the situation or extent of their endurance.

News of the action travelled across regional presses, prompting broadly sympathetic reports in newspapers in Cardiff, Leeds, Truro and Plymouth (Editorial, 1977a; Editorial 1977b; Editorial 1977d; Editorial, 1977j). 'Serious' art critics entered the discussion on 31 October, when Caroline Tisdall – then the most seasoned critic of performance art in the country – noted that the political implications of the feat allow it to transcend its own 'Colditz-style' stunt quality (tacitly rebuking Sarah Kent's earlier remark). For Tisdall, 'the word passage has both physical and mental meanings', to 'underline the fact that there are still people in our society who are prepared to undergo severe strain of their own free will for social and political belief. We all know that really, but often in the abstract' (Tisdall 1977). She adds, 'Trengove's week of deprivation removes this abstraction', through his act of sustained and seemingly unmediated 'exhaustion and isolation' (*ibid.*). Tisdall attends to the aspects of the *Passage* that follow the writings of Freire, intuiting his key themes of emancipatory struggle, limit-acts and the ontological vocation of becoming more fully human through one's political endeavours. The *Observer* was the only broadsheet to dismiss the performance outright: 'When art imitates Colditz', its columnist sniffed, 'it's time to leave' (Editorial 1977i).

On 31 October 1977, seven days into the dig, other sustained metaphors appeared across journalistic accounts of Trengove's subterranean progress: Minsky returned to track his progress, reporting that the 'mole man is seven feet from freedom' (Minsky 1977b); another reporter wrote that '[h]uman mole Kerry Trengove surfaced last night amid a shower of rubble' (Editorial 1997e; see also Editorial 1977c); and in a further article, Trengove is a metaphorical 'badger' (Editorial 1977f). Reporters in Sheffield and Leeds likened *Passage* to 'an eight-day-long Houdini act', invoking the image of the great escapologist Harry Houdini to suggest, perhaps, the sleight of hand, superhuman or modern sideshow aspects of Trengove's act (Manning 1977; Editorial 1977e). Journalists noted the strangeness of the duration of Trengove's inhabitation of the cell and the repurposing of daily activities of survival – working, eating or sleeping – as practices of art (**Figure 1.5**). Throughout, they reported the challenges Trengove faced in the final days of the tunnelling expedition, including multiple drywalls, iron bars embedded in the foundations, a power cut and problems with his oxygen supply. John Roberts reflects that Trengove's action was depicted in the popular press as 'mad' and 'dangerous' and that journalists were 'out to use Trengove' in the service of prejudices against modern art that 'turn speculation into idiocy' (1982: 63). Yet, in fact, beyond those in the *NME* and *Observer*, reports were generally respectful, detailed, coolly distanced and courteous – even when bemused.

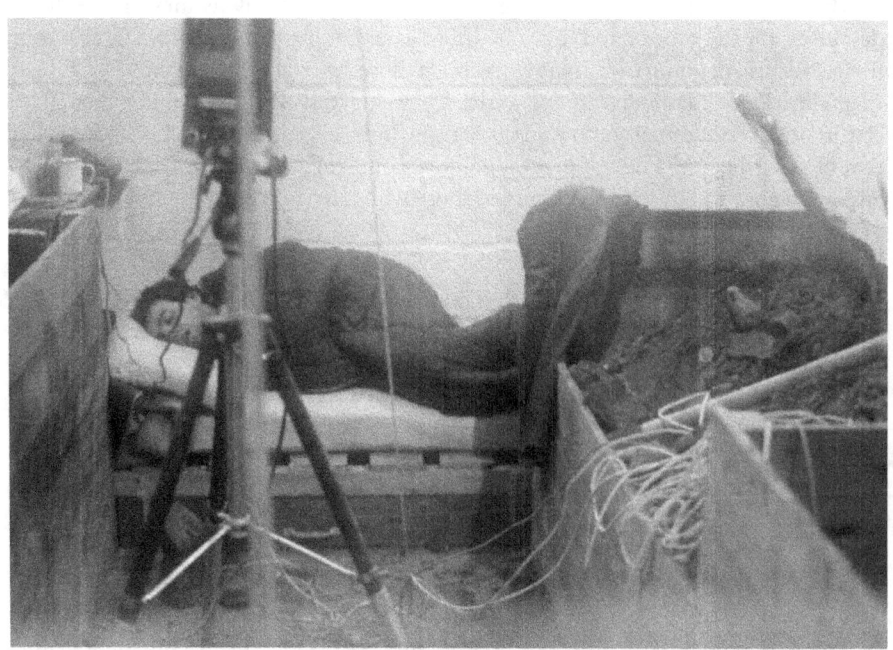

1.5 Kerry Trengove, *An Eight Day Passage*, photographs from a durational performance, The Acme Gallery, London, 25 October to 1 November 1977

Included in the Acme Gallery's archives is a four-page typescript of an unpub-lished article by filmmaker Marilyn Halford (a note suggests it had been sent to *Time Out*, *Miss London*, *Artscribe* and *Readings*). Her draft response is broadly critical of the performance and specifically complains of Trengove's apparent capitulation to – or encouragement of – media interest or hype. Halford writes,

> Kerry Trengove showman extraordinaire has, by use of himself as focus, captured the media, and so the public. By straining limits . . . one's mind b[are]ly likes to imagin[e], he has placed himself in a position upon which TV, radio, newspapers, district surveyors and the man next door have been able to act, depending upon their talents and opportunities.[3]

She adds that as the days progressed, Trengove was objectified or monumentalised to the detriment of his dialogic imperatives: 'Kerry's social presence became fainter and fainter, he became incorporated with the cell, so that . . . I looked at Kerry as [an] exhibit rather than a friend' (Halford, untitled text: 3). Her criticisms primar-ily concern Trengove's aspect as a 'showman'. This is a term Trengove would have recoiled at, for he was concerned centrally with distancing himself from theatricality and spectacle, as well as from any possible commercialisation of his work. Halford writes that she was troubled by 'the premise of displaying the physical duress under which many people find it necessary to place themselves, in order to liberate creative energies' (4). She is not concerned by the comparison to prisoners or detainees, but rather by her impression that as a 'showman', 'puppet' and 'manipulator of the media', Trengove had 'allowed himself to be acted upon by those who need an energy source on which to feed', suggesting his lack of agency in the event, his own tacit victimhood over the course of his exertion and an exploitative dimension that may have over-whelmed Trengove's dialogical structure (4).

Despite the popular coverage he received (and notwithstanding Halford's criti-cisms), Trengove did not enact a media blitz and neither did he encourage its attention beyond conceding to interviews – many of which were conducted via the telephone provided for social interaction with his audience. Owing in great part to press interest, the performance was well attended. The visitors' book covers 11 closely lined page; attendance was counted at 2,537 (an impressive average exceeding 300 visitors per day).[4] Visitors added their name and details and some offered notes. Over two pages, the British-Filipino performance artist David Medalla wrote a letter to Trengove on the final day of the performance, at 9.03 p.m. (half an hour after Trengove's emer-gence from the tunnel). He describes it as 'a stunning experience: You, immured for a period of time (for longer than I, in my imagination, could conceive I could – I would – be capable of doing), and you emerging: it was a rebirth for all of us who were here and also for others who were not here.' Medalla compares the scene to a medi-eval altarpiece: 'waiting for you to break through . . . [we] were like the peasants and shepherds and magi and little children in those magical paintings waiting/attending

---

3 Marilyn Halford, untitled text, November 1977, pp. 1–4 (p. 1), Acme Gallery Archive, Acme, Box 3, Hanging File, Folder: 'Kerry Trengove, *Eight Day Passage* and *Solo*'. Subsequent references in this paragraph appear in parentheses.
4 'Acme Gallery: Visitors Book 1977', Acme Gallery Archive, Acme, Visitors Books series 1976–82.

an ephemeral and wondrous moment.'[5] Trengove's endurance prompts in his friends
and audience members – here, in Medalla's testimony at least – a breathless admira-
tion, even a kind of love.

In his open attitude to the media, Trengove did not compromise the importance
of his work, or the impressions his performance would have on sympathetic audiences, including his peers. He entertained the attention of journalists by talking freely
and seriously with them throughout the performance – and he instructed Jonathan
Harvey (director of the Acme Gallery) to exhibit the news clippings on a 'media
wall' that accumulated notices and commentaries over the course of the *Passage*. As
Michael Archer notes, 'by grasping the mocking attention of the press and putting it
to good use, Trengove found the wider impact which his literal attempt to break out of
the artificial confines of the art gallery seemed to demand' (1991: 25). Yet the revolutionary aspects of his work were likely lost on his expanded audiences and left wanting
in much of the attention granted by the media, in favour of accounts that – however
sympathetic – may have sensationalised the feat in apolitical or counterproductive
terms.

Endurance and masculinity

In photographs from the 1970s, Trengove's face is compelling, rugged. It's handsome,
even. Jovial and asymmetrical, his eyes are jolted out of horizontality as if weighted
by something external at their far corners. The skin of his cheeks is vertically creased
and weathered, which, alongside his ruffled hair, gives his appearance an unpam-
pered, roughly sketched demeanour. While his friends recall Trengove's gregarious
and perhaps overwhelming personality (made more rambunctious by his excessive
drinking), Trengove's supposed impression of bullish masculinity *in performance* is
offset by his evident criticality about its deployment: he devises consistent situations
of co-authorship and collective, relational exchange, suggesting an interest in mutual
entitlement and equitable potentials for discovery. *An Eight Day Passage* is not readable persuasively or substantially as one of brute intensity for a passive, stunned and
silenced audience, as might befit a properly egoistic, self-aggrandising, phallic spectacle. Yet, Roberts notes elsewhere, contemporary critics tended to dilute Trengove's
politics by reading his persona as (he thinks erroneously) 'egoistic', 'self-aggrandising'
and 'bullishly masculine' (Roberts 1992). While masculinity remains operative
throughout the work, Trengove positions himself in a critical relation, enabling a
farther-reaching political efficacy.

This counteracts the assumption that endurance-based actions inevitably secure
the artist's ordeal as being in the service of opportunism, narcissism or bravado – even
when camouflaged in the mythic image of an artist-hero overcoming an ordeal, thus
taking charge of the institution, the audience or one's own fate. Art historian Guy

5 David Medalla, unpublished letter, 1 November 1977, in 'Acme Gallery: Visitors Book 1977'.

Brett describes feats of endurance and duration in performance art of the 1970s as 'Promethean' with direct reference to Trengove and notes the old-fashioned tang such activities may attach to the concept of the artist; he argues that the heroic refusal of 'stereotyped modes of behaviour, control and freedom' might be at odds with other projects in the decade that instantiate new experiences and voices – especially those by women and people of colour (Brett 2008: 253). Indeed, in the 1970s, British-based artists such as Rose English, Rose Finn-Kelcey, Rasheed Araeen or David Medalla were profoundly important for their refusal of the 'Promethean' vigour of action-based artists. Their self-reflexive works in performance refused what Roberts calls Trengove's 'almost story-book heroism' (1980: 40), by claiming less phallic models of behaviour and adventure.

For Donald Kuspit acts of endurance embody 'the feel of power' and signal the exultation of 'wrestling with the angel of death' (Kuspit 1988: 38), perhaps recalling Medalla's account of Trengove's sanctification. Acknowledging what he considers more sceptical or cynical readings of such actions as 'the usual daredevil flirtation with death' or 'an ironical form of self-mythification', Kuspit tends towards an old-fashioned myth of the heroic artist (epitomised, for him, by Chris Burden) who transcends his ordeal to reach creative transfiguration by way of 'his own power of endurance', twinned with 'composure [as] a sign of great ego strength' (1988: 38–9). Such accounts may privilege what Jennifer Doyle calls 'an awful cliché, cemented in a romantic tradition that exalts some psychic struggles as heroic and abjects others as weak and self-indulgent' (Doyle 2016: 318). The quarrel concerning which ordeals qualify as reasonable and which others are indulgent or regressive runs deep in the study of performance art. Lisa Tickner's earlier critique pits feminist performance and criticism against what she calls the 'heavily expressionistic, sado-masochistic, messy and perhaps *macho* performances' of Burden, Hermann Nitsch and Stuart Brisley, who tended to attract encomiums for the resemblance of their ordeals to catharsis, rite, sacrifice or alienation and to their valorisation of 'pain, risk, and premeditated self-abuse' (Tickner1980: 60, emphasis in original).

Similarly, for Amelia Jones, such ordeals may signify 'laconically macho' displays (Jones 1994: 568) and an uncritical 'bad boy' aesthetics (1994: 573), which shore up the familiar spectacle of masculine invincibility. Jones usefully identifies the performance of masculinity in art as 'the ritual display of phallic attributes, specifically in relation to the masculinized function of the artist', supported by feminist art history's prior accounts of the artist as 'a quintessentially phallic figure' (1994: 546–7). Endurance art, she writes, must reckon with 'the transcendental and singularly masculine conception of artistic authority put into place within modernism – a conception that relies on the veiling of the actual body of the artist such that his divinity (his phallic prowess) can be ensured' (1994: 547). In her analysis, such performances may either bolster the myth of masculine transcendence (as Burden did) or seek to dismantle it (as would Vito Acconci, among others).

Burden's performances are a useful litmus test for extremity – and for seemingly untrammelled displays of masculine bravado. I invoke him here, briefly, to pose a question about the active negotiation of masculinity and privilege in Trengove's performance. Trengove's endurance in the *Passage* sits in suggestive counterpoint to

Burden's long occupations of gallery spaces. While Burden typically remains transfixed to open the art institution to potential critique, Trengove attempts to leave his
self-imposed imprisonment in the gallery and to undermine physically and hence
symbolically the integrity of institutions of art. In *Bed Piece* (1972), for example,
Burden stayed in bed in a gallery – mute, unresponsive and inactive – for 22 days.
Burden's performance of endurance requires the gallery to reorganise itself around
the exceptionality of his way of taking up space and time: its organisational structure
is reconstituted, as if to better accommodate the demands he places upon it. *Bed Piece*
may suggest a period of endurance that activated the role of the audience as participants and their attendance as witness or vigil, disallowing the more inevitable function of the audience as passive consumers. Without providing instructions on his care,
Burden relied on donations of food and water from the employees of the gallery (the
Market Street Program, Venice, California) and his audience, who became activated
as participants – as carers or as jailers – for the duration of his self-imposed incarcera-
tion. If such activation forced some audience members to rethink their ethical duty
towards the artist, it also exploited their susceptibility to turn them into unpaid immaterial labourers, encouraged not to dialogue (for Burden remains mute) but to return
with provisions to sustain the artist's pointedly pointless act of endurance. Burden's
exceptional passivity, here, may act as a surrogate for – that is, a tool to recalibrate or
extend – his own privileged access to the space of the gallery and his own steadfast
dominion over it.

In *Bed Piece*, Burden's mission is to survive his own solitude, to eke out an existence amid the promise of boredom, desperation and loneliness. An act of passive
resistance, it is as much a performance of the artist's stubborn refusal neither to make
art nor to leave the gallery. Trengove's *Passage*, on the other hand, discloses a renun-
ciative logic: a laborious and incessant refusal to claim the entitlement to such spaces
that his privilege might authorise. He takes up the challenge to work through his
ordeal – and through the physical structure of the gallery. If such privileged access is
a masculine one, his resistance to it resembles what Amelia Jones describes as the way
performance 'ruptur[es] the very binary model of gender that it engages – opening
provocative cracks in the fabric (or flesh?) of masculinity', as opposed to shoring it up
(1994: 548). While Burden's performance resolved to reclaim and restyle the gallery
space in his own untarnished image, Trengove sought to demolish it.

Irregular experience and revolutionary aesthetics

In an unpublished interview, conducted during the preparation for the *Eight Day
Passage*, Trengove explains the acuteness with which he sought to reject the commercialisation of art and performance. He recounts that he began to appear in his works
in 1969 and at the same time began to activate his audiences as participants. He cites
an early work he made around 1970 (whose title has been lost) that used waste and
industrial materials, which the audience was invited to rearrange. 'That had quite an

effect on me', he remarks, adding, 'I didn't make another "art object" after that.'[6] He continues, 'I just couldn't see how the defence of art categories and their individual attempts at formal manipulation were any longer art currency' (Trengove, untitled interview: 1–2). He explains his resistance to the commodity form in more detail: as 'an efficient business system', the 'market place' of art 'must perpetuate the idea that art's primary status is that of a commodity, an educational prop for museums, a means of investment décor for apartment walls' (2). This necessitates his 'attempting to extend the idea of what art is, by altering its traditional function and place of being', by privileging ephemeral modes, the performing body, his own immaterial labour and unmanageable or uncontainable durations (2). He describes himself as deeply invested in the ethics of art: paraphrasing a (seemingly apocryphal) statement by Lenin, Trengove explains, 'he said that in the arts aesthetics would give way to ethics as the primary concern of the artist. I think this is happening now', in and through performance (2).

In his turn to ethics as a means of overcoming aestheticism and his commitment to bridging art and life, Trengove's approach in the *Passage* and in his public thinking emphasises the primacy of *experience*, over and above the production of objects and unitary definitions of art, recalling the aesthetic theory of John Dewey. Presented as a series of lectures in 1931 and first published as a book in 1934, Dewey's *Art as Experience* is a pragmatist rethinking of the philosophy of art, arguing for a materially grounded and de-idealised understanding of art as co-extensive with the experiences of everyday life. His theory sought to revoke the traditional aesthetic hierarchy – operative since the Enlightenment – by which art is 'isolated from the human conditions under which it was brought into being and from the human consequences it engenders in actual life-experience' (Dewey 1934: 3). Dewey sets out to unknot the paradox of the aesthetic suspicion of art. Experience is his key to undermining or overwhelming the strong modal claims that aesthetics tends to make for art – namely, authoritative claims as to the essential or universal qualities of art and aesthetic experience, which rarely include (or stand up to) specific examples. Dewey opposes the aesthetic tendency in which art is abstracted as a 'general significance . . . cut off from [its] association with the materials and aims of every other form of human effort, undergoing, and achievement' (*ibid.*). His solution is to forge a philosophical sublation (a dialectical overcoming) of the false polarity of art and life: 'to restore continuity between the refined and intensified forms of experience that are works of art and the everyday events, doings, and sufferings that are universally recognized to constitute experience' (*ibid.*).

Dewey's description of artworks as 'intensified forms of experience' is striking in the context of Trengove's *Passage*, as a work that explicitly ramps up the intensity of the labour, commitment, risk and duration we may associate with art and, in the same operation, returns such extremity to life, both in terms of the bare life of the prisoner and the augmented life of the sportsman (both represented in the process and

6 Kerry Trengove, transcript of untitled interview, Acme Gallery Archive, Acme, Box 3, Hanging File, Folder: 'Proposal for Show, 24–9 October 1977', pp. 1–8 (p. 1). The interviewer is named only as 'P'. No date is given. I have corrected spelling and punctuation in my quotations. Subsequent references in this section are given in the text as 'Trengove, untitled interview', followed by a page number.

auditory words of the performance) and the 'real' life of the miner or manual labourer, suggested by Trengove's central activity. For Dewey, the efficacy of art is confirmed by the physiological effects it provokes in the viewer, by, say, the 'bristling of the skin, shivers in the spine, constriction of the throat' and other 'organic "clicks"', such that aesthetic experience is not fully and exclusively physical, but is 'more than intellectual, because it absorbs the intellectual into immediate qualities that are experienced through senses that belong to the vital body' (1934: 216). Such perceptual phenomena are both extreme and entirely uncontainable, demotic and familiar. The dailiness of art – as that which, in his extremity, Trengove manifested so compellingly – is precisely the theme of Dewey's aesthetics. He prompts the reader to imagine aesthetic experience 'in the raw':

> in the events and scenes that hold the attentive eye and ear of man, arousing his interest and affording him enjoyment as he looks and listens: the sights that hold the crowd – the fire-engine rushing by; the machines excavating enormous holes in the earth, the human-fly climbing the steeple-side; the men perched high in the air on girders, throwing and catching red hot bolts. (1934: 4–5)

The experience of art, he suggests, should be theorised in accordance with the aesthetic judgement that attends pedestrian experiences such as those listed, to provoke a democratic, socially inclusive basis for the new philosophy of art. The political efficacy of such a position is clear: 'Even a crude experience, if authentically an experience, is more fit to give a clue to the intrinsic nature of [a]esthetic experience than is an object already set apart from any other mode of experience' (Dewey 1934: 11).

Dewey distinguishes 'experience at large' – the continuous process of existence, in which a living organism interacts with its environment – from '*an* experience', showing that while the former is an inchoate process without resolution, it coheres into experiences, is demarcated and classified and begs our attention, under certain conditions that ensure the stuff of experience 'runs its course to fulfillment' (1934: 35, emphasis in original). He writes about events or undertakings after which one might say, 'that *was* an experience' – a memorable meal, a stormy night sea crossing, or a brush with danger or death (1934: 36, emphasis in original). 'Such an experience is a whole and carries with it its own individualizing quality and self-sufficiency. It is *an* experience' – and, typically, an overwhelming or extreme one (1934: 35, emphasis in original). He sees these qualities in works of art.

After Dewey, and particularly after the late 1950s, when artists read and digested Dewey's ideas – the originator of Happenings, Allan Kaprow was a noted student (Kelley 1993: xi–xii) – art actively aspired to the shape and force of the profound yet demotic experiences Dewey celebrated. Kaprow's appropriation of Dewey was still in the air in the 1970s, and would have set a profound scene for Trengove's *Passage*, which manifested Dewey's enlivening account of what it might mean to undergo – or to prompt in others – a full-blooded experience.

At its heart, Dewey's pragmatist theory of art is a relational one. His communitarian philosophy of art is explained in the conviction that works of art 'are not remote from common life [but] are widely enjoyed' as 'signs of a unified collective life' (1934: 81). To the degree it 'exercises its office', Dewey writes, art 'remake[s] the experience of the community' with the feasible effect of sustaining 'greater order and unity' (*ibid.*). Later, he reiterates this thesis in different terms:

> Communication is the process of creating participation, of making common what had been isolated and singular; and part of the miracle it achieves is that, in being communicated, the conveyance of meaning gives body and definiteness to the experience of the one who utters as well as to that of those who listen . . . Art breaks through barriers that divide human beings, which are impermeable in ordinary association. (1934: 244)

Trengove's emphasis on the social possibilities that extreme action might engender complements and extends the relevance of Dewey's theses. By firmly embedding a broad community of individuals in the researching and making of the work – through recorded dialogues with some 60 interviewees – and by forging opportunities for round-the-clock conversations with the artist during the extent of the *Passage*, Trengove gives stunning reality to Dewey's account of the communicative potential of art as an experience of 'making common what had been isolated and singular'.

Trengove's work may be characterised as part of a general shift in art of the late 1960s and 1970s, away from objects and towards processes – a transformation influentially described by art historian Lucy Lippard as the 'dematerialization of the art object' in the period (Lippard 1997). John Roberts addresses the new art of ephemerality and social relations as 'a fundamentally cognitive activity', adding that after art's conceptual turn in the 1960s, 'the pleasure taken from engaging with art was held to be not necessarily confinable to looking at discrete objects', prompting the development of what he terms 'post-object aesthetics' (Roberts 1992). He theorises Trengove's *Passage* as one among various actions that broke with the 'fetishism of form', typifying a contemporary political effort in art: '*not the aestheticisation of the social environment, but instead, the socialising of the aesthetic*', by privileging process and breaking down traditional divisions of labour, such as those between artists, craftsmen, technicians and manual labourers (*ibid.*, emphasis in original).

Between 1970 and the early 1980s, Trengove pioneered what would later be called *relational aesthetics* or, more broadly, the *social turn* in art and its study. 'Relational aesthetics' is a term coined by the critic-curator Nicolas Bourriaud to describe a politics of art that he deemed typical of developments in performance and interactive art in the 1990s. In 1998, Bourriaud defined relational aesthetics as 'an art taking as its theoretical horizon the realm of human interactions and its social context, rather than the assertion of an independent and *private* symbolic space', deeming this relatively new apart from a few loosely historicised works of performance (Bourriaud 2002: 14, emphasis in original). Stressing the cultural novelty of 'relational' art practices, Bourriaud observes performances and installations that function as 'social experiments', which investigate or upend the 'uniformity of behavioural patterns', explaining opportunities and imperatives of art that fit Trengove's working practices of some two decades earlier (2002: 9). The social emphasis in Trengove's performance has been noted elsewhere, including by John Roberts in an obituary; he explains the importance of relationality in the *Passage* and his other works of the 1970s as 'opportunities to talk and argue, points of open contact between spectator and art-work that the routine day-to-day life of the art world obliterated' (1991: 24). This emphasis on co-creation through dialogue, collaboration and the active co-creation of knowledge demonstrated that Trengove's key discovery 'was not the simple linguis-tic fact that the production of meaning was a shared act, but that such a process was explicitly a social one, and therefore potentially pedagogic' (*ibid.*).

Writing after Trengove's death in 1991, Roberts anticipates Bourriaud's theory of the art of the coming decade, but situates Trengove's relational approach to aes-thetics within a solidly Marxist framework. Roberts explains the importance of Trengove's committed reading of Paulo Freire's *Pedagogy of the Oppressed* (published in Portuguese in 1968 and in English in 1970), stating 'it would not be an over-exaggeration to say that to understand this book is to understand [Trengove's] art', such that Freire's revolutionary praxis for a decolonised and dialogical approach to teaching was the ground for Trengove's 'distrust of traditional aesthetics' and prepared his faith in the power of art 'to "intervene critically" in reality' (*ibid.*). Viewed in the light of Freire's controversial book, Roberts suggests, the *Passage* shows that 'politics in art was not a univocal process of address in which the audience got "the message", but a process by which meanings were returned transformed to the context from which they emerged, to be used and transformed again'; *Passage* and Trengove's subsequent per-formances were therefore 'metaphors of self-activity through collaborative exchange' (Roberts 1991: 24). Or, as Freire puts it, '[k]nowledge emerges only through invention and re-invention, through the restless, impatient, continuing, hopeful inquiry human beings pursue in the world, with the world, and with each other' (Freire 1996: 53).

In *Pedagogy of the Oppressed*, Freire draws on his experiences working as an edu-cator with non-literate, socially disadvantaged people in Brazil at mid-century and articulates a revolutionary praxis for the liberation of those living under economic and state oppression. His general theory requires that the members of the colonised *lumpenproletariat* gain the tools to model their own liberty through learning. This new praxis is centrally dialogical and does away with what Freire criticises as the tra-ditional 'banking' model of teaching, where information and skills deemed useful by the oppressive class are implanted into the grasp of the oppressed class whose subjects must respond dutifully by 'receiving, filing, and storing the deposits' (1996: 53). The new praxis of learning and teaching is one modelled on co-operative thought rather than the instrumentalisation of knowledge and the 'false generosity' of granting (as opposed to enabling) growth, to produce 'the individual's ontological and histori-cal vocation to be more fully human' (1996: 37). Freire's central tactic for enabling the oppressed class to inhabit their proper 'ontological vocation' is a relational one: 'Dialogue, as essential communication, must underlie any cooperation. In the theory of dialogical action, there is no place for conquering the people on behalf of the revolutionary cause . . . Dialogue does not impose, does not manipulate, does not domesticate, does not "sloganize"' (1996: 149). Hence, in Trengove's design for the *Passage*, what might otherwise have become a superhuman feat to be witnessed from afar – and thus, perhaps, an oppressive, phallic spectacle – is retooled via Freire as dialogic and equitable, as an opportunity for a richer practical encounter with political self-determination.

For Freire, decolonial liberation requires that the educator recognises one's tacit function as an oppressor and reinvents him- or herself as a conduit for revolutionary action: 'Conversion to the people requires a profound rebirth. Those who undergo it must take on a new form of existence', he writes, suggesting the importance of a test of will and the visible strain of physical and intellectual transformation as fundamental steps in one's social deconditioning – one's active refusal of complicity in an oppressive discourse (1996: 43). Both oppressor and oppressed alike reinvent themselves in the face of what Freire calls 'limit-situations', which reveal the limitations imposed upon the subject, by undergoing 'limit-acts', conceived by the subject as attempts to overcome one's material restraints – precisely through a practice of endurance, a test of will or mettle or, say, a performance of extremity. He writes,

> Once perceived by individuals as fetters, as obstacles to their liberation, these situations stand out in relief from the background, revealing their true nature as concrete historical dimensions of a given reality . . . As critical perception is embodied in action, a climate of hope and confidence develops which leads men [*sic*] to attempt to overcome the limit-situations . . . As reality is transformed and these situations are superseded, new ones will appear, which in turn will evoke new limit-acts. (1996: 80–1)

The relevance of Freire's revolutionary praxis to Trengove's performances is suggested by Trengove's commitment to processes that dramatise the thesis that '[f]reedom is acquired by conquest, not by gift'; thus he conceived actions that function ideologically as parables or metaphors for 'limit-acts' or the ordeal of realising in oneself and enabling in others 'the indispensible condition for the quest for human completion' (1996: 29). The task of creating a literal passage through physical and psychological endurance, over frightening distances of time and densities of space, thus resembles Freire's description of the emboldening nature of duress and struggle – perhaps recasting the *Passage* as a kind of personal conquest. The commitment to sourcing and representing the voices of those who have been subjected to oppression – in the *Passage*, through interviews with tortured detainees – also chimes with Freire's teaching in facilitating another's ontological vocation: 'their primordial right to speak their word', to name the world so as to transform it (1996: 69).

Yet Freire's praxis is concerned precisely with the specific circumstances of education in developing world contexts; the correlation or applicability of his methodology to the distant milieu of performance art in galleries in Europe in the 1970s is perhaps tendentious. If we take Trengove at his word and pursue the parallels between his own method and Freire's praxis, stumbling blocks appear, especially if one consents to Roberts' suggestion that Trengove's actions function as 'metaphors of self-activity' in the spirit of Freire's pedagogy. Who is the oppressed class in Trengove's set-ups, including the *Passage*? In his struggle, does the artist metaphorise the embattled constituent of an oppressed class, on 'the frontier between being and being more human' (1996: 83); or the teacher striving towards conversion to the people, digging through the foundation of the institution to come to 'comradeship with the oppressed'? (1996: 43). Is the audience – embedded in dialogical, horizontal relations – imagined here as standing in for the oppressed class, yearning for freedom from the yoke of their oppression? Who is their oppressor, the artist or the spectre of other non-dialogic artists? Or the art world and its institutions, including the gallery Trengove disassembles through his digging action? These analogies feel patronising – to audiences, but also to the camouflaged subjects of real oppression, Freire's own comrades: 'those who are oppressed, exploited, and unrecognized', 'the unloved', 'the helpless, subject to terror' and 'the tyrannized' (1996: 37). My sense of the gravity of their suffering smarts under a comparison to that of a self-willed artist or his self-selecting observers. Such analogies or homilies – however well-intentioned – reduce the function of the artist and of art and at the same time would perform a kind of hagiography, setting up the performance as a totem to the benevolence and transcendence of the artist (which I have argued against, here).

Yet Trengove does not evangelise or self-aggrandise. If the *Passage* acts on a metaphorical level, its metaphoricity is not a direct substitution between a single element or constituency in the work and a world outside it, but a function of discourse that allows the totality of the work to speak to a social reality that it seeks to manifest and transform. If the *Passage* functions at the level of metaphor, it is not in an attenuated, abstracting manner, but reflects Paul Ricoeur's theorisation of metaphor not as mere substitution (a figure that stands in for another) but as 'the rhetorical process by which discourse unleashes the power that certain fictions have to redescribe reality', suggesting an ontological function grounded in the transformative right to language (Ricoeur 1977: 7). Art historian Darby English writes of the troubled play of metaphor in endurance performance in a compelling discussion of William Pope.L's long-distance crawls in urban space, commenced in New York in the late 1970s. He describes Pope.L's supine elaboration of an 'aesthetics of dispossession' that indexes the experience of homelessness in the artist's (and the rough sleeper's) incidental performances of public horizontality: by crawling in a costume through the street, Pope.L may mimic and comment upon the 'compulsory ascendancy' (English 2007: 281) that marginal subjects are required to aspire to, which stigmatises the horizontal body and celebrates 'dignified verticality' (2007: 267). Pope.L's painful crawls, English writes, are not minor dramas about or theatrical narrations of the destitution of homelessness (which the artist and his family had experienced), but, rather, work 'to collapse on a small scale a pre-existing order "structured" by race, class, gender, and sexuality though an insubordinate identification, or voluntary dispossession' (2007: 288).

Indeed, Freire allows for such substitutions and broader applications beyond the proper scholastic sphere of his research. He acknowledges the significance of secondary representation, adding in a footnote that '[t]he coding of an existential situation is the representation of that situation, showing some of its constituent elements in interaction' (1996: 86, n. 21). For Freire, broader experiences of representation can be crucial to the project of liberation, suggesting that the authentic work of revolutionary *praxis* includes, or is comparable to, the project of a revolutionary *aesthetics*, as two edges of the same ideological imperative, namely, to 'perceive the reality of oppression not as a closed world from which there is no exit, but as a limiting situation which they can transform' (1996: 31). This parallelism does not rely upon representation as a simulation or analogy, but as a working through: performance here is the coding of a situation as a critical, sympathetic and co-operative activity.

In his own voluntary dispossessions, Trengove adopts the tenets of revolutionary praxis and the body postures of those who have sought it or attained it, not to mimic them or for mere fabulation, but to explore them, to inhabit them thoroughly – *to collapse them on a small scale* – with care and without violence. As English writes, an endurance action by Pope.L (and, I think, by Trengove) may make 'painfully clear' that 'to aestheticize dispossession is not necessarily to metaphorize it or to make it pretty', but, rather, to attend to 'what makes dispossession particularly devastating for some by exploring the mode of its connection to all' (English 2007: 288). Moreover, implicit in Freire's praxis is a commitment to politics as a totality from which super-structures, such as art, cannot be detached. In *Theatre of the Oppressed* (published in 1974) – a book indebted to Freire (even if the author addresses him cursorily [Boal 2000: 96]) – Augusto Boal makes this position clear. 'Nothing is alien to politics', he writes, 'because nothing is alien to the superior art that rules the relations among men' (2000: 12). If politics includes aesthetics, the theatre artist suggests, then actions willed under the sign of art are not outside, subordinate to or weak approximations of politi-cal action; rather, they function at the level of an experience to re-describe reality and transform the situation.

Trengove began to actualise his interests in Freire in the design of his early works in performance, beginning in 1973 (in works that have never been discussed in art history). *Postal Piece* (1973) consisted of two 50-ft greenhouses filled with plants that he sold to visitors over the course of the performance. The visitors were engaged by the artist in conversation about botany, ecology, gardening and farming and invited to write a postcard or letter to Trengove on a prearranged date to report on the usages and development of the plant they purchased, thus prompting 'a natural dialogue' (Trengove, untitled interview, 3). Exchange or communication was foregrounded in early works like *Postal Piece* through sale, conversation and letter writing – and with greater ambition in the *Passage*.

'One of the things that excited me about the greenhouse', Trengove recalls, 'was that quite a number of people couldn't understand what a plant salesman was doing in an art exhibition', suggesting his enjoyment in trafficking non-art experiences or activities including socially distinct practices of labour into an art context. He was also readily aware of the political efficacy of 'sidestep[ping] the preconceptions of what art should look like' (*ibid.*). When asked if he minds the fact that his role as an artist is not always immediately obvious, Trengove replies:

> New systems have come into being which have directly affected the historical structures, including art. As in nature these structures must adapt or die. A new and less exclusive general theory is emerging which affects art as much as it does technology or politics. It's been said that new theories win recognition not by their general acceptance as much as by the dying off of their opponents. For this to happen, for me anyway, it's not necessary for it to be read as art, at least for the moment. (Trengove, untitled interview, 6)

Trengove's explanation is exuberant. He clearly comprehends and even relishes the need to exceed or explode the limits of form, here in his reflection on the *Postal Piece* – and, of course, in anticipation of the epic accomplishment of the *Passage*. Pressed on the topic, Trengove describes this emergent 'general theory' in terms of the creative responses by women's liberation, civil rights and anti-war movements, which successfully attracted and manipulated media coverage to create and sustain social change. He adds that artists and audiences alike are more attuned to being 'constantly under pressure to readjust our conceptual frameworks to balance all the new technological and social innovations', which can be taken up in one's social and artistic responsibilities (*ibid.*). In a distinctly Freirean mode, Trengove states that the artist's present function is to demonstrate and enact 'freedom of action': 'The people who take up this ethical role will become the . . . only [artists] with the unique freedom to work between the systems and institutions without being committed to any one of them' (Trengove, untitled interview, 7). He is not saying that everyone is an artist (an idealism) or that the artist must lead the way (a moralism); rather, he is calling for an anti-disciplinary, post-medium practice of art, against the limits of form, beyond the reach of any institutional embrace, as the basis for art as a project for social change.

Working

In Trengove's account of his own work, the *Postal Piece* spurred him on to blur the lines between artistic and skilled manual labour, which he outlines further in his new ethical mandate for aesthetics as 'the unique freedom to work'. Of performances and installations in the late 1970s, John Roberts writes, '[b]oat-building and . . . cooking, hole-digging and dog-handling have all been seen at the ACME Gallery over the past few years': he references Trengove's *Passage* and his subsequent, canine collaboration piece *Solo* (1979); and other works including Bobby Baker's *Edible Family in a Mobile Home* (1976), a participatory installation consisting of a deceptively homely, habitable cake sculpture; and Ron Haselden's *Working 12 Days* (1978), an installation involving the wreck of a wooden lifeboat, which Haselden found beached on Canvey Island, cut into pieces with a chainsaw and meticulously rebuilt in the gallery (its spectacular effect was heightened by mechanising the tensile steel that held the boat together). 'The cult of the work-in', Roberts continues, 'is among us': it finds its apotheosis in Trengove's work, which 'combines the workshop with the theatre of ideas' (Roberts 1980: 40).

With the social turn in performance studies, the question of labour and the material conditions of production trump the seemingly uncritical 'magic' of creative expression. Socially turned and demystified, the prior myth of the solitary, inspired artist whose creative inspiration transcends her or his material labour is exposed as an alibi for the fantasy of the genius-creator. Ignoring the reality of work would obscure the artist's substantive and inevitable interactions with agents of collaboration, delegation, outsourcing, commissioning, funding, documentation, dissemination and reception. Typically, the modes of performance that demystify the reality of labour do so in tandem with the abandonment of traditional forms of artistic creativity – hence the lack of 'artistic' flourishes in the scenography of a work such as the *Passage*. A blatant anti-aestheticism thus runs deep in much performance art of the 1970s, where appropriation and the de-skilling of art were crucial activities in its paradoxically creative avoidance of creativity proper. The actions that characterise performance art may be idiosyncratic, excessive, subtle or rigorous, without resorting to the wishful obscurantism of creativity or of *expressing oneself*. This in itself constitutes a strategy of extremity – as an overrunning or undermining of the traditional demonstration of creative acuity, technical capacity or flair. Trengove is apposite in this regard: his performances – as attested by the artist and by media responses – barely register as art at all.

Work emerges as a problem for post-object aesthetics in the 1960s and 1970s when the question of *how much* work has been involved in the production of art becomes unavoidable, typically because the degree of exertion seems insignificant or negligible (especially proportionate to the implied cultural value or presumed price tag of the resulting work of art); otherwise, the amount of work required seems extravagant in its physical excess, muscularity or durational capaciousness. Of the former tendency, Bruce McLean's works are extreme representatives. In *Taking a Line for a Walk* (1969), McLean walks down Cleveland Road in suburban London, pulling a piece of white string in his wake, creating a mobile image that is definitively lightweight, in both substance and apparent meaningfulness. Similarly, in *Floataway Sculpture* (1967), he throws sheets of hardboard, linoleum and woodblock into Beverley Brook, allowing the current to drag the materials into casually constructed sculptural formations that exist only for the moment his camera documents them. McLean playfully stages variations on the least possible amount of labour required to produce a work. In their activity and as props for rather slight events, McLean's action sculptures barely attain the assumed discreteness, stability and value of sculpture; in their formal border-crossings, they also confirmed a new series of limits for performance art.

Of the tendency towards excessive labour, Trengove's *Passage* is of course apposite (even if historically camouflaged). Its lengthy duration and the requirement of physical exertion or duress commit it to a context of endurance-based performances in the UK and Europe in the 1970s. For example, since the 1970s, Nigel Rolfe's performances have typically involved specialised though pedestrian materials, such as raw pigments, soil, meat, rope and urban detritus, manipulated in barely planned processes of discovery over extended durations – what he calls 'sculptures in motion' (Coogan 2015: 112). In *Running Man* (Belfast, 1978), for example, a large floor-frame held a morass of upright sticks, through which Rolfe ran, fell and clambered, becoming trapped and then freeing himself in a repetitive, exasperating and physically exhausting activity. For Rolfe and his peers, including Anne Bean, Stuart Brisley and Alastair MacLennan (and farther afield, artists such as Marilyn Arsem in the United States) long durational performances would foreground extended acts of seemingly inefficient labour – practices of work removed from productivity, object-production and rationality – to manifest and investigate a series of aesthetic axioms concerning immediacy, endurance, non-repetition, difficulty, risk, ephemerality, change and an explicit resistance to commodification.

In performances of the 1960s and 1970s, specifically, a new world of excessive and impractical work is realised in, and as, the practice of art, as art reorients itself to reflect the modern economic base upon which labour was reformulated. For Shannon Jackson, this is founded in great part on the achievements of feminist art by women, such as the 'Maintenance Art' of Mierle Laderman Ukeles, whose cleaning interventions in museums and other spaces – such as *Hartford Wash: Washing/Tracks/ Maintenance: Inside* (1973) – prompted a methodological and political transition 'from a discrete notion of an art *work* to a process-based notion of the *work* it takes to make art' (Jackson 2011: 92, emphasis in original). The quantification of work in relation to the created and displayed object or artefact demands an address to the types of labour involved – activities that are often unskilled, administrative, manual, menial, invisible, immaterial, flexible, affective or obscure – as well as an analysis of the social and economic conditions in which they are undertaken. Moreover, by the 1960s, the meaning and value of art becomes alienated from its mythical origin in artistic intention and resituated in the intellectual labour of the viewer through the conviction that an audience completes and activates the aesthetic, political and cultural work of this or that art (Molesworth 2003: 29–30).

Trengove's *Passage* is enabled by these shifts in the understanding of what constitutes labour, the material conditions for work, the scale of effort involved (or denied) in 'dematerialized' art and the direct appropriation of recognisable acts of labour. These material transformations also illuminate his selection of particular modes by which to metaphorise or actualise his readings in Freire's revolutionary pedagogy. In his attention to the activation of audiences, the problem of labour and its effects on the perceived limits of form and his struggle for a new, ethically progressive revaluation or reconstitution of aesthetics, Trengove was attuned politically and aesthetically to the zeitgeist of the period – and gave profound form to the need to overcome and remake the category of art. This was enabled not discretely by reading Freire (or Brecht), but by his sensitivity towards – and his resolve to change – the situation he worked in. Specifically, the mode of labour appropriated or approximated by Trengove – digging and working in a tunnel – referenced the contingent labour of coal mining, which was profoundly topical in the popular imagination, after historic strikes led by the National Union of Mineworkers (NUM) in 1972 and 1974. In his authoritative history of the mineworkers' labour movement in Britain and Northern Ireland, Seumas Milne describes the success of industrial actions in the early to mid-1970s as 'shattering experiences' for the Tories, which 'laid the ground for what became a twenty-year vendetta against the miners: a single-minded and ruthless drive to destroy the NUM and, if necessary, the bulk of the British coal industry in the process' (Milne 2014: 6). In 1972, led by Arthur Scargill, 10,000 miners went on strike, picketing the Saltley coke depot in Birmingham, signalling what Milne calls 'the cutting edge of a new working-class assertiveness' (2014: 7). If the industrial action of 1972 was 'the single most successful mass-picketing operation in the postwar period', a further long-term dispute in 1974 created an energy crisis in England, forcing the infamous Three-Day Week (from 1 January to 7 March) and precipitating a general election that felled Edward Heath's Conservative government (2014: 13). The mineworkers (and in synecdoche, their figurehead, Scargill) would epitomise the new industrial and political militancy of the period, Milne writes, emboldening working-class activists in their reasoned ability to humiliate and demoralise the ruling political class.

The relation between the miners' strikes and the specific act of tunnelling as a form of work in the *Passage* is complex. Trengove's exertion is substantial in the context of scenes of endurance in performance and equivalent in some ways to the physical demands and human privations of a working week in the life of a miner. Yet the same density of labour and deprivation is slight in comparison to the struggle of the striking miners, whose legacy of personal, familial and industrial interruption the *Passage* might seem to appropriate or paraphrase. Perhaps the latter comparison is unfair. The literature Trengove produced does not index the miners directly, even if his action is ghosted by their labour and their contemporaneous activism. Moreover, the range of contexts he summons explicitly, especially in the creation and staging of recorded interviews with political detainees and athletes, renders the metaphorical relation to the striking miners as a sympathetic one: Trengove's own exertion (which is substantial and sustained) might err towards that of sportspeople, whose privations are self-imposed, conscientious, painful and goal-orientated (rather than precocious, obscure or phony); and through the voices of the former detainees, as tortured and tumbledown subjects, the ghostly miners circulate among similarly authentic agents of the limit-experience of political and human destitution. The experiences of detainees, athletes and miners – and their testimonies as 'limit-acts' (Freire 1996: 80–1) – construct a continuum of human struggle, from the horrible to the merely hard: Trengove's own labour slips and slides amid these poles of human physical and psychological extremity. His refusal to identify his own struggle with those of other classes of activists performs a productive ambivalence, in place of a fixed identification that would be politically questionable.

As the art critic Michael Archer wrote in 1985, 'Trengove sees his claim to the role of artist lying in an attitude of responsibility towards the world. It would not be sufficient to rely for credentials upon the carrying on of some particular activity such as "painting" or "sculpture"' (Archer 1985). In the same publication, Trengove would write, '[t]he imagination knows no limits, cannot be contained. Painting, sculpture, drawing are not absolute terms; they are inventions, flags of recognition, flags of convenience' (Trengove 1985). The imagination may be more susceptible to limits than Trengove suggests, but the politics of form waits, it would seem, for transgressive recombination or other tactics to undermine its regulation. Of Trengove's political imperatives and casual disregard for posterity, Archer writes, 'Trengove certainly takes delight in overstepping limits, but his pleasure is not malicious or anarchistic. His spirit is an inquisitive one', driven to explore a given problem from 'the other side', resembling the antic strategy of 'someone who lifted up the carpet to show people what was underneath' (Archer 1985).

Trengove's later artworks involved sustained labour in the form of research and practical experimentation, including international fact-finding expeditions to explore a dizzying range of topics: militarisation in Northern Ireland (*Points of Defence*, Belfast, 1980); cohabitation with rutting stags in France (*Enclosures*, Lyon, 1980–81); and the flight habits of endangered kestrels in Mauritius (*Voices in the House of the Dead*, 1982). As such, Trengove would continue his investment in anomalous kinds of labour, through practices of art that strived for active politicisation, proletarian authenticity, an expanded palette and new materials and practices of making. Archer explains,

[In his] performance works of the seventies and the installations which followed, there has been a physical and formal distinction between the analytical, perhaps didactic side of Trengove's art, and its sensual counterpart ... a co-extension of the actual and the possible. (Archer 1985)

Archer's characterisation of Trengove's works as 'a co-extension of the actual and the possible', in his wonderful phrase, entails the intellectual rigour of the artist's research; it also includes his social and formal extremity, as an 'eccentric', a 'maverick' and 'an imp of the socially perverse' as Archer describes him (*ibid.*). This appreciative portrayal as a fabulist, activist and oddball frames Trengove's working method of embedding himself, often frighteningly deep, as a labourer (miner, dog-handler, war correspondent, lay scientist, preservationist or eco-critic), within a chosen context, situation or process. Trengove himself describes his performances and intermedial practices as an experimental pursuit of '[t]hat moment in art when one is beyond reason, when instinct liberates from puritan suspicion, when vision and velocity are one' (Trengove 1985). His unreasonable quality therefore was not mere attention seeking, but the effect of his serial attempts to find unfamiliar ways of working in new environments through which to trigger unprecedented forms of artistic production – as, I argue, exemplars of the performance of extremity.

After the *Passage*

After the *Passage*, Trengove's performances of extremity continued his key principles, including the design of limit-acts, opportunities for dialogue and work and the central refusal of familiar practices, materials, durations and styles. In *Solo* (17–30 June 1979), Trengove lived in Acme Gallery with four dogs for two weeks. He undertook continuous activity from 11 a.m. to 6 p.m., based on a 40-minute cycle: 30 minutes training one of four dogs, 'each chosen for its lack of behavioural skills in the human world'; and 10 minutes of conversations with visitors (**Figure 1.6**). After each 40 minutes, he would move on to working with the next dog, enabling him to collaborate with each non-human animal around ten times each day. Trengove writes that over 13 days, *Solo* would involve 'conditioning and reinforcing (training) particular behaviour in each of four dogs' and 'conversations at scheduled times with visitors to the gallery during which issues raised by the work may be discussed'.[7] *Solo* continues some of the key imperatives of the *Passage* in its use of durational goal-oriented action, taped speech (interviews with behavioural professionals) and opportunities for a relational encounter and dialogue with visitors. Yet the performance design is imperfect: the dogs can consent neither to their collaboration nor their reconditioning; they may participate actively but they cannot enter fully into a

---

7 Press release for *Solo* (17 to 30 June 1979), Acme Gallery, Acme Gallery Archive, Acme, Box 3, Hanging File, Folder: 'Kerry Trengove, *Eight Day Passage* and *Solo*'.

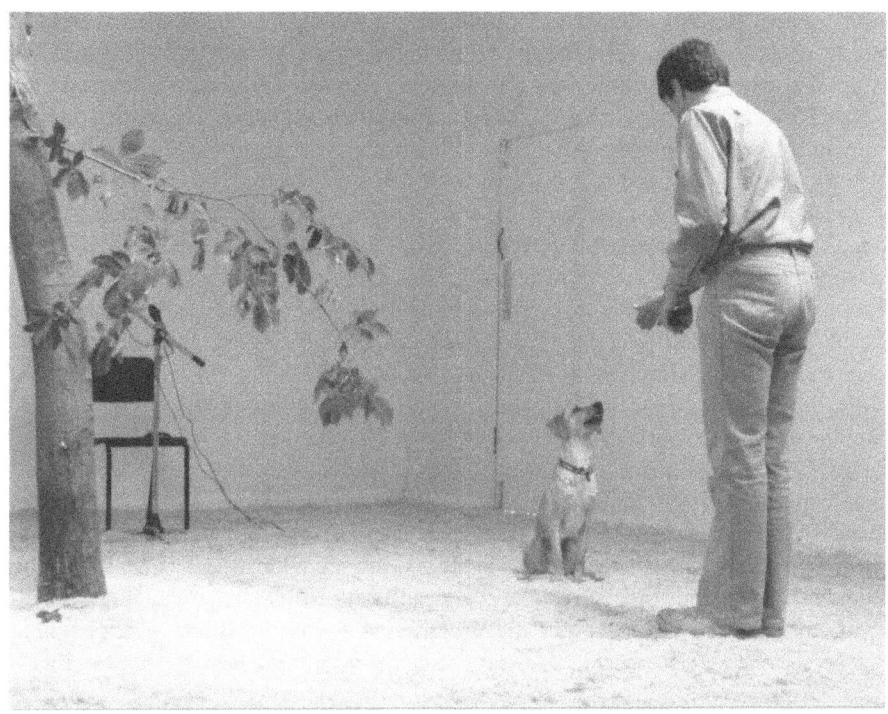

1.6 Kerry Trengove, *Solo*, photograph from a durational performance, The Acme Gallery, London, 17–30 June 1979

dialogical experience or take charge of their learning, even though legitimately they co-author the performance.

While his interviews and personal statements confirm Trengove's political imperatives, he was also keen to find novel means to evidence and analyse his desires and their potential effects. To this end, after *Solo*, Trengove commissioned a behavioural psychologist, Peter Butcher, to study him, publishing the ensuing clinical report in the catalogue for *Zoos*, a group exhibition (of four artists including Trengove) at the Institute of Contemporary Arts, London in 1982. Butcher considers Trengove in terms of the logic of a 'vision quest', describing his primary concerns as 'encouraging creative responsibility for personal and social change', through activities 'designed to raise questions about stereotyped roles and modes of behaviour, to stretch and break the imposed limitations of cultural, political, personal, physical and mental enclosures' (Butcher 1982: 58). Trengove undertakes his 'quest' actions through 'a process of self-imposed initiation, deconditioning and new learning', re-creating the function of 'the artist as explorer becoming the artist as ethnologist', specifically by animating 'the animal within', through acts that echo those of animals (like the mole, who tunnels, burrows and lives underground) or require close interspecies proximity (training dogs or living among kestrels or deer) (*ibid.*). Trengove's performances are instances of 'exemplary action' that assist the subject in progressing towards 'full humanness', Butcher adds (*ibid.*). Specifically, I think, Trengove's exemplarity is a model of extremity: he achieves the unthinkable by way of acts that seem less than human, superhuman or otherwise redefined in proximity to the non-human animal.

Key strategies, then, included co-authoring (with human collaborators and non-human animals), dialogue, detailed and lengthy research with individuals outside the art world, with whom recordings were often produced and displayed during performances and the staging of strategic processes of training, conditioning and deconditioning as the stuff of performance. In an artist statement titled 'My Frame of Reference', written shortly prior to the *Passage*, Trengove notes a democratising impulse: 'In the area of human activity we call the arts, the only common factor is the act of creation itself; this activity is not solely limited to the arts nor to those whom we refer to as artists.'[8] The palpable oddness of his work – both in terms of its content and form, as well as his discursive framing – is part and parcel of its extremity. He reiterates the function of performance art as a type of direct action: 'I fight against any form of categorisation. For me art is an act of dissent, and an act of resistance. It is a moral action, perhaps the last spiritual process available to man' (Trengove, 'Notes from the Project'). In his passionate commitment to Brecht and Freire, Trengove had conceived a limit-act, of a sort, with which to investigate and represent the historical reality of other people's oppression, other subjects' ontological vocation of finding or gaining *more life*, spurred by Freire's argument that 'the objective of any true revolution . . . requires that the people act, as well as reflect, upon the reality to be transformed' (Freire 1996: 111). Even if this was camouflaged by the media's framing of his action – as human mole or modern-day Houdini, as a prankster and showman extraordinaire – Trengove held fast to his ideological convictions during the *Passage* and subsequently in the varied works he continued to produce until the end of his short life.

For so robust a feat, and one so well recorded in its lifetime, the action now feels strangely evanescent. This is not surprising, I think, for the nuanced means by which Trengove attempted to erase his own history and – in the *Passage* – to tear down, literally and figuratively, the sustaining foundations of the art institution. By dismissing his own historical remains in the long term – refusing to produce saleable documents or traces and eventually mandating the destruction of his archive – and by using his privileged access to the gallery in a subversive mode, he seeks to dismantle the structure that might otherwise support his posterity and celebrate his achievement. As such, he undercuts the quality of masculine endeavour in his greatest work, by undoing his own entitlement to critical, historical and institutional acceptance.

After the completion of the *Passage*, media interest in the artist died down quickly, never really to pick up again during his lifetime. The action incurred the threat of legal repercussions, but neither Acme Gallery nor the artist was prosecuted.[9]

8 Kerry Trengove, 'Strategies for Change', unpublished proposal to Acme Gallery, Acme Gallery Archive, Acme, Box 3, Hanging File, Folder: 'Proposal for Show, 24–9 October 1977'.
9 On the fourth day of the dig, the Secretary of Acme Housing Association was served with a Notice of Irregularity by the District Surveyor's Office, on account of Trengove's lack of planning permission, and his probable undermining of party walls. Henry Lydiate of the firm Artlaw reported the legal implications of Trengove's performance in *Art Monthly* (1978: 37–8). Harvey explained to Lydiate that the 'contractor' – Trengove – was unavailable, and therefore could not be instructed to cease building activities until he emerged from the other end of the tunnel. Acme also received a notification from

Jonathan Harvey contracted builders to return the space to its previous style. They dismantled the breezeblock cell, disposed of the materials and repainted the walls. They filled the tunnel with its displaced rubble and smoothed the ragged hole with concrete, leaving no scar in the Shelton Street floor. A thin slice of a large West End building, the ground floor of 43 Shelton Street is now a generic-looking clothes shop. The upper galleries have been converted into six luxury apartments. The history of the action is turned to dust and papered over. As Jean Genet asks of the algebra of every loss: 'How could one detect the secret of the disappearance of things?' (1969: 48). What will have come of the magic of the passage, exertions hitherto barely known, the voices of the combatants and the dialogues proffered and sustained? Thus spoke the tunnel.

---

chartered surveyors representing the neighbouring property (E. A. Shaw & Partners, letter to Acme Housing Association, 28 October 1977, Acme Gallery Archive, Acme, Box 3, Hanging File, Folder: 'Kerry Trengove, *Eight Day Passage* and *Solo.*') As the action was due to finish the next day, Harvey ignored the letter.

2

A criminal touch

Yes, they are criminals. This means, in all good logic, that they have committed one or more crimes and that they are liable to punishments set down in the statute book. But by virtue of the ambiguity of the term, society convinces them – and they let themselves be convinced – that this objective definition actually applies to their hidden subjective being. The criminal that they were to others is thus ensconced deep within them, like a monster . . . Their failings and errors are transformed into a permanent disposition, that is, into a destiny. (Jean-Paul Sartre, *Saint Genet*)

Ulay remains a thief, a nomad, historically wild. His particular crime was extraordinary in form and dutifully documented. In its repercussive wash, too proliferative to hold or name, he accepts the charge of criminality and its consequences. Conceived as a poetic sensibility of active outsidership and extending beyond the discrete event of his illegal misconduct, criminality is to some extent Ulay's permanent disposition as an artist – that is, as an *artivist*, to cite his own neologism, which emphasises the activist dimension, as well as an atavistic sensibility, inside his commitments to art. Ulay tells me, 'I certainly carried out a criminal act. I was, at the very least, a thief. And it's a strange thief who surrenders. I was put in prison' (Johnson 2015: 22).

The criminal act in question is the core of *There is a Criminal Touch to Art* (*Da ist eine kriminelle Beruhrung in der Kunst*), in which Ulay stole a nationally significant painting from the Neue Nationalgalerie in Berlin in 1976. A performance action – and thus a work of art in its own right – his pilfering of Carl Spitzweg's oil painting *The Poor Poet* (1839) from a highly secured museum is a performance of extremity. It takes precedence in its extreme reanimation of the anti-art sensibility in avant-garde aesthetics – literally, here, an attack on art (on a particular object). It does such work, I argue, in order to provoke a kind of national insult: an attempt at irritating – with political effects – the artist's implication within a sense of German national identity in the post-war period. The action thus comments on art worlds, the material realities of privilege and poverty and collective feelings of pride, propriety and hypocrisy. Ulay's indomitable action – the pilfering of a national treasure – suggests an attempt to strike free of the bounds of art or performance art as formal categories. Yet another set of limits – of the law and civil retribution – revealed themselves to be less malleable, more rigid and insurmountable in their delimitation of creative or subjective freedom, however unfathomable or anomalous the shape such freedoms might be urged into taking. Throughout Ulay's performances in the period – including an earlier project involving tattooing and elective cosmetic surgery, among other works of performative photography – he enacts an extreme position to provoke a seemingly violent conceptual slippage.

When the case against Ulay came to trial in Berlin in early 1977, he recounts, 'I was convicted and sentenced to 36 days in prison, or a fine of 3,600 Deutsche Mark. *I chose neither*' (Johnson 2015: 22, emphasis in original). Ulay conscientiously assumed his crime, larceny, for the theft of what art historians Rosemarie and Rainer Hagen have called 'the German painting best-loved by Germans' (2003: 393). Ulay bears the ethical mantle of his deed, but rejects outright the penalty and, implicitly, the monstrous burden of contrition that would otherwise attach itself to the criminal or the crime: he fled the country before sentencing. Ulay accepts the formal identity bestowed upon him – he is a thief, an outsider, the architect of a criminal act – but through his action seeks to critique or reject his national identity, namely, his German-ness. He also disavows his guilt, namely, what Jean-Paul Sartre calls (with reference to Jean Genet) 'the Other's gaze [that] supervenes and cuts him off from himself' (Sartre 1963: 37). Genet's friends orchestrated his pardon (from a life sentence for serial theft), while Ulay did eventually serve out a short sentence for the crime. Apprehended a few years later passing through Germany in transit to Agadir, Morocco, Ulay was jailed for 10–14 days – he cannot remember precisely. Like Genet, Ulay is magisterially unrepentant.

Ulay's extremity, it might be said (here, as if in the margin), begins with his name. Pronounced '*U-lie*' (the latter part resembles 'lie' as in *lying*), it is derived from the first syllable of his middle and last names by birth: (Frank) Uwe Laysiepen. Jacques Derrida writes – in the course of an analysis of Genet – that a name may appear to be a natural occurrence (a birthright) or an effect of commerce (a brand), like 'an act without a past' (Derrida 1986: 7). However, to give someone or something a name is always 'to sublimate a singularity and to inform against it, to hand it over to the police'. He writes, '[t]o "arraign" is to ask for identity papers, for an origin and a destination. It is to claim to recognize a proper name. How do you name without arraigning? Is that possible?' (1986: 7). In Ulay's act of self-naming, with an im-proper name (it resembles a moniker or nickname), he stakes a claim to being without social identification: muddling the drama of being given over to the police, he upends the social function of naming (*who does Ulay think he is?*) Indeed, the lone name proliferates in the novels of Jean Genet – Mimosa, Divine, Darling, Querelle. The lone name (or byname or cognomen) stages what Genet himself calls the 'sibylline effect of arbitrariness in the immaculate choice [that] . . . remarks and abolishes, to the point of infinity' (cited in *ibid.*). The logic of self-obliteration, twinned with self-fashioning – so germane to

Genet – is redolent too in Ulay's work (beginning with his name), to the extent that it signals the political and aesthetic stakes of his prime performance of extremity, namely, *There is a Criminal Touch to Art*.

Ulay's action is legible as a work of art, even if it had few direct precedents to license or legitimise such an extreme strategy in art's name. Its aesthetic extremity depends upon this singular quality and consists of Ulay's appropriation of a distinctly anti-art technology – the criminal practice of art theft – as a means to extend, renew or revolutionise the formal parameters of art, specifically through performance and through the secondary medium of film. The action may be without precedents and formally extreme, as if materialising from the ether. Neither does it lack formal precursors in Ulay's own prior works. Moreover, the fact that this exemplary performance of extremity has been subjected to broad oversight (or, perhaps, active dismissal) by historians and theorists of contemporary art and performance does little to undermine the aesthetic boldness, historical perspicacity and political charge of *There is a Criminal Touch to Art*. I ask what Ulay's reluctant mastery of extremity tells us about the apparent limits of the aesthetic and of avant-gardism in the 1970s and the effects of their transgression in terms of aesthetics, appropriation and identity.

Daylight robbery

On Sunday 12 December 1976, at one o'clock in the afternoon, Ulay entered the Neue Nationalgalerie in Berlin, descended the main staircase and walked into the Biedermeier rooms in the museum's basement floor. Marina Abramović followed with a lightweight Super 8 camera to record the action (they had met in Berlin two weeks earlier and quickly struck up an enduring relationship). In the extant footage, Abramović begins with a close, frontal shot of Spitzweg's *The Poor Poet*, Ulay's target in the theft. The lighting is dark and the painting itself is almost blacked out by the shot's low contrast. The crux of the 'Berlin Action' (Ulay's shorthand for the performance, which also distinguishes it from the film) was startlingly abrupt. As shown in a series of stills edited into the film, Ulay approached *The Poor Poet*, lifted it off the wall in a swift scooping motion and turned towards the camera with the painting in his arms (**Figure 2.1**). Abramović's subsequent footage captures Ulay running quickly through the galleries. Security guards apprehended Abramović, but they failed to find her footage, as she had swapped out the hot reel and hid it in her boot. When the guards confiscated her camera, they found it loaded with an empty reel.

The film *There is a Criminal Touch to Art* (1976) was produced by gallerist Mike Steiner and edited by Wilma Kottusch; it consists mostly of extensive footage by Jorg Schmidt-Reitwein (Werner Herzog's cameraman on 17 movies, including many of his best of the 1970s) alongside Abramović's reel; it also incorporates found footage from radio and televised news and further collaged elements, as well as a brief voiceover by Ulay. The film begins with clippings from newspapers, including headlines accompanied by images of the painting and of museum officials, published in the immediate

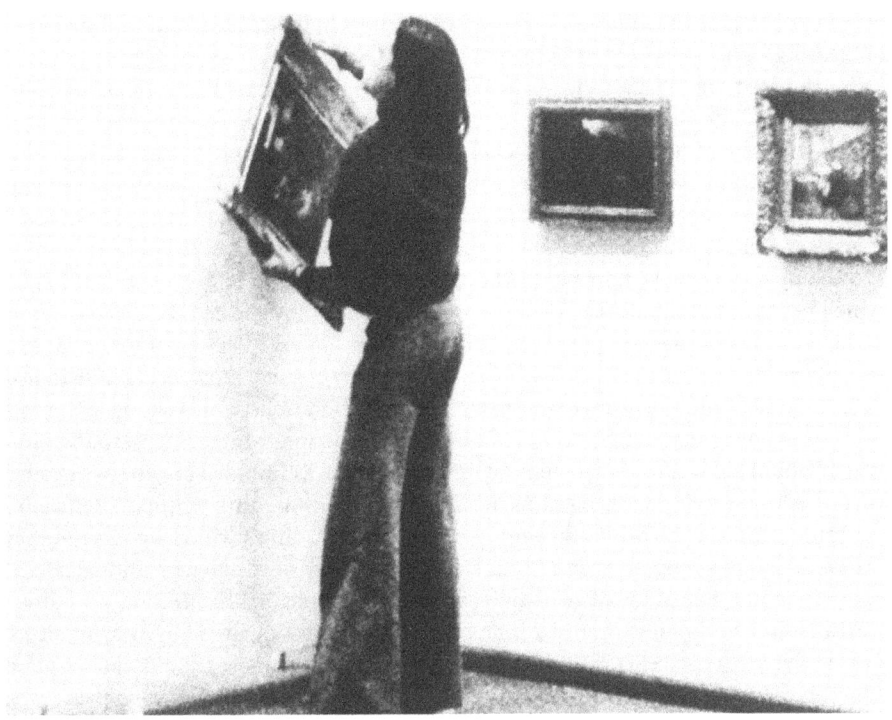

2.1 Ulay, *There is a Criminal Touch to Art* (1976), film stills from the Berlin Action, Gelatin silver print, 20 × 25 cm, series of 18 works

aftermath of the heist. They read, for example: '*Berlin: Linksradikaler raubte unser schönster Bild*' ('Left radical steals our most beautiful painting'); and '*Der Spitzweg-Dieb flüchtet mit dem Millionen-Bild durch den Notausgang*' ('Spitzweg thief flees through emergency exit with painting worth millions').

In the film's first shots of Ulay, prior to the theft itself, we see the artist in a long black leather trench coat, with shoulder-length hair. He stands on a wooden ladder to attach a large reproduction – about 2½ metres wide – of Spitzweg's painting above the entrance of the Hochschule der Bildende Künste (Academy of Fine Arts) in Charlottenburg, Berlin, a short walk from Bahnhof Zoo. Hanging the reproduction, he unrolls it to block the academy's doors. Ulay explained, 'Education at the art academy in Berlin at that time was pretty backwards. Performance was out of the question, as were video, photography and installation. They were still only teaching traditional forms: painting, sculpture, and graphic art' (Johnson 2015: 19). By commencing the action with a stunt that implicated the Hochschule, Ulay would use the ensuing theft to comment on a series of inequities in German art and culture, including the institutional marginalisation of performance art and other experimental practices, of which Ulay was an established pioneer. Without expecting or presuming that the establishment might endorse his actions, Ulay would directly associate his intervention directly with spaces of art beyond the museum, by quoting – or in his words, criminally 'touching' – a series of institutions in the unique temporal structure and cartographic shape of the performance.

After blocking the entrance to the Hochschule, Ulay carries the wooden ladder to his vehicle. Ulay's Citroën HY van – with its distinctive corrugated side panels painted black – was the same model as a French police van and symbolically associated with the student uprising in Paris in May 1968, lending Ulay's own intervention a particular political intonation. (It also has biographical resonance: Ulay and Abramović lived together in the van at the time and would continue to do so until they ran it into the ground during a collaborative performance in Paris, *Relation in Movement* (1977), in which Ulay drove it in a circle for 16 hours, while Abramović called the 2,226 circumnavigations from a megaphone in the passenger seat.) We see Ulay get into the car and the shot shifts to the vantage of the cameraman's snow-swept windscreen. Accustomed to inhospitable filming scenarios, through his collaborations with Herzog, Schmidt-Reitwein had stipulated that he would film the core action from inside a separate car, which would allow him a swift getaway if Ulay's plan was rumbled or otherwise failed (hence Abramović's recruitment as an abetter in the museum). Schmidt-Reitwein's car follows Ulay as he drives through Berlin in the morning's winter light, until they arrive at the imposing glass and black steel architecture of the Neue Nationalgalerie, some four kilometres away, at the Kulturforum complex in Kreuzberg – a stone's throw from Checkpoint Charlie. Much of the drive is accompanied by Ulay's voiceover, as the artist recounts a 14–line statement. The latter was a terse point-by-point itinerary or plot, which he produced as a two-page score titled '*Korrespondenz zum Verhältnis*' ('Correspondence to the Relationship') (Ulay 2016: 210–1). He mailed this to a number of national newspaper desks on the Saturday, knowing that the postal system's weekend closure would prevent it from arriving until Monday morning, the day after the completion of the action.

There is a Criminal Touch to Art is not a document of performance precisely, but a carefully designed, structured and edited film work. The footage of the streets and cars, with Ulay's van generally in view, is interspersed with shots of the museum's revolving door spinning empty, suggesting or anticipating the key tactical challenge of the heist. The footage also tracks the route Ulay will take down the staircase, anticipating his entrance and hurried escape. The camera pans inside the museum's cantilevered first-floor pavilion, taking in its arch-modernist style (designed in the 1960s by Mies van der Rohe). At one point, a guard approaches and places his hand over the camera lens, breaking up the panning shot of paintings and sculptures. The guard demands that the cameraperson stops filming. A woman's voice can be heard reasoning with the guard, as if in presentiment of the much more egregious 'criminal touch' to come: the theft whose extremity will dwarf the minor infraction constituted by filming without a licence. The museum will have been under particularly tight security at the time, as was the rest of Berlin, owing to the ongoing threat of terrorist activities led by the Red Army Faction/*Rote Armee Fraktion* (RAF). After a guerrilla campaign from 1970, anti-capitalist agitators including Andreas Baader, Ulrike Meinhof and Gudrun Ensslin had been arrested in 1972, prompting an escalation of terrorist attacks by the remaining RAF militants. These activities culminated in the 'German Autumn' of 1977 (a series of kidnappings, assassinations and aircraft hijackings), whose extremism was provoked by the suspicious deaths – in police custody – of Meinhof in 1976 and Baader and Ensslin in 1977. Therefore, Ulay's theft took place in what he remembers as 'a dangerous time to be in Berlin', during the escalation of terrorist attacks following Meinhof's alleged suicide, adding to the anxious tone of the lead-up to Ulay's misadventure (Johnson 2015: 20).

Ten minutes into the film, Ulay arrives at his second destination, the Kulturforum, parking his car at the rear of the museum. Ulay brought pliers to clip two networked wires upon which the painting hung (McEvilley 2010: 213). He knew that doing so would trigger the electronic security system and the exits would lock automatically. After entering the museum's revolving doors, he opened an emergency exit and propped it ajar (the film doesn't show this activity). In the 1970s, museum security conventions required that wall-mounted artefacts were fitted with one or more security features, including magnetic reed switches, displacement sensors or electromagnetic induction devices, among other options (Tillotson 1977: 104). Ulay assumed, however, that the emergency exit would remain unlocked if tampered with. In museum security terms, this is referred to as a 'defeat of system' manoeuvre, a countermeasure that compromises an otherwise effective security setup (the museum's alarm system and magnetic contact devices) (Hunter 1983: 383). Ulay cut the painting's induction wires, grabbed *The Poor Poet* and ran.

Less than a minute after snatching the painting, Ulay had scarpered from the museum. However, a security guard had begun to give chase as Ulay left the Biedermeier gallery, meeting him at the foot of the staircase as Ulay leapt up them and out of reach, jetting out the main door towards his car, whose aged engine he had been forced to leave running during the heist as it was prone to take several attempts to start. Schmidt-Reitwein's footage shows Ulay leaving the museum and sprinting past the museum's modernist frontage, with the painting tucked under his right arm, peremptorily wrapped in nylon (a sack, whose size Ulay miscalculated – too small to envelop the frame). We see three security guards give chase (although one stops abruptly). One guard is about ten feet behind Ulay and the second equidistant to the first. Near the car (though the footage misses this too), Ulay tripped and fell supine into the snow. He recalls his legs seizing – from fear or excitement – then falling: he was down long enough for the guard to grab hold of his ankle, though Ulay quickly shook himself loose and fled to the van.

'I stole the painting using my hands and feet', he tells me of the 'Berlin Action', with 'no technology, no assistance, nothing. I knew I could do it' (Johnson 2015: 20). Such a seat-of-the-pants approach – borne, for Ulay, from two weeks of improvisatory research in the museum – seems cavalier or wild, but is not in fact atypical in historical incidents of art crime in museums. Despite the tendency in popular films and novels to attribute art thefts to debonair white-collar connoisseur-thieves or to high-level organised crime syndicates, Anthony M. Amore and Tom Mashberg write that the reality often tends to be 'far more grimy and far less romantic' and involves 'petty offenders' or 'lone wolf' individuals: for example, they recount the opportunistic theft of Leonardo's *Mona Lisa* (1503–17) from the Musée du Louvre, Paris in 1911, by a patriotic Italian housepainter, Vincenzo Peruggia (it was retrieved in 1913) (Amore and Mashberg 2011: 8); and – 50 years later (strangely, to the day) in

1961 – the technologically savant theft of Goya's *The Duke of Wellington* (1812–14) from London's National Gallery in 1961, through an unlatched bathroom window, by elderly retired truck driver Kempton Bunton. The *Duke* was initially held for ransom, but returned voluntarily in 1965, and Bunton served a three-month prison sentence (incidentally, for the theft of the frame, which was never recovered) (2011: 10).

There is a Criminal Touch to Art shows Ulay drive towards and past the cameraman's vehicle. The latter follows Ulay at a distance – perhaps 20 metres or so behind – and drizzle spots the windscreen through which Schmidt-Reitwein records the convoy. The distance between the vehicles grows and other cars intervene, until Ulay's van is out of sight. The camera continues to film the grey, barely populated streets of West Berlin. The second vehicle soon catches up with the first, until one is driving directly behind the other.

Ulay's Citroën stops in the sleeting snow, in a car park beside a graffitied wall, less than a kilometre from his third destination in the action, Künstlerhaus Bethanien, a studio and exhibition complex for international artists – predominantly, at that time, American residents at German academies. Undertaking the remaining trips by foot was part of Ulay's plan to avoid detection and capture. He recalls that the distinctiveness of his car posed a problem: 'Berlin cab drivers listened to the police radio, and if they received a signal they could identify me or block the roads. So after a short drive I parked the car on the outskirts of Kreuzberg, took the painting, and ran, ran, ran, through the snow' (Johnson 2015: 20). The film shows his protracted excursion. He holds the painting under his right arm, with the front facing his body and the nylon sack wrapped over the top of the frame. In his other hand he carries a holdall. He runs across streets, along pavements, past shops and bars, winding through passers-by, followed by car and camera. His long jog eventually slows to a brisk walk. During the kilometre on foot, filmed in real time, his body and the shot are in constant motion. The frame, composed through the wet windscreen, is scrubbed by the window's wipers and jolts with the terrain, cut by passing cars. The jog-trot rhythm suggests the anxious tension in Ulay's body and his highly wrought focus. He does not look at the camera.

At Bethanien – eight kilometres from the museum, continuing a vaguely straight cartographic line from the Hochschule – Ulay pins a small colour reproduction of *The Poor Poet* to its notice board, affixing it crookedly over an existing poster. 'Touching' Bethanien connects a sequence of venues across Kreuzberg: an art academy, a museum and an exhibition space, which are blocked, perforated or 'defaced'. In truth, the latter is tentative and only gestured to; indeed, no lasting damage is incurred deliberately at any of the three venues and neither by the painting, though all lose face, perhaps.

From Bethanien, still grasping the painting, Ulay again runs, heading northeast to what was then a predominantly Turkish neighbourhood, crossing a park and a bridge to reach it, towards the final appropriated venue of the 'Berlin Action'. He stops at a phone booth and calls the police. We hear him report the theft of *The Poor Poet* and provide an address on Muskauer Strasse, near to where he stands. The footage cuts from Ulay telephoning the police to his entering the humbly decorated home of a Turkish *Gastarbeiterfamilie* (the German term for 'guest worker family' is given in Ulay's 14–line statement of 1976 [2016: 211]). An unidentified woman holds an

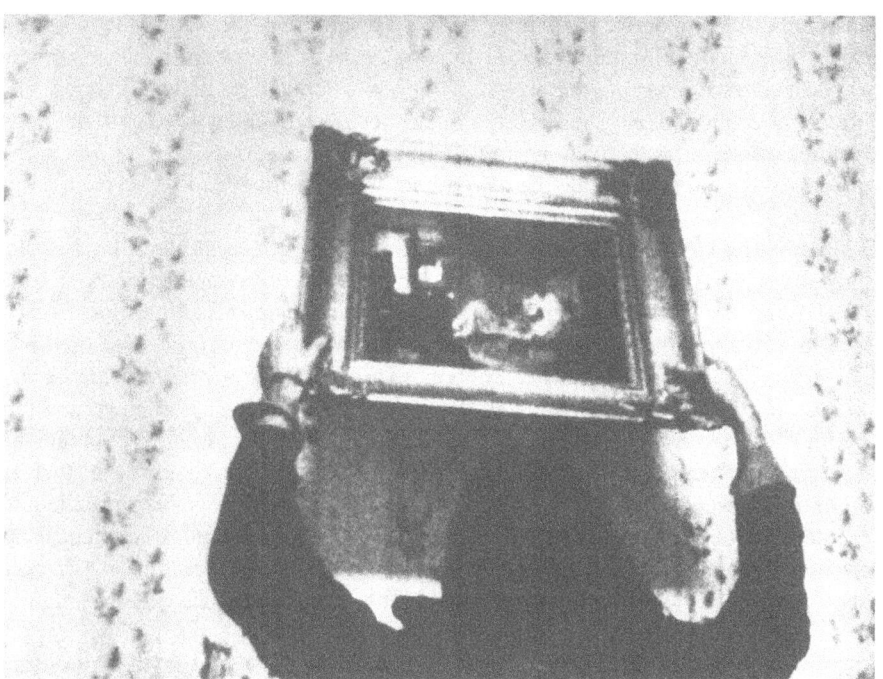

2.2 Ulay, *There is a Criminal Touch to Art* (1976), film stills from the Berlin Action, Gelatin silver print, 20 × 25cm, series of 18 works

infant in her arms and smiles or laughs at the ensuing event, directing her bemusement towards the camera. An older child stands by somewhat aloof and watches with his mother. Ulay recalls, 'I had chosen a Turkish family at random, and visited them before the commencement of the action. I told them we were shooting a film (which was true), and asked if we could bring a cameraman to shoot in their home. They agreed. I left them in the dark about the details, so they wouldn't be investigated or interrogated by the police' (Johnson 2015: 21). Ulay removes a long, framed, glass-fronted reproduction – a painting of a reclining, clothed figure partnered by floating cupids – from the sitting room's decorative wallpaper. He replaces it with the smaller, square Spitzweg in its heavy ornate frame. (**Figure 2.2**)

In the safety of the second-floor apartment, we finally see a lucid image of Spitzweg's painting. The camera pitches and shows the patina of the canvas and the contents of the painted scene – obscured in the footage from the museum – as if the apartment of the Turkish *Gastarbeiter*, in a working-class neighbourhood of the city, is the ideal or rightful setting in which to view *The Poor Poet*. The painting's hyperbolic depiction (or appropriation) of poverty and poetry, diluted in the century since its creation and mystified by its celebration and canonisation as a national treasure, is emphasised, clarified and re-contextualised by the actual poverty and pedestrian poetry of the modest family home. It is a romantic gesture on Ulay's part, in its suggestion of the humility, dignity and authenticity of working-class life. The sequence ends on a stilled image of the canvas, followed by an inter-title stating the full duration of the action: 30 hours from the mailing of the statement to the artist's arrest. The film does not record the arrival of the police and the museum director. The phone call requested that Dieter Honisch, the recently appointed director of the Neue Nationalgalerie, visit the painting in its adapted milieu. '[Honisch] arrived with the police', Ulay remembers, 'saw the painting in its new setting, and retrieved it. I was arrested. That was the whole action' (Johnson 2015: 21).

After the conclusion of the 'Berlin Action', the film continues with a visual epilogue of sorts. With a cigarette in his mouth, Ulay leans against layers of large reproductions of newspaper reports pinned to a wall; he unfixes and rolls away each layer to reveal another story beneath. '*Kunstraub war eine „Aktion"*' ('Art theft was an "action"') reads one headline. Another splash reads '*Irrer raubte in Berlin das weltberühmte Spitzweg-Gemälde*' ('Lunatic robs world-famous Spitzweg painting in Berlin'). The headlines narrate the return of the painting to the museum, celebrate the intervention by museum officials and address (or mock?) the revelation of the theft as an *Aktion*/action or performance. The news establishment was palpably ambivalent to the status of the theft as a work of art in its own right (akin to, but more emphatic than, the bemusement prompted by Kerry Trengove in 1977). Moreover, this ambivalence about art was written into the work itself or otherwise latent in Ulay's conception of the action.

In my analysis of Trengove's *An Eight Day Passage* (1977), I presented a social and creative context for artists using pedestrian activities – including manual and affective labour – as a series of means to enact and provoke a formally extreme experience. What further actions provide a context for the precise experience manifested in Ulay's 'Berlin Action', which, too, lifts a type of labour (though an illicit one)? A precedent for theft as the technical and political basis of a critical art action can be seen in a rogue, untitled performance by Pierre Pinoncelli, a French artist who held up a bank in Nice in 1975, using a sawn-off shotgun, robbing the teller of the token amount of 10 francs. Though formally similar, Pinoncelli stole money not art and the threat of violence represented by the shotgun is absent from Ulay's action. In its comparative subtlety and conceptual clarity, a stealth performance by the American performance artist Christopher D'Arcangelo provides a more apposite context for Ulay's intervention. On 8 March 1978, in one of his little-known *Museum Pieces* (1975–79), D'Arcangelo visited the Louvre in Paris, removed Thomas Gainsborough's *Conversation in a Park* (1740) from the wall and placed it on the floor. After his guerrilla re-installation of the frothy pink and green painting, D'Arcangelo attached to the wall a printed statement, which asked, in part: 'When you look at a painting / where do you look for that painting? / What is the difference between a painting installed / on the wall and a painting installed on the floor?'[1] D'Arcangelo's text raised the question of the codes of conduct and reading prompted by institutional spaces of art. His action highlighted the privilege endowed by or withheld from the viewer by museums.

---

1 Christopher D'Arcangelo, untitled draft of statement, MSS 264 Christopher D'Arcangelo Papers, Fales Library Special Collections, Downtown Collection, New York University, New York, Series I, Box 3, Folder 5: Louvre – Writings and Statement 1978. In the performance D'Arcangelo used a French translation.

By making unfamiliar the incidental viewer's sightlines, he stages how an institution manufactures the physical locus of looking: whether we look parallel to or down upon a painting may distort the perceived value of the object one encounters and therefore changes the meaning it is empowered to produce.

Over and above the precedents and contexts that lend Ulay's action its politics, what enabled the theft to be conceived as an 'action' and licensed the artist to conceive it as a work of art in its own right? In his sensitivity to the nuanced manner in which an object or event accrues meaning and attains the status of art – and perhaps on account of his own natural reticence – Ulay is productively evasive or ambivalent on the topic of how, precisely, the theft transmuted into or qualified as an aesthetic artefact. 'It's not up to me to declare the action a work of art', he tells me, shifting the necessary authority away from himself. 'Doing so', he continues, 'was not important enough as a motive for doing the action. I succeeded in doing it, and that was all that mattered to me' (Johnson 2015: 22). In its ambivalent relation to the project of the historical avant-garde and more substantially in its extremity – that is, to the extent that it struggles against its own ontological security as either a criminal act or an art action – Ulay's 'Berlin Action' both subscribes to, and breaks with, the politics of aesthetics in the twentieth century. It figures itself as a work of art, however tentatively, yet it does so through an attack on art and its institutions.

Appropriating criminality

In its attack-mode sensibility, Ulay's action is definitively iconoclastic. Iconoclasm denotes an assault on the residual power of images, including that of individual works of art. In a book on the powers attributed to images, visual studies scholar W. J. T. Mitchell describes iconoclasm as '[a] kind of theatrical excess in the rituals of smashing, burning, mutilating, whitewashing, egg- and excrement-throwing [that] turns the punishment of images into a spectacular image in its own right'; iconoclasm requires, he continues, a reciprocal act that seeks to compensate for the insult or violence experienced in the viewer and thus attributes a kind of vital power – its own 'lives and loves' – to the targeted work of art (Mitchell 2005: 126–7). As Mitchell suggests, iconoclasm can involve vandalism, theft or other strategies of a conservative or progressive nature, which the agent uses to intervene into the function of an artefact and more broadly into the cultural value of art. If the historical tradition of iconoclasm involves phobic attacks on the sanctity of art, including by defacing or destroying sacred images, the critical development of contemporary art has often involved the appropriation of destructive activities such as 'erasing, burning, cutting, nailing into, stepping on, piercing, torturing, perforating, and pissing on paintings', in Michael Darling's evocative inventory of performance-oriented iconoclasms that lead to productive aesthetic ends for post-war art (Darling 2009: 26). So, too, Yoko Ono desublimates the iconoclastic desires of art audiences with her participatory work *Painting to Hammer a Nail In* (1960): a painted monochrome board that becomes a vector for our potential interaction with the object, as the audience-participant is invited to grab a hammer (attached to the painting) and drive a nail into its surface, perhaps reminding us of the popular drive towards aggression in encounters with art. Perhaps, in the shadow of her foundational performance *Cut Piece* (1964), in which audience-participants complete the work by snipping away the artist's clothes with scissors, the aggression we enact towards the painting manifests the object as a proxy for the artist or for a vulnerable or scorned community or constituency.

In Ono's *Painting to Hammer a Nail In*, Ulay's misuse of *The Poor Poet* or in performances like Niki de Saint Phalle's *Tir* actions of the 1960s, in which she fired shotgun blasts into paintings loaded with balloons or cans that spilt paint onto the canvas beneath, the iconoclast perceives or instils a magical quotient in art or in a specific work, as if to identify a punctum that can be activated or killed by a creative interaction with the vessel. The psychoanalyst Adam Phillips defines magic in terms of what the witness seeks to encounter in it, namely, 'people's wish to half-knowingly put their trust in the untrustworthy' – whether it be one's mystified faith in the occult, escapology or art (2001: 129). Magical thinking thus entails neither elaborate sophistries nor gnostic odysseys (though these occur at strategic moments in my larger narrative – and without shame) but, rather or in addition, a productively mystifying split in one's improvised systems of belief. What mindful effect does Ulay seek when he puts his trust in the untrustworthiness of *The Poor Poet*? In its iconoclasm, the 'Berlin Action' sought to irritate the institutions of art and the state – indeed, the film is sometimes referred to by the title *Irritation*, to distinguish it from the live action it documents – specifically though the cultural and political values inculcated in *The Poor Poet*, as a popular, nationally treasured 'master' work. Indeed, Spitzweg was an exemplary target in this regard: Adolf Hitler was a noted and prolific collector of the painter and his circle (Hitler's Fuhrermuseum – now the Linz Collection – lists a total of 50 paintings by Spitzweg); his friend, the Nazi architect Albert Speer recalls Hitler's fondness for Spitzweg's 'staunch middle-class genre quality' and 'affable humor' (Speer 1970: 44). Controversially, the dictator's affection may evoke the possibilities for nationalist investment that Spitzweg's nostalgic style of genre painting may sublimate or tacitly enable.

The 'Berlin Action' was conceptually sophisticated in its design, in part thanks to its reliance on appropriation is several ways. First, Ulay clearly appropriates in the criminal sense of the word, when he removes or filches the painting from its original or legitimate home, the museum. Second, he sites the same object in a new venue – legitimate in a different sense – so transposing the object from one kind of space (institutional, public, national) to another (domestic, private, 'foreign'), thus appropriating and resituating a borrowed element in the way one does in collage, quotation, sampling or plagiarism. Third, he appropriates a non-art or anti-art activity (art theft) as a practice of artistic production, by then an established strategy associated with emergent postmodernism. The yearning of Ulay's theft to the status of a work of art in itself is perhaps announced in his naming of the activity as an 'action'. That is, he deploys then-current terminology to describe the theft as a particular instance of performance art – moreover, one with local precedents, not least the art-criminal activities of Vienna Actionism (*Wiener Aktionismus*) in the 1960s. Its core artists,

Otto Mühl, Hermann Nitsch, Günter Brus and Rudolf Schwarzkogler proposed revolutionary effects for – and were criminalised on account of – the appropriation of low, base or daily practices, including animal sacrifice, desecration of corpses, eating, drinking, wounding, shitting, pissing and vomiting as abjected techniques for a new praxis of performance art. The status of Ulay's action as a work of art is also achieved by affording it a title and by orchestrating effective documentation that may circulate in perpetuity, to sustain the life of an otherwise ephemeral, incorrigible incident.

Appropriation in and as the practice of art may instantiate a semantic crisis that leads artists and audiences into limit-experiences, by pushing for the recognition of previously alien experiences (alien, at least, to art) as the stuff of aesthetic cognition (the topic, in part, of Chapter 1). Appropriation also expands or radicalises the experi-ence of aesthetic sensing, provoking the viewing subject to relearn art as a sensibility, an orientation to perceptual experience, rather than a fact of creation and rational judgement. The effect of appropriation may be dizzying and thus shocking, Thomas McEvilley notes, as the introduction of appropriation as a central technology of artistic production brings with itself the risk (or threat) of 'infinite regress': exponen-tially greater feats that aim to collapse the categories of art and life (McEvilley 2005: 236). This suggests extremity as a cumulative phenomenon: extreme actions may incite grander fiats of excess; but they might as well provoke containment, by requir-ing other artists to restate their oppositional identity by a new and more profound contravention of perceived limits. McEvilley presses his point by narrating a series of performed gestures of grandiose artistic one-upmanship: including Yves Klein's appropriation of the fundament by signing the sky in an untitled action of 1949; and Ben Vautier's 'signing' of Klein's death in 1962, as if to appropriate another's dying (an event definitively not of Vautier's making) as one's own artistic concept. Such actions may suggest aesthetic tomfoolery, hoaxing or grandstanding. McEvilley writes that Klein, Vautier and others are serious in their prankishness, as authors of acts of 'sympathetic magic' – that is, attempts at 'an appropriation of a piece of reality into a sheltered or bracketed zone of contemplation', inviting a situation of dissociation, dizziness or semantic bewilderment when a sympathetic viewer attempts to concep-tualise the aftereffects of such acts of regress (2005: 238). Moreover, the challenges of performance art are provocative for McEvilley because the conceptual vertigo inaugu-rated by the genre in the late 1960s and 1970s also led artists and audiences into ethi-cally and politically murky waters, in which '[c]onsciousness is violently retextured by imposing a new conceptual overlay on its experiences' (2005: 9).

Moreover, Ulay has subsequently described the 'Berlin Action' in terms that emphasise its additional prescience, as an appropriative strategy that one might call *guerrilla curating*. He tells me, 'I loaned or borrowed the *Poor Poet* – without permis-sion, of course' (Johnson 2015: 22). Rather than *stealing* the painting, which suggests an intention to retain it in perpetuity or sell or ransom it to generate filthy lucre, Ulay *borrows* the painting – its return is latent in its mobility. Not so much violating sacred spaces, Ulay *touches* (and thus connects) relevant sites or scenes to revalue and rework the way language attaches itself to actions and objects, which accrue significantly dif-ferent meanings when appropriated into the space of performance or the broader space of the aesthetic. 'My action was conceptual', he explains (*ibid.*), even if it departs

from the typical low-intensity and emotional aridity of his contemporaries in conceptual art, such as Sol LeWitt's geometric drawings, Joseph Kosuth's philosophical alle-
gories or Lawrence Wiener's wordplay – each of which looks urbane but anodyne in
Ulay's shadow. By appropriating and re-contextualising *The Poor Poet*, he was careful
not to damage the work: rather than detract from its symbolic appeal, he 'added an
additional value to the painting' (*ibid.*). As a guerrilla curator of sorts, Ulay was able
to insert the painting and its history into a new context, through which it accrued new
meanings – as might any object relocated and inflected by effective curatorial practices
(itself at times a creative and legitimate process of appropriation).

The possibility or validity of strategies such as appropriation relies, perhaps, on
the revelation of the contingency of the art object – or art action – in the twentieth
century. Citing Marcel Duchamp's 'readymades' as a point of origin for this transformation, Martha Buskirk argues that in neo-dada, minimalism, pop art, conceptual
art, land art and performance art – game-changing art forms at mid-century – the
smuggling of unprecedented objects and activities into the languages of art criticism
and theory necessitated a radical revaluation of key concepts for art criticism and
art theory. '[T]he use of unexpected materials, particularly ones that carry cultural
associations that extend beyond the museum's walls', Buskirk writes, required new
practical and theoretical positions concerning the dialectic between form and content,
the name of the artist (or author function), medium specificity, appropriated models
of industrial production and so on (Buskirk 2005: 10). The individuality of the artist
was undermined by some of these procedures, stymying the modernist authority
of the genius artist and offsetting the hegemonic priority of virtuosity or skill; yet
at the same time, such procedures and revolutions re-establish the influence signified in the name of the individual artist, as suggested by McEvilley's examples; for
appropriation to take effect, the artist's signature must authorise an object, action or
procedure – Klein's sky, Klein's death – as pertinent to the radically inclusive (though,
paradoxically, radically selective) horizon of art. 'Presentation under an artist's name',
Buskirk writes, 'ensures not only that a range of different forms of expression will be
read as works, but that heterogeneity within the series of works will be read as a decision that itself carries meaning as a play on the very idea of authorship as a form of
unity or internal consistency' (*ibid.*). This operative priority of the name of the artist
is intensified in the work of artists like Ulay who adopt a distinctive cognomen yet
prefer not to acquire or refine a signature style: the objects, actions and positions he
makes or takes up have no internal consistency, it seems, no default style to bind them,
emphasising the radical contingency of the work of art and the authorising function of
the creative will. As Guy Brett writes of another such artist without a signature style,
Rose Finn–Kelcey, her '[p]hysical objects [and performances] looking so different
from one another are tied together by the artist's name. It is interesting to speculate
on what would happen if they had all been signed with a different name, if the artist,
true to a mischievous streak, had given herself a pseudonym for each one and kept the
secret' (Brett 2013: 9–10). A resistance of continuity across an oeuvre – such mischief
– heralds its own extremity.

Works of art are also contingent in another sense: for their fuller meaning and
value to be readable, such activities tend to invoke their own specific historical,

cultural, social and political conditions of emergence and reception. It is on the back of paradigmatic shifts that formally and affectively unsettling or otherwise alien activities – including Ulay's appropriation of art theft as a practice of art making – are viable interventions into the spaces and languages of artistic production, in and beyond what I call the performance of extremity. As the Brazilian artist Hélio Oiticica put it, concerning his own auto-destructive process, '[t]he challenge . . . is not the actual destruction of the painting itself, but rather its transformation into something else' (Darling 2009: 14). The conceptual imperatives of Ulay's action departed from vandalism, towards strategic, iconoclastic or (after Oiticica) transformative misuse. The destructive quality remains operative, nevertheless: in a museum or gallery, even merely *touching* an art object constitutes a kind of harm, for direct contact leaves a mark or residue, however minimal or reversible, as it interferes with the material as well as symbolic integrity of the object.

Art crime

Ulay's description of his light-fingered 'Berlin Action' as an unlicensed 'loan' from the Neue Nationalgalerie is provocative and potentially tongue-in-cheek. Its symbolic charge relies on the malefic status of art theft (like that of its sibling, art vandalism) as a culturally despised activity. Art and crime – and, it would seem, curation and theft – seem to belong to different categories of experience or activity. As criminologist Thomas Bazley writes, conventional thought assumes that 'art is a positive contribution to our world', whereas crime 'conjures images of human behaviour at its worst and would seem to stand in stark contrast to art as a positive feature in our lives' (2010: 1). His assumption of the humanistic essence of art inflects the cultural politics of its theft: the removal of a work from the possibility of future witness may deprive a constituency or class of its sustaining pleasure – and the thief may actively seek to achieve this effect, in a proto-terroristic sense – to invoke powerful feelings of loss, hurt or anger in those for whom the stolen work has sentimental, historical, national or other kinds of value. For Bazley, implicitly, Ulay's action would fall short of the essential condition of art, for it lacks the transcendent, uplifting nature suggested in the humanist definition. His action is *merely* criminal in nature.

Paradoxically, art thefts often draw upon and affirm the cultural and economic value of art. Writing about the theft of two of J. M. W. Turner's paintings from the Schirn Kunsthalle in Frankfurt in 1994, the curator Sandy Nairne notes that art theft inevitably 'focuses attention on which works of art are worth stealing and, by implication, which are not', capitalising upon and thus signalling the complex hierarchy of economic, cultural and sentimental values among works of art (Nairne 2011: 9). Significant works may be prone to theft simply because the thief seeks to bank a token of the financial worth of the object (usually a painting, jewel or antique). Yet, frequently, thieves are motivated by ambitions independent of monetary gain: the cultural or national status or other symbolic function of a work ensures that an act of theft will be instilled with meanings that signal or trigger a militant quality in the crime, because the disappearance or destruction of the work provokes reverberations in the culture at large, including negative or ugly collective and personal feelings.

Therefore, some thieves actively harness the culturally loaded effects of art theft, in order to pass comment on the national and other functions of art institutions or specific works. As Robert Tillotson noted in the 1970s, thefts are prompted by 'rational' motivations, including ransom or resale; or by the 'fetish' incentives of thieves acting on 'the need to challenge authority – political, religious, or even parental; and the drive to possess an object which has taken on metaphorical, symbolic, or mythical connotations' (Tillotson 1977: 70). Amore and Mashberg write that guerrilla or terrorist thefts frequently participate in 'class warfare', attracting a 'false Robin Hood mystique' as thieves seek to smash the institutions that uphold oppressive values (Amore and Mashberg 2011: 15). Guerrilla thieves liberate or undermine an artwork's symbolic capital, in the course of what appears to be a victimless crime (the burglaries by Bunton and Peruggia, noted here, fall into this politicised or fetishistic category – as, of course, might Ulay's larceny). More generally, though, the public impact of art theft depends on the values coded or inculcated in 'master' works, the totality of which is materially undermined – but also symbolically affirmed – by the action of removing a specific work from public consumption or enjoyment, as well as from the more abstract visual space of cultural awareness, such that any art theft may have a guerrilla quality.

Also frequently iconoclastic, the history of vandalism sets a precedent or context for Ulay's 'Berlin Action'. When carried out by artists or political activists, vandalism replaces kidnap (artnap) with active destruction or desecration of a culturally valued artefact. Its practice is generally more fanatical than that of theft. In historical instances, artist-vandals often describe themselves as making an example of an existing work, modifying or improving it through their violence against it, while hitching their own original performance to the cultural values associated with its target. Beginning, perhaps, with the Suffragettes – via Mary Richardson's iconoclastic, feminist attack on Diego Velásquez's *Rokeby Venus* (aka *The Toilet of Venus*, 1647–51) at London's National Gallery in 1914 – activists may damage or destroy a work as an act of political protest or social commentary, in the service of a greater ideological purpose, which gains traction through the specific form and context of an act of destruction. Interestingly, tactical vandals seem more likely than thieves to identify as artists. Perhaps it is more feasible or efficient to destroy or damage a canonical work – often opportunistically, by stabbing or slashing canvases or smashing sculptures – than it is to orchestrate its theft (or unlicensed loan). Moreover, a violent intervention is perhaps more politically transparent, as vandalism seems to involve no reasonable opportunity for financial gain, hence the perception of its radicality, in contrast to the potential self-interest associated with theft.

Artists seem to become vandals in order to self-aggrandise or mythicise themselves; or, for Bazley, as 'expressions of a grudge, or envy' (for example, a non-achiever's hatred of perceived excellence in others) (2010: 143); or, more interestingly, still, to further an aesthetic manifesto (including conservative ones). At the Museum of Modern Art, New York in 1974, the artist Tony Shafrazi (now an influential gallerist) used spray paint to vandalise Pablo Picasso's *Guernica* (1937), covering it with the (curiously unenlightening) phrase 'KILL LIES ALL', to protest against continued American involvement in the Vietnam War. Shafrazi's vandalism is a classic example of the misuse of a canonical work – Picasso's painful homage to the human losses incurred in the Spanish Civil War – to comment on current issues that art may fail to address. The trashing of Picasso's painting throws into relief a hierarchy of grief, in that the 'death' of a revered object (and the historical casualties it memorialises) seems to garner more powerful outpourings of collective loss and rage than the mass-deaths of nameless Vietnamese civilians. Setting a precedent of sorts for Ulay, Shafrazi explicitly described his intervention into the museum as a work of art in its own right and titled it the *Guernica Action* (Gamboni 1997: 192).

More recently, in 1997 the Russian performance artist and prolific vandal Alexander Brener destroyed Kasimir Malevich's *Suprematism (White Cross)* (1922–27) at the Stedelijk Museum, Amsterdam, by spraying a large green dollar sign on the white monochrome, describing his intervention as a 'dialogue' with Malevich concerning the institutionalisation and commodification of revolutionary art (Piotrowski 2012: 22–3). Like Shafrazi, Brener's action provokes a semiotic exchange – however blunt – by altering, heightening or theatricalising the meanings lodged within a canonical, culturally legible work of art. The activity has a political effect, even if the means of achieving it are slight, boorish or pyrrhic. Yet despite the relevance of these actions, Ulay is not a vandal. 'Vandalism was not my intent', he explains, to distance himself respectfully from the active destruction or damage of works. 'There are art *destroyers*, and there are others, like me, who give a second value to existing art works by temporarily *misusing* them' (Johnson 2015: 22, emphasis in original).

Perhaps more in tune with Ulay's action, the Canadian artist Istvan Kantor (aka Monty Cantsin) sustained this critique of art's commodity status by interrupting Jeff Koons's retrospective exhibition at the Whitney Museum of American Art in New York. In his stealth performance in 2014, Kantor sprayed a large 'X' on the museum wall in his own blood and signed it in black ink. The exhibition was compromised and Kantor's anti-commercialism was made plain, but Koons's garish works remained undamaged. In each instance, the artist-criminal chooses a significant work, namely, one that is known as a superlative statement of a value perceived by the attacker as toxic: Koons for his corporate formalism; Malevich and Picasso for the way their revolutionary spirit has been contained and commoditised by institutions. Similarly, Ulay's singling-out of *The Poor Poet* was certainly significant, as a cipher for the German-ness he sought to demolish in himself.

The Poor Poet

If the history of vandalism and theft shows that an intervention may be politically, polemically or fetishistically meaningful in terms of its specific form and context, what is at stake in Ulay's choice of target in the 'Berlin Action'? In other words, why steal a painting by Carl Spitzweg and *The Poor Poet* in particular? Spitzweg was both an inspired choice and an incidental one; the painting and its cultural history enabled a precise series of political effects when Ulay stole and reinstalled it in the course of his performance of extremity.

Spitzweg was born in 1808, lived in Munich and became a practising pharmacist after qualifying in 1832. In the late 1830s, he taught himself to paint by copying Dutch masters in the Pinakothek (the Neue Pinakothek now owns Spitzweg's surviving copy of *The Poor Poet*). As an amateur, he began to paint his own quaint scenes around 1837, including detailed 'painted drawings' or illustrations, depicting the lifestyle of the petit bourgeoisie, a milieu to which he belonged (Norman 1987: 124). In the mid-nineteenth century, Spitzweg created a broad range of works including paintings of bourgeois individuals and groups, landscapes, pastoral scenes, neoclassical sketches of nudes and statuary (some of which are fragrantly homoerotic), architectural drawings, cartoons and society portraits. He took early retirement from pharmacy and took up painting professionally after a large inheritance provided him with lifelong financial security. Spitzweg would become popular among the masses after his death in 1885, but was considered a hack by the intelligentsia during his lifetime (Wichmann 1985: 9). He has been the subject of a number of posthumous monographs and exhibition catalogues. However, little of substance has been published on his work in English, beyond commentaries in surveys of 'great art' aimed at a general readership; the main German-language monographs remain untranslated.

The Poor Poet is a monument of German popular painting. Indeed, a poll in Germany ranked the painting as at one time the people's second favourite work of art, after the *Mona Lisa* (Hagen and Hagen 2000: 393). Spitzweg painted two near-identical versions (a third, different version is also extant). Perhaps owing to its national significance, the same version Ulay stole has been prone to theft. On 4 September 1989, some thirteen years after Ulay's action, two men entered Charlotteburg Palace (one on foot pushing the other in a wheelchair), again snipped the security wires upon which two of Spitzweg's paintings were hanging – *The Poor Poet* and *The Love Letter* (1846), on loan as part of the *Art of Biedermeier* exhibition – assaulted a guard and escaped with the pictures (Hagen and Hagen 2000: 393). They have never been recovered (indeed, 36 paintings by Spitzweg are currently missing).

Painted in 1839, *The Poor Poet* was one of Spitzweg's earliest works. It resembles an illustration and recalls Norman Rockwell's sentimental narrative paintings of a century later. Painted in oils on board, it is relatively small in size, measuring just over 14 × 17 inches (35 × 43 cm) without its garishly large frame (**Figure 2.3**). In the lower third of the picture, the eponymous poet lies upon a mattress, entrenched in his poetic reverie and oblivious to the poverty of his surroundings. He lies swaddled in a heavy coat, scarf, hat and blanket, propped up against voluminous white pillows. Holding a feather quill in his lips and with spectacles perched upon his nose, the poet reads a sheaf of his papers. The flea he holds between the pinched fingers of his right hand has punctured his attention – or, according to a different reading, the poet is 'scanning out a hexameter that he has written on the wall', to count out its syllables (Stauble 2013: 182). Tattered tomes with broken bindings sit piled beside the bed. Above the reclining figure, a large, broken umbrella is fixed to the ceiling to shield the poet from his

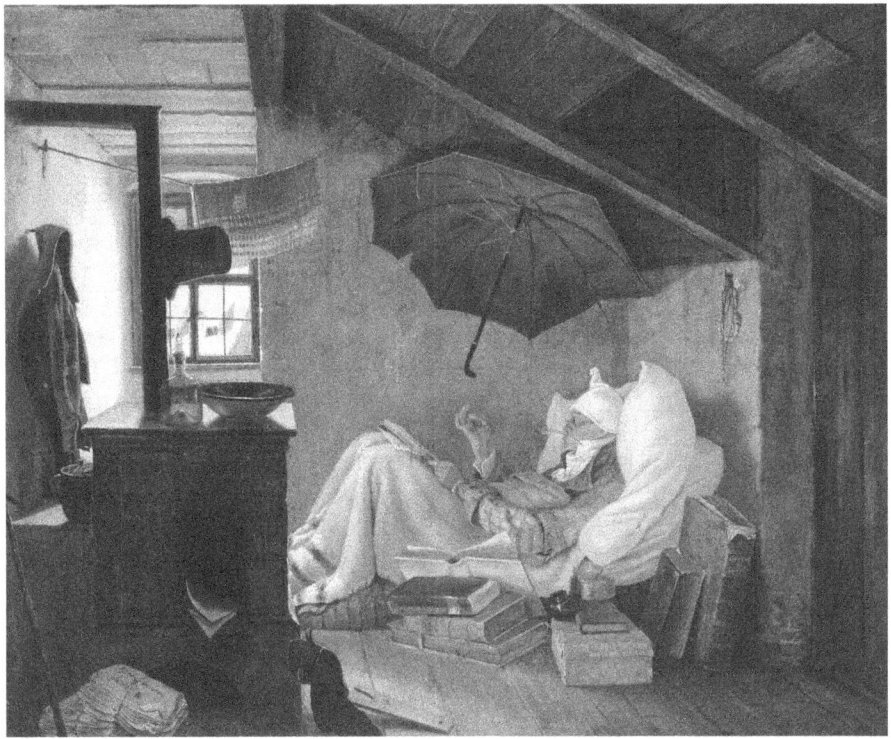

2.3 Carl Spitzweg, *The Poor Poet* (*Der arme Poete*) (1839)

leaky roof. A rosary hangs nearby. Illegible poems are written directly onto the muddy wall, a white line of which bifurcates the painting, laterally across its centre.

The narrative force of the painting enmeshes the poor poet in the solitary act of poetic invention, and pairs this spectacle with that of the black wood-burner on the left-hand side of the scene. As the poet hones his craft, a stack of manuscripts hangs from the burning stove, for the writing of manuscripts has exacerbated the poet's extreme poverty, preventing him from affording firewood. He is burning his poems to stay warm and to dry his possessions: his wet boots at the corner of the stove, a hat hung on the chimneystack and a towel suspended on a washing line. A further stack of poems, wrapped in string, sits on the floor, awaiting the fire. The top sheet of the stack is partially legible and reads 'Operum meor- fasc- III' – that is, 'Operum meorum fasciculum III' or 'My work, part three' (Norman 1987: 124). Others have given different readings, such that the hat perched upon the stove's flue suggests that the oven is cold, therefore emphasising the 'wretched' situation of the poet's material extremity; his persistence in his craft becomes a testament to his magical transcendence of the situation of impoverishment through poetic reverie (Hagen and Hagen 2000: 395).

In either reading, *The Poor Poet* recalls another impoverished Romantic, Colline in Giacomo Puccini's *La bohème* (1896), who sings the aria '*Vecchia zimarra*' to his tattered pauper's coat, operatically envisioned to be as world-weary as his own stolid self: 'Never has your poor worn back bowed before the rich and powerful', Colline sings. 'Deep in your calm cavernous pockets, you have protected philosophers and poets.' For the neo-Romantic poet Patti Smith, Colline 'bids his ragged but beloved coat farewell as he imagines it ascending the pious mountain, while he remains behind walking the bitter earth' (Smith 2015: 159–60). Smith captures the poetic boon of such spectacles of self-abnegation in penury, which exceeds the banal facticity of its scene, from a miserable wet room to a crappy old coat.

The scene of Spitzweg's painting typifies what Geraldine Norman describes as the signature affect of the Biedermeier, *Gemütlichkeit*, an untranslatable German term suggesting a snug, genial quality, combined with a righteous state of spiritual grace (Norman 1987: 8). Yet as McEvilley notes, the poor poet of Spitzweg's painting is 'completely self-absorbed' and represents 'a metaphysical system that is entirely self-sufficient, creating new world-elements by the warmth of burning old ones' (McEvilley 2010: 171). Stolid and bland, the illustrative scene may just as well poke fun at the Romantic vision of the artist in his solitary quest, demarcating the Biedermeier artists' difference from the contemporaneous development of German Romanticism in painting and literature, particularly by Caspar David Friedrich, and Johann von Goethe and Friedrich von Schiller, respectively. The painting's apparent mockery of idealist aesthetics were duly noted by Spitzweg's contemporaries and maligned in such terms: the jury of the Kunstvereins Munich, of which Spitzweg was a member, rejected *The Poor Poet* as unsuitable for exhibition (Wichmann 1985: 173). Indeed, his work was received so coldly by his peers that Spitzweg refrained from signing subsequent works, replacing his signature with a lozenge symbol, known as a '*Spitzweck*', to avoid further vilification (Stauble 2013: 182).

The scene of *The Poor Poet* is a theatrical one and depends on a tension at the level of narration. Whether the painting is a paean or a farce, the act of poetic invention is depicted as transcendent, as suggested by the image of the poet immune to the duress of his situation, in the cold, wet environment of his cloisters. At the same time, the apparent burning of the manuscripts suggests that the poems themselves, once created and refined, are superfluous, so much literary flotsam, in the grander scale of personal survival or the trials of existence, for they can be sacrificed without concern to ensure the warmth of his home and the dryness of his boots and hat. The effect is one of dogged persistence. If Spitzweg meant to pillory the Romantic position, the effect is difficult to secure in the present. As satire, still, Spitzweg's illustration conjures the inescapable fact of poverty and sufferance, as well as the insignificance of duress beneath the gravitas of creative inspiration. The dialectical image it produces is enjoyable to read, hence perhaps its attractiveness to audiences, but the two sides of the dialectic are mired in cliché, which is intensified in the caricatured visual style of the painting and muddled to the extent that its satirical quotient may be missed by the viewer.

The iconicity of *The Poor Poet* in national terms and its easy popular allure can be understood as the fundamental conditions of meaning that license the political effects of Ulay's audacious action. This lends his ensuing performance of extremity a more fervent political effect. 'When I was at school in Germany in the late 1940s,' he recalls, 'I had a textbook, and its only colour image was a reproduction of *The Poor*

Poet. That tells you how iconic the painting was for German identity in that period. Everybody identified with it . . . I thought if I got my hands on it, *hell might break loose*' (Johnson 2015: 18, emphasis in original). The habitability of 'German-ness' as a national identity had taken a seemingly irreversible nosedive after the rise of National Socialism in the 1930s, the material realities of German national expansionism during the Second World War, incredible discrimination, genocide and the horrific revelations concerning the Holocaust in the 1940s. As historian Gerd Knischewski argues, a fragile national identity in post-war Germany struggled to evince and accept collective guilt, which similarly prevented individuals from admitting personal involvement in, and culpability for, the atrocities of the regime and the war. In the early post-war years, during and after the uncovering of the full extent of Nazi war crimes, he writes, Germans preferred 'to claim for themselves the status of victims who, if not having been brutally coerced into compliance, had most definitely been skilfully manipulated by the [National Socialist] regime' (Knischewski 2008: 104). He continues,

> They felt further victimized by the (Western) Allies who had subjected them to carpet-bombings during the war, had accepted the brutal expulsion of Germans from their former eastern territories, and conducted a denazification process which Germans perceived as ambivalent, unpredictable and unjust. (2008: 104)

This created a tense situation for post-war German nationals – and particularly so for Ulay, owing to his personal history as a child of the war and his later leftist political sympathies. The young, perhaps, took upon themselves the victimised subjectivities described by Knischewski, by acknowledging national (if not personal) responsibility for atrocity or else punished that aspect of themselves that reflected or enjoyed their embattled sense of national belonging. As such, immediate generations of post-war Germans were subjected to what historian Gitta Sereny describes as a kind of generalised subjective destitution. As she wrote in 1972, 'the Nazis committed not only physical but spiritual murder: on those they killed, on those who did the killing, on those who knew the killing was being done, and also, to some extent, for evermore, on all of us, who were alive and thinking beings at that time' (Sereny 1995: 101).

Ulay was one of those 'alive and thinking beings' and his intellectual and political activities were directly formed by his family's experiences of the Second World War. He was born in a bomb shelter on 30 November 1943, in the industrial town of Solingen, North Rhine-Westphalia, Germany – a city that would be mostly destroyed by British air raids in 1944. Ulay had a profound sense of the injustice of war, owing in part to the dreadful injuries suffered by his father (who was conscripted, with shocking misfortune, into both world wars, was disabled in the second and died in 1957) and his mother's mental breakdown. Ulay told his friend Thomas McEvilley about his mother's (and his own) traumatic experience of the war, especially during an attempted escape from Germany to Lithuania in 1944:

> Unfortunately, while fleeing to the East [my mother] ran into the Russian front which was headed West. She was raped by Russian soldiers – and I was taken from her. The Russians

took little boys, never little girls, to bring them home and make them stay with them like souvenirs from the war. My mother made a tremendous effort by offering herself as a woman to get things like vodka or [cigarettes] to buy me back with. (McEvilley 2010: 167)

After the war, Ulay told me, his mother 'disappeared into her solitude, and had no contact with the outside world until her death' in the early 1980s (Johnson 2015: 24). Stripped of a family and its comforts, Ulay lived in a boarding house for much of his teens, before finding employment in a factory producing meat grinders (Westcott 2010: 86–91). The war, including his memories of the *Trümmerfrauen* – the self-organising widows of war who tended and cleared the rubble of his birthplace – and the aftermaths of war, including the drudgery and solitude of early adulthood and his turn to activism in the mid-1960s, seemingly incited in Ulay a heightened sense of disgust for Germany's collective criminality, national victimhood and lack of authentic social and individual contrition and guilt.[2] This exemption or negation was expressed ruefully in a work Ulay created in Paris in 1974, a printed funeral card for himself that reads '*Mein Abschied als einzige Person*' ('My Farewell as a Singular Person'). By picturing a funeral for himself and sloganising his demise, Ulay killed off – not finally, but serially and theatrically – the part of his identity that gave him pause, prompting a conceptual self-erasure, a presentiment of social death and a concomitant commitment to collaboration.

For McEvilley, the cultural history of *The Poor Poet* licenses the politics of Ulay's theft, as it represents the artist 'turning away from his German heritage to the cause of the despised and the alien' – towards the *Gastarbeiter* or towards his own criminality – as a personal mutation that 'brought to the surface and articulated the musculature of an extraordinary strength that had been striving toward expression for years' (McEvilley 2010: 225). This is manifested in Ulay's flight from (or loss of) family life, his sympathy for anarchist organisations (particularly the Provos in Amsterdam, with whom he was affiliated) and his earlier experiments in performance and photography – which McEvilley sees as confrontational antecedents to the 'sheer heroism' and 'awesome loneliness' of his ultimate crime (*ibid.*). The punch line of the action, his dramatic gifting of the painting to the Turkish family, in the course of his guerrilla act of curation, adds a further layer of symbolic efficacy to *The Poor Poet* in this equation. The material poverty of the *Gastarbeiterfamilie*, suggested by the modesty of their home and its location in a 'ghetto' neighbourhood, presents an unadorned version of the low income and social marginalisation that attends or constitutes the experience of being poor. This is in contrast to the poverty of Spitzweg's poet, whose penury is self-imposed, romantic and socially valorised – as evidenced by the national pride taken in the painting and its institutional valuation as a priceless cultural artefact (the painting was not technically priceless: a newspaper report cut into Ulay's film values it at two million Deutsche marks).

Ulay's action in removing the painting from the museum redresses the imbalance between romanticised and actual poverty, exploitation and destitution, although in

2 Tevž Logar discussed the *Trümmerfrauen* of Solingen and their influence on Ulay's later commitment to social art practice at a symposium to accompany Sophia Yadong Hao's exhibition *Ulay: So You See Me* at Cooper Art Gallery, Dundee, 2 December 2017.

a temporary, provisional or symbolic way. When the highly valued painting passes into the temporary care of the poor, the passage of the material wealth (which can never practically be capitalised upon) undertakes a theatrical movement from those who revere *The Poor Poet* to those whose poverty arouses no poetry in the collective imagination of the masses.

The hypocrisy at the heart of *The Poor Poet* concerns its brazen caricature of historical, fantastical poverty, in counterpoint to its audience's assumed disdain towards less picturesque situations of actual poverty. Exposing such a situation consoled Ulay in his long-term imperative to neutralise his own national identity and to embarrass his abandoned homeland, Germany (by 1976, Ulay had been living in self-imposed exile for eight years). Ulay's de-romanticisation of poverty reflects John Roberts's argument that after the general casualisation of labour and the specific 'proletarianization of cultural production', poverty is no longer 'the existential source of artistic self-transformation – a way of defining the artist's "otherness" – but the very means out of which the artist produces a transformative or emancipatory relation with the world: "another world"' (Roberts 2015: 31). Ulay does not identify with the poor poet, but, rather, critiques its romantic function in the painting and the attendant values affixed to the figure and the whole. He deploys his critique – through his forcible relocation of the painting – to create a new means of viewing the economic disparities at work in the art world and in the broader regime of the social, as signalled by his *criminal touches* across four sites in the city. Or, as Ulay tells me in typically more diffident terms, 'I needed to deal with my German-ness. I wanted to *irritate* it, and I did it best by stealing Germany's favourite painting' (Johnson 2015: 21).

Extremity or the last resort of kings and common men

Ulay's drive to irritate and unsettle his own national identity had found form long before he entered the Neue Nationalgalerie in December 1976. In the summer of 1968, aged 24, Ulay fled his home in Cologne, Germany, leaving behind his wife and child (McEvilley 2010: 178). Abandoning domesticity and avoiding military conscription, he headed first to Czechoslovakia, where his arrival coincided with the Prague Spring – a period of violent clashes instigated by radical student agitators in favour of economic decentralisation from the Soviet regime (Hobsbawm 1995: 398–9). Ulay moved on to the Netherlands, where he fell in with the militant Provo movement (McEvilley 2010: 180–1); he has remained predominantly in Amsterdam ever since.

The process of forensically examining, deconditioning and reconstituting one's own identity was by 1976 a well-established strategy for Ulay, particularly through enduring periods of performance research into identity and bodily integrity, beginning with his auto-Polaroid projects of the early 1970s. McEvilley sums up Ulay's 'performative photography' projects as methodical and prolonged investigations into the varied facets of his identity: 'For two years he dressed continuously as a female and entered the social milieu of transvestites and transsexuals. For another year he presented himself as mentally defective [*sic*] and sought out the company of people with extreme physical abnormalities, miming their self-image to erode his own' (2010: 39). For Amelia Jones, these works cumulatively signify Ulay's investment in denaturalising normative male (and, tacitly, white, able-bodied) privilege – 'to loosen the binds of normative masculinity (or femininity) in a heteronormative, patriarchal culture', as Jones puts it – in a manner she reads as both feminist and queer (Jones 2015a: 6). The immersive durational projects, undertaken by Ulay between 1970 and 1973, resulted in a cache of Polaroid prints, many of which remained private or hermetic until the recent publication of his full-career catalogue raisonné (see Bojan and Cassin 2014). The connections to these earlier series of performances of extremity demonstrate that Ulay's theft of *The Poor Poet* is therefore not simply a publicity-garnering feat of audacity and masculine bravado or an art prank, but a conceptual project that seeks to continue to undermine the vestiges of unity and authenticity in identity – both gendered and national – by weakening its icons or inflecting them with new and debilitating meaning. Ulay undermines his own identity by sabotaging his German-ness.

Many of his early performative self-portraits are illustrative in this regard. In a compelling series of Polaroids titled *Soliloquy* (1974), Ulay slices the tips of each finger with a Stanley knife and drags his bloodied fingers down a white tiled wall (**Figure 2.4**). In one image, the camera closes in on his action to frame his screaming face, partly concealed by a hood that comes down over his eyes and nose; his bleeding hand is splayed against the grid of the wall's black grouting and its passage has left messy hieroglyphs of blood. Written on the wall is the word *Unglück*: he is unhappy, miserable, luckless or wretched. Earlier in the series, Ulay stands in a fur coat (brandishing an erection) and writes the word on the wall, alongside the initials 'P.B.F.B' – those of a lover, Paula – and the insignia of a crudely sketched dagger. In other images in the series, Ulay writhes and grimaces in a blank-sheeted bed, in various states of apparent hysteria, intimate exposure and performed unrest. The series sequences surprisingly direct images, using a performance of ordeal – here, for the camera – to attempt to visualise one's hurt in the body (both psychic and physical), collapsing emotional and visceral pain. As in lived experience, here one is a surrogate for or indistinguishable from the other. *Soliloquy* is a far cry from the later disavowals of pain and its density in the *Relation Works* (1976–79, with Marina Abramović) for which he is best remembered. Of the later works, Ulay states, '[t]he unwritten rule in our work was that regardless of whatever either of us can bear, which can differ of course, we would always stop before the performance became pathetic. It was not our idea to make people empathise with us, or with our pain' (Johnson 2015: 34).

In *Soliloquy*, however, before his strategic distancing from the utility (or distraction) of pain, the handwritten word and the expressionistic scrapes made by the artist's bloodied fingers are significant: each type of writing is obscured or illegible, as if to say that the nature of pain can never be properly explained. We struggle to put our pain into words, to give it a shape that would manifest, authenticate or record its texture, density and tensile strength, the photographs might seem to say. In Ulay's cries and in his shattered writings on the wall, as in our own more measured statements, the hurt subject struggles to stage the particularity of a psychic or

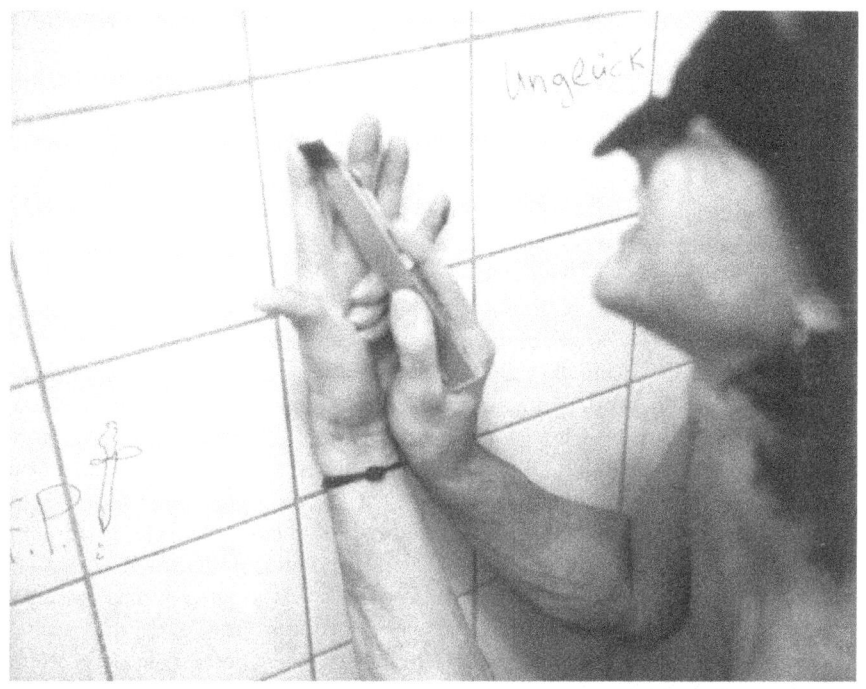

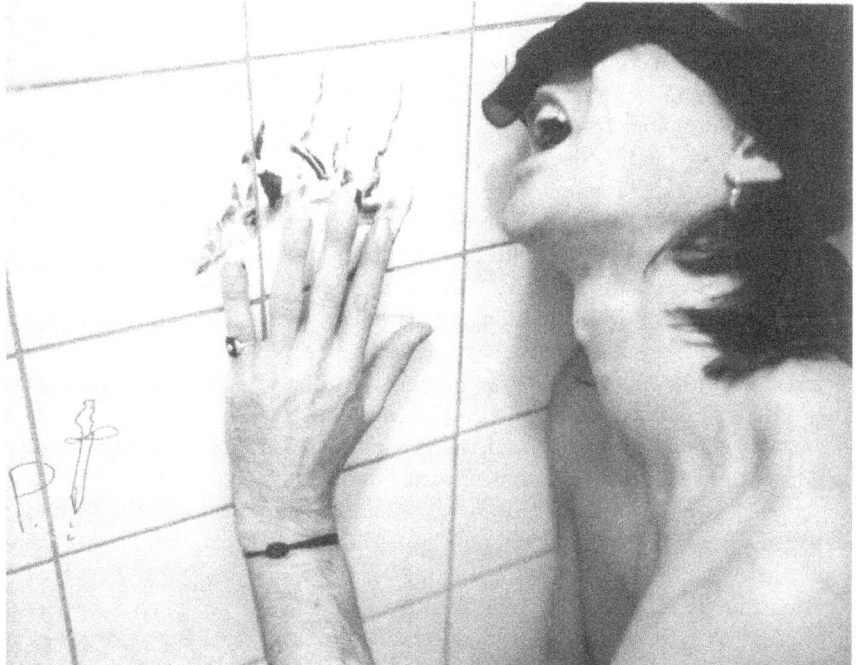

2.4 Ulay, *Soliloquy* (1974), from the series *Renais sense*, Polaroid type 107, 8.5 × 10.8 cm

psychical injury. Ulay's choice of the word 'soliloquy' – a speech directed towards no particular object – is telling in this sense. The obstacles to representing pain itself – beyond showing its superficial signs, like a gash in the skin or a scream in the mouth – does not prevent us from listening intently to how others try to make their pain known. Other images in Ulay's oeuvre of the 1970s rehearse a similar strategy, such as a Polaroid, *Diamond Plane* (1974), in which a glittering brooch of an airplane – a memento from a departed lover – is stabbed into his chest leaving a long bloody flight path on his skin. In a further work, *Bene Agere (In Her Shoes)* (1974), Ulay wears a lover's shoe and carves the limit of its leather into the skin of his foot with a blade, as if permanently to mark the fetishistic split between his body and her remainders. Its main title, *Bene Agere* ('well and good') sits in uncomfortable counterpoint to the *unglücklich* quality of *Soliloquy*: the speech the latter suggests is one of psychic or emotional desolation, for the homeliness of inhabiting the lover's shoes is nowhere to be seen in Ulay's drastic self-image. The broader mass of Polaroids similarly performs and interrogates the legibility of gender, sexuality, desire, pain, romance, wellbeing, ability and national identity.

If *There is a Criminal Touch to Art* contests the relation between performance art and documentation in the course of its attack on national identity, Ulay has been invested consistently in staging the incapacity of both performance and its documents (particularly photography) to represent, expose or capture truth and authenticity: of the self, a situation or the nation. In 1972, this gave rise to a potently invasive attempt to go *beneath the surface of the image*, perhaps to transcend superficiality, while also making a spectacle of the artistic search for meaning and truth. This approach lays a fecund ground of sorts for his later performance of extremity in Berlin in 1976. The project in question, *GENE.T.RATION ULTIMA RATIO* (1972) was a pioneering work using tattooing and cosmetic surgery – likely the first appropriation of the latter as an artist's technique and an early use of tattooing for such purposes – soon after the first significant artistic appropriation of tattooing, VALIE EXPORT's *Body Sign Action* (1970), in which a garter and the perimeter of hosiery were tattooed onto the skin of her thigh. Ulay commissioned a tattooist in Amsterdam called Pier de Haan to tattoo the title of his work in the skin of his forearm. After four weeks, Ulay commissioned a plastic surgeon to remove the healed tattoo and graft a piece of unblemished skin from the underside of the same arm. Using a Polaroid camera and a remote shutter, Ulay documented both processes and titled the resulting series *Tattoo/Transplant* (1972) (**Figure 2.5**). In order to achieve the photographs, the surgeon used a nerve block, leaving Ulay conscious and physically able to use his right hand to hit the shutter-release, while the operation was undertaken on his left arm. He hired a nurse to be in attendance to remove and replace the Polaroid films. After its excision, Ulay preserved the tattooed skin in formaldehyde solution, subsequently air-drying it to create a totemic, leathery relic of the action, now framed as a work of art: though shrunken, it is still partly legible.

The title *GENE.T.RATION ULTIMA RATIO* suggests the phrase 'Generation Last Resort', in reference to the 'ultima ratio regum' – or 'Last Resort of Kings and Common Men' – issued by royalty as a signal for the declaration of war. Inserting a 'T' bounded by full stops in 'generation', Ulay refers additionally to the emergent

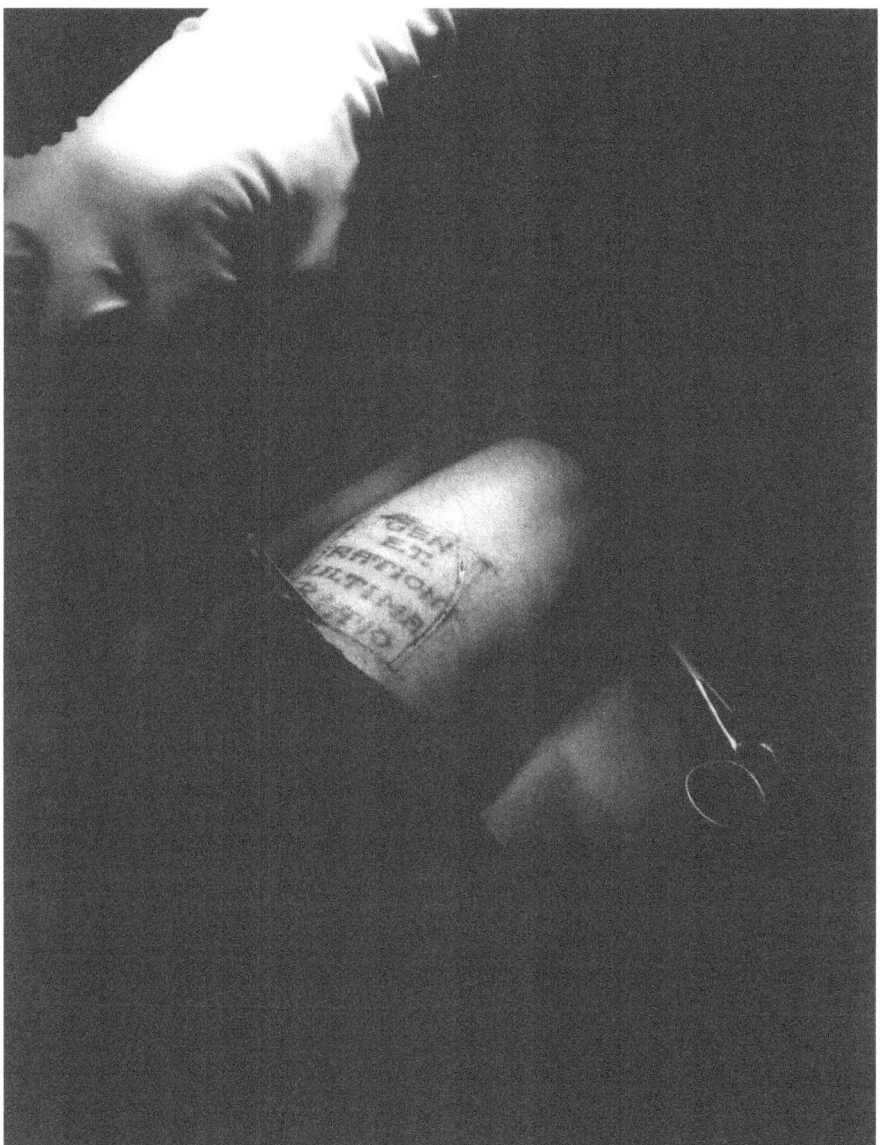

2.5 Ulay, *GEN.E.T.RATION ULTIMA RATIO* (1972), Polaroid type 107, 10.8 × 8.5 cm

popular discourse on genetics, signalling his imperative to challenge the shape and design of his body, in contradiction to its genetic constitution (to my eye, Ulay also nods to Genet, to foreshadow his own spectacular criminality to come). Responding to the work, art historian Beate Söntgen notes its biomedical prescience, as 'a painful but nonetheless self-inflicted . . . procedure . . . determined by external conditions beyond individual authority, by the threatening possibility of the formation of man through the hand of science' (Söntgen 2016: 115). As a *last resort* and a call to arms, Ulay's semi-private performance and implicated project of performative photography approximated a battle cry and appropriated the mark of the outsider and the criminal (the tattoo) as a project of what Söntgen usefully calls 'self-ascertainment' (2016: 116), only to obliterate the sign of his singularity via medical technology (cosmetic surgery).

His 'last resort' stages his keenly felt difference – national, evolutionary, sexual – akin to the way generations of people in affluent societies have sought to manifest (however awkwardly or inefficiently) our collective alienation through practically similar strategies of body modification, including tattooing, piercing and scarification. The excision of the skin that hosts the mark seems to stage Ulay's self-determination and subjective agency, while also representing the apparent impossibility of such an enactment, for the effacement of the sign reiterates his will at the expense of his previous attempt at the same future. The activities that make up his performance are as powerful as they are futile, for neither the tattoo nor its obliteration can enact the subject's freedom from the constitutive limits and prohibitions of the social or from the weight of history. The surgery brings him back full circle and Ulay is healed – but scarred. (Seated close, some 40 years on, I see the patch of transplanted skin, shiny and hairless on his forearm.)

As Mechthild Fend notes, Ulay's choice of tattooing was still potent in terms of German national identity: 'the act of tattooing letters into a person certainly also resonated [with] another "ultima ratio", the national socialist final solution and the dehumanising practice of tattooing numbers into the [fore]arms of concentration camp prisoners' (Fend 2009: 50–1). If the appropriation of tattooing implied its unspeakable misuse in the Nazi era, Ulay neutralised the tattoo's ability to brand its wearer with a linguistic sign of abjected ethnic, religious, political or sexual identity, replacing its toxic signification with a permanent scar. *GENE.T.RATION ULTIMA RATIO* was thus invested in an attempt to rewrite or remove an aspect of Ulay's national identity, to anticipate in some ways the later extremity of *There is a Criminal Touch to Art*. 'In many ways I tried to de-Germanize myself', Ulay says of his performances of extremity in the 1970s: 'I wanted to respond to a situation, and found my way to do it' (Bojan and Cassin 2014: 117). The brutal or drastic aspect of his solutions was as much a product of his temperament as an effect of the extremity of the historical situations he responded to.

At a formal level, *GENE.T.RATION* established Ulay's programme of destroying and rebuilding our understanding of the limits of art or its categories. In the documents, the spectacle of blood, fat-pebbled viscera and lacerated skin materialises the conceptual slippage between the body and a work of art and between performance and photography, perhaps akin to the way his theft of *The Poor Poet* materialises a slippage between art and crime. This propensity for enacting vehement conceptual slippages has three key characteristics that remain relatively constant for Ulay. First, his aesthetic philosophy is primarily, wilfully, paradoxically anti-art. The anti-art or anti-aesthetic sensibility is strident but paradoxical because, as Hal Foster observes, it aims at a 'negation of art . . . in the anarchic hope of an "emancipatory effect"', while at the same time reaffirming art – a radical new version, at least – as 'a time of pure presence, a space beyond representation' (1983: xv). Foster argues that for an anti-aesthetic practice or theory to be critically active, rather than self-deluding rhetoric, it must function as 'a critique which destructures the order of representations in order to reinscribe them' (*ibid.*) – a telling description in the light of Ulay's action of writing and unwriting in *GENE.T.RATION* and his guerrilla curating in the 'Berlin Action'. Second, the conceptual slippages frequently occur because Ulay appropriates surprising technologies and styles to enact the ephemerality of corporeal and performed identities, pushing the content of one sphere of knowledge, practice or being into another. Finally, he is profoundly concerned with abandoning corporate, decorative or functional approaches to aesthetics in favour of a searching ethical programme for artistic production and reception. For Ulay, 'aesthetics without ethics becomes cosmetic' (Iles 1988: 18). All three convictions are conditioned by the problem of the limit. In its use of anomalous body practices, *GENE.T.RATION* is an imaginative practice apparently freed from the bounds of form, overextending the category of art to stray into the alien territories or techniques of tattooing, surgery and genetics. In the 'Berlin Action', however, any similar dream of transcendence comes up against an insurmountable limit, namely, that of the law.

In *GENE.T.RATION*, specifically in the surgical procedure recorded in the gruesome Polaroid series, the sight of Ulay's bloody meat emerging from the sectioned skin ruptures the familiar logics of substitution and simulation that we associate conventionally with the practice of art. The effect is in a continuum with the shock of his appropriation (the obliteration of the difference between art and crime) in the 'Berlin Action'. Like other photographic actions, detailed earlier, the promised permanence of Ulay's tattoo and the scandal of its removal (that is, the precocity and extravagance of its excision) provoke a conceptual slippage in our understanding of what art does – and thus the work sets a provocative precedent for the 'Berlin Action', as a similarly scandalous departure from the conventions of artistic approximation and verisimilitude, displaced by the appearance of immediacy. Ulay's transplant and theft both enact the material conflation of the body and art. As elsewhere in the performance of extremity, the life of the artist is collapsed violently into the practices it undertakes: respectively, through the permanent scarring of his arm and the assumption of formal criminality as a conceptual scarring of character. Such actions bring with them a forbidding kind of finality, an incorrigible singularity. In a word, they epitomise Ulay's extremity. The latter takes the form of appearing to go too far with regard to what is acceptable or reasonable: the social disaster of criminality in the case of the *There is a Criminal Touch to Art*; or the physical destitution of excessive self-injury in the case of *GENE.T.RATION ULTIMA RATIO*.

Yet in the late 1980s, he would relinquish his stardom at the peak of his celebrity, withdrawing from the spotlight to throw himself even more fully to the wolves of perversity, secrecy, monasticism and a permanently peripatetic life. Among his criminality and his wildness, which retain their own inveterate clarity, Ulay remains unwilling to stake a claim to certainty, stability, credibility or coherence. Today he is quite the survivor – of obscurity and of extremity (and of cancer). Maybe he's just stubborn, happy or generous, too prone to letting go or much too careless with his grandeur. His calm is that of an iconoclast.

3

The dirtying intention

A child already knows that graffiti is more obscene than the organs or gestures it evokes because the dirtying intention is affirmed in all its purity. (Simone de Beauvoir, 'Must We Burn Sade?')

COUM Transmissions was multiple by its very nature and kaleidoscopic in form and appearance and remains difficult to pin down in the wake of its collapse. COUM was initially an alter ego for Genesis P-Orridge.[1] Then, all at once COUM was: an art collective of unstable membership whose core included P-Orridge and Cosey Fanni Tutti;[2] a pidgin language; a philosophy or makeshift ethic; and a way of life. From the early 1970s, COUM posed a grisly and uncompromising threat to received ways of making and exhibiting art and occupying public space, through a dizzying range of activities, aesthetic provocations and stunts. The very question of what art is, does and should feel like – and how we might seek to speak to it – would come under attack in COUM. This set of imperatives was re-articulated at COUM's prompting, under different styles and with different stakes, in the space of performance, extensively in the courts and in the press. The theme or strategy of obscenity – or, more precisely, indecency – is a defining force in COUM's scandalous performances of extremity in the 1970s, via what the feminist philosopher Simone de Beauvoir

---

1 The artist now identifies as Genesis BREYER P-ORRIDGE, having undergone *Breaking Sex* (1999–2007), a project of surgical and behavioural modifications to merge identities with the late Lady Jaye BREYER P-ORRIDGE and create a 'pandrogynous' post-transsexual entity without gender. I have retained the obsolete name 'Genesis P-Orridge' to discuss works undertaken before the advent of *Breaking Sex*; I credit the artist's newly adopted name where appropriate to refer to texts produced in the present.

2 Other key members, at various times, included Fizzy Paet, Spydeee Gasmantell, 'Reverend' Les Maull, Tim Poston, Lord Biggles, Foxtrot Echo, Peter 'Sleazy' Christopherson and John Lacey. From here on, I refer to Cosey by her first name, as is conventional in discussions of her work.

describes as 'the dirtying intention', signalling not simply the precocity or puerility of making things – objects, images, utterances and social interactions – filthy or low. Reflecting in the present upon the past, Genesis BREYER P-ORRIDGE articulates a parallel insight: that obscenity resides not in the thing that provokes the indecorous-ness or insult of scandal, but in the scandal itself. The distortion is what we ought to take offence at: 'There is nothing more obscene', the artist explains, 'than people trying to intimidate and violate you in such a way that you feel you have to censor your thoughts, and censor how you relate to your own body and personal existence' (interview with the author, New York, 19 March 2016). The 'dirtying intention' is paradoxically 'pure'; the vilification of the truthful imperative by the scandalising frame is sordid and cheap.

In its subversions, COUM questions how the sensibility through which one frames one's enactments can bring about powerful effects, including those of state oppression, silencing and discipline. It therefore may shed light upon the common distribution of what is, or is not, allowed, expected or true in a given conjugation of space and time. The drastic nature with which the law and the media, in the name of a spuriously defended public good, came down with prohibitive and punitive force upon COUM's artistic activities in the 1970s demonstrates both the seeming obscen-ity of the group's coercion and regulation and the firebrand novelty, surprise and importance of COUM's actions.

P-Orridge writes, 'COUM is a search for temporary definitions. A series ov arbi-trary statements fixing in more concrete terms thee eternal, non-existent paradox of time, for no reason' (P-Orridge 2000: 65).[3] As an ethos or sensibility, COUM remained definitively undefined. COUM's project – as 'an absolute collision that leads to a penetration wondrous to behold' (*ibid.*) – began as a thought-experiment in the late 1960s and in its freethinking, freak-out, consciousness-expanding nature was very much of that time. In 1976, COUM became especially radicalised in its public perception when, at the age of 26, P-Orridge suffered a series of critical run-ins with the law and broadcast media, which soon prompted the artist's (and the group's) conceptual and practical withdrawal from the art world. P-Orridge reflected on these changes in a text called 'Scenes of Victory' of 1978, writing in sardonically simple terms: 'COUM has changed. That is good' (P-Orridge and Christopherson 1979: 65).[4] Thus, the positive change announced prosaically in the statement refers to the abandonment of art as an identifiable category of creative production – a retire-ment of sorts from a conversation into which the artist had been introduced – and a compensatory embrace of even more ambivalent or ambiguous aesthetic commit-ments. The effect involved COUM's deliberate formal dispersal of aesthetic practices that were already remarkably ephemeral and uncontainable – a 'series ov arbitrary

3 Here and throughout, P-Orridge's strategic misspellings are preserved as in the originals. These include the use of 'thee' for 'the' and 'ov' for 'of'; and elsewhere, 'E' for 'I', 'yoo' for 'you', 'butter' for 'but', and prolific introductions of 'coum' to colonise various words (for example, 'coumplete').

4 'Scenes of Victory' prefaces several pages of found images, quotes and commentaries (or 'heresies') that were collectively produced with Sleazy in 1976 and previously published as a standalone provocation in *Studio International* magazine (see P-Orridge and Christopherson 1976: 44–8). The text cited through-out refers to the republication of 'Annihilating Reality', which consists of both parts.

statements' – and a conceptual retreat to still more remote and esoteric aesthetic lands.

Coummentary

Neil Andrew Megson was born in Manchester, England on 22 February 1950. After attending the University of Hull for one year from 1968, Megson abandoned formal education, taking up the eccentric, gender-neutral name Genesis in 1969. The full name Genesis P-Orridge was acquired by deed poll in January 1971. P-Orridge founded COUM Transmissions in December 1969 and it grew in membership and visibility from 1971, after a series of performances in and around Hull in the northeast of England. Born in Hull in 1951, Christine Carol Newby joined COUM in late 1969 and took on the psychedelic name 'Cosmosis', soon shortened to 'Cosey'; in 1974, Robin Klassnik suggested (on a postcard) the full name Cosey Fanni Tutti, a play on *Così fan tutte*, the title of Mozart's *opera buffa* of 1790. The moniker – which stuck – is a malapropism that puns on the title's generalisation about women and the resemblance between '*fan*' and 'fanny' (in England, slang for vagina), with a saccharine soupçon of *tutti frutti* that suggests a pleasurable but nutritionless confection. It also emphasises cosiness in amusing counterpoint to Cosey's characteristically blank, cool, severe or pokerface quality in performances, shoots and interviews – and ironicises the far-from-cosy threat her work would come to pose to a shockable and fainthearted popular press in 1976.

After popular campaigns against COUM in Hull and a documented campaign of police harassment (Cosey 2017: 129–30), in June 1973 P-Orridge secured a lease on the Death Factory, a workspace provided by Space Studios at 10 Martello Street, adjacent to London Fields in Hackney, East London, which became COUM headquarters – and their new home.[5] The name 'Death Factory' came from the macabre (but apocryphal) belief that London Fields covers a seventeenth-century bubonic plague pit (Cosey 2017: 190).

The performances of COUM Transmissions between 1971 and 1976 consisted primarily of provocative live actions in public and alternative spaces and in art venues, as well as experiments in sound, mail art and installation. Merging art and life, COUM's performances and objects explored the aesthetics of the urban industrial wastelands in which P-Orridge, Cosey and their collaborators were raised, with allusions to and enactments of sex, scandal, crime, wounding, atrocity, and occult ritual. Enacted in the streets of Gross-Gerau, West Germany (and revived in a different version in Kiel later the same year and elsewhere), *Omissions* (1975) was a typical performance (**Figure 3.1**). Describing the plan for the first performance, by Cosey

5 This and the preceding biographical information on P-Orridge is given in a three-page CV, Institute of Contemporary Arts Collection, TGA 955/7/7/72, Tate Archive, London, 'Papers relating to the exhibition *Prostitution* by COUM Transmissions'. See Ford on P-Orridge's early years (1999: 1.8–16), Cosey's arrival (1999: 1.17–21), the Hull years (1999: 2.4–22), and the move to London (1999: 3.7–10).

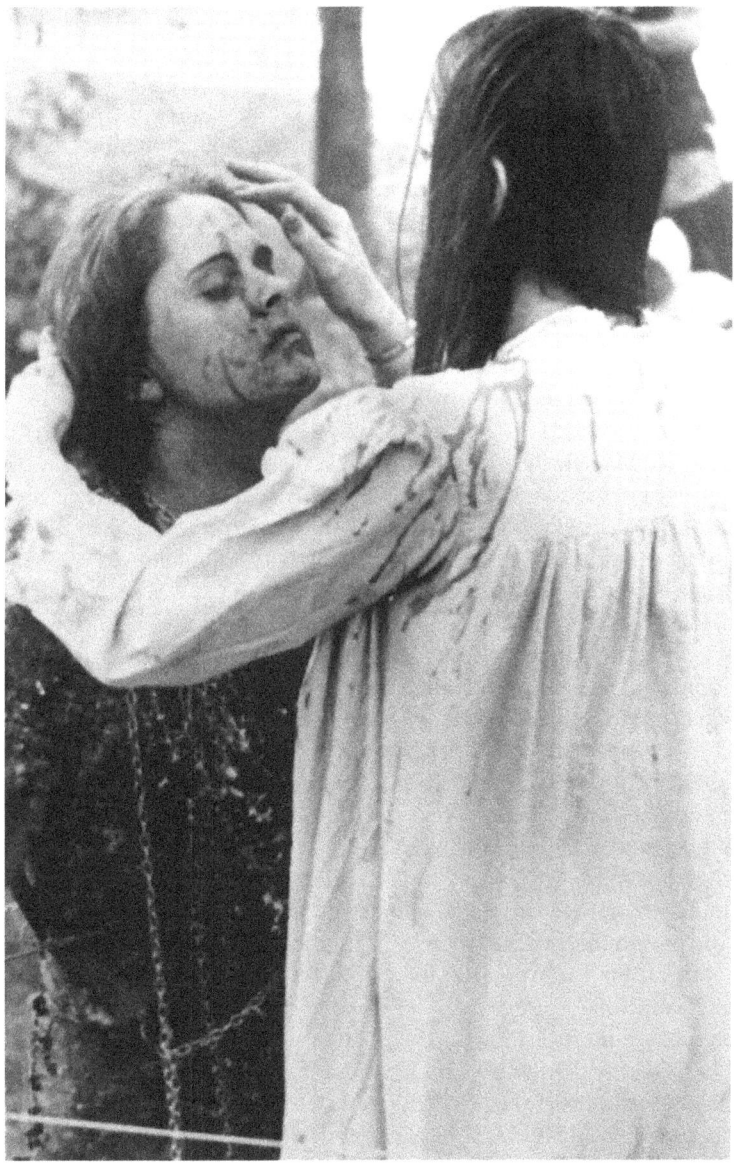

3.1 COUM Transmissions, *Omissions* (1975), performance, Kiel, Germany

and fellow COUM associate Fizzy Paet (aka Peter Waudby), P-Orridge writes in diary form:

> [COUM] pour petrol into gutters and light it whilst Cosey . . . masturbates on lit candles in street, Fizzy covered in used tampax, milk bottles tied to his fingers filled with blood and maggots, Cosey fingering her cunt, hits them [the bottles] with hammer and smashes

them. They eat raw eggs and puke, then they try to wash in vomit, then piss themselves and fuck, milk syringed up their arse. (Ford 1999: 5.6)

The bloody, pornographic action kick-started three days of public performances by COUM; Cosey recalls 'the first [action was] stopped by police and the remaining ones moved from the main thoroughfare . . . away from any children' who happened to pass by (2017: 165).

COUM's aesthetic could be unnerving, repellent, indecent or obscene, with its reclaiming of thematic 'omissions' (the feasible contents of a life that are omitted from polite representations) and its fascinations, here, with bodily emissions and other indecorous materials. But it was never exclusively so. If COUM could disgust and outrage, it was also eccentric, farcical and strategically infantile, typified by its first poster artwork, a portrait of P-Orridge as a schoolboy propping up a tuba, framed by the slogan *Yes COUM are Fab and Kinky* (1971). In performances, writings and ephemera, COUM characteristically mingled acts and images of physical extremity – sure to outrage or repel casual and informed audiences alike – with a deliberately silly, tasteless or camp sensibility. The effect is profoundly jarring.

With the reinforced intensity and productivity that followed P-Orridge and Cosey's translocation to London came an escalation of COUM's strategic attraction to scandal and intrigue. This was not merely promiscuous and neither was it always active or conscious. However, P-Orridge theorised the public nature of COUM's interventions and the active pursuit of media coverage as political necessities. 'No social ticket is required, no venue', P-Orridge writes, as the work reaches audiences beyond the self-selecting constituencies comprising the art world (P-Orridge and Christopherson 1979: 65). Specifically, COUM attempted to 'use the press to record our activities like a diary' because 'it was far more effective propaganda/information dispersal to be written up [in] the NEWS section of daily papers than in a back page column of a specialist Art journal' (*ibid.*). The ramifications of this adaptation were significant for P-Orridge, as it both exploited and undermined the purported impera-tives of the press and exempted COUM from the institutional apparatus of art. 'The threat is biggest for the art world, the art market', P-Orridge declares. 'Solving art problems is coincidental' (*ibid.*).

As a means of interrogating COUM's 'threat', I explore two specific controversies that led to COUM's permanent renunciation of the art world (some 40 years later, COUM is categorically defunct; P-Orridge and Cosey are still active, yet remain incor-rigibly marginal). In April 1976, P-Orridge appeared in court, charged under the Post Office Act 1953, after a case was brought for sending indecent materials through the mail. The ensuing trial, *General Post Office* v. *Genesis P-Orridge* (*G.P.O.* v. *G.P-O.*) was appropriated by P-Orridge, transformed into a performance event and renamed the *Mail Action*. It enabled P-Orridge to combine, muddle and compare the spaces of art and law, art and pornography and mail art and performance art – so as to 'cut up' these domains, in William Burroughs' practical sense of creating new texts by splicing existing ones, to absolve oneself of superegoic injunctions and subjective inhibitions (Burroughs 1993: 61). P-Orridge's performed intervention did not affect the outcome of the trial and neither could it change the law nor prevent the future prosecutions of similarly inclined artists. Rather, I argue, the *Mail Action* allowed P-Orridge to frame, recode or erode the purported autonomy of art and theatricalised the reach of the law across the freedom to be an artist. Particularly, it put into stark relief the inhibited freedom to create and disseminate 'indecent' or objectionable art.

Six months later, in October 1976, Genesis P-Orridge and Cosey Fanni Tutti would become household names after the scandalised reception of COUM Transmissions' exhibition *Prostitution* at the Institute of Contemporary Arts (ICA), London. Better known than its forbear, it prompted a media furore on account of its provocative, sexualised content, including active appropriations of hardcore pornography, particularly in the light of the group's receipt of public funds at a time of economic austerity and heightened political and social conservatism. As with the *Mail Action*, ontological problems concerning the forms, techniques, contents and categories of production proper to art and performance were taken publicly to task via the fallout of *Prostitution*. These contestations were enacted not in the courts but in the press and Parliament. So, too, the range of experiences art might invoke were also regulated, against COUM's own imperatives and with different stakes. Under the sign of indecency, the courts and the press were to lay claim to their responsibility to sustain conservative ideals, including the social principle of decorum and the moral principle of decency. Beyond their apparent reach, aesthetic principles also came under scrutiny, including the aesthetic distinction between art and pornography, delimiting the scope of the performance of extremity with grave effects, even for a troupe of experimenters as provocative and unrestrained as COUM.

The year 1976 was a pivotal year for art and controversy in Britain. As Richard Cork noted: '[i]t is difficult to recall a period in recent history which produced the flurry of scandalised attacks we have witnessed over the past 12 months', adding that the effect upon the public's reception of modern art had been 'undeniably disastrous' (Cork 1976: 11). The controversies included media outrage over the Tate Gallery's purchase of '120 ordinary firebricks', in the form of Carl Andre's minimalist stacked sculpture *Equivalent VIII* (1966); Mary Kelly's *Post-Partum Document* (1973–79), a conceptual artwork containing, in part, 'a tabulated row of soiled nappy-liners' (*ibid.*) at the ICA in London; and (opening at the same venue three days after Kelly's closure) COUM's *Prostitution*, which, Cork writes, made P-Orridge 'a national laughing stock' and a target of popular hostility (*ibid.*). For historian Alwyn Turner, references to Kelly and COUM 'became a journalistic shorthand for the monstrosity of modern art' (2008: 161). The effect suggests the facility of art scandals as a popular technology to demean the extremity of new cultural practices in the 1970s.

In the *Evening Standard*, journalist Maureen Cleave reflected somewhat sympathetically upon the greater implications of the *Prostitution* scandal, but warned that the cumulative threat of 'a stream of Orridges, bolstered by nappy exhibitions and people in Nottingham sweeping litter into "artistic piles," is another matter' (Cleave 1976: 19). Her column makes reference to *Post-Partum Document*; and to funds received by Ray Richards (of Ddart Performance Group, noted in Chapter 1) to make sculptures out of sweepings in the streets of Nottingham. Cleave suggests that in 1976 the best of British art risked being undermined or supplanted by the work of mediocre but attention-grabbing artists; this complements Cork's suggestion (which he debunks subsequently) that artists had been caught in the act of 'perpetrating a confidence trick' against a gullible public (1976: 11). The mood of generalised moral disturbance brought to a flashpoint the threat seemingly posed by the performance of extremity to the state and to popular values as inculcated by the press. In a compensatory manoeuvre, COUM crystallised the material impositions of the state upon artists and art. Both dynamics provocatively staged the mid-1970s in Britain as a period of culture war.

Culture war consists of a historically and geographically localised moment in lowering national tolerance for mischief, filth or cultural insurgence; it is typified when serial scandalous eruptions in the state of art, literature, cultural production and subcultural self-fashioning provoke, as Wendy Steiner puts it, 'a landscape littered with the remains of vilified artworks and discredited orthodoxies' (Steiner 1995: 209). Culture war in the twentieth century – especially in the late 1980s and early 1990s in the United States, but also including the eruptions of hostilities in Britain in the 1970s – involved the punishment of artists and experts, for example through reactionary strategies including institutional backlash, defunding, blacklisting, indictments for obscenity or indecency and reductive critical readings of contemporary art. In a landmark study of deviance and public outcries, published in 1972, Stanley Cohen noted that the question of popular scandals – or 'moral panics' as he terms them – is a question of social reaction or 'the organized system of social control', to the extent that this compensatory effect outweighs any substantial qualities of the 'warning' or trigger itself (Cohen 2002: 19). In other words, objects of analysis are never scandalous in themselves; scandal is a property of the observing group subject to the influence of community leaders (often including the press), whose social responses conspire to create and sustain a social response that then becomes readable in its vitriol. The treatment of COUM in 1976 and the seemingly causal relationships between the *Mail Action* and *Prostitution* and other scandals in the immediate period – including, in addition to art scandals, the rise of punk as a popular form of cultural agitation – suggest a formidable cultural war in the UK that tends not to be identified as such, beyond Simon Ford's useful observation of a direct correlation between COUM and Cohen's concept of 'moral panic' (Ford 1999: 6.22).

Couming on strong

Set amid the social, cultural and economic ferment indicated by culture war, the performances and mail art of P-Orridge and/or COUM (the slippage, here, is deliberate in the period) participates in a series of avant-garde strategies aimed at critiquing the institutional practices of art and of granting aesthetics a more vital relation to the concerns, sensory experiences and creative processes of everyday life. As P-Orridge writes, COUM 'found the art world on every level less satisfying than real life' (P-Orridge and Christopherson 1979: 65). This dissatisfaction prompted COUM to query and unbind the artificial division between the aesthetic domain and its purported outsides – including popular, macabre or pornographic cultures – and to privilege the vital margins of life over the artificial, ineffectual promises of art.

Indeed, later in 1976, Chris Burden's public dismissal of P-Orridge both staged COUM's formal overwhelming of the gains of even the most advanced performance art of the period and fuelled the political ardour of P-Orridge's strategic withdrawal from the art world. Burden and the conceptual artist John Baldessari reportedly stormed out of COUM's performance of *Cease to Exist No. 4* (LAICA, Los Angeles, 23 November 1976), 15 minutes into the piece. P-Orridge recalls, 'I was naked. I stood on tacks. I drank a bottle of whisky and gave myself enemas with blood, milk and urine, and then broke wind so a jet of blood, milk and urine combined shot across the floor in front of Chris Burden and assorted visual artists'; further gruesome feats included Cosey 'trying to sever her vagina [up] to her navel with a razor blade' (Mullen 2003). Burden was vocal in his disgust. 'This is not art,' Burden declared in a public statement, 'this is the most disgusting thing I've ever seen, and these people are sick' (Mulholland 1998: 226, n. 54). P-Orridge embraced this intended de-legitimisation and pathologisation of COUM's performances of extremity and quipped in retaliation, 'E told you we don't do art [but] you wouldn't believe me; take Chris Boredom's word for it, he MUST be right' (Mulholland 1998: 226). Controversially, but presciently, P-Orridge's performance of extremity revealed how performance art – despite the rigour of its own trangressions – was quick to develop its own orthodoxies, a fact that sustains, perhaps, the so-called (that is, selective) institutionalisation of performance art in the present. (Mentioning Burden to BREYER P-ORRIDGE today still garners a jocular eye-roll.)

The *Mail Action* stages P-Orridge's and/or COUM's placement both inside and outside the broader narratives of art criticism and history in the 1970s. The group – and particularly P-Orridge – participated expressly in ongoing discourses on the politics of marginal art forms and arguably never floated fully free from the domain of art, despite COUM's anti-art sensibility and the explicit restating of the dream of such an escape. In 1975, P-Orridge pitched a neo-avant-garde conception of COUM's anti-aesthetic sensibility in persuasive terms, writing: 'Performance art is not "about" entertainment, nor does it claim to produce an art-form which is concerned with beauty, aesthetics or a high standard of moral life. It is not [an antidote to] poverty, ignorance, atrocious housing, speculation or politics' (Ford 1999: 5.8). P-Orridge suggests that art cannot provide a solution to the specific material conditions of contemporary life; neither is there in the frequently rarefied and self-serving practice of performance art an antidote to the limitations – formal, moral and legal – against which the performance of extremity tends to strain. 'Performance art', P-Orridge continues, 'is concerned with Experience – direct, first-hand, individual interpretation of action. It uses as its *base* the imaginative interpretation of life itself, the raw material being drawn from the everyday' (*ibid.*, emphasis in original), recalling John Dewey's conception of art as a form of invigorated experience, embedded in the rhythms and practices of daily life.

In P-Orridge's hands, Dewey's 'crude' experience (Dewey 1934: 11) suggests a raw, pedestrian event, like the spaces and rituals of the law, of intimacy, or even the consumption of pornography. Dewey's aesthetic philosophy addresses the fact of an artist's (or perhaps viewer's) experience that the work of art emerges from, namely through the material conditions of production, labour, execution and exhibition. The logic of experience also serves to frame the desiring attachments, investments and participations provoked or enabled by COUM's work (specifically, here, by the pornographic aspects of the postcards in the *Mail Action* and the works exhibited in *Prostitution*, but also, more broadly, by COUM's performances) and by the personal cost of making art, including the emotional burden for P-Orridge of the trial and its outcome.

This unresolvable project of blurring art and life has a long history, in art practice as well as in the development of philosophical aesthetics. Dewey's philosophical challenge – and ethical plea – towards the blurring of art and life has since become a received truth of sorts in our understanding of the social fabric of art. While the democratising imperative would come to a kind of fruition in pop art, Happenings or land art, Dewey is open to stronger stuff, including experiences of 'perturbation and conflict . . . the sense of which haunts life' (1934: 17). Yet suffering, pain, affront or inflammation of the senses (including that provoked, perhaps, by porn) must have a transformative effect if it is to qualify as '*an* experience': 'To put one's hand in the fire that consumes it is not necessarily to have an experience', Dewey observes. 'The action and its consequences must be joined in perception. This relationship is what gives meaning; to grasp it is the objective of all intelligence' (1934: 44). For Dewey, 'with the vast extension of its scope to take in (potentially) anything and everything, art would have lost its unity, were there not a core of common substance', namely, the forging of profound feeling, efficacy or consequence in the experience of making of receiving art (1934: 191). Dewey's claim for the categorical indiscriminateness of art, bound by a 'common substance', anticipates Jacques Rancière's more recent proposition: 'Art exists as a separate world since anything whatsoever can belong to it' (Rancière's 2013a: x). Neither Dewey nor Rancière claims that everything already is a work of art, nor that art as a discrete category has ceased to exist by succumbing to the greater stakes of life. Rather, each philosopher retains his own understanding of the function of art and the contingency of aesthetic experience. For a democratic aesthetics, no trans-historical limit may be placed upon a particular object or event that would disallow its ideal aspiration or strategic elevation to the dizzyingly expansive common substance of art.

By proclaiming the source and style of art to be 'the raw material being drawn from the everyday' (Ford 1999: 5.8), P-Orridge realised the specifically democratic potential of performance art, but also of mail art. This is relevant in terms of the centrality of mailed artefacts – dirty postcards – to the *Mail Action*, as well as to P-Orridge's social involvement in the mail art scene in Britain and internationally at the time. John Held writes, '[w]hile mail art may not appeal to a commodity-based art mainstream, it obviously strikes a receptive chord with the general public', perhaps because it offers an alternative to 'expensive artworks and hyped-up art stars'; moreover, the postal letter or postcard as an artistic form 'democratizes art' (because anyone can participate), 'decentralizes art' (because the pre-digital 'eternal network' renders geographical distance insignificant) and 'dematerializes art' (as the importance of skill, technique and materials is undermined). Mail art 'fulfil[s] a prophecy of the historic avant-garde in bridging art and life' (Held 1991: xiii). Contemporary examples of mail art in COUM's immediate social and artistic milieu were indicative and influential – for example Robin Klassnik's *Yellow Objects* (1973), for which he distributed 8,000 self-addressed envelopes with a call for donations of yellow artefacts, which were mailed to the artist and displayed indiscriminately as part of a 'postal sculpture' in an expanding window display at the ICA. Klassnik harnessed the performance-oriented nature of audience participation, creating an installation that grew daily according to improvised responses to a predetermined script or score, drawing mail art into the orbits of performance art, installation and relational art. Superficially, the performance-installation was a direct influence on COUM's creation of a 'media wall' in the same venue during *Prostitution*, as discussed in this chapter. Indirectly, but structurally, P-Orridge's appropriation of an indecency trial as the *Mail Action* was a canny response to the ephemerality of performance art and mail art, enshrining (as Klassnik did) the democratic values of dematerialisation, while, in the same stroke, harnessing publicity and notoriety to ensure greater attention from audiences and the longer reach of cultural and critical memory.

The scandal of Ulay's crime was its explicit criminal premeditation and the artist's radical openness towards capture and punishment (*it's a strange thief who surrenders*). P-Orridge's crime takes up a more ambivalent orientation in terms of the will to agency, criminality or penalisation. The artist's assumption of the role of criminal is partly accidental – or at least incidental to the work of creating the postcards, during which process their criminal status was perhaps unknown, dissociated or sublimated. The air of criminality hovers, obscurely, over P-Orridge's artistic labour, including the act of creating the cards. Yet P-Orridge stages very explicitly the will to aesthetics, embraces criminality after the fact and aestheticises the ensuing drama; whereas Ulay actively appropriates and thus purposefully orchestrates a criminal act, P-Orridge does so unwittingly, yet follows up by self-consciously appropriating the ensuing trial as a work of art in itself. What, precisely, is at stake in expropriating art into spaces that remain categorically alien to it and claiming the pedestrian spaces of a life as the stuff of art and of aesthetic experience? How does the *Mail Action* vacillate upon the border between art and its outsides, be these the volatile terrains of pornography, performance, correspondence or life? How does COUM – by stealth – enact slippages or border-crossings between performance art and crime, art and porn, as peculiar demotic variations on the categories of art and life?

The *Mail Action*

On 17 January 1976, Genesis P-Orridge was charged with five counts of indecency under section 11(1)(c) of the Post Office Act 1953, a piece of legislation that governed proper use of the postal service. By sending five collaged postcards through the Royal Mail, P-Orridge had contravened a law that states: 'A person shall not send or attempt to send or procure to be sent a postal packet which . . . has on the packet, or on the cover thereof, any words, marks or designs which are grossly offensive or of an indecent or obscene character.' Until its repeal in 2001, the Act complemented the existing obscenity legislation – including the Obscene Publications Act 1959 – by providing legal means for the state to prosecute the dissemination of formally 'indecent' materials. Writing in 1979, P-Orridge's barrister Geoffrey Robertson explained the difference between obscenity and indecency as models of legal censorship. The proof of *obscenity*, he writes, depends on the offending object's potential, 'taken as a whole', 'to deprave or corrupt' its consumers and cause objective social harm (Robertson 1979: 348). However, the criminally *indecent* artefact is that which might embarrass or outrage the citizenry's perceived sexual modesty (1979: 1). While obscenity is understood to actively harm the individual or social body, indecent materials are illegal because they are 'a public nuisance, an unnecessary affront to people's sense of aesthetic propriety' (1979: 174). In what resembles a legal anomaly, P-Orridge was committing a crime neither by producing or owning the postcards, nor by purchasing or repurposing legal, commercially available pornographic images and writings. Yet once the adulterated cards entered the postal system, the artefacts became formally 'indecent'. A crime had been committed.

P-Orridge was initially charged with sending two cards. Subsequent counts were added to the prosecution's case on 3 February 1976 after investigations uncovered three further, older cards (P-Orridge 2002a).[6] Of the five cards, two were seized and never returned. The original cards were stamped prominently with COUM's studio address (the Death Factory at 10 Martello Road, London Fields), suggesting P-Orridge had little knowledge of or concern for the probable illegality of the activities in question – or, alternatively, ensured conscientiously that any ensuing controversy would attach itself to COUM Transmissions, named brazenly on the cards. Indeed, P-Orridge does not claim to have prompted or anticipated the charge or the ensuing furore: 'we were totally surprised, because we had been doing it for years and nobody had bothered'.[7] Noting the safety of the 'contented bubble of mail art', P-Orridge continues, 'you could do what you wanted and nobody gave a shit about it so we just kept sending out these cards. We sent out hundreds of "Queen postcards"' – that is, cards combining collaged images of the Queen and pornographic (and miscellaneous) found imagery (interview with the author, 2016). However, only a small number of the proliferating postcards were the basis of the concomitant trial.

While the *Prostitution* debacle was engineered as a media spectacle, P-Orridge remembers being somewhat naïve about the ramifications of the mail art project. Cosey (who lived with P-Orridge) documented the serving of the legal summons by a policeman. Asked whether this had somehow been planned in advance, which might therefore disclose some prior knowledge or anticipation of legal problems to come, P-Orridge explains: 'That's just us. We were documenting everything. That's how we were working at that time' (*ibid.*). Pushed on the issue, P-Orridge explains the use of

6 Unless otherwise stated, factual details concerning the trial are drawn from the same unpaginated source.
7 The artist presently identifies in the plural, hence the uses of 'we' in place of 'I', and similar.

photography here, but also during the trial, as well as the transmutation of the trial into a performance and the decision to retain (and subsequently reproduce and disseminate) the paperwork the *Mail Action* produced:

> It's been an ongoing part of our practice to treat even the most apparently banal moments of life as potentially amazing or significant . . . We were perceiving everything as performance art, even when there was no one watching, no audience of any kind. It all becomes a part of a triggered performance piece, which in a way is far more interesting, because you are as ignorant of the . . . results that might happen as anyone else on the other side of it – in this case the police. Suddenly you are all involved in this spontaneous event, with no knowledge of tomorrow. (*ibid.*)

The offending postcards merge pornography and other imagery on the fronts and carry messages, stamps and other attachments on the backs. One postcard was sent to Lord Biggles (Ian Goodrich) on 11 October 1975. The front carries a relatively inoffensive found image of a woman grasping a male lover, collaged against a background of chains, with a patterned sheet pasted across part of both images. The back includes a section of text cut from the porn magazine *Club International*. 'I could hear Angelo breathing heavily', the text begins, 'and after a couple of minutes his penis began to harden again, filling my mouth with its rigid flesh.'

A second card was sent to Tim Poston – a lecturer in mathematics and COUM collaborator – at an address in Geneva on 12 October 1975 and consists of appropriated elements collaged onto a souvenir postcard. The resulting work shows a drawing of a farmer sprinkling seeds onto the lawn of Buckingham Palace. Directly next to an inset portrait of the Queen, a pornographic image shows a hand reaching up between garter-clad legs. The fingers part and probe the cleavage between the buttocks; in combination with the agricultural cartoon perhaps the resulting collage insinuates an erotic euphemism, namely, the heteromasculine entitlement to 'sow one's seeds'. On the back, a handwritten message from P-Orridge reads, 'The lady on the front has her mouth shut because her teeth are filed to points', in reference to the unsmiling Queen. P-Orridge recalls the image of the Queen as a central imperative for the overarching project. The forced proximity between images of Queen Elizabeth II and commercially available pornography entailed a mischievous attack on the perceived corruption of the monarchy. 'As we all know', P-Orridge explains, while laughing, 'the most perverted, debauched and unpleasant people, sexually, are usually the aristocrats who can be untouchable. Go and check out Gilles de Rais if you want to know about that', P-Orridge adds, in insouciant reference to the fifteenth-century noble – and prolific serial killer of children (*ibid.*).

In formal terms, the collage acknowledges the mutual commercial availability of both pornographic images and tourist-oriented representations of the Queen. 'We never used images that weren't available from newsstands', P-Orridge notes. 'They were always already available to the public.' By attaching one to the other – the image of pornographic display on top of the anodyne royal souvenir postcard – the surprising new configuration places conventionally disparate or discrete categories of mass-produced commercial representations of women on a promiscuously even footing, suggesting P-Orridge's imperative 'to symbolise corruption on a very deep level – and hypocrisy, double standards, and all that good stuff that power usually generates' (*ibid.*). The Queen on a postcard clashes with a pornographic image of sex, prompting discursive contiguities between dissimilar categories: regal and kitsch, vulgar and natural, hifalutin and top shelf. The effects of such recombination or blurring muddles the assumptions we may make about the form and content of each category of collaged source material and the ensuing object.

The three cards that came under additional legal scrutiny had been sent on 9 August 1974, 29 November 1975 and 5 December 1975. The sole surviving work uses a reproduction postcard of René Magritte's *Time Transfixed* (1938), in which a locomotive steams from a fireplace, jutting at full pelt into an empty, painted room (**Figure 3.2**). Magritte's apparent gesture towards the train as phallic substitute is desublimated brusquely in P-Orridge's appropriation. In P-Orridge's collage, a reclining woman is anally penetrated, afore the fireplace, as two hands (the man's) hold open the folds of her vulva. The train rams the penetrated woman in the neck, nearly perpendicular to the penis that enters her from below. In its original French, Magritte's title – *La durée poignardé* – translates literally as *Impaled Duration*; P-Orridge returns to the painting a suggestion of physical impalement, rather than the cognitive activity of transfixion adopted in its decorous English title. Like the first card, the back of the third has two paragraphs pasted from a pornographic magazine. It describes an 'adulterous fuck' in close detail, adorned by a signature and various rubber stamps, including 'FILE UNDER COUM', which suggests COUM as a self-sufficient category of indecent, illicit and wilfully illegitimate activities.

The Magritte postcard was sent to 'Ted Glass', a fictional artist P-Orridge included surreptitiously in *Contemporary Artists* (1977), a mammoth encyclopaedia of 1300 artists' biographies compiled by P-Orridge and art critic Colin Naylor (1977: 342). The entry is accompanied by a half-page reproduction of one of Glass's fallaciously attributed photographs – depicting a broken mirror – as well as a forged artist statement. The latter reads in part: 'My art is sometimes distrusted and disliked . . . People like sham artists that soothe them with aesthetic platitudes. They dread having to face reality in any form' (*ibid.*). The statement is loaded with irony, as it was written by P-Orridge and credited to a 'sham' artist, namely Glass. The statement was reprinted in edited form in 'Scenes of Victory' (P-Orridge's co-authored artist statement discussed in the opening pages of this chapter), suggesting a playful and serial slippage between P-Orridge's performance of identity and the construction of alter egos – staged throughout COUM and, here, obliquely, in the photograph of a cracked, distorting mirror that illustrates the Glass biography.

The address used on the postcard, 210 West 14th Street, belonged to Marcel Duchamp's long-term studio in New York from 1943. Duchamp was not a friend of COUM – he died in 1968 – but P-Orridge's use of the address sets up a playful relation between Glass and his supposed contemporary Duchamp to riff on the latter's identity as a prankster of sorts and to pun on the received name of Duchamp's most famous work, the *Large Glass* (1915–23). This elaborate and mostly secret or unnoticed ruse was folded into the ongoing mail art project. The use of a fictional recipient suggests P-Orridge planned to send the most graphic card without incriminating a correspondent or hoped to ensure it a longer journey, by using the postal system's

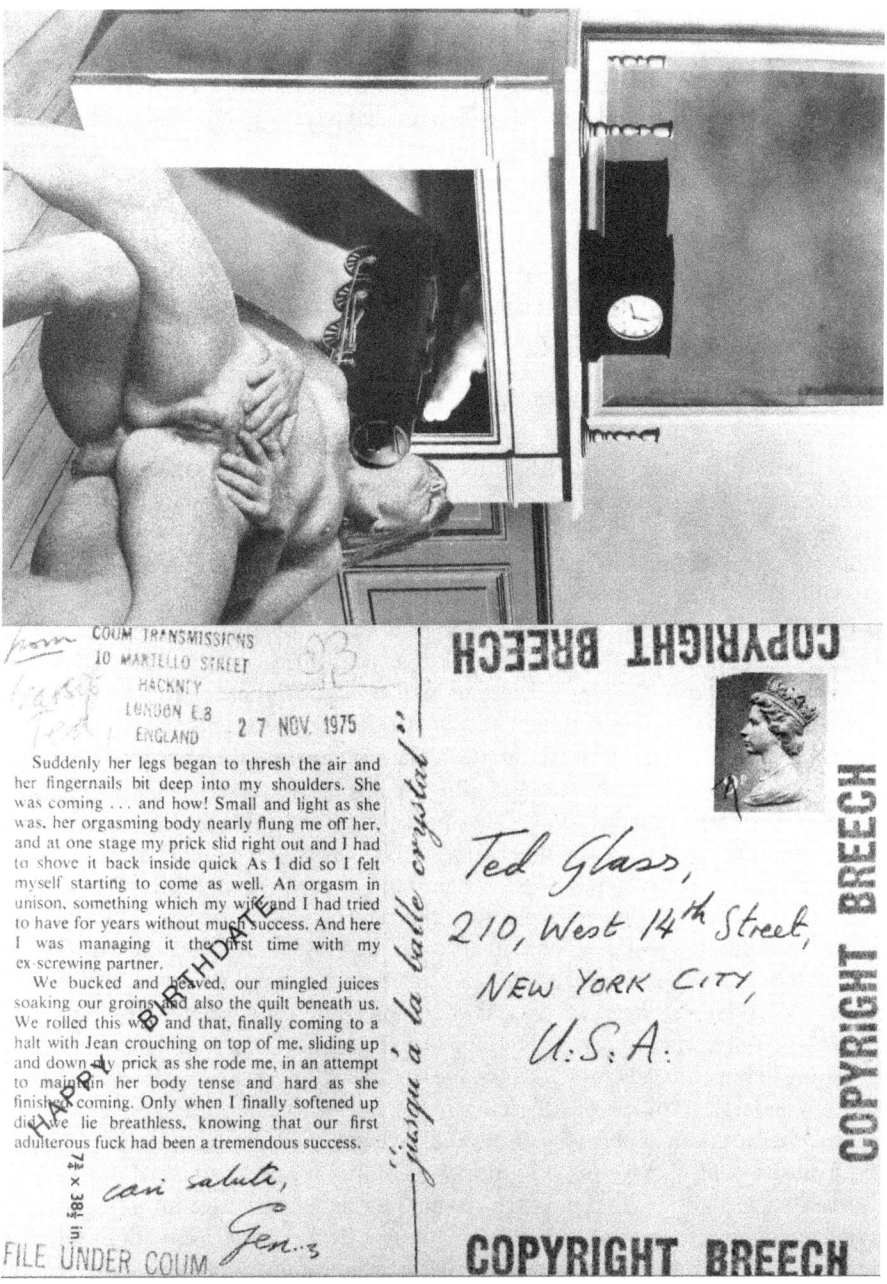

COUM TRANSMISSIONS
10 MARTELLO STREET
HACKNEY
LONDON E.8
ENGLAND   2 7 NOV. 1975

COPYRIGHT BREECH

Suddenly her legs began to thresh the air and her fingernails bit deep into my shoulders. She was coming . . . and how! Small and light as she was, her orgasming body nearly flung me off her, and at one stage my prick slid right out and I had to shove it back inside quick As I did so I felt myself starting to come as well. An orgasm in unison, something which my wife and I had tried to have for years without much success. And here I was managing it the first time with my ex-screwing partner.

We bucked and heaved, our mingled juices soaking our groins and also the quilt beneath us. We rolled this way and that, finally coming to a halt with Jean crouching on top of me, sliding up and down my prick as she rode me, in an attempt to maintain her body tense and hard as she finished coming. Only when I finally softened up did we lie breathless, knowing that our first adulterous fuck had been a tremendous success.

Ted Glass,
210, West 14th Street,
NEW YORK CITY,
U.S.A.

COPYRIGHT BREECH

FILE UNDER COUM   Gen.

3.2 Genesis P-Orridge, *Untitled* (*Time Transfixed*), postcard with collaged elements sent to 'Ted Glass', 27 November 1975

conventions for undeliverable mail (or dead letters) to extend the circulation of the artwork. Indeed, other mail art pieces received by P-Orridge around the same time were reworked and re-posted via the 'return to sender' protocol to continue the evolution and travel of a work rendered collaborative by P-Orridge's intervention. The use of an art-historically pungent address demonstrates that P-Orridge privileges the process of transit or passage – the administration, carriage and delivery of the postcard and its accrual of stamps, graffiti and other signs of its activation as a significant object. Indeed, other cards bore a rubberstamp mark designed by P-Orridge consisting of the literal command, 'KEEP ME POSTED' (P-Orridge was a pioneer of rubberstamp art, an established but barely historicised subgenre of mail art in the 1970s). Each work is thus transformed into a tool in a task and becomes a trace of a series of performed actions, thus anticipating or engineering the performance of the *Mail Action*, in which their function as props and documents would be exaggerated.

Unpublished correspondence with other artists including the mail artist Pauline Smith show that such experiments with the formal characteristics of the postal service had been established in P-Orridge's practice several years earlier, including strategic use of the postal system's 'return to sender' facility. Smith found notoriety with her 'Adolf Hitler Fan Club', a mail art project that prompted tampering by postal workers and several raids on her Ealing flat by Special Branch officers – including, astonishingly, a raid on 5 April 1976, the morning of the *Mail Action*. The fullest statement of P-Orridge's theory of mail art was composed in a letter to Smith in January 1974, after P-Orridge creatively recycled her cards and mailed them back 'return to sender', prompting Smith to complain about their apparently disrespectful treatment. 'Thee reason E have bin sending em all back to yoo is cos E find hoarding boring', P-Orridge explained in COUMspeak. 'Yoo sed to moi that [your postcards were] meant as circulars & yoo'd er hoped that people would either sling em, or send em back altered, or triggered. Well E went hom sweat hom and E did it' – that is, the artist dutifully cannibalised, digested and returned Smith's original works.[8] The letters to Smith – as instances of mail art – demonstrate P-Orridge's conviction that art should be anti-commercial, intimate, collaborative and disposable. In the same letter, P-Orridge valorises '[p]ersonal coumunication' over isolated production in the creation of a work of art: 'Everything else is a luxury . . . and E dont care if they get slung in bins, E really dont.' P-Orridge suggests a key avant-gardist principle for COUM, namely, to overcome dialectically the categorical separation of art and life, so that the latter might absorb – or wishfully destroy – the former. At the very least, P-Orridge would manage to compromise the cultural capital attached to COUM's works of art, such that they might circulate in a democratic relation of equivalent value to other consumable (and disposable) objects of use. P-Orridge's interest in pornography was not therefore puerile or exhibitionist, but part and parcel of an attempt to theorise and extend the politics of art, by rethinking in practice its mediation, co-authoring and circulation.

8 Genesis P-Orridge, letter to Pauline Smith (13 January 1974) Pauline Smith Papers, TGA 801/1/12, Tate Archive, 'Correspondence Filed Under 'P''.

As a performance event, the *Mail Action* would be formally innovative, appropriating the existing space of the court and the existing structure of the judiciary process, to frame and recast a series of contested themes in contemporary aesthetics: morality, sexuality, the body and indecency. Its prescience and novelty were noted at the time: in *Art and Artists* magazine, for example, Colin Naylor described the *Mail Action* as '[p]erhaps the most important art event of the British Calendar' and 'the best art show in town' (Naylor 1976). The action commented on the status of art versus that of pornography; and the contemporary redefinition and revision of the historical avant-garde attempt (indexed in P-Orridge's invocation of Duchamp) to activate the blurring of art and life. As noted, it did not directly influence or overwhelm the course of the law's applications, not least because P-Orridge's own imperatives would have been subjugated, to a great extent, to the formal restrictions placed on activity within the court, as well as to the will of the artist's lawyers, as those endowed with the power to speak, act and be heard with proper effects in the judiciary process.

In *The Wreckers of Civilisation*, an exhaustive survey of COUM (and of its subsequent manifestation as the industrial music pioneers Throbbing Gristle), Simon Ford gives a concise overview of the trial and notes the adaptation of the proceedings into a performance, yet stops short of theorising the *Mail Action*, except for a useful observation that it ended P-Orridge's primary investment in mail art and drew to a close the intense central period of COUM's productivity (Ford 1999: 6.10–13). However, the trial catalysed P-Orridge's further theorisation of COUM's work, particularly in writings to friends and testimonies to the court. In a formal instruction to solicitor David Offenbach, P-Orridge writes, 'I want to be part of popular culture, involved with everyday life and responses, not an intellectual artist, in an ivory tower, thinking I am special, revered and monumental . . . I don't want to be separate from anything' (P-Orridge 2002a). To Offenbach's question, 'Why use postcards?', P-Orridge replies, 'I want my art to circulate and be acces[s]ible in structure, to be popular and amusing as well as significant and aesthetic . . . Thee person in thee street has some marvellous, ready-made, mediums at his disposal and I want to remind them they are there for everyone to use and explore' (*ibid.*). From the utopian naivety with which P-Orridge approached the *Mail Action*, to consistent pronouncements made in the present ('Change thee way to perceive and change all memory', BREYER P-ORRIDGE tells us in recent spoken word performances), P-Orridge has long been an artist whose critical and political ethos discloses an idealist understanding of aesthetics. Of the abstract power of art as a tool to defamiliarise the everyday, P-Orridge writes in suggestively idealised terms,

> Once Art is brought into line with everyday life and individual experience in public situations, it is exposed to the same risks, the same unpredictable coincidences, the same interaction of living forces. COUM is therefore both a serious and tragic emotional stimulus combining the fruit of experience to create precious, yet expendable, moments in time. COUM is a mirror of all it coums across and all who coum across it, in any of its forms. (P-Orridge and Christopherson 1979: 65)

In COUM's provocative example – and most profoundly in the *Mail Action* – the category of art vacillates by its forced encounter with other categories of the aesthetic, including that of life and other categories of representation, including pornography. Jacques Rancière makes clear:

> The property of being art refers back not to a distinction between modes of doing, but to a distinction between modes of being. This is what 'aesthetics' means: in the aesthetic regime of art, the property of being art is no longer given by the criteria of technical perfection but is ascribed to a specific form of sensory apprehension. (2013a: 29)

Thus, the status of a cultural text as art – here, a trial and the postcards it brought under legal scrutiny – is not determined by a demonstration of formal quality, aptitude or achievement, but by its promiscuous recombination of source materials, as if to wrestle with what Rancière terms elsewhere a 'distribution of the sensible' (2013b), as the ideological structures of inclusion and exclusion that govern what can be sensed, known or understood in aesthetic terms. In specific 'scenes' that contest the regime of intelligibility, objects may bear more strongly upon our assumption of what is thinkable and what is not, Rancière argues, by causing the limit between categories to 'vacillate' (2013a: ix). In such a situation of extremity, the emancipated spectator challenges the codes of visibility that conventionally allow a scene to be understood as a subject of the discourse of aesthetics (2013a: ix–x). This, of course, is heightened in situations where art erupts into a space that is traditionally immune to it; or where art appears in unlicensed ways in spaces that exist to police or validate what counts as art.

As a scene of vacillation, the performance of extremity confounds our understanding of assumed distinctions between art and its others, be they illicit or indecent artefacts or events and activities that seem to belong more properly to other walks of life, including the criminal, juridical, mundane, intimate, pornographic or esoteric. In the translation of a trial into a performance event and the transformation of erotic postcards from playful missives into tokens of punitive control, P-Orridge's *Mail Action* performs what Rancière describes as the common substance of the aesthetic: that is, 'the power of a form of thought that has become foreign to itself' (2013b: 18).

Art on trial

The trial was originally set for February 1976, but was postponed for two months to allow P-Orridge and Cosey to perform at *Arte inglese oggi (English Art Today) 1960–76*, at Palazzo Reale, Milan. In the intervening months, P-Orridge set to work appropriating and recasting the imminent trial as a performance action. What made it a performance per se? 'Sending out the invitations was the first part', the artist recalls. 'That was when it became a performance' (interview with the author, 2016). Visually modelled on a wedding invitation, the cards are made from embossed, textured white card and printed in silver cursive script. Each reads: 'Coum Transmissions request the presence of _____ at thee trial of Genesis P-Orridge. G.P.O. v G.P.-O. "Mail Action" at Highbury Corner Magistrates Court, 51 Holloway Road N.7, April 5th 1976 at 2 pm.'[9] Indeed, the use of specifically designed wedding invitations – which also served as mail art works in their own right – to legitimise an action as a performance had precedence for COUM: the card for the *Mail Action* was modelled on an earlier use of the same design for COUM's performance *The Marriage of Fizzy Paet and Tremble* (1973), a wedding action at the Manchester Arts Festival, in which Fizzy (on roller skates) married P-Orridge and Cosey's pet dog Tremble in a interspecies wedding ceremony in a derelict church (Ford 1999: 3.7).

The recasting of the trial as a performance also involved using the new title *Mail Action* in the accompanying literature, beginning with the bespoke invitation cards. The appropriation of the trial also depended on a sophisticated publicity campaign to disseminate the invitations, including the notification of diverse international press contacts at *Artforum, Studio International, Melody Maker, NME, Time Out, Mayfair, Playboy, Penthouse* and the Press Association. On 1 April, P-Orridge also posted invitations to a long list of friends, acquaintances, peers and high-profile figures in the art world (P-Orridge 2002a). By encouraging a diverse reception, P-Orridge orchestrated a sympathetic art world audience for the performance despite its unconventional setting in a courthouse. The mailings provoked postal responses from invitees (including a friendly endorsement of sorts from Charles Manson, at Folsom State Prison, who wrote: 'Gen – you must be a retarded person – or maybe you're in another universe' [P-Orridge 2002b: 7]). The performance artists Bruce Lacey and Jill Bruce replied with a repurposed wedding invitation acceptance card, with 'wedding' crossed out to read 'trial' and a witty handwritten note: 'Is Dress Optional?'

Moreover, P-Orridge repurposed the trial as a performance by 'deciding to collect everything, with some kind of publication or book or folder in mind, and making sure that everything that happened was documented' (interview with the author, 2016). The desire to produce a lasting document was provoked, P-Orridge recalls, by recognising the landmark nature of the proceedings and in order to produce a sort of monument to it. 'To us it was a significant event,' P-Orridge explains, 'not because it involved us, but because it was art under siege. It was the establishment trying to censor and intimidate the artist into self-censorship' (*ibid.*). The key document resulting from this approach to the *Mail Action* is a book of textual proceedings, *G.P.O. Versus G.P-O.: A Chronicle of Mail Art on Trial*, published as a limited edition by artist John Armleder's imprint, Galerie Ecart, Geneva in 1976. Serving as a document of the legal proceedings and as an exhibition catalogue of sorts for the *Mail Action*, it provides a vast amount of factual and contextual information about the event and the social and cultural milieu in which COUM was active. Letters of support, notes, affidavits, legal documents, invoices, receipts and other artefacts are collected in facsimile alongside the extant cards. The book reproduces a number of documentary photographs taken by Cosey and art critic Barbara Reise, which show the audience in groups outside the courthouse, posing together and larking about with P-Orridge after the unique appropriation of – and astonishing conclusion to – the trial. In a letter to Sir

---

9 *Mail Action* invitation card, Barbara Reise Papers, TGA 786/5/2/43, Tate Archive, London, 'COUM 1973–1976'.

Norman Reid, P-Orridge describes the book project as 'a complete moment in time, prese[r]ved as information' and 'a work by a collection of people in a non-chosen context', proposing the book as a document of performance, an archival collection and a work of art in its own right.[10]

On the afternoon of 5 April 1976, P-Orridge arrived for the *Mail Action* wearing an appropriately theatrical costume, described by journalist Duncan Campbell as 'resplendent', consisting of a 'lurex suit, red socks, silver finger nails, and with his hair just growing back on the crown of his head' – actually, a triangular tonsure on the forehead – 'from where he had recently shaved it' (Campbell 1976: 9). The *Mail Action* lasted an hour and a half and involved addresses from the defence and prosecution and testimonies from an impressive celebrity roll call, amassed and cast by P-Orridge and the artist's legal team. The audience consisted, furthermore, of 'a battalion of London's avant-gardesmen', in the words of the journalist for *Time Out* (Campbell 1976: 8). Specifically, the audience included Cosey, Reise, Naylor, Smith, Lacey, Bruce and the filmmaker and performance artist Ian Breakwell, all of whom are shown together in extant photographs of the event, including those taken by Reise – one component of the action's fairly extensive documentation (**Figure 3.3**). Their presence suggested the importance of the event to the London art world calendar and demonstrated a resistant show of force by friends and peers against the situation of what P-Orridge diagnosed as an instance of 'art under siege'.

At the trial, P-Orridge admitted sending the five cards, but pleaded 'not guilty' on account of believing that the cards were not indecent. The defence consisted of a notable legal team, namely, barrister Geoffrey Robertson and solicitor David Offenbach. Robertson was renowned for defending the editors of the British counter-cultural magazine *Oz*, convicted under the Obscene Publications Act in 1971 in the longest obscenity trial ever conducted in Britain (and exonerated on appeal) (Miles 2010: 299); and, later, the defendants in cases brought by the 'vindictive' moral crusader Mary Whitehouse concerning *Gay News* for blasphemy in 1977; and Michael Bogdanov, director of the play *The Romans in Britain*, for soliciting an indecent act in 1982 (Miles 2010: 308). These services prompted Whitehouse to describe Robertson spiritedly in her memoir as 'The Devil's Advocate' (1982: 167). P-Orridge retained Robertson on the advice of the Welsh porn baron David Sullivan, whom Cosey knew through her contributions to Sullivan's magazines *Playbirds* and *Whitehouse* and her acquaintance with porn actor Mary Millington (Sullivan's girlfriend) (Cosey 2017: 180). The question of indecency and obscenity was topical in the porn industry: earlier in 1976, Robertson's mentor John Mortimer QC had successfully defended the Soho bookseller Johannes Heinrich Hanau on charges of obscenity after distributing some 38,000 copies of the explicit memoir *Inside Linda Lovelace* (Sutherland 1982: 138; Whitehouse 1982: 127). Yet owing to the specific charge of indecency, Robertson was less hopeful in this instance and warned P-Orridge of the realistic risk of a fine of £500 and the lesser risk of up to 12 months in prison.[11]

---

10 Genesis P-Orridge, letter to Sir Norman Reid (9 August 1976) Sir Norman Reid Papers, TG 15/6/14, Tate Archive.
11 Genesis P-Orridge, letter to Sir Norman Reid (30 March 1976) Sir Norman Reid Papers, TG 15/6/14, Tate Archive, London: 'Miscellaneous Correspondence 1976–79'

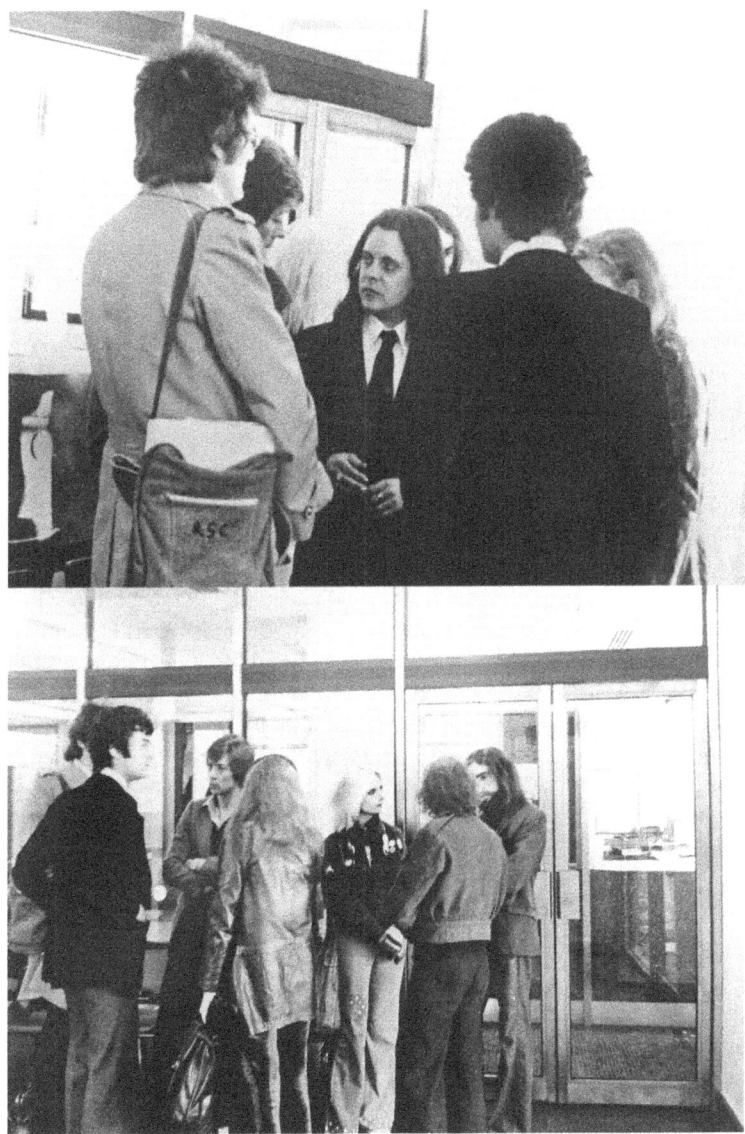

3.3 COUM Transmissions, *Mail Action* (1976), documentation of solo action by Genesis
P-Orridge, Highbury Corner Magistrates Court, London. *The group includes Genesis
P-Orridge (top centre), Ian Breakwell, Richard Cork, Colin Naylor, David Offenbach
and Pauline Smith.*

P-Orridge was tried by three magistrates, rather than by jury. The prosecutor presented the offending cards and read salacious quotations from the collaged messages,
like 'to my delight I felt his tongue running up and down my slit' and 'we bucked and
heaved, our mingled juices soaking our groins', to prove P-Orridge's transgression

of the objective criterion of indecency (Campbell 1976: 9). P-Orridge's legal team attempted to counter the prosecution's case with a demonstration of the legitimacy of the artist, the works and mail art as a form by reading affidavits by Sir Norman Reid (director, Tate Gallery); art critics Reise and Naylor; Gerald Forty (director of fine arts, British Council); Beat novelist William S. Burroughs; and artists Mark Boyle, Allen Jones and Bridget Riley (with whom P-Orridge had recently exhibited in Milan during *English Art Today*).

Each witness attested to P-Orridge's merits as an artist and argued the incontrovertible status of the postcards as works of art. For example, Riley described P-Orridge as 'an artist of integrity and dedication', whose performances were 'inventive, decorative and amusing'.[12] In his affidavit of 1 April 1976, Forty testified to the chief clerk that 'Genesis P-Orridge is a professional and wholly committed artist with a serious approach to his work, and if at times it has a mischievous and provoking quality, this is an essential element in an art which is designed to stimulate and to call into question many of our accepted attitudes' (P-Orridge 2002a). As a friend and mentor of sorts, Burroughs wrote an affidavit on 22 March 1976 to certify that he considered P-Orridge 'a devoted and serious artist in the Dada tradition. The postcards in question were certainly not intended to titillate nor to offend, but to instruct by pointing up banality through startling juxtapositions' (P-Orridge 2002a). Burroughs was certainly well placed to understand P-Orridge's mischievous but sincere investment in déclassé subject matter and most likely sympathised with P-Orridge's victimisation as a subject of censorship, after noted trials against the publishers of his own novel *The Naked Lunch* (1959). Forty and Burroughs evoke the seriousness or earnestness of P-Orridge's creative endeavours and frame the postcards and their mode of dissemination in terms of a carefully conceived aesthetic strategy – namely, to *épater la bourgeoisie* – thereby, in part through Burroughs' references to Dada, staging the historically legitimate foundations of P-Orridge's avant-gardism.

Stripped of substantive legal recourses in the trial, P-Orridge's legal team sought to defend the merits of the artist's mailings. It had the contradictory effect of declaring the autonomy of P-Orridge's art – its singular status as aesthetic production – detaching it from pornography and from letter writing, as well as from other domains of cultural and social life. While P-Orridge frequently claimed to obliterate the distinction between art and life, the defence restated the objective difference between art and other practices of representation, inadvertently forcing COUM back from its free-floating aspect into the discrete category of art. Nevertheless, as Robertson notes, rebuttals by the defence of artistic merit are inadequate against charges of indecency, for 'in determining whether an article sent by post is "indecent", the courts have imposed an objective criterion, so that the character of the [sender] and the purpose of the mailing are irrelevant' (Robertson 1979: 183). He adds, 'it follow[s] that an offence might be committed for the most laudable purpose', for example, when an

---

12 Bridget Riley, letter to the magistrates (2 April 1976) Genesis P-Orridge Papers (uncatalogued), Tate Archive, London: 'G.P.O. v G.P.-O. (Trial Documents) file'. The letter was not reproduced in P-Orridge's book of documentation.

original work of art – which need not be deemed obscene if shown in a gallery – is sent using the postal service; or when indecent material is mailed by '[s]pouses who exchange frank love letters' (*ibid.*). Indeed, P-Orridge later collected clippings relating to relevant offences, including a case brought successfully in June 1976 against Sheila Heywood, a landlady in Penge, who broke the law by posting a pornographic image (of a person resembling her male lodger) to a friend as a joke.[13]

Richard Cork and Ted Little – art critic for the *Evening Standard* and director of the ICA, respectively – were called to speak at the trial as experts, though their testimonies were summarily dismissed when the magistrates found the defence of artistic merit to be irrelevant (Mather 1976: 2). P-Orridge's defence was under collapse. At the close of proceedings, after a ten-minute recess for deliberation, the three presiding magistrates returned their verdict. P-Orridge was found guilty on all five counts and ordered to pay a then-sizeable fine of £100 plus £20 in legal costs (Campbell 1976: 9). (The legal team cost a further £150.) Little complained to the press that the trial and its outcomes had been 'a tremendous over-reaction' and was cautious of its broader cultural implications (Mather 1976: 2).

Barbara Reise recorded her impressions of the court proceedings as an audience member. Reise was a contributing editor at *Studio International*, for one critic 'surely the most internationally respected writer of her generation writing out of England' (McEwen 1978: 2) and a close friend of P-Orridge from 1975 until her untimely death in 1978. In her unpublished trial notes, Reise states that the legal team's defence was '[t]oo wordy, too abstract, too redundant' and overstressed P-Orridge's 'international reputation'. The contention of the work's purported indecency, Reise observes, remained intact.[14] Ian Breakwell concurred with Reise's impression, commiserating to P-Orridge in a letter on 6 April 1976 that he 'feared the worst as soon as your lawyer opened his mouth' (P-Orridge 2002a).

Indecent exception

As a legal event, *G.P.O. v G.P.-O.* was 'precedent-setting', writes Duncan Campbell, in that 'it established that a person can now be prosecuted for sending "dirty" postcards even though they have offended no-one, and traditional in that the arguments really came down to one person's art being another person's porn' (Campbell 1976: 8). Journalist Ian Mather corroborated its landmark aspect, noting that the trial was the first time the Post Office Act had been used to prosecute an artist (Mather 1976: 2). Reflecting on the *Mail Action*, P-Orridge confirmed its significance as a forgotten instance in a series of 'real authentic suppressions of freedom of art' in the period (email to the author, 22 December 2014).

---

13 Unattributed clipping in Genesis P-Orridge Papers (uncatalogued), Tate Archive, London: '*G.P.O. v G.P.-O.* (Trial Documents) file'.
14 Barbara Reise, unpublished notes, Barbara Reise Papers, TGA 786/5/2/43, Tate Archive, London.

P-Orridge's barrister, Geoffrey Robertson QC tells me, 'Of course I remember this "trial" at Highgate Magistrates Court – the utterly humourless bench of elderly lay justices, the bumptious and outraged fat clerk, the baby-faced provocateur of a defendant and his sweet and supportive-in-mischief girlfriend. Oh for a jury trial! Conviction was a foregone conclusion' (email to the author, 3 December 2014). Robertson is affectionate in his portrayal of 'baby-faced' P-Orridge and 'sweet' Cosey and playful in his recollection of the dreary magistrates and their 'bumptious' routines. The status of the proceedings is thrown into question in Robertson's suggestive placement of the word 'trial' in scare quotes. Writing elsewhere, Robertson notes the inadequacy of legal definitions of 'indecency' and their usage in court, arguing that by lacking the detailed criteria that qualify prosecutions for obscenity, charges of indecency rely on the working definition of 'something that offends the ordinary modesty of the average man', which is too 'vague and arbitrary' for objective usage in criminal proceedings (Robertson 1979: 176). Robertson suggests that indecency and obscenity charges, alike, depend substantially on the vagaries of social acceptability: 'Criminal trials are mechanisms for deciding who is telling the truth, but in obscenity trials there is no truth to tell – only a clash of opinions, as a captive audience is invited to score a polite debate between bewigged protagonists' (Robertson 1979: 6).

In indecency cases, which do not involve juries, the situation can be just as theatrical yet even more specious, as the judges are not required to evaluate the work as a whole (in contrast to the test of obscenity); there can be no defence of the work as having particularly merits, as the *Mail Action* demonstrates, nor an appeal to community standards. Moreover, Robertson notes that the defence against indecency involves a losing battle, namely the attempt 'to convince a bench of lay justices that anything pertaining to sex is not "indecent"', when '[w]hat "offends the ordinary modesty of the average man" is decided in most cases by what offends the extraordinarily prudish modesty of the average magistrate' (Robertson 1979: 175–7). Hence his mordant observation to me that P-Orridge's conviction was, regrettably, 'a foregone conclusion'.

Indecency is, however, a strategic mode that proposed profound challenges for the practice and criticism of art. The vigour with which P-Orridge and COUM courted distasteful, shocking or provocative ideas and images may have been couched in conceptual terms, yet contemporary critics noted a distinctly prurient aspect to such pursuits. In 1978, COUM published the following statement: 'We have moved into the public arena and are using popular cultural archetypes. We live our lives like a movie, we try to make each scene interesting viewing. We use the press to record our activities like a diary' (P-Orridge and Christopherson 1979: 65). Yet if COUM were invested in recycling and recasting 'popular archetypes', they were not 'popular' in the sense we might expect from 'pop' usages by contemporaries such as the painters Richard Hamilton, Pauline Boty or Roy Lichtenstein, in their appropriations or depictions of cartoon imagery, consumer artefacts, pin-ups or celebrity.

The pages of 'Annihilating Reality', compiled in 1976 and appended to the written statement of 1978, are illustrated with a different order of found images in P-Orridge and Sleazy's montage: a medical photograph of the compression of a carotid artery; Cosey naked in *Playbirds* magazine; a detainee in a Nazi concentration camp; a police photograph of the horrific outfit worn by the 'Beast of Jersey', Edward Paisnel (a serial child rapist who displayed Satanic affectations); Sheba, the 'champion tassel twirler of 1972'; a lesbian couple illegally married in a church in 1975; genital piercing and tattooing; the 'Great Beast' Aleister Crowley; Iggy and the Stooges; rubber and piss enthusiasts; the burial site of a victim of Ian Brady and Myra Hindley; and a mug shot of Charles Manson (P-Orridge's sometime pen pal). The images are grisly, perverse or titillating. Interspersed with these photographs are art images, with a preponderance of documents of performance art, by the Kipper Kids, Hermann Nitsch, Otto Mühl, Rudolf Schwarzkogler, Gina Pane, Monte Cazazza, Ürs Luthi, Enrico Job, Ralph Ortiz and Jerry Dreva (P-Orridge and Christopherson 1979: 66–71). As P-Orridge asks in the same document, 'Is crime just unsophisticated or "naïve" performance art?', begging the question of the relation between the objective crimes documented in the portfolio and the accompanying photographs of grisly-looking performance art actions.

In 1979, John Roberts cautiously observed the excessive, negative or nihilist tone of COUM's repertoire, writing, 'Hackney is not Dachau. The morality becomes inverted; a cruel milieu is taken up as the image of fashionable ennui. These are creeping signs of decadence. They have to be watched' (Wilson 2015: 230, n. 73). Pressed on the topic of COUM's interest in seemingly prurient imagery, P-Orridge reflects that COUM were not interested in the inherent power of criminality, morbidity or the macabre as shock tactics, but were committed to exposing how different categories of representation were arbitrarily yet dramatically separated and charged with drastically different values. P-Orridge tells me,

> [T]his label 'crime' or this label 'art' changes society's perception of the same action. What does that mean? We didn't have an answer but we were curious about the line between . . . when [an image or idea is] unacceptable [or] acceptable – and that line is always shifting. Something about that line, like the line between awake and asleep, between alive and dead, or male and female – it is blurry to begin with, and if you strip it down, there's nothing there. And so it becomes this odd, convoluted philosophical question about where [one's] position is in this flux. (Interview with the author, 2016)

Prurient, puerile or indecent (or not), COUM interrogated the nature of distinctions between art and life, art and crime, art and pornography and other socially divisive and enduring categorical separations. Appearing to some as an indiscretion, a crime or a 'creeping sign' of negative potential, the frequently unpalatable content and form of COUM's performances of extremity are orchestrated in a conceptually searching interrogation of how and with what effects the discourse of art (and of what seems to be an opposing face) is constructed, policed and perhaps overturned.

Taking exception to modal claims about the proper objects and tactics of art, P-Orridge used indecency as a means to explore the limits of performance, reinventing oneself and one's practices as exceptions to the rule of moral, social or aesthetic decorum. As such, in contemporary writings and artist pages, including mailed screeds and the unsettling montage in 'Annihilating Reality', P-Orridge articulated a coherent strategy towards becoming – and remaining – categorically marginal to the institutions of contemporary art, including the gallery circuit and its attendant market. Still, ever the contrarian, in the *Mail Action* P-Orridge also leaned quite confidently upon support from the upper echelons of power in the art world, suggesting a nuance, ambivalence or contradiction in the artist's stated or staged relationships to extremity, decency and the politics of artistic legitimacy. In a short preface to the collected documentation from the *Mail Action*, P-Orridge writes, 'often E work in a way coumwhat disparaging of the Art World. Yet, when E went to all my friends in that world . . . not one person refused to help me' (P-Orridge 2002a). For example, as noted, P-Orridge called upon the influential museum director Sir Norman Reid in a series of affectionate and amusingly candid letters. P-Orridge's first unpublished letter was written in COUM's signature style, on letterhead paper topped with a phallic, spunk-dripping logo. Primarily requesting support in the form of a written affidavit, P-Orridge includes legal information, sample letters, commentaries and anecdotes, noting, for example, Tate's own recent embroilment in scandal. 'E realise this is a bit boring', P-Orridge writes of the imminent trial, adding that support from Reid is 'possibly after the [Carl] Andre thing a bit difficult tactically for you', with reference to the 'Tate bricks' dispute earlier in 1976. P-Orridge also mentions a limited-edition print of the Magritte postcard and encloses six copies for the Tate Gallery's consideration, adding: 'Maybe if E win thee case you can sell them in your shop (I doubt it).'[15]

Prostitution

The *Mail Action* exposes the reductive impositions of clear boundaries and categories – art, pornography, indecency and obscenity – categories P-Orridge had already been eager to upset or displace, not least through the choice of content in the postcards that precipitated the criminal charges. The court's gallery of visitors becomes an audience and the three magistrates are cast as unwitting performers in P-Orridge's luridly costumed spectacle. While persisting as a legal procedure, the trial also becomes a conceptual space, continuous or coterminous with the enabling appropriation of the postal service and its avenues of transit and travel, which had been so artfully apprehended and sabotaged by the objectively indecent procedures of P-Orridge's mail art.

As a performance of extremity, in *Mail Action* P-Orridge performed a limit-text of the appropriation and recasting of an institutional space, namely the semi-public space of the magistrate's court. The usage exceeds the logic of site-specificity on account of its unwelcome, unauthorised and partly invisible nature (its status as performance was not visible to the magistrates, at least). Moreover, the *Mail Action* throws into relief the way COUM provoked a vacillation of the aesthetic as a category of object or event, by encouraging it to bleed into pedestrian, specialised or non-art spaces, languages and practices. Such a vacillation of the category of art would set the scene for the subsequent scandal of *Prostitution* at the ICA, which again claimed and

15 Genesis P-Orridge, letter to Sir Norman Reid (30 March 1976), Sir Norman Reid Papers.

re-inscribed a given space – here, a differently institutional one, that of a gallery – in both licensed and unlicensed ways.

In a letter to Reid in August 1976, P-Orridge explains the emotional toll taken by the trial: 'E am beginning to feel more like my old self'. The letter continues, '[s]ince thee trial E was very depressed, paralysed as far as keeping up coumunication with people went & even now E get severe depressions, feelings of hopelessness, like anti-matter negating all my energy. Butter E have not stopped COUM activity, its just slow.'[16] P-Orridge discloses that COUM was 'bankrupted' by the fine and associ-ated costs and fees, explaining that this has slowed and curtailed ongoing projects. Legal troubles and mail tampering persisted too: in September 1976, Cosey wrote to Hungarian mail artist Endre Tot, imploring him to cease sending P-Orridge indecent postcards as the police had visited the Death Factory to investigate P-Orridge: 'They are under the impression he sent them both to be clever, thinking he could get away with [indecency] by pretending someone else sent them', Cosey writes, noting the realistic prospect of twelve months in prison if P-Orridge were charged on a fresh offence while on probation.[17]

In October, the *Prostitution* controversy would embroil P-Orridge and Cosey in much deeper trouble than the 'anti-matter' of the *Mail Action*. Indeed, the trial in early 1976 provided what P-Orridge calls 'the map for *Prostitution*'. In prepara-tion for COUM's retrospective at the ICA, P-Orridge recalls in an interview, 'We . . . were planning to deliberately trigger another furore', in contrast to the fact that 'with G.P.O. v G.P-O. we didn't do it on purpose. It was a surprise.' P-Orridge was 'dis-gusted and outraged' that the state had 'changed the goal posts' by reinscribing 'some-thing that is commonly available' – namely, top-shelf pornography – and decreed that the artist's individual usage of the material rendered it illegal. Or, as P-Orridge's puts it, the situation seemed to testify that 'my mind makes it criminal. My touching it and reassembling it makes it criminal.' This anomaly provoked a characteristically mis-chievous, antiauthoritarian streak in P-Orridge, who remembers thinking: 'Well, OK, if I'm a criminal, fuck it, let's enjoy it' (interview with the author, 2016). P-Orridge claims not to have informed the other collaborators in COUM of this reckless strategy and deliberately prompted a media backlash as a kind of subterfuge:

> We bought all the different newspapers and main magazines available. We made a list on index cards of all the news editors, assistant news editors, the people who review theatre and art, and so on . . . Secretly we posted invitations to all of them, without telling anyone else in COUM. To see what would happen. We had a good idea it might explode on them. By golly, it did. (*ibid.*)

Prostitution was on show at the ICA from 19 October to 26 October 1976 and included three key components alongside a suite of planned live events. The core

16 Genesis P-Orridge, letter to Sir Norman Reid (9 August 1976), Sir Norman Reid Papers. Misspellings and oddities in punctuation are in the original.
17 Cosey Fanni Tutti, letter to Endre Tot, (1 September 1976), Genesis P-Orridge Papers (uncatalogued), Tate Archive, London: 'G.P.O. v G.P.-O. (Trial Documents) file'. Mail tampering occurred for at least a decade and P-Orridge would write to the Postmaster at Royal Mail to complain about receiving tampered mail (two complaints from 1980 and 1989 are held in the same folder).

consisted of Cosey Fanni Tutti's *Magazine Actions* (1973–77) – a series of sexually explicit portraits of the artist appropriated from some 40 pornographic magazines; the original exhibition design had them mounted on a wall, but fears over the legality of their public display meant that the ICA enclosed them in portfolios, to which viewers had to request privileged access (only members of the ICA were eligible to view them) (Cosey 2017: 202). On the adjacent wall were mounted extensive documentation of performances, including photographs taken by audience members without COUM's bidding, as well as props and ephemera including sex paraphernalia (such as whips, a blood-smeared dildo, Vaseline and anal syringes); knives and a curtain of chains; and box sculptures made by P-Orridge from Cosey's used tampons, Sleazy's photographs and other materials (Miles 2010, 344; Battista 2013: 45; Cosey 2017: 209). A third component, situated opposite the planned wall of the *Magazine Actions*, was a 'media wall', namely, a mounting array of press cuttings, which proliferated across the perilous course of the exhibition. Alongside the three exhibited elements, COUM scheduled live performances on the raucous opening night. The event was titled *Music from the Death Factory* and included a strip show, performances by Throbbing Gristle (consisting of P-Orridge, Cosey, Sleazy and Chris Carter) and the band Chelsea performing as 'LSD' (featuring future pop-punk sensation Billy Idol). Several performance interventions into the exhibition were also planned.

Two officers from Scotland Yard's Obscene Publications Squad visited *Music from the Death Factory* and sent a report to the Director of Public Prosecutions. No action was decided, but the ICA pre-emptively cancelled COUM's additional live performances (Dovkants 1976: 1). If earlier in the year COUM had appropriated the abstract space of the trial and the concrete space of the courtroom as venues for performance, the critical punch of *Prostitution* depended in part on a subcultural intrusion into the relatively august space of the ICA. However, it involved more robustly an analogous act of appropriation, namely Cosey's recasting of her own experiences of modelling as surreptitious interventions into the porn industry and her concrete appropriation of pages from magazines – clipped and framed – as individual works of art, namely, the *Magazine Actions* (**Figure 3.4**). Cosey performs a range of actions in the photographs and takes up a dizzying range of characters: named personae like 'Tessa from Sunderland' or various stereotypes from the traditional porn repertoire. When the photographs were placed under lock and key and made available for private viewing upon selective request, the ICA's curatorial compromise simulated the under-the-counter dynamic of consuming illicit pornography and theatricalised the pornographic function of the source materials as the essential aspect of the finished works.

The *Magazine Actions* have endured as the most profoundly articulate and memorable works from *Prostitution*, as well as, arguably, of COUM's output in the period. Indeed, three prints from the series were purchased by Tate for its collection in 2013, after five of P-Orridge's 'tampon sculptures' from the exhibition were acquired in 2012, lending the contents of *Prostitution* some belated legitimacy in recent years. The meaning or effect of the *Magazine Actions* is produced by the appropriation of pages from commercially available pornography and their isolation and re-presentation as discrete works of art, as well as by the recasting of Cosey's immaterial labour – posing

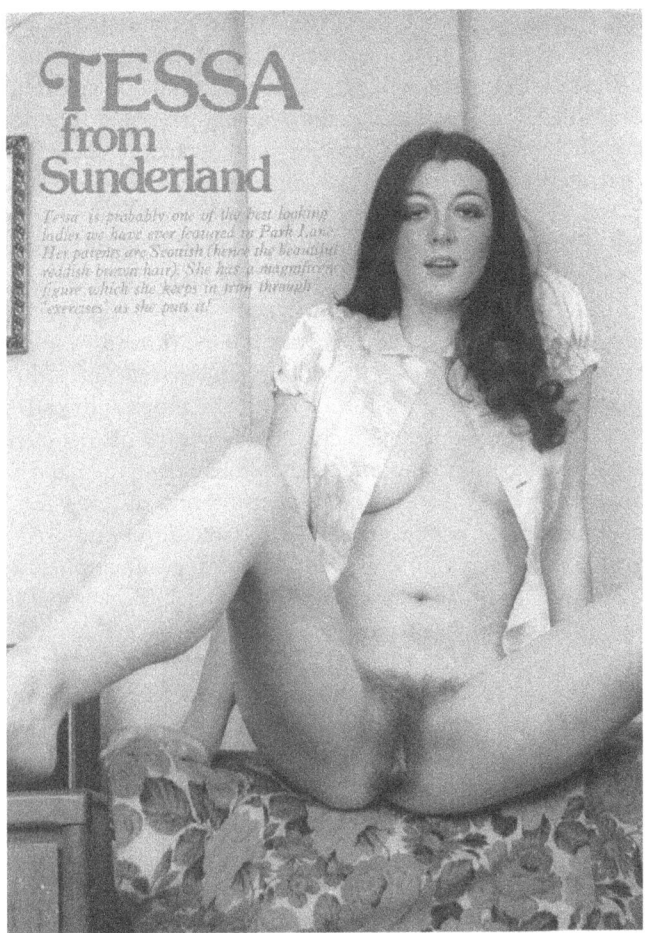

3.4 Cosey Fanni Tutti, *Tessa from Sunderland, Park Lane, Issue 12* (1975–76), Magazine
Action, colour print on paper. Courtesy the artist and Cabinet, London

for pornographic images – as a surreptitious conceptual art project. The strategic
power of the work is activated in COUM's description of the *Magazine Actions*
as assisted self-portraits: in the poster-cum-press release for *Prostitution*, COUM
account for the series as 'ways of seeing and using Cosey with her consent, produced
by people unaware of her reasons, as a woman and an artist, for participating'.[18]
Cosey is no longer solely the passive, prostituted object of the photographic gaze (or,
subsequently, subject to the private masturbatory gaze); rather, she declares herself
an agent of self-representation, under whose control the photographer is unwittingly
subordinated.

18 Poster for *Prostitution*, Institute of Contemporary Arts Collection, TGA 955/7/7/72, Tate Archive,
London, 'Papers relating to the exhibition *Prostitution* by COUM Transmissions'.

At a closer level of detail, the works make meaning through the internal resonance between the images themselves – of Cosey and male and female co-performers variously kissing, licking, groping, holding or displaying each other's body parts and otherwise performing the aesthetic tropes of orgasm or ecstatic pleasure – and the overlaid texts, written by porn writers or sub-editors, added to accentuate, narrate or explain the visual content of the source pages. While this relation is practical in its original design upon the page, Cosey's (and therefore COUM's) central procedures of appropriation and display, as strategic interventions into the aesthetic nature of the imagery, recast the ways the text and images work together as a form of unbidden collage. In Cosey's direct appropriations of commercial pornography, the individual pages are framed (literally and figuratively) as works of art and migrate to be consumed within – and thus against – the institutional spaces and protocols of art. In these formal transformations and spatial transits, the relations between images and texts – including the para-texts that circulate around them, including wall labels, promotional matter and press – demand new practices of reading from the viewer. In a striking intensification of this effect, a journalist in the conservative tabloid newspaper the *Sun* narrated the perceived moral bankruptcy of *Prostitution*, describing it as a collection of 'pornographic pictures, sticks and flails – and the 36–24–36 charms of stripper Shelley', who performed at the opening; its journalist also cites the (now-disgraced) Tory MP Nicholas Fairbairn's salty depiction of it as 'an excuse for exhibitionism by every crank, squint and ass in the business' (Deves 1976: 3). Yet by being printed on page three, the article is flanked by an imposing pinup shot of 'lovely Jackie Sewell': aged 18, smiling Jackie bares her breasts and wears a feather boa to preserve her modesty. Demeaning one appropriation of pornographic content (*Prostitution*) while normalising and profiting from another (the 'lovely Jackie'), the hypocrisy of the newspaper's moral position is breathtaking.

The nature of the political effects produced by COUM's works and their reception is at least potentially feminist, as confirmed by more recent exhibitions of the *Magazine Actions* as pioneering works of sex-positive, post-porn, anti-capitalist or 'black sheep' feminism.[19] Siona Wilson anticipates and extends this reading when she reads the works as feminist and queer, in their ability to undermine and reconstitute stereotypical assumptions about gender, sexuality, subjectivity and the 'symbolic codes of sexual difference' (Wilson 2015: 136). These codes are articulated blatantly or painfully in the pornographic captions and commentaries of the source texts and in framings such as Fairbairn's or the *Sun*'s – and so artfully ironicised and exposed by Cosey (and thus by COUM) in their appropriations of the images as *Magazine Actions*. That said, Cosey has since attempted to debunk feminist readings of COUM, in part by refusing to claim her own practice as feminist (Cosey 2017: 171–2), but also by describing the distribution of labour in COUM's living and working arrangements as exploitative and traditional in gendered terms (2017: 111).

19 Cosey's work was included in the major survey shows *WACK! Art and the Feminist,* Museum of Contemporary Art, Los Angeles, 2007; and *Pop Life: Art in a Material World,* Tate Modern, London, 2009–10; and alongside the art of three other 'sex-positive' artists in *Black Sheep Feminism: The Art of Sexual Politics,* Dallas Contemporary Art Museum, 2016.

The bulk of the ensuing controversy around *Prostitution* took place in the pages of newspapers. This occupation of newspaper print space would fold its effects back upon the ICA itself, when Fairbairn demanded in Parliament that Education Minister Shirley Williams investigate the venue's use of public funds, namely £200 from the ICA's public disbursement and a further £800 directly to COUM from the Arts Council (through a Performance Art Bursary); in the same smear, Fairbairn also labelled COUM with the pejorative but immortalising epithet 'the wreckers of civilisation' (Ford 1999: 6.22). The *Sun* stoked a daily campaign against *Prostitution*, writing that 'even a stripper' was shocked by the 'sick' and 'disgusting' exhibition; and indignantly reported 'beastly' COUM's use of tax revenues, protesting: 'Even a penny of public money is too much to spend on this squalid rubbish . . . Mr. Orridge is prostituting Britain – and sending us the bill' (Wesley 1976: 2). The ICA's Arts Council grant was suspended pending an internal review and both Ted Little (director) and Robert Loder (chairman of council) resigned from the ICA in protest (Miles 2010: 345).

Articles about *Prostitution* were often accompanied by graphic images of key performances by COUM, which fanned the scandal's flames, yet also recalibrated the exhibition as a vector for the democratic goals set out in P-Orridge's polemical writings on the politics of art. COUM consolidated its strategic appropriation of the media to gain widespread dissemination (an analogue precursor of sorts to the viral technologies afforded by online media). The experience was, once again, distressing and isolating for P-Orridge, who wrote to Barbara Reise (on the back of a hand-altered photograph from a performance with Throbbing Gristle (**Figure 3.5**)), 'It's all pretty sick really, everyone running for cover, leaving us as a target/sacrifice and

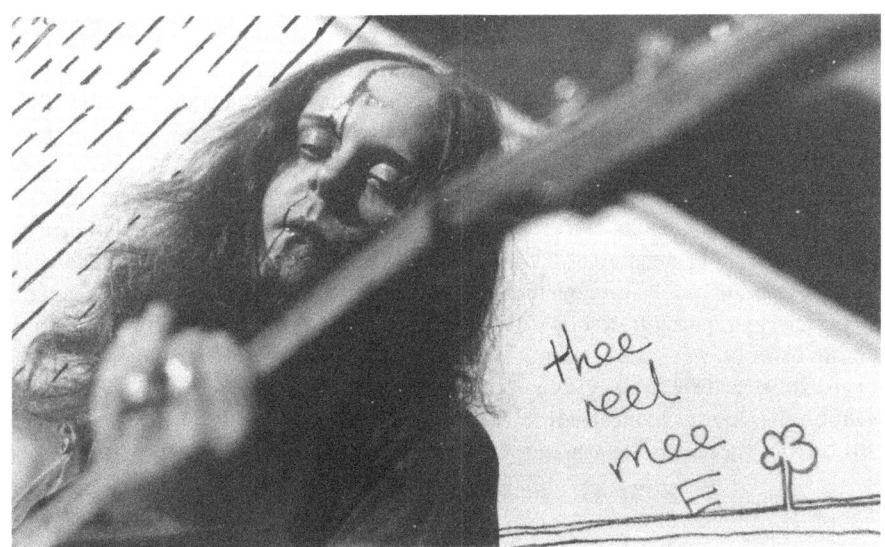

3.5 Genesis P-Orridge, *Untitled* (*Thee Reel Mee*), postcard with collaged elements sent to Barbara Reise, 28 October 1976

then blaming us for being there alone. Your card was very welcome and helped me survive'.[20] The experience was also personally damaging to Cosey: the news coverage of *Prostitution* prompted her mother never to speak to her again (Cosey 2017: 207).

In a searching chapter on the opportunities and challenges *Prostitution* poses for feminist art history, Siona Wilson has emphasised the central place of performance art in the ways it produced meaning and ensured its own controversial reception. Although she misidentifies the earlier charge against P-Orridge (as obscenity rather than indecency), she acknowledges briefly the importance of the *Mail Action* as a spur to the exhibition's greater impact, noting that 'the treatment of the trial as a performance event sets a precedent for *Prostitution* in both the use of the media and the parodic attack on established norms of heterosexuality' (Wilson 2015: 96). Wilson gives due care to the way Cosey's *Magazine Actions* functioned as a complex, constitutive and (arguably) co-authored part of COUM's larger exhibition. Noting that the works were documents of prior performances, the mode in which they are exhibited in *Prostitution* as a practice of 'contractual reattribution' conceptually muddles the nature of the images as documents; or, as Wilson writes, 'the evidentiary logic of photographic documentation of a live action – the contractual status of the photographic image – coincides with the Duchampian logic of the readymade' (Wilson 2015: 108–11). Cosey's (potentially collaborative) activity of selecting, framing, signing and grouping the images recreates the images as documents of the performance of extremity and as works of conceptual art (namely of appropriation), in a sexualised and politically acute variation on Duchamp's avant-gardist strategy of claiming banal or pedestrian objects – a urinal, a shovel or a bottle-rack – as works of art (the urinal is at least potentially sexualised).

For Wilson, Cosey usurps the authorship of a named male photographer as a feminist intervention into the gendered nature of authorship, given the traditional manner in which women have been prevented from claiming (or are subsequently denied) their own right as the author of the effects of their own creative labour, including most egregiously in porn, but also, differently, in art history (Wilson 2015: 118–19). The politics of authorship is particularly controversial – and sensitive – here as while Cosey's participation in the porn industry is unquestionably a product of her own initiative, it is often unclear whether the *Magazine Actions* – the rigorous recasting of her modelling as the foundations for a conceptual artwork undertaken by stealth – should be attributed to Cosey or (collaboratively) to COUM, as made vivid in long-standing public disagreements between P-Orridge and Cosey on this issue.[21] The issue is put partly to rest by Cosey's recently published memoirs in which, citing diaries from 1973–75, she accounts for her participation in the porn industry in terms of an explicit artistic strategy: as part of 'a pursuit of self-discovery' by way of an intervention that 'wasn't [conceived] solely for art, for feminist ideals, or for Gen' (Cosey 2017: 162). That is, in her account, Cosey entered the porn industry independent of

20 Genesis P-Orridge, letter to Barbara Reise (28 October 1976) Barbara Reise Papers, TGA 786/5/2/43, Tate Archive.
21 After the inclusion of the *Magazine Actions* in the Tate Triennial, Tate Britain in 2006, P-Orridge publicly challenged their attribution to Cosey without reference to COUM (see BREYER P-ORRIDGE 2006: 15; and Cosey 2017: 408).

P-Orridge's encouragement (or alleged opportunism and exploitation) deliberately to create self-directed materials for collage and strategic recombination.

Wilson also takes seriously the function of the media wall, arguing that it stages COUM's prescient understanding of the way critical reception is constitutive to the social construction of a work's meaning and its social and historical significance, which is articulated in *Prostitution* by actively folding the press coverage into the work itself, to create a 'feedback loop' at the core of the exhibition (2015: 97). 'Thus *Prostitution* should also be read as an extended improvisatory performance existing temporally as well as spatially', she argues: one that, 'following the group's name, is structured by the logic of *transmission*' (*ibid.*, emphasis in original). For Wilson, this suggests COUM's participation in art as a 'mediatic formation', through what she describes as Cosey's and P-Orridge's privileging of the form of dissemination over the content – or 'political message' – of art (2015: 103). Interestingly, the same claims can be extended to Kerry Trengove's *An Eight Day Passage* (1977), discussed in Chapter 1, on account of Trengove's inclusion of a similar wall of cumulative newspaper cuttings and his participation in (or tacit courting of) press interest. Trengove's borrowing suggests the prescience of COUM's usage and its utility for other artists seeking to map – or capitalise upon – media interest in the performance of extremity.

Wilson's reading usefully proposes *Prostitution* as an anomalous instance of performance art. In tandem with the *Mail Action*, it may demonstrate COUM's incorrigible capacity to extend or refashion the limits of performance, now, in its extremity, stretched far beyond the form's assumed shapes and sizes. The media wall also performs the multiple ways the later scandal of *Prostitution* was forged on the back of the *Mail Action*, from COUM's active harnessing of press and public outrage – in order not to be crushed by it – to the folding of the public and press outrage into the substance of the exhibition, to the extension of the mediatic formation of mail art, conceptual art and performance art. The result was a cumulative performance of extremity made notable in the *Mail Action* and notorious in *Prostitution*.

Across both events – the trial-cum-performance and the exhibition-cum-performance – COUM harnessed the explosive and divisive power of two supplementary discourses that are deemed antithetical to art, namely, pornography and crime; and in so doing, COUM investigated the nature of contemporary sexuality in Britain and its surprisingly consistent (though contradictory) potential to inflame official and incidental audiences. The stridency with which P-Orridge was disciplined in the conclusion of the *Mail Action* and the vilification of P-Orridge and Cosey during and after *Prostitution* suggests the power of sexualised representation to incriminate its makers, as well as the apparent nervousness with which the state (and its surrogate, the press) perceived and patrolled such transgressions. Across the two events, the notoriety COUM garnered attempted a semiotic flattening of representation, in stark contrast to the expansive and particularised means by which the two events framed and freed up sex and sexuality. Writing about the literary pornography of the Marquis de Sade in 1951, Simone de Beauvoir identifies this particular power of non-literary pornography in its uses and its dismissals. She writes, 'removed from any social, familial or human base, eroticism loses its *extraordinary* character. No longer conflict, revelation, privileged experience; no longer revealing dramatic relations between individuals, eroticism reverts to its biological coarseness' (de Beauvoir 2012: 73, emphasis in original). De Beauvoir does not make a moral value judgement about the difference and refrains from elevating 'voluptuous' representations – deep depictions (such as de Sade's) that convey or uncover the 'singular affective complexes' of sex – from the coarsely biological symptoms afforded by pornography, suggesting that indecency retains an almost scientific, empirical aspect, even if its horizon of appearances is limited to those exhibited in or on the body (*ibid.*).

This returns me, here, in conclusion, to the potential significance of pornography for the performance of extremity. De Sade 'elaborates an immense system' of sexual anomalies, de Beauvoir writes. This seemingly administrative approach to sexual extremity overcomes 'banality', despite the frequent inanity of the content and form of pornography:

> [B]eyond their repetitiveness, their clichés, and their clumsiness, he attempts to communicate an experience whose particularity, however, is to want to be incommunicable. Sade tries to convert his psycho-physiological destiny into an ethical choice; and with this act through which he assumes his separation, he claims to set an example and make an appeal: here his adventure takes on a substantial human significance. (de Beauvoir 2012: 45)

Thus, what some other writers have dismissed 'with calumny and omission' – as perversion or irrelevance – de Beauvoir approaches seriously, with an analytical, philosophical eye (2012: 44). The performances and objects of COUM Transmissions neither attain the immensity or breadth of de Sade's literary transgressions, nor do they plumb as drastic a depth of depravity – although COUM's frequent flirtations with, say, the crimes of Hindley and Brady or their fascination with Gary Gilmore's execution (which they mimed in a postcard on its occasion in 1977) betray an attraction to nadirs of sexual decorum and deliberate evacuations of moral righteousness. Yet the status of the pornographic endeavour for COUM, in both the *Mail Action* and *Prostitution*, is notable for the apparent sincerity with which P-Orridge and Cosey were able to investigate the deep and tangled natures of art, crime, pornography and sex in the particular political moment they inhabited. From twinning the image of sex with that of the seat of power, respectability and decorum (namely that of the Queen), to situating the banality of pornography within the augustness of an institution of art (one that happened to be within spitting distance of the Queen's ceremonial home), sex was returned to its complex function as a perennial problem for performance.

The *Mail Action* and *Prostitution*, then, must be read as pivotal landmarks in a history of the performance of extremity in the 1970s. The *Mail Action* in particular serves as an evocative snapshot of imperatives at the margins of culture: to 'cut up' institutions, consolidate new and eccentric aesthetic languages and destroy art's already-beleaguered autonomy. In the 1970s and since, in multiple, unpredictable and redoubtable ways, P-Orridge, in particular, has always insinuated the 'what if?' of performance, of art and life. *What if?* What if by provoking the situation or intimation of extremity, through its images and its actions, what if performance art is not (just) the provocation of the limits of bodily experience – the feelings, affects, emotions, sexual impulses and erotic events that might feel *too much* – but, too, the testing of the limits of thought? What if performance art stages the limits of what can be known, such that knowledge, rationality and the concept of conceptuality itself, are so tortured in the event and thus reconstituted by the baffling, bizarre, deranged actions that often characterise its practice, that the common knowledge of what we thought we knew – the categories of art, life, sex, crime – might seem as new unto itself? If COUM never quite renounced art, it was surely not a failure of nerve but, rather, a concerted refusal to see art as a category distinct from, or superior to, the broader horizons of *a life strangely lived*. COUM's reconstitution of life would be permanent, all-encompassing and inextricable. As P-Orridge announced, in decisive mock-visionary terms, 'There is no such thing as art there is only coum.'[22]

---

22 Genesis P-Orridge, letter to Pauline Smith (13 January 1974) Pauline Smith Papers, TGA 801/1/12, Tate Archive.

4

Impossible things

You can't force a story that doesn't want to be told. (Eileen Myles, *Chelsea Girls*)

Anne Bean's work is formally enigmatic and materially hidden – or *occulted* – from view. It seems it cannot properly be found in history or identified through the cognitive habits encouraged by art criticism, for, taken together, Bean's performances, public interventions, drawings, videos and writings are actively pursued as a 'continuum', and she strives to diminish the distinctiveness or iconicity of each in favour of a democracy of forms and effects. Pressed on this principle of the blurring of art and life and her antipathy towards iconicity, Bean tells me,

> By being a continuum, art includes all the life 'in between'. It's just the truth of it. That's how the work happens, in among other practices of life. So, those moments in a life that happen to have a photograph or a bit of video attached, they are simply butterflies caught in a net. The photograph or the video does not *exclude* the enormous and much more exciting territory of what led to that moment, and how different ways of working shifted and flowed. The work, and the life, and everything in between – the *fluidity* of it – all of it is equally valid. (Johnson 2015: 64, emphasis in original)

Her performances, then, ought never to be identified forensically as discrete objects or actions, or collectively isolated in their totality as a project distinct from her pursuit of a life. This is part of the evanescent substance of her extremity.

Bean invents a new term to define her work: 'I tend to say "life art", she explains (in a variation on 'live art'), before adding, '[m]aybe one doesn't need any nomenclature at all. More and more, my work comes from asking how performance comes about in an everyday life situation'; as a summation of her orientation to art, she continues to ask, 'How can one seamlessly integrate one's work into just living?' (Johnson 2015: 56). This impossible endeavour involves the obliteration of the conventional distinction between art – its instances of production and presentation, as well as its objective form – and the durations and activities of life that lie beyond it for the artist; a life can no longer, here, be represented as left unadulterated by what is done in or as art. Nor might an individual butterfly be picked from the net to be subjected to scrutiny as evidence of its (or the artist's) own significance. As she writes in a note on her online archive: 'The flight is the thing. Not the pinned butterflies' (Bean 2016).

Amid Bean's mutually connective series of works of the 1970s, she performed her series *Imposters* as interventions, in Reading in 1970 and in London from 1971. Bean and friends would create 'im-posters' – impossible posters, non- or anti-posters – by wheat-pasting large blank sheets (or sheets featuring a single suggestive word) to walls or 'cancelling' existing posters by overlaying them with new images and texts. In one such action, in East London in 1971, Bean searched out posters for the Whitechapel Gallery's first *East London Open* exhibition (2–21 February 1971). The *East London Open* was an open selection platform presented annually from 1971 to 1976 (and re-launched as the *Whitechapel Open* in 1978). In 1971, it used the tagline 'Who Selects the Selectors?' to foreground the ideological constraints of curatorial and institutional practice, suggesting that the gallery's selection of curators reflects and sustains aesthetic imperatives at the institutional level. Regardless, Malcolm Jones's submission to the Whitechapel's open call was rejected for what Bean remembers as 'practical reasons' that complicated, exceeded or closed the 'open' nature of the exhibition.[1] In an elliptical response, Bean, Jones, Natasha Lawrence and Martin von Haselberg sought out advertisements for the exhibition and covered them with new posters featuring an image of Jones's work stencilled with the word 'cancelled' across it in black letters, as though by their negation they might open the *Open* (**Figure 4.1**). A photograph shows Bean with a powdered face, wearing a lace bonnet and flowing smock (one of her everyday experiments in extreme couture), engaged in conversation with a policeman. Approached for suspected vandalism, she attempts to explain the semiotic trouble posed by the action: as the poster had been rendered an 'im-poster' or impossible object, one could not be held liable for its damage. The 'poster', now cancelled at an ontological level, had ceased to exist and could no longer be subject to vandalism. Von Haselberg's photographs show the uniformed policemen writing down Bean's and Lawrence's explanations on a small pad. Baffled by the artists' philosophical expositions of the former poster's thorny ontological status, he let Bean and company go with a caution.

Bean's works in performance often proposed ontological trouble for artist and audience alike. In *Digging a Hole in Water* (1973), Bean performed a *kōan*: a Zen practice of active meditation devoted to the inauguration of 'great doubt', akin to the riddle of one hand clapping (**Figure 4.2**). Invited to perform at Essex University, Bean asked a number of her peers to present a *kōan* each towards a curriculum of non-standard intellectual experiments, suggesting a kind of anti-university premised

---

1 Anne Bean, 'Holding Infinity in the Palm of your Hand' (performance-lecture), *Performance and Politics in the 1970s*, organised by the author and Nicholas Ridout, Whitechapel Gallery, London, 31 May 2015.

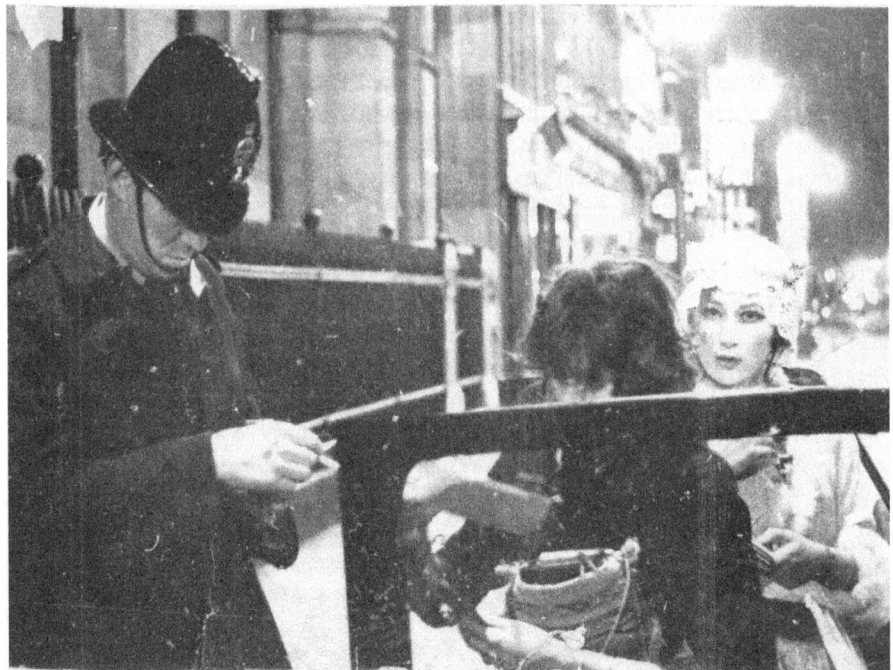

4.1 Anne Bean, *Imposters* (1971), action with Natasha Lawrence and Malcolm Jones, London

on performance. Her own *kōan* involved the impossible attempt to dig through the surface and density of a lake. In a document from the action, Bean stands half-submerged, slinging a shovelful of water, while engaged in a Sisyphean task of apparent meditative intensity that lasted for over three hours. The sole photograph is the only material consequence Bean could hope to achieve in the action; any significant transformation is registered in her commitment to the impossible undertaking and in the concentration, belief or thought that her commitment might engender.

Moreover, in her work's occulted aspect, as well as in her sensitivity to problems of belief and doubt, Bean's performances draw upon and internalise a set of esoteric reference points and unfamiliar ways of being, thinking and doing that are metaphysical in nature or form and inscrutable at heart. She reinvents the art/life continuum through the performance of a para-science: happily imperfect, impractical and untenable. The artist's quest for enigmatic and forbidden contents and forms is a reasonable one, especially in and after modernism in its revolutionary stages. Indeed, mystery, ineffability or illegibility may be defining circumstances (or aspirations) of much art, especially since the implosion at mid-century of the myth that a work retains a final internal coherence or kernel of truth, which can be disclosed and affirmed by learned acts of judgement. Lost to truth, art attains (or returns to) a kind of primordial weirdness, perversity or esotericism. In addition, by encouraging it to remain barely known, Bean's practice of art finds itself at a conceptual limit: the limit of the visible, the intelligible or of receptiveness to criticism and historicity.

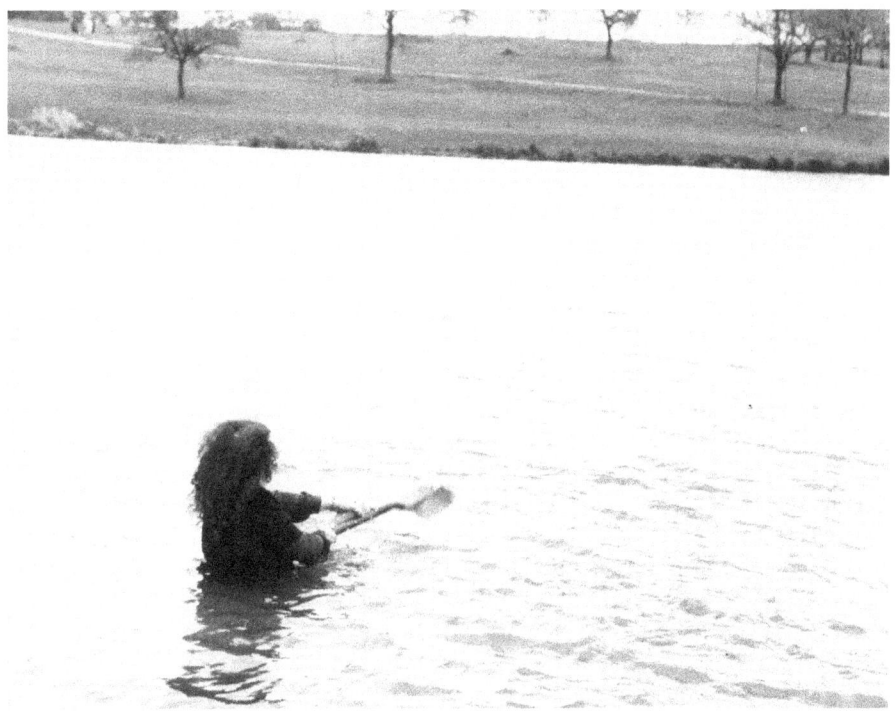

4.2 Anne Bean, *Digging a Hole in Water* (1973), Essex University

There is a gap in the process by which knowledge emerges from or envelops any work of art. It is tempting to try to assuage this impasse, to suture the splits in art's meaning or to broker a compromise in the rift between intention and manifestation or performance and context. In Bean's practice since the late 1960s, the enigmatic condition of art is magnified or focused by her valuation of process over the production of finite objects or finished works of performance. The sensuousness of her thought and its attendant values have remained more or less consistent: her performances are never scripted in advance beyond a basic score, never repeated or re-performed (though sometimes 'reformed' or reinterpreted anew) and inconsistently documented. Working principles in her performances include the privileging of her body as a living, thinking, creative, exploratory thing; her refusal or emphatic side-lining of photographic and audio-visual documentation; practices of differing durations, from the very short to the very long, necessitating an eclipse of the conventions of theatrical or cinematic time; the use of *povera* or pedestrian materials, including found or pre-loved objects; and the permanent disavowal of a signature style. Bean often refrains from making key decisions until the day of a performance – decisions that then remain provisional and may be abandoned in the course of a performance, should its undertaking require it. 'The very nature of [performance] is about some sort of profound communication', she has stated, which prompts a mode of experimentation that can sometimes feel 'traumatic', because fiasco, backfire or ontological risk are inherent in the process: although her approach can and does invoke profound effects, 'one can completely miss' or fail in achieving that goal.[2] Nevertheless, whether hit or miss, no single performance may take precedence over another.

The creative and destructive potential of materials is indicative here. The animation of that which the self comes into contact with – as a vitalist imperative for the artist – consistently involves Bean's subordination of her own self to chosen materials, such as the slow *durée* of melting ice, the drip of honey, wilting flowers or the freezing of skin in snow and the petrification of transitional or magical objects (in her embalming of children's toys, for example); or the quick and dangerous temporalities of flames, fireworks, explosions, breaking glass or the swirling undertows of a river in which her body might be dragged under to spontaneously drown while swimming in a lover's boat's wild wake. Each animated material, in encounter with Bean's body, seems bigger than she, much older, bolder, additionally vital or more profound than the singularly aesthetic or the merely human.

In the developmental arc of *Unlimited Action*, then, Bean enables a shift from exemplary, isolated performance actions that promise limit-experiences – Kerry Trengove's tunnelling action, Ulay's grand larceny or Genesis P-Orridge's appropriated trial, for example – to the means by which a practice at large challenges the viewer to acknowledge the limit of an artist's visibility and of her work's intelligibility. Bean's work also complicates how we write about art and performance, faced with the challenge not to isolate and celebrate individual works or confer iconicity and exemplarity upon them in the course of our attention. Bean puts the historian in an extreme methodological position, one that is exacerbated by the absence (or strategic inaccessibility) of much of her archive.

The flight is the thing

The Whitechapel Gallery's archive holds a letter to Bean, written by the curators of *Short History of Performance Vol. 1* (2002) a major retrospective of performance art of the 1960s and 1970s – also sent to other performance artists, including Yoko Ono, Carolee Schneemann, Paul McCarthy, Vito Acconci and Stuart Brisley. The letter invites Bean to participate in the opportunity to 're-live a small number of pivotal performances, once again bringing them in direct relation with an audience or group of participants'.[3] Bean replied with a postcard to Tarsia to politely decline, writing: 'I have to be honest and say that I don't consider any of my work [to be]

2 Anne Bean, the Kipper Kids and Nikki Milican, 'Meet the Artists', unpublished presentation, *National Review of Live Art*, 2003. A002555 National Review of Live Art Video Archive, Theatre Collection, University of Bristol. Subsequent references are given in the text as 'Bean, Kipper Kids and Milican 2003'.
3 Iwona Blazwick and Andrea Tarsia, form letter (4 March 2002) *Short History of Performance Vol. 1*, Exhibition Folder, Whitechapel Gallery Archive, Foyle Reading Room, London.

either renowned or pivotal.'[4] More than mere humility or insouciance, Bean's refusal signals an axiomatic belief concerning the status of her performances, the nature of the relationship between them as a continuum and art's role as an anchor for the broader edifice of a life.

Ever the contrarian, Bean subsequently consented to participate in the Whitechapel survey of performance art of the 1960s and 1970s, yet still avoided iconicity by working collaboratively. She returned to the performance *Death to Grumpy Grandads* staged by the group Bernsteins (Anne Bean, Peter Davey, Malcolm Jones, Jonathan Harvey, Chris Millar, Brian Routh and Martin von Haselberg) in 1972. The work came about when Jill Jones (a housemate) scrawled the titular epithet in lipstick on the walls of the group's shared home – a squat in a chemists' shop called Bernsteins on Mile End Road in Stepney, East London – in response to their apparently interminable and unrelentingly serious conversations about G. I. Gurdjieff and P. D. Ouspensky, theosophy, philosophy and the occult. In 1972 and again in 2002, the seven friends sat for one hour, tasked solely with laughing with, or at, each other for the duration of the performance, with each performer moving through periods of shallow laughter, raucousness, hysterics, sighs, sobs, giggles and tears. In the first performance and the return, Bean demonstrated her commitment to bridging art and life: turning a fragment of experience (the lipstick curse) and an augmented practice of living (collective laughter) into the bare premise for a work of performance, first in private, then, some 30 years later, in a public forum.

Throughout the continuum of her work and life, Bean sustains the dream of a democratic acceptance of any practice, action or thing as the stuff of art. In 1969, Bean immigrated to England from South Africa and studied under the painter Rita Donagh at Reading School of Art. Donagh recounts that Bean embodied 'the feeling that anything could be art', which was particularly fresh and current in the late 1960s and early 1970s, when Bean studied under her; Donagh continues, 'it was just how you did it, and what you did. Anne really understood that everything she did was her creative work' (Bracewell 2007: 263). One upshot of Bean's embrace of 'the *fluidity* of it' includes a seemingly militant refusal to value the results of her democratic practice of art: the selective 'butterflies caught in a net' (Johnson 2015: 64, emphasis in original). Elsewhere, in a public discussion with the Kipper Kids, Bean states, 'I feel nothing we've done has been significant.' Martin von Haselberg replies, 'Thanks a lot, Anne!' prompting peals of laughter from the audience. In her reply, Bean clarifies her position, mollifying the perceived insult that enables the joke, by explaining their collective ethos in the 1970s:

> I think it was about *not* being significant, about small gestures, about being together, about trying things out, about risking and experimenting. It was about present time, and not documenting, about free floating and being open to different situations and . . . explorations. There are wonderful iconic performances [by other artists] . . . but I think there was very much an attitude [among us] of things being of the moment, and not of the marketplace. (Bean, Kipper Kids and Milican 2003, emphasis in original)

4 Anne Bean, postcard to Andrea Tarsia (18 March 2002) *Short History of Performance Vol. 1*, Exhibition Folder, Whitechapel Gallery Archive.

In her refusal of iconicity and her attempt at creative self-actualisation, Bean performs a paradoxical, ambivalent or enigmatic project towards being both historically *impersonal* and creatively, personally *singular*. This suspension of significance or dominance and the clashing obligation to a superlative selfhood, with which it is held in tension, suggests Bean's formal elaboration of an anti-masculinist, implicitly feminist, anti-capitalist, anti-spectacular stance as an artist. It is a non-position or invisible position without station that is assuaged only by her rigorous and difficult commitment to collaboration, which has been a profound aspect of her working life since the early 1970s.[5]

Bean's collaborative performances with the Kipper Kids (whose own work is the subject of the next chapter) confirm her refusal of institutional decorum, twinned with her engagement with physical and other kinds of risk, resulting in performances that appear happily throwaway, pleasurable and dangerous in equal measures. Documents of a performance with the Kipper Kids at Vanguard Gallery, Los Angeles in January 1979 show Bean wearing a dress pinned with sliced salami and, later in the same performance, drenched in paint. The photographs, published in *High Performance* magazine, show her adding painted handprints to the Kipper Kids' bare buttocks and wearing an evening dress with Harry Kipper's hand covering her genitals (his body is concealed behind a curtain) and singing in a white leotard that has been scrawled with magic marker breasts, cock and balls and pubic hair. She is also shown, in the dressing room, showered clean, with the still-costumed Kipper Kids in all their chaotic muck-slathered glory. The accompanying interview ends with a testament to the physical and material risks posed by Bean's performance. Flanked by a photograph of his facial bruising, Christopher Hill writes, 'the marks on my face are the result of an accident I suffered backstage during the Bean performance at the Vanguard Gallery. In addition, my camera was damaged by flour thrown by the Kipper Kids during the act. I lost $60' (Hill 1979: 20–3). Yet the blurring of art and life means that by trafficking art into life and life into art, the resulting practices can sometimes seem to barely register as works – or as art – at all. Many of her performances are presented without audiences as such and remain undocumented. As performances of extremity, Bean's superlativity does not necessarily depend on the muscularity or violence or individual nuttiness of individual activities or actions (though some works do attain these anomalous marks of esteem); rather, her extremity is constituted by the formal challenge she poses as a whole to received notions of the categories of art and of performance art.

The pursuit of an impossible practice in performance finds form in Bean's prolific continuum of works since the late 1960s in two shapes. First, I argue that

5 Bean's other collaborative practices in the 1970s include performances as lead singer in the art-concept band Moody and the Menstruators, which started as a prank of sorts in 1973, yet accidentally accrued music-world recognition. Described by Michael Bracewell as 'alternately feckless, disquieting, funny, cool, without purpose, compelling and clever', and compared to Gilbert and George, and Bruce McLean's 'Nice Style' Pose Band, the 'Moodies' are acknowledged as a key influence on the development of bands including Roxy Music (2007: 261); they performed as a warm-up for Lindsay Kemp's dance company, and were courted by Malcolm McLaren and Barry Flanagan, who each sought to manage them. They were profiled in *The Sunday Times*, and even hailed by a German newspaper as '[t]he biggest music sensation since the Beatles' – then disbanded within a year of their formation before being corrupted by fame (Bracewell 2007: 174).

she seeks to *actualise* herself, not in a final, authentic fashion – which subjectivity, arguably, cannot sustain – but as a perpetual work-in-progress, as though this unfinished work of the self could be the subtle, provisional triumph of a deconditioned subjectivity. Second, she seeks to animate objects as vital things, as if to be subjected to or enchanted by them, such that they might act distinctly from the volitions and desires of self-fashioning, through a practice of magical thinking or occultation. This argument entails a strange or perilous route through and about the work of Anne Bean – and an esoteric direction in which to pursue the performance of extremity – beginning with the assimilation of her works into a continuum that also includes her life, then taking in the theosophy of G. I. Gurdjieff and the dubious critical methods of magic and the occult, ending up at the persistence of her refusal to be fixed or found by history – perhaps as an attempt to escape notice.

Escaping notice

Owing to Bean's absolute refusal of the significance of individual works and projects, the avoidance of notoriety or fame and the terms upon which she affirms the radical continuity between performances and between her work and her life, it is counterproductive to isolate her particular performances from the broader wash in which they swim. To do so would be to risk the conferral of iconicity – a status or circumstance that the artist and her works deliberately resist – and the ensuing hermeneutic activity of close reading would misread the works. Rather than ignoring the whole continuum for fear of breaking it, my provisional solution is to feel out a series of knots, barbs or prickles along the continuum in a manner that might do something other than artificially quarantine these emergences from the mutual effects of other contingent works, into or against which they make meaning, in symbiotic, sympathetic or synchronistic respects. This requires a calibration of sorts for art and performance scholarship (my problem, not hers) and, as noted, a shift or spanner in the working methods established or adopted in this book.

Bean's formal provocations undermine the traditional disciplinary approach (in the history of art, cultural history, literary studies and so on) of selecting, according to rationales or criteria, one or more case studies, which the scholar then places under a certain scrutiny. At the same time, the attempt to bring the continuum as a whole into view – that is, to see Bean's work as demanding our attention, despite her secrecy – requires, at least, an attempt to describe or explain some typical (which is to say atypical) works that constitute the continuum as it existed in the 1970s. Doing so might partly negate her political imperatives, but it also breaches the critical quietude that otherwise greets her and draws the continuum out of the wilderness in which it is suspended. It may do so without, one hopes, disarming or defanging the work, segmenting or segregating her 'life art' or condemning it to the commercial vagaries of the marketplace. The performances I discuss throughout are to be treated as a number of sites of difference along a continuum: the critical mission (prone to misfire like the performances) is to sustain them as contiguous analytic artefacts dotted around the interconnected skeins of a web.

A resistance to visibility and to registering as a permanent trace or as wilfully significant art – or as art at all – also appears in the work of Bean's peers in the 1970s. For example, the British artist Annabel Nicolson undertook striking, fleeting works, such as the durational performance *Sweeping the Sea* (1975), in which she swept a shoreline in Southampton, on the south coast of England, over an extended period. Performed as a poetic exploration of a seemingly impossible task – of cleaning or sorting the sand and pebbles or of brushing away the lapping waters – the piece had no formal audience, beyond the walkers and beachcombers who happened to pass by, and is documented by a single, ghostly photograph of Nicolson lunging her broom into the shallow shifting tide. 'On a grey day in July she was seen sweeping the sea', the artist writes in a note on the performance; '[p]erhaps it was deliberate this trick of making herself part of the background of being just slightly out of focus' (Nicolson 1977). Her reflection on the action gives a sense of being unfocused in time, of evading full recognition even by those who pass her by in her immersion on the beach and afterwards in our equivocal encounters with her documents. Writing in the third person, she also gives the impression of having difficulty in identifying with, or laying claim to, her own action. Similar works in the period involved Nicolson disentangling frosted grass with a hair comb in *Combing the Fields* (1976); lying motionless on soil, turf or alongside and atop a tree trunk in the six photographs titled *Sleeping like a Log* (1976); and *Looking for Seals* (1976), a discreet and self-explanatory action undertaken amid Cornwall's caves and surf. In a handmade book self-published by the artist in 1977, Nicolson commented on the incipient task of evading capture or delimitation by history or by criticism, through fleeting accounts of works in which she 'seeks to remain inconspicuous' amid public interventions, including the marathon walking series *Redefining the Contours of Britain* (1974–76) (Nicolson 1977). As David Toop writes, the near-mystic substance of Nicolson's performances takes the shape of 'passing through rural communities as a woman of mystery, searching for the ineffable, the minor incident barely worthy of comment, or the more serious business of vanishing footpaths' (Toop 2013). For Nicolson, as for Bean, the forgetting of their performances is not (merely) a historical travesty – a dereliction of duty by critics or historians – but an effect built into the forms they pioneered.

Disappearance, enigma and ineffability are particularly germane to Bean's (and Nicolson's) surprising experiments in extremity. After 1960 and especially after the advents of postmodernism and poststructuralism, there is almost nothing to find in art, no intrinsic meaning and no coherent subject-position outside language from which to look. In her psychoanalytic approach to the impermanent or ephemeral sculptures of Eva Hesse, Mignon Nixon writes that 'art is enigmatic – not filled in but hollowed out', meaning that the architectural 'hollow' of the space of art's presentation and reception (the contingent 'milieu' of art) is emptied of meaning, but sympathetically completed by the hollowed-out subjectivity of the viewing subject; indeed, art is 'a hollow that can receive another hollow' (Nixon 2006: 171). This sympathetic relation between entities without substance or coherence creates an ideally inexact and ambivalent situation of organic sensing – or *aisthesis* – which may give rise to theorisation or to thought: 'art acts on the viewer as a proposition', Nixon writes, 'but one that is enigmatic' (2006: 173). For Amelia Jones, in a different but synchronistic vein, the enigmatic nature of performance art, specifically, relies on its constitutive ephemerality and its incessant slippage into the past, including in the duration of its experience as a live event and subsequently when one engages with its documentation. Moreover, its elusiveness depends on the formal impossibility of subjective 'presence' to the material. Jones writes,

> We engage with art or performance because we want confirmation of (our own) presence, paradoxically by relating to works produced by another in the past. We want to defer endlessly the 'eternal return', the way in which we are continually opened to the other . . . even as we want fullness within our own enunciation of self. We seek this in performance art by clinging to a notion of the 'original event'. But . . . there is no original event; or, strictly speaking, there 'was' an event, but it was never . . . fully 'present'. (Jones 2010: 11)

For Jones, the aspiration of performance to authenticity, hermeneutic fullness and pure presence – including stated claims by artists or critics and the silent claims of certain works themselves – signal an 'impossible' ambition at the core of performance. This central enigma is accentuated, Jones notes, by uncritical attempts to reclaim or master the lost object or event – most egregiously through re-performance and institutional endorsement – that belie 'the impossibility of that fantasy of a return', to authenticity, to an origin or to presence (2010: 12).

Bean's *Imposters* series was explicitly interventionist in form, activating the urban environment by altering or neutralising found objects, and relational in its provocation of a philosophical conversation with an incidental audience – including with a policeman. In other performances from the period, Bean foregrounds her political agency and uses suggestive imagery and explosive action to engage with risk, negative affects and personal culpability. In *Raw/War* (1971), Bean sliced the tip of her finger and used the blood to paint her lips. Standing before a large sheet of plate glass, she used the same finger to write 'RAW' on it, turned the glass around to reveal a palindromic approximation of the word 'WAR' and rammed her head against the pane until it shattered, lacerating her scalp in the process. She painted her face with the issuing blood, along with spittle and pigment. For Bean, *Raw/War* enabled her to imagine fear and danger in a way that created what she describes as a relation of 'direct simpatico with a fearful situation, like hiding in a building with the windows being blown in', in affinity with the experiences of individuals in conflict or crisis (Johnson 2015: 61). While performance can never fully approximate such an experience, the use of physical wounding, disruptive effects and formal unpredictability create a relation of symbolic equivalence that is provocative for herself and for her witnesses.

In a similarly abrupt performance series in 1970, Bean realised that walking with a dog allows one to shout a word (the dog's name) in public without the particular affront that other loud interruptions seem to cause. She acquired a dog, named it 'Mortality' and walked it at various public spaces, including Heathrow Airport, Glasgow Central Station, a street market in London and the countryside, creating unauthorised or stealth performances by screaming the dog's name – 'MORTALITY!' – to the surprise, amusement and probable annoyance of passers-by. The resulting series, *Mortality* (1970) used performance to shock incidental audiences into questioning social decorum, the proper and improper usages of public space and one's own habitual relations (as governed by law, ritual and decorum) to life and death. Many of Bean's performance in the 1970s created incidental audiences and took place in short blasts of time, yet many others were durational, open-ended or otherwise integrated into the practice of life. A long, meditative performance, *Ghost of a Shadow, Shadow of a Ghost* (1972) inaugurated an endless process: Bean made a hardboard cut-out of a foetal shape based on her own crouching body, placed it in sunlight and excised the shadow the silhouette cast on canvas; the resulting canvas is then placed in sunlight and Bean cuts out the next shadow in another sheaf of canvas, potentially (though not actually) ad infinitum (**Figure 4.3**).

From 1976, the turn towards expanded durations and media took a more comprehensive turn for Bean. She moved into Butlers Wharf with Paul Burwell, an artist who used drumming as a sculptural technique to create performances on both an intimate and industrial scale. Situated on Lafone Street in London's Shad Thames, Butlers Wharf was a converted studio complex covering 200,000 square feet, in which Bean and Burwell lived and worked, alongside artists Derek Jarman, Andrew Logan and Stephen Cripps and X6 Dance Space – until the buildings were destroyed by fire in 1979. From 1983, Burwell, Bean and Richard Wilson collaborated as the legendary Bow Gamelan Ensemble, a sound art group that created fantastical machinery, spewing ear-splitting noise, debris and steam and explosive showers of sparks and light. At Butlers Wharf, frequently in collaboration with Burwell, Bean's performances overtook or merged with daily practices of living, actively to blur the hierarchical distinction between art and life. She recounts,

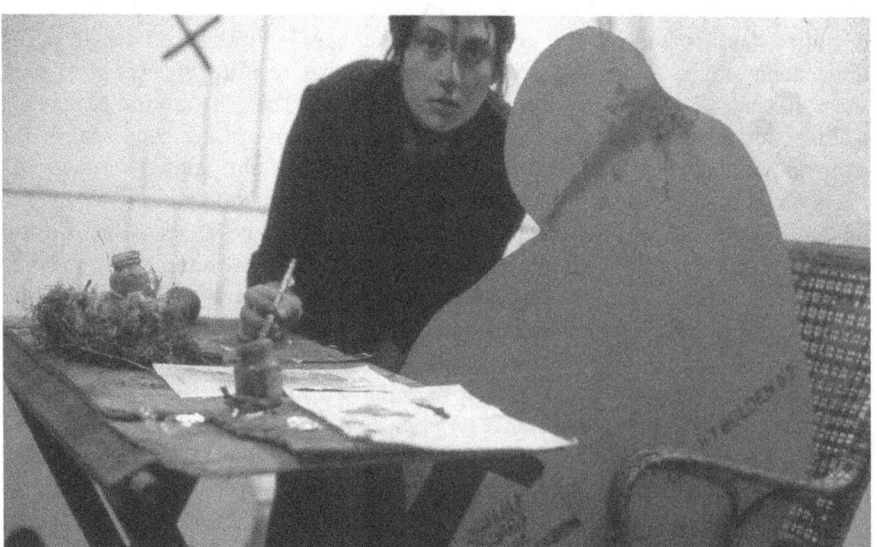

4.3 Anne Bean, *Ghost of a Shadow, Shadow of a Ghost* (1972), Reading University

[M]any days would be spent with whatever was in the kitchen, in true laboratory style – seeing if bacon dripping fat on to different surfaces would make different sounds, or throwing poems into a liquidiser to reform texts, or whatever, until one's whole life became a sort of laboratory. I have mostly lived my life in that mode. (Johnson 2015: 60)

Similarly, the live-work space of the studio at Butlers Wharf, the 'laboratory' mode she engineered, the influence of Burwell's drumming practice and the technological devil-may-care-ism of Cripps – with whom they lived and collaborated – enabled experiments that elided the distinct or discrete status usually afforded performance art (I return to Cripps in the Conclusion). Without beginnings or ends and with or without audiences, Bean's generally undocumented experiments broke with many of the traditions associated with performance art, installation and noise, as emergent genres of art in the 1970s. She recalls, for example,

I had a drum kit in my studio in Butlers Wharf, which I connected to lights, and I wired metal drumsticks to a car battery. When I drummed, and completed the circuit on the edge of a drum rim, or on a cymbal, the battery would light up one of several small headlamps, so that different rhythms would strike up different shadows. (Johnson 2015: 48)

Playing her assisted drum kit created bridges between action, sound and light, as the act of drumming triggered the synchronous production of percussive sounds and lighting effects – so that the drum kit (and the performance) was 'lit by its own lights'. The constructions would be played in various situations, including the parties she organised at Butlers Wharf, attended by the punk rock royalty who constituted her wider circle, including Jayne (then Wayne) County and the Electric Chairs, Sid Vicious and Nancy Spungen, the Jam, the Buzzcocks and Siouxsie and the Banshees (Toop 1992: 11). The process led to specific works, too, such as *Echoing Tower Bridge* (1976): in a rowing boat on the Thames, Burwell played an electrified drum kit that provided light effects, while Bean swam behind the boat's passage with red lifeboat lights attached to her ankles. Passing riverboats lit the scene along with follow spots operated by friends perched on the balcony of their home in Butlers Wharf. If living there created or enabled a 'laboratory' scenario, in her imbricated practice of art and life, one finding of the prolonged experiment at home and in the river was that the artist might 'see sound and hear shadow' (Johnson 2015: 48). Performance art urges the experience of living into risk and broaches the unnameable, in part by rerouting the traditional separations and functions of sensory experience.

By the late 1970s, Bean's performances – presented in Britain and internationally – used experimental noise and sound alongside actions, gestures and materials in intuitive, exploratory ways, often with jarring or explosive effects, whether in intimate, incidental settings or in more high-profile events. An example of the latter is her contribution for William S. Burroughs at the legendary *Final Academy* event (curated by the artists Roger Ely, Genesis P-Orridge and David Dawson, London, 1982), where she performed *The White Man's Got a God Complex*, an improvised

cover of the proto-hip-hop track of 1971 by the Last Poets, sung effervescently to percussion by Burwell (an audio recording is extant). Her public actions were frequently
raucous and sometimes dangerous. Describing Bean's performance *Low Flying
Aircraft* (DTLA, Los Angeles, 1980) in an editorial note, Linda Frye Burnham writes,
'Anne Bean sang, threw ice at the audience, doused herself in olive oil and lit smoke
bombs. Paul Burwell accompanied her with live music' (Bean 1980: 120).[6] In the
first of two full-page photographs by Charles Hill covering the antic performance at
Public Spirit: Live Art LA (a legendary festival convened in Los Angeles by Linda Frye
Burnham, Paul McCarthy, Barbara T. Smith, Chip Chapman and John Duncan),
Bean kneels in an oil-soaked nightgown, on a bench raised above a large amount of
melting ice. The background shows sculptural shapes made from Mylar or tinfoil and
a large array of musical equipment, including amplifiers, speakers and tubular bells
(**Figure 4.4**). In the second photograph, Bean sings in a room full of billowing smoke.
She wears a smoking jacket, loose-fitting trousers and a mortarboard-like hat made
from a piece of mirrored material with a hole cut for the head. She holds a microphone and screams into it, holding her unseen audience in an intimidating staring
contest of sorts. Another reviewer echoes Burnham in her description of the 'frenzied
excitement' of Bean's performance: 'Drenched in oil, she attacked certain members of
the audience with flying ice cubes and proceeded to light off different coloured smoke
bombs. This last phase of the performance ended the display because the audience
was forced to evacuate the gallery and run down to the street below to avoid smoke
inhalation' (Anawalt 1980: 134).

The art historian Guy Brett notes Bean's use of different shapes of time across her
works, from brief disruptive actions (perhaps like *Raw/War* or *Low Flying Aircraft*) to
works with extended or non-delimited durations. Brett describes this relation to time
as a strategy of vexation or of interrupting the institutional reception and containment of performance:

> The instantaneous and the long-drawn-out are both measures which are foreign, in excess
> of, or outside the rationalised time which the institution of art increasingly imposes on the
> production of artists, and which it demands in exchange for fame and power . . . Bean has
> questioned the notion of fame and career and has even said she would prefer to remain
> anonymous, not through any saintly abnegation of the self, but from a desire for freedom,
> not to be tidied-up or narrowed down. (Brett 2006: 27)

Brett's commentary reminds us of the stakes of breaching Bean's self-imposed invisibility. By tearing through a series of moments along her continuum, I remain in an
ambivalent position between her need to stay silent and without station and my commitment to knowing (and honouring) what she has done. With what effects does an
artist remain anonymous or refuse to appear? With what effects does she privilege

---

6 *Low Flying Aircraft* was used as a title for various projects, including a record released on 7-inch vinyl by
   her art-concept band PULp MUSIC in 1979. In the latter, Bean sings and screams herself hoarse, with
   percussion by Burwell using drums, bells, and liquid-filled tubes, and Cripps using '10 CO_2 cylinders,
   goldfish, explosives, keyboard, wind instruments, fireworks, electrics, tapes, percussion'. Stephen Cripps,
   'PULp MUSIC', unpublished notes in 2013.90 Stephen Cripps Drawings Collection (uncatalogued),
   Henry Moore Institute, Leeds.

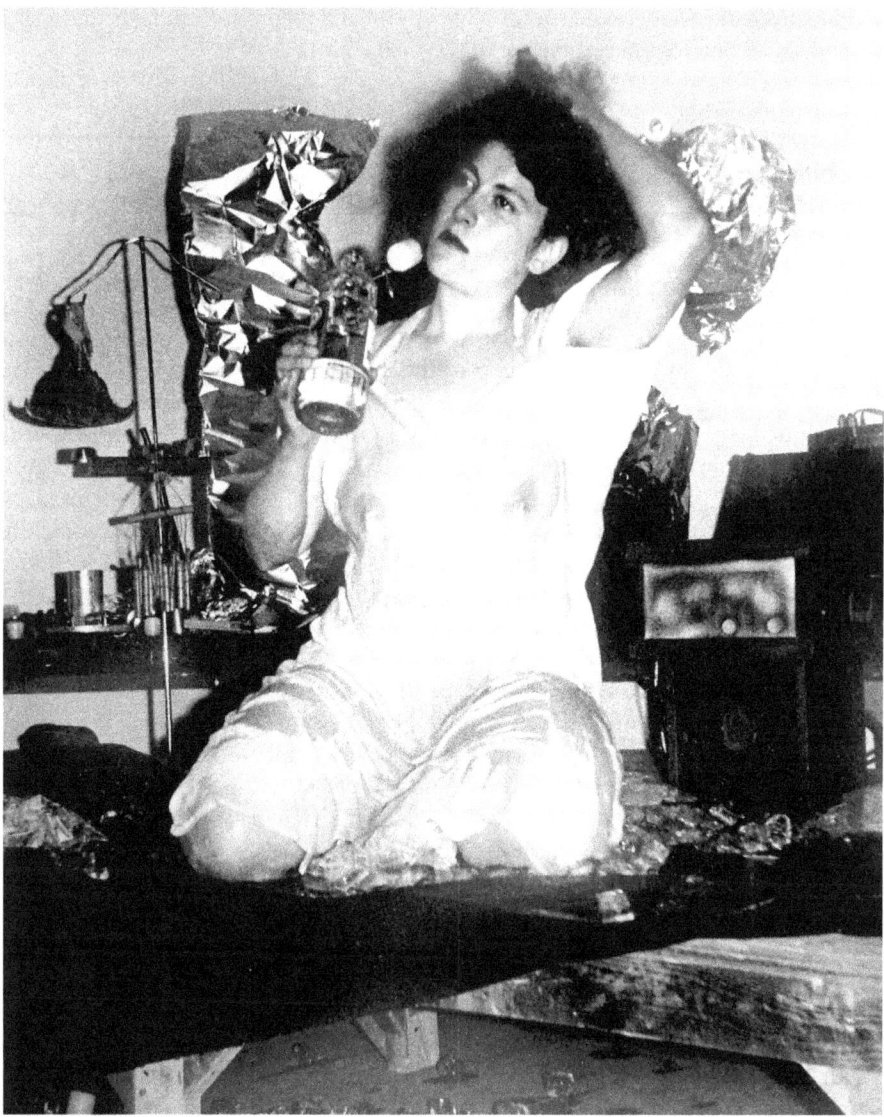

4.4 Anne Bean, *Low Flying Aircraft* (1980), with Paul Burwell, Vanguard Gallery, Los Angeles

the slices in time explicitly given over to the production of 'art' and the things so produced? And what is the effect upon the remaining swathes of time that constitute the day, the night, the week, month or year? If such an endeavour – the creation of a continuum between works of art and between art and life – is 'impossible', what are the stakes of committing oneself to the pursuit of wilfully untenable acts, to redefine the world of one's experience? How is such an impossible or untenable project the basis for the blurring of 'art' and 'life' and what is the shape and texture of the 'life art' so inaugurated? What are the specifically cultural and theoretical contexts that make this praxis an ontological reality?

Hanged for a sheep as for a lamb

Born in 1950 in Livingstone, Northern Rhodesia (then a British colony and since 1964 the Republic of Zambia), Anne Bean's conflicted identity as a white, Jewish woman in colonial Africa seemingly influenced her orientation towards individuality, ritual and fabulation. According to the journalist and gay rights campaigner Peter Wildeblood, Northern Rhodesia at mid-century was an 'impossible' place, 'surrounded by glittering rocks and twisted thorn-trees, the coughing of leopards and the honking of hornbills' (Wildeblood 1957: 26). The politician Tony Benn, posted there on active service in 1944, testifies that the country was blighted by apartheid: of a visit to a hospital, he recounts the shock of 'the absolutely appalling conditions of squalor under which the Africans [of colour] were treated, within a stone's throw of a well-equipped modern hospital for white patients', noting that the spectacle of racial disparity in the country consolidated his commitment to socialism (Benn 1979: 14).

As her friend Chris Millar recalled in 1983, moreover, Bean 'tells me how she swam in the crocodile infested waters, only thinking of the swim and not the danger or the lack of it. She was making a Universe which didn't incorporate the possibility of being eaten by crocodiles', suggesting her imaginative response to dealing with crisis, risk, danger or terror (Millar 1983: 6). This idea of a singularly created (or fictively inhabited) 'Universe' dovetails neatly with Michael Taussig's anthropological account of the 'magical' invocation of 'other worlds', through the alchemy of mimesis or mediation. The effect is 'magical' or requires 'magical thinking' because any imperative to represent – not to mimic but to forge a new object or action in mediated form (say, in performance art) – entails the practice of estranging one's sense of an entity or environment in and of itself. Via the sympathetic power of active ideation or of what Taussig calls the 'Law of Similarity' (the conviction that enacting or forcing a fantasy produces its desired effect [Taussig 1993: 47–9]), magical thinking prompts 'the capacity of the imagination to be lifted through representational media . . . into other worlds' (1993: 16). Bean's sense of difference and her solutions – activating public space, reclaiming one's autonomy in the face of danger – were perhaps presentiments of impossible things to come.

In 1968, Bean left Livingstone to study fine art in South Africa at the University of Cape Town. During her time there, she made her first forays into performance art, through live interventions into public space that committed her to investigate the fact of racial inequality during apartheid and the social construction of blackness and whiteness. *Net Blankes* (1969) was one such response, in which the young artist sat on benches marked 'Whites Only' (the English translation of her original title in Afrikaans), with parts of her body painted black: the palms of her hands or one side of her face. The performances evaded the mimetic minstrelsy of blackface while asking how much of a person – of skin, constitution or sense of self – must be visibly black before one is excluded from segregated spaces; as such, *Net Blankes* enabled a bitingly subtle intervention into public discourse. Bean put herself at risk in the actions: she recalls, 'I was always threatened, taken in for questioning and moved on by the police', yet nevertheless felt 'strong, angry, scared' (Bean 2005). The works were intuitive, provocative, itinerant – and perhaps formally savant, in the sense that her conservative education in Cape Town, the limited availability of critical resources about performance and contemporary art and the pioneering nature of her actions did not admit her much knowledge of the full political potential of performance art or its emergent historical genealogy.

Net Blankes functions as a telling example of the aspiration of mimetic representation to the function of magical thinking. For literary scholar Leigh Wilson, magic is 'the realization of a still-unfinished reality [that] . . . works through harnessing the vital materiality of the world' (Wilson 2013: 14–15). Aesthetic experimentation is ideally suited to engage this practice of magical thinking – or Taussig's 'magical mimesis' (1993) – because, for Wilson, it 'mediates between the world as it is and the world as we would like it to be as a result of our actions. It makes it possible to act in the world in such a way that, if successful, the action would change the world, even though we know we may fail' (2013: 27). The *Net Blankes* series may have little material efficacy, beyond the posing of an oblique question to passers-by, but it enabled Bean to address a political question that possessed her – namely, of the situation of racial inequality and the terms of racist scorn and privilege – and to mediate a crisis in everyday life that curtailed her happiness or subjective coherence. No documentation exists of these performances and their transient or ephemeral nature prevents them from circulating or persisting as iconic, beyond their status as hearsay or legend. Translating the racist assumptions of her contemporary state of social existence into a series of live performances, devoid of spectacle but directed towards a situation of a politically and creatively aware practice of life, Bean precipitated the central question she still asks of herself some 45 years later: 'How can one seamlessly integrate one's work into just *living*?' (Johnson 2015: 56, emphasis in the original).

Bean's political commitments, namely, her openness to deploying her experiments towards explicit political contexts, are a common thread, as claiming the right to speak or feel one's privation or pain. We see it in *Net Blankes* and *Raw/War* as well as in other early works like *I Speak through Blood-Stained Lips* (1970). The latter was performed in the course of *The White Room*, a three-week collaborative 'live-in' performance led by Rita Donagh at Reading School of Art, featuring contributions by Monica Ross and other artists. Here, Bean staged a spontaneous response to the previous day's freshly reported atrocity, namely the Kent State massacre of May 4, 1970, in which the Ohio National Guard violently quelled an anti-war protest by unarmed students on a university campus, killing four and wounding nine. Bean cut her fingers with a Stanley knife, anointed her lips with the issuing blood and read aloud a newspaper report of the shootings. In a simple but poignant action, the news of bloodshed was spoken through 'blood-stained lips', making the speaker more viscerally intimate – via the Law of Similarity – with an event that was far away in cartographic terms but close enough politically, not least in terms of the regime she had just recently fled. *I Speak through Blood-Stained Lips* can never collapse the violent difference between the artist's experience (cutting her fingers) and that of those caught up in a massacre, just as *Net Blankes* is irremediably split by Bean's inability to fully inhabit the life experiences of a person of colour under apartheid, however much she swims in crocodile-infested waters. Yet the 'magical quotient', as a quality of her aspiration, to some extent distinguishes her fantasy of transcendence from merely wishful or benevolent thinking: the Law of Similarity enables the artist, rather, to entertain the distance of the gap between performance art and social efficacy.

If magical thinking is redolent as a method of reading, here, Bean's performances have regularly engaged the problem of magic and occult actualisation in more direct ways. For example, her film *The Days of Thy Youth* (1973) is a short, provisional study in a 'laboratory' mode – that praxis in which she tells us she has sought to live much of her life (Johnson 2015: 60). Bean performed *The Days of Thy Youth* at Reading School of Art in 1973, in private, recording the action on 8 mm film with optical sound. Bean selected a passage from the Old Testament, namely: 'Remember now thy Creator, in the days of thy youth' (Ecclesiastes 12: 1) and learned to speak it backwards. Lining up and lighting a long series of white candles, Bean moved down the series blowing out each candle and speaking the biblical phrase in phonetic reversal. Completing the action, Bean edited the footage, reversing it, along with its soundtrack. The effect is a short film-performance in which the artist speaks in an eerie incantation – the ecclesiastical words, reversed into an approximation of their original phonetic shape, are intelligible, yet uncanny, ghostly sounding (anticipating a core technique of the filmmaker David Lynch). Each de-familiarised word is matched by the phenomenon of a candle being blown *into* flame, as if the occult action might blow a dead thing into life by the manipulation of the Law of Reversal.

The act of learning biblical text in phonetic reversal along with the visual trickery of Bean's inverted flame sought to enact the occult practices of the 'Great Beast', Aleister Crowley. Crowley was a poet, magician and noted mountaineer, but better known until his death in 1947 as a target of public hatred in British newspapers: he was vilified and exiled for his blasphemy, junk addiction, queerness, sexual predation, polyamory and formidable eccentricity. Crowley's occult Law of Reversal held that the temporal inversion of text, image and human processes like walking, talking or thinking could summon hidden, secret, unconscious forces (the phonetic reversal of the Lord's Prayer is also a reputed ritual in the Satanic Black Mass). Crowley's law is staged in Bean's incantation and theatricalised in her apparent action of visually inverting the process of flammability. A contemporary technique subject to the Law of Reversal is the playing of phonograph records backwards to expose a message 'backmasked' into a text: it was a topic of countercultural recovery at the time of Bean's *The Days of Thy Youth* as a result of scandals concerning its supposed abuse by Led Zeppelin, Pink Floyd, the Beatles and the Rolling Stones, who used it to create musical effects, but were also rumoured to have trafficked Satanic dispatches and other tokens of subliminal persuasion into their records. (What would the history of performance art disclose when subjected to the Law of Reversal?)

Bad theory

'There is . . . something to be said for moments of methodological naiveté', writes the philosopher Jane Bennett, concerning the intellectual possibilities that attend to thinking counterintuitively about our practices of cognition and interpretation (Bennett 2010: 17). 'But how to develop this capacity for naïveté?' she asks. 'One tactic might be to revisit and become temporarily infected by discredited philosophies', she suggests (for her, in the course of rethinking the micropolitics of things) (2010: 18). Bennett suggests that our understanding of pressing questions – of ontology, episte-mology, metaphysics, *poiesis* and praxis – may be recalibrated by pausing or eclipsing the received hierarchies of knowledge and by practising, even temporarily, naïve or *brut* methods of thought.

In the early 1970s, Anne Bean lived and worked in a co-operative setting with a number of other artists as Bernsteins. Bean tells me the collective 'spent a lot of time there, asking what we were trying to do, philosophically and conceptually . . . We were reading Gurdjieff and Ouspensky, and thinking seriously about being and doing, wakefulness and mindfulness' (Johnson 2015: 51). Their art of living entailed inter-mittent undocumented performance actions in private or in secluded semi-public places, long and committed conversations and extensive reading of what Bennett calls 'discredited philosophies'. With Millar, in particular, Bean conversed extensively, over terrestrial days and astral weeks, on topics concerning philosophy, theosophy, the occult and art, prompted by their ongoing discoveries as young artists, their shared enthusiasm for Ouspensky's writing and subsequently through close readings of Gurdjieff and other occult thinkers, including Helena Blavatsky, Austin Osman Spare, Aleister Crowley and Israel Regardie (Bean, conversation with the author, London, 5 July 2015).

The 'occult' refers to a broad and arcane set of 'hidden' philosophies, histories, cryptozoologies and obscure practical techniques – of necromancy, thaumaturgy, synchronicity, the paranormal and clairvoyance – gathered from aged *grimoires*, sixteenth-century magical diaries, mystic dream logs, documents of oneiric travel, etherograms, telepathically transcribed texts and other eccentric sources. As phi-losopher Eugene Thacker describes it, the occult assumes 'the idea of an occulted world which both makes its presence known and yet in so doing reveals to us the unknown . . . Against the humanist world-for-us, a human-centric world made in our image, there is the notion of the world as occulted, not in a relative but in an absolute sense' (Thacker 2011: 52). In occult philosophy, Thacker continues, 'we enter the human world of hide-and-seek, of giving and withholding, of all the micro-exchanges of power that constitute human social networks. We as human beings actively hide and reveal things that, by virtue of this hiding and revealing activity, obtain a certain value for us as knowledge' (*ibid.*).

As Bean told writer Michael Bracewell of her time at Reading in the early 1970s and after, 'Gurdjieff was a seminal influence', because he influenced a 'pre-punk thought', namely that 'everything's unreal' and 'everything's an illusion', so 'you can create your own being. It's called "self-re-membering"', she adds (Bracewell 2007: 265). Bean's small cabal in Bernsteins took seriously this work of 'self-re-membering', in the course of their research into the occulted word of human experience – as demonstrated by Bean's pilgrimage to Gurdjieff's Institute for the Harmonious Development of Man, at the Château du Prieuré commune in Fontainebleau-Avon, Paris (and, later, her experiment in Scientology, during which she lived for six months at the cult's British headquarters at Saint Hill Manor in East Grinstead, West Sussex) (Millar 1983: 4–8). Brian Routh recalls their collective education in Bernsteins through Gurdjieff and its influence on his performances as one of the Kipper Kids:

> Gurdjieff taught a Stop Exercise – people move around and someone says 'stop', and you'd freeze and take account of yourself, physically and emotionally – until someone released you from the exercise by saying 'enough'. So we incorporated that into the show – but when we stopped, we grabbed a cup that was hanging from the ceiling, and drank a cup of whisky each. (Johnson 2015: 70)

Indeed, their appropriation was transparent to some audiences: a critic reports of one performance in 1979 that the Kipper Kids' 'use of Gurdjieffian stop exercises signalled consumption of alcohol' (Adderley 1977: 51). However, Routh jokes about the lightness of his readings and invokes the cultural familiarity of Gurdjieff's teachings when he quips, 'We were influenced by the writings of Gurdjieff [but] we just read the back covers of Gurdjieff books, rather than the actual content', then laughs (Johnson 2015: 70).

George Ivanovich Gurdjieff was born in Alexandropol in the Greek Caucasus (now Armenia) in 1866 and came to wide public attention from around 1915, on account of his eccentric balletic rituals (or 'sacred dances'), his lectures on the occulted life and his general school of thought – first in Moscow, then in Paris and London and through national tours in the United States, until his death in 1949 (Ouspensky 1950: 16). He had an imposing appearance, with what his protégé Ouspensky described as 'the face of an Indian raja or an Arab sheik' and an overall attire that 'produced the . . . almost alarming impression of a man poorly disguised' (1950: 7). Celebrated by his disciples as a true mystic, guru and philosophical genius, as dramatised in Peter Brook's laudatory cinematic portrait *Meetings with Remarkable Men* (dir. by Brook, 1979), Gurdjieff is dismissed by his detractors as a cultist, showman, charlatan or huckster. For example, Anthony Storr labels Gurdjieff a 'confidence trickster' whose excesses garner him a damning comparison to Reverend Jim Jones (architect of the Jonestown Massacre in 1978, in which 909 disciples died) (Storr 1996: 11); he proceeds to describe Gurdjieff as 'ludicrous' and 'bombastic', a 'dictator' and probable 'chronic schizophrenic' (1996: 28–9).

However, Gurdjieff's thinking on agency, consciousness and truth laid the groundwork for an emerging popular turn to secular mysticism, which achieved mainstream appeal in the 1960s through a series of countercultural innovators, including: the Western appropriation of Zen Buddhism in the writings of Alan Watts; Allen Ginsberg's oneiric celebration (in his poem 'Howl' of 1956) of poets who 'studied Plotinus Poe St. John of the Cross telepathy and bop kabbalah because the cosmos instinctively vibrated at their feet' (Ginsberg 2001: 59); teachings at Black Mountain College and at the Jack Kerouac School of Disembodied Poetics, Naropa; and the psychedelic and psycho-nautical revolution spearheaded by Aldous Huxley and Timothy Leary, among others. Gurdjieff's original ideas about the 'man-machine' in which one's human potential is imprisoned and the discovery and release of one's 'astral body' (Ouspensky 1950: 31–2) are perhaps clichés today, owing to the extensive popular usage by which they have become acclimatised and contained. Gurdjieff also actively cultivated an aspect of charlatanism about himself. As Ouspensky recalled, 'no ordinary demands could be made of [Gurdjieff], nor could any ordinary standards be applied to him . . . He might say one thing today and something altogether different tomorrow, and yet, somehow, he could never be accused of contradictions; *one had to understand and connect everything together*' (1950: 36, emphasis added). The latter sentiment must have seemed profound for Bean.

In the early 1970s, Bean and her collaborators in Bernstein's chemist shop grappled with an arcane book of Gurdjieff's called *Beelzebub's Tales to his Grandson: An Objectively Impartial Criticism of the Life of Man*. Dictated by the guru in the 1920s and published in 1950, this tome of 1,135 pages is written in a circumambulatory, arcane, funny and challenging manner. Bernstein also read closely Ouspensky's analytic portrait of Gurdjieff, *In Search of the Miraculous* (also published in 1950). *Beelzebub's Tales* is framed by a profoundly ambitious prolegomena, in which Gurdjieff sets out his attempt '[t]o destroy, mercilessly and without any compromise whatsoever, in the mentation and feelings of the reader, the beliefs and views, by centuries rooted in him, about everything existing in the world' (Gurdjieff 1992: frontispiece). In the book, Beelzebub circles the universe in a spaceship called the *Karnak* and imparts to his grandson Hassein a copious, novelistic, obtuse and sometimes baffling account of the occulted life of man. He takes in such concepts and philosophical enigmas as the 'law of falling', genuine 'being-duty', the cause of the genesis of the Moon, the 'arch-absurd', the 'arch-preposterous' and the relativity of time, while attempting – though his wildly elliptical style – to put the reader into a profoundly receptive and experimental state of perception. As Hassein listens to his grandfather's ceaseless schoolings, he tells Beelzebub, 'Things I never thought of before are now a-thinking in me' (1992: 72).

I want to take seriously Bean's statement about studying Gurdjieff for lessons about 'being and doing, wakefulness and mindfulness' and towards active 'self-re-membering', particularly as it may tell us of the limits of thought and praxis in performance art in the 1970s (Bracewell 2007: 265; Johnson 2015: 51). This prompts me to pursue Gurdjieff's account of the 'definite and peculiar psychic data crystallized in my common presence during my preparatory age'; and to provide an honest engagement with the critical potential of 'mindfulness', as an actualizing of new ways of thinking and being and of 'wakefulness' towards the vital nature of things (1992: 24). It would be facile (and convenient) to laugh at Gurdjieff and his followers in this context and patronising to excuse Bean her youthful diversion. As per my pursuit of Kerry Trengove's established interests in Paulo Freire, so too I pursue Bean's contemporary investment in Gurdjieff, as twin effects of an attempted fidelity to what artists concerned themselves with learning in the 1970s. Gurdjieff might seem like 'bad theory' in comparison to Freire; or relative to the robust interdisciplinary framework provided by reading George Kubler – as Rosalind Krauss has done – to get closer to the praxis of Robert Morris, who read Kubler's *The Shape of Time* (1962) while rethinking the function of process in post-minimalist art-making (Krauss 2013: 91). So what if Gurdjieff seems less intellectually weighty, less serious, less sane? In the spirit of the limit, I will account for Gurdjieff's school of thought and its implications and pursue some of his apparent influence on Bean's unique approach to art and performance in the 1970s, including her appropriation of what Ouspensky calls 'the connectedness of everything [Gurdjieff] said' or, how 'his ideas were not detached from another, as all philosophical and scientific ideas are, but made one whole' (Ouspensky 1950: 28).

The core of Gurdjieff's philosophy is to propose methods for unlearning or de-habituating inhibitory tendencies in the human subject. He writes of the accumulation of 'mentation by form' – or thought by rote or ritual – by which an individual conservatively relies upon an idea that is 'fixed as a result of specific local influences and impressions' and which 'evokes in him [sic] by association the sensation of a definite "inner content"' or 'habitual meaning'. De-habituating thought – actualising 'mindfulness' – requires a thinker to become aware of received thinking and to acculturate oneself to 'a different "inner content"' or new ideas concerning a given word, object, practice or thought (Gurdjieff 1992: 14–15). Passive thought occurs in the 'waking consciousness' (which for Gurdjieff is also 'fictitious consciousness') whereas proper 'wakefulness' requires the thinker to access the 'subconscious' (paradoxically, 'your real human consciousness') (1992: 22–3), staging at its core a kind of hackneyed post-Freudian ego psychology, though additionally embellished and narrated.

In his attempt to de-habituate thought and language and to avoid or retrain 'mentation by form', Gurdjieff introduces new words to explain his worldview and reveals a series of 'cosmic laws' that govern the shape and structure of consciousness and corporeality. 'Actualisation' is a key term, which he defines in a typically inventive fashion: 'during the transition of the fundamental sacred laws into the ilnosoparnian process, similitudes of the whole arise on planets, and . . . contribute to the formation of the various "systems of being-brains"', giving rise to 'world-creation' and 'world-maintenance' (Gurdjieff 1992: 81–2). Gurdjieff's most influential construction, however – including for Bean and her co-conspirators, is the esoteric ethic of 'being-partkdolgduty', borne of the 'ilnosoparnian process' of mind, as the formal terms for what Bean terms 'self-re-membering'. Being-partkdolgduty marks the achievement of a 'subjective being-conviction formed by [one's] own logical deliberation', as a state of grace from 'those convictions . . . that depend exclusively upon the opinions of others'. The latter suggests a conforming subject-position – 'the abnormal conditions of external ordinary being-existence' – that establishes 'as a norm' the influence of the 'inner evil god', namely 'self-calming' (Gurdjieff 1992: 99–100). Gurdjieff's critique might seem arcane, but it is also an occulted version of what Michel Foucault would later identify more gravely as the disciplinary production of 'docile bodies'. Foucault writes,

> [B]eneath every set of figures, we must seek not a meaning, but a precaution; we must situate them not only in the inextricability of a functioning, but in the coherence of a tactic.

> They are the acts of cunning, not so much of the greater reason that works even in its sleep and gives meaning to the insignificant, as of the attentive 'malevolence' that turns everything to account. Discipline is a political anatomy of detail. (1991: 139)

Self-calming or docility, as the product of what Foucault terms a malevolent function of discipline in the form of tacit self-schooling, is productively undermined in Gurdjieff's teaching, in order to accrue personal sensitivity to one's 'instinctive sensing of reality' and a strategic diminution of the hegemony of 'sane logic' (Gurdjieff 1992: 127). Instinctive sensing equates to a hallucinatory version of what Foucault terms, above, the small 'acts of cunning' by which a creative subject survives the distribution of accountability, productivity, conformity and other styles of docility.

Many of Bean's works in the period enact a refusal of sane logic in the service of a specialised, alien, but individually necessary action. For example, in *Homecoming* (1972), Bean purchased 20 lbs of sea salt and several sacks of sand, travelled to the shore and emptied them on Peacehaven Beach, Sussex. She undertakes the arduous task of transporting the materials, carrying them across the beach and piling up pyramids of sand and salt. She waits as the sea laps upwards with the tide, reclaiming the sea's constitutive elements, namely the salt that distinguishes it from other bodies of water and the sand upon which we might stand. The action is pointless in practical terms, incidental and a miniscule contribution in the grand sense of how much the beach might need or register these activities. Yet, like her *Digging a Hole in Water* or Annabel Nicolson's *Sweeping the Sea*, Bean's *Homecoming* refuses the very logic of productivity or accountability. No account can make biochemical sense of the contribution Bean makes to the elemental makeup of the Sussex coastline or the water of the English Channel; neither can we quantify the shift in the cleanliness or order of Nicolson's swept sea. The duration and exertion of each action dwarfs the efficacy of each artist's intervention. Yet the poetry of *Homecoming*, like that of *Sweeping the Sea*, is profound, even if its profundity is directed towards a private operation upon the performing self – and precisely because it is written or spoken in a minor key. The psychic displacements undertaken in the performer – Gurdjieff's 'world-creation' and 'world-maintenance' (1992: 81–2) – dwarf the physical displacement made visible in the action of adding sand and salt to surf, digging a hole in water or sweeping the sea. If discipline is a political anatomy of detail, these anomalous actions are resistant to its vocations.

Provocatively, for Gurdjieff being-partkdolgduty is inhibited – not facilitated – by art, even though he humbly describes himself, early in his book, as 'simply, a teacher of dance' (1992: 46). Of art he writes,

> This definite concept, now existing there under the name of 'art', is one of those automatically acting data, the totality of which gradually and imperceptibly, yet very surely converts [human subjects] – beings who have in their presence all the possibilities for becoming particles of a part of divinity – merely into what is called 'live meat'. (1992: 412)

Gurdjieff assumes a constitutive difference between 'art' – codified as a normative and inhibitive set of practices, styles and institutions – and instinctive aesthetic sensing or *aisthesis*. His manifesto on art describes a means to revalue the practice of art at a remove from 'terrestrial' values; he calls for an aesthetic revolution – a cosmic 'arising' in Gurdjieff's terminology – that could progressively be integrated into the path to being-partkdolgduty. He calls this art of actualisation 'afalkalnas' and defines it as 'various works of man's hands which have entered into the everyday life of people', including rituals, ceremonies and occult occurrences (1992: 420). A. R. Orage writes, in his influential commentary on *Beelzebub's Tales*, that according to Gurdjieff, '[a]n artist should not be a special kind of man, but every man should be a special kind of artist' (Orage 1985: 93).

Gurdjieff's position (and Orage's commentary) directly anticipates formal developments in the new art that became more fully recognised later in the 1950s (the decade Gurdjieff's book first appeared) and into the 1960s. For example, Allan Kaprow's Happenings proposed and enacted an expansive practice of de-skilling, based in part upon his teacher John Dewey's thinking on art and experience, which dovetails (in a subdued way) with Gurdjieff's. Another equivalent context may be found in the emergence of Fluxus as a model for making art based on seemingly simple or usefully transparent games and pedestrian instructions, particularly in the work of George Maciunas, George Brecht and Yoko Ono: 'Art is not merely a duplication of life', Ono proclaimed in 1966. 'To assimilate art into life', she continues, 'is different from art duplicating life' (Ono 1996: 738). Similarly, Gurdjieff anticipates the 'social sculpture' (*soziale Plastik*) of Joseph Beuys, which held that 'Sculpture = Everything' and – in his much-quoted and perhaps misunderstood credo – 'every man is an artist'. Beuys' slogans stood in for his more complicated equivalences and less quotable theses concerning the utopian potential of art, such as his statement in 1971 that 'Art equals man equals creativity equals freedom. Every man is creative, and hence he is free. Freedom and creativity make him fundamentally able to determine, to form, and to change. This is true both in the realm of art – whose task is to create awareness of such possibilities – and in society' (Alonso 2010: 191). In practical terms, for Beuys, creativity was to be detached from the production of stable objects and epitomised by or assimilated into all aspects of human life, such that '[e]ven the peeling of a potato can be a work of art if it is a conscious act' (Beuys 1990: 87). Of a piece with these developments and emerging from his own 'sacred' public performances, Gurdjieff calls for a reintegration of creativity as an undifferentiated part of everyday life. Specifically, his own avant-gardism celebrated the strategic invocation of 'reciprocal thrusts' between the artist-performer and members of the audience and the production of 'inexactitudes' of meaning – or sites of semiotic ambivalence – in activities that would secure collective 'cosmic arisings' in and as performance (1992: 421).

Cosmic arisings in the common integral vibration

Bean's 'life art' performances of the 1970s, then, are not illustrations of theosophy or philosophy per se, despite her serious readings of the postulations I have been surveying. Rather, her works inhabit the key principles of such theosophy, including the ambition towards art as a process not of aesthetic production but of aesthetic sensing. As such, she searches out, through performance, the possibilities, potentialities, dead ends and new realities associated with doing and being for art.

Further approaches furnished by Gurdjieff include Bean's incitement of reciprocal thrusts between the artist and the audience and her commitment to try to let meaning go, to provoke – to use Gurdjieff's word – 'inexactitudes', which the newly manifested situation of reciprocity might hold or bear. So, when Bean performs *Shouting 'Mortality' as I Drown* (1973), the durational commitment to the task and her refusal to document the action may complement or confirm a commitment to these preceding principles. Naked in a bath of water, the artist submerges her head and face and screams 'Mortality', repeatedly, through the water, creating a muffled, gargled speech. As her action progresses, the artist incrementally comes closer to drowning. At the point when she is too tired to continue and she brings herself as close as bearable to drowning, she articulates the nature of mortality, as the common property of bodies, in which one's finitude can be delayed or embraced, by the commitment of a body to testing its own vital limits, subject still to external factors beyond one's control.

Bean's performance is concerned with her own perceptual exploration of how it feels to take life and death into one's own hands. She stages the privilege of doing so, for other bodies outside the situation of art or performance will be subjected to the crisis of death or near-death experiences without agency in the event; in its course Bean inhabits the pleasures and pains and perceptual novelties of sound, of feeling and of embodiment that accompany such an endeavour – what Gurdjieff calls the cosmic 'totality' of being 'live meat' (1992: 412). In *Shouting 'Mortality' as I Drown*, the audience may share in some of the sonic oddities of her act. They hear her aquatic screams, the choking, coughing and frantic splashes of the drowner. They may feel a sympathetic anxiety, feelings of fear, even of horror – at watching someone drown or commit herself injury – and feelings of guilt or shame at one's inaction in such a scene. Similarly, in *I Speak through Blood-Stained Lips* and *Raw/War*, Bean's audiences are drawn to or repelled by her self-injury and by the bloody spectacle of her consensual action and its complicated relation to distant, unseen victims of violence. These constitute some of the precise reciprocal relations (or 'thrusts') set up in the performances. They are exceeded by that which the audience cannot gain access to, namely, what it feels like for the artist to undergo the struggle: her drowning or, elsewhere, her cutting and its pain. This occlusion of the reach of our affinity – a break in the range of reciprocity – occurs again and again in Bean's works of the 1970s, either by occultation of meaning, leaps of faith or plain nuttiness of expression. The artist lays claim to a specialised variety of experiences, furnished by the singularity of her subject-position in each action and the precise materialities of water, of breath and of voice – or elsewhere of burning wood, trajectories of unstrung wire, blood, elemental matter and fear, which cannot be predicted, represented or conveyed.

The new wakefulness that Gurdjieff advocated – and which Bean was provoked by – relied on a learned practice called 'instinctive sensing', which, for Gurdjieff, 'permit[s] the "exchange of substances," or "reciprocal feeding" of everything existing' (1992: 129). The 'common-cosmic' foundations of 'everything existing' – the human and non-human forms of the world – suggest a continuum as well as a kind of animism or non-theistic vitalism, as qualities that occur throughout Gurdjieff's practice (and so, too, though circuitously, in Bean's). He calls the common-cosmic substance 'eth-ernokrilno', 'the primordial substance with which the whole universe is filled', as the 'omnipresent active element' and 'principal cause of most cosmic phenomena' (1992: 129), suggesting, perhaps, atomic particles, genetic material, DNA or light; or 'star-seed' as the extra-terrestrial fundament of human life (Leary 1973); or 'orgone energy' as orgasmic *prima materia* (Reich 1948). With Timothy Leary and Wilhelm Reich, Gurdjieff discloses a common claim that we are connected to the world in a chiasmus or network (here a cosmic, psychonautic, cybernetic or orgasmic bond) and that the human subject is not superior to or independent from non-biological or inert matter. If the preceding adventures in theosophy seem eccentric, this methodological extrem-ity belongs nevertheless (at least obscurely) to a recent turn towards new philosophi-cal investigations that contradict common-sense understandings of matter and event and which stage anew our carnal place among the carpentry of things.

Philosophy, in the past decade, has given rise to new materialisms – variously, speculative realism, object-oriented ontology, neo-vitalism or guerrilla metaphysics – which seek, by differently nuanced means, to speculate upon the vitality or onto-logical self-sufficiency of objects, beyond their reliance upon the human subject for substance, meaning or coherence. Jane Bennett explores the potentialities of inert matter as constitutive to human experience, including by narrating quotidian events – encountering litter or a power blackout, for example – as situations that 'present non-human materialities as bona fide participants rather than recalcitrant objects', in order to ask: 'What would happen to our thinking about nature if we experienced materialities as actants'? (Bennett 2010: 62). Similarly, for Graham Harman, another key thinker of the realist 'turn' in philosophy, the task at hand is to find methods to recognise the 'reality' of 'entities as genuine forces to reckon with in the world, as real players exerting influence outside themselves even while hiding behind their exposed surfaces' (Harman 2005: 11). The entity or object, as a 'real force throwing its weight around', Harman continues, 'demand[s] to be taken seriously', beyond or despite the philosophical tendencies to quarantine one's concerns to the human sphere and to naturalise both the autarchy (or tyranny) of anthropocentrism and its horizon of discrete perceptual phenomena (2005: 17).

As the sober counterpart to Gurdjieff's concept of the '"reciprocal feeding" of everything existing' (1992: 129) (or for that matter, the wacky vitalism of Reich and Leary), Bennett and Harman rethink philosophy as a means of valuing or honouring the animate life of non-human entities, which are otherwise dismissed or displaced by the assumed prior authority of human lives. For Harman, whether the philosopher (or artist?) turns one's gaze to 'lemon meringue, popsicles, Ajax Amsterdam, reggae bands [or] grains of sands', each entity is authentic in its existence apart from its rela-tions to other things or to the assumed authority of a human author of experience (Harman 2005: 19). Or as Bennett writes, one might write 'to rattle the adamantine chain that has bound materiality to inert substance and that has placed the organic across a chasm from the inorganic. The aim is to articulate the elusive idea of a mate-riality that is *itself* heterogeneous, itself a differential of intensities, itself *a* life', such that any object may be experienced as 'itself aquiver with virtual force', reanimating the parts played by human and non-human 'actants' in the theatre of our collective consciousness (Bennett 2010: 57, emphasis in original).

The poetic (and agentic) re-animation of non-human materials as described by Bennett and Harman announces a novel means of understanding the strange, unlikely or screwy approaches to objects and materials in early performance art, as a highly specialised and de-structured outland of the world of things. Why, how and with what effects would an artist – say, Anne Bean – manipulate, experiment with, refashion, destroy or transfigure a series of materials: cancelled posters, a dog, shards of glass, a gush of blood, a bath, breath, salt, sand or sea? (What of Hannah Wilke's chewing gum, folded into labial forms? Marina Abramović's bullet and gun? VALIE EXPORT's box cutter, amputated cuticles and milk? Ulay's amputated scrap of tattooed skin? Or Bruce McLean's string, dragged along the street? William Pope.L's flower in a pot, carried on a crawl? Allan Kaprow's jam, licked from the bonnet of a car? Yoko Ono's cloth or Jack Smith's glitter? Or Tomislav Gotovac's litter, collected in a square and arranged into pleasurable constructions on the floor?) How can such laboratories of matter be considered practical experiments in the discovery of the animate life of objects? What is the effect of theorising thems, first, as a novel deployment of Gurdjieff's supposedly crackpot worldview and, second, as a surprisingly apposite and topical question at an ontological level?

One of Bean's earliest works anticipates these questions and chimes neatly with Bennett's and Harman's proposals for a new ontology of things. In a long, sensuous description, Bean recalled to me the genesis of her piece *Falling in Love with a Chair* (1969), first performed in private, as an action that emerged intuitively on one of her first nights in England, while seated on a simple chair made of wood and reeds:

> There was this intensity of the situation, a whole new life, having come straight from Africa and sitting in this room, in England, feeling cold, which was unusual, and everything was completely outside my reality, yet, strangely, completely inside it. There was a feeling of excitement, and fear, and potential. Then, I'd recognised that here was the chair holding me, and the wood had come from a tree, and the reeds had come from grass. I felt the displacement of this chair from its initial place in nature. I felt a strange connection to this chair, wondering what sort of forest the wood came from, and what the tree looked like, and where the reeds came from, and so on. I felt at home with its displacement. Sitting there, alone, I realised I was touching this chair, very sensually. It led me into a strange dance with this chair. I later thought of it as *falling in love with a chair* . . . It was *alchemical*, in all the very best senses of the word, as a transmutation of material. (Johnson 2015: 59, emphasis in original)

Bean's secretive performance in some ways inaugurates her subsequent lifelong commitment to pursuing performances without predicted ends or results – here by feeling out the sensibility of her own 'displacement' (from Africa, apartheid and/or anthropocentrism) that became akin, obscurely, to the displacements of materials from unknown forests and estuaries to a solitary chair in an English student dormitory. Her account is distinctly redolent of Jane Bennett's project to revitalise 'the sex appeal of the inorganic', namely, as 'another way to give voice to . . . [the] shimmering, potentially violent vitality intrinsic to matter (Bennett 2010: 61), as a positive force of the object that might demand our sensual attention and erotic interaction. The 'transmutation of material' proposed by Bean's solitary dance was clearly a profound one for the artist. It inaugurated a new orientation to performance (and to England), and staged a scenario – dancing with a chair – that Bean has since returned to (as a 'reformation' of the original piece in 1996, for a video in collaboration with artist Nina Sobell; and as a live solo work – with a chair made from fluorescent tubing, mapped by thermal-imaging technology – at the National Review of Live Art, Glasgow in 2003). In each instance, starting with the first performance in 1969, at the outset of her pioneering practice as a performance artist, Bean begins to dislodge the narcissistic anthropocentrism of conforming thought – and of art or aesthetics – by dancing with a non-human entity in a choreography that does not subordinate the same entity to traditional human needs or experiences. 'Humanity and nonhumanity have always performed an intricate dance with each other', Bennett writes; amidst environmental disaster, overproduction of commodities, and dwindling resources, she continues, 'today this mingling has become harder to ignore' (2010: 31).

The hidden or occulted life of the chair – its harvested wood and reeds and their transmutations and displacements on account of biological as well as human agencies – are exposed as ineradicably alien to the self, yet also as promiscuous substances of a common world. Evoking the speculative realist and vibrant materialist turns in philosophy (and an embarrassing, naïve cousin, Gurdjieff's theory of ethernokrilno), Bean's dance partakes in a philosophical emphasis on the interconnectedness of things, as an ontological reality of the cohabited human/non-human world. For cultural theorist Steven Shaviro, in his overview of speculative realism, animating the life of entities beyond our direct control provokes the uncanny effect of actively knowing objects and materials in 'continual interpenetration' with each other (Shaviro 2014: 39) – that is, as a *continuum* of objects, actions and lives – such that entities exist in synchronicity with other inhabitants of a universe of things, yet retain their own identities as 'autonomous centers of value' (2014: 89). Here, then, the vitalist imperative reminds us of the general theory of Bean's practice, namely of performances in a continuum with each other and of performance art as an indivisible part of (her) life. Of the anthropomorphic conventions of thought, Shaviro writes: '[w]e need to break this habit in order to get at the strangeness of things in the world – that is, at the way that they exist without being "given" to or "manifested" by us. Even the things that we have made ourselves possess their own bizarre and independent existence' (2014: 66–7) – a chair, perhaps, with which one might fall in love.

Keep moving

At the end of the 1970s, Bean would come to feel that Gurdjieff's influence had crystallised into a self-limiting rule, until she found it necessary to break with it (conversation with the author, London, 5 July 2015). In works such as *Two Ps and a Bean* (1983), perhaps Bean sought or staged a departure of sorts: here and after, she intensified her method and introduced new strategies, but, strikingly, sustained the bare principles learnt from her discipleship to Gurdjieff, including the supreme value of wakefulness and the power of instinctive, aesthetic sensing. Her use of collaboration and physical risk in the action seemingly outstrips her earlier forays: while her previous perfor-mances demonstrated a commitment to exploring and complicating the reciprocity of audiences and artist, the heightened vigilance required by this performance provokes an extreme she had not previously approached.

In *Two Ps and a Bean*, Bean collaborated with Paul Burwell and Paul McCarthy (the two Pauls the Ps of the title). In a striking series of photographs by Linda Frye Burnham, we see Bean, Burwell and McCarthy standing amid wreckage inside a ter-raced house, clambering from a window and otherwise wreaking havoc (**Figure 4.5**). The performance came about after Bean and Burwell met McCarthy in Los Angeles in 1980, during the course of *Public Spirit*, in which all three were contributing artists. (In *Public Spirit*, Bean and Burwell presented *Low Flying Aircraft*. McCarthy presented *Monkey Man* [1980], a messy naked action; and *A Penis Painting Appreciated* [1980], in which he painted a canvas using his penis as a brush.) After 1980, McCarthy con-tacted Bean and Burwell to find a London venue for him to perform in, but they had no luck in securing him an invitation. Bean and Burwell therefore suggested the three of them collaborate in a stealth action in an appropriated space, namely a derelict Victorian house next door to their own home in Bow, East London. In the resulting

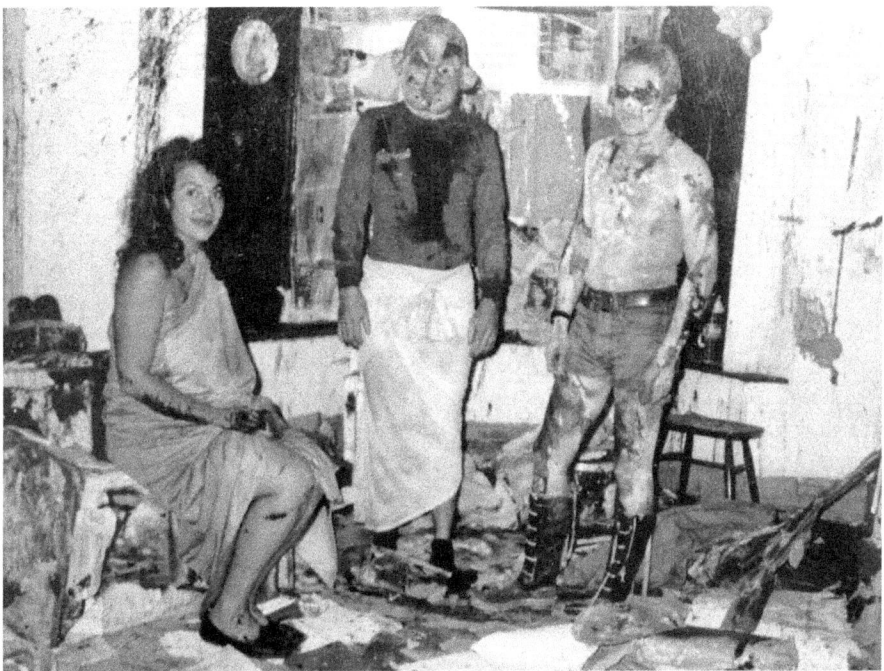

4.5 Anne Bean, Paul Burwell and Paul McCarthy, *Two Ps and a Bean* (1983), Bow, London

performance, the three artists occupied separate rooms and floors. Bean dug a ragged hole through the dividing floor from upstairs, showering Burwell and his drum kit with building materials and props. Bean also dropped large glass spheres through the opening, making thunderous sounds – and a machete – as Burwell protected himself flimsily with an umbrella. Bean sang through a tube into the space, climbed through the hole and fell to the floor. As Bean took over on drums, Burwell scaled the side of the building using a ladder, smashed a window and entered McCarthy's space. McCarthy staged a messy performance, wearing a trademark cartoon mask and Burwell chased McCarthy through the house, spraying the interior and its occupants with ketchup. Throughout, the audience moved in a panicked, highly vigilant manner, bearing or escaping the assaults of image, sound and hurtling debris. Bean recalls,

> the audience inevitably were caught up in the mayhem, running for cover, not knowing which way to go, what to see, what floor would give way, what glass would fly, what stair-case was safe. We all – performers and audience – genuinely had to have our wits honed and alert and seemingly antithetically, this is often the safest as well as the most enlivening situation we can be in. (La Frenais 2016: 3)

She summarises this situation of hyper-vigilance with a quote from Sun Ra: 'I would tell people on this planet that there are forces: their job is to slow you up. And you [sic] supposed to keep moving.'[7] Citing the Arkestral musician and Afrofuturist theoso-phist suggests that perhaps overcoming one esoteric touchstone opened the gates to new possibilities, including the psychic push of motile futures and astral pastures new.

I believe in nothing but

Methodologically speaking, Bean poses problems for those of us who seek to engage with her continuous history as a 'life artist' (Johnson 2015: 56). Her personal archive has little or no material existence, beyond the scant images and texts she has published on her website (and possibly a suitcase of slides she alluded to, but declined me access to). From conversations with Bean, I understand her propensity towards ephemerality and her attitude of resistance towards archival sedimentation and intellectual capture. Yet I contacted her regardless, pushing my luck perhaps, to ask to look at whatever she may have saved from her early work, be it notes, journals, sketchbooks or docu-ments. She replied, 'Numerous electro-chemical archives and repositories abound [but] all paper work, sketch books etc. have been ditched at various junctures. I mourn not (I have written that twice and deleted so it will just have to stay now)' (email to the author, 30 June 2015). Her process entails active destruction (owing perhaps to her full engagement with and contribution to punk culture in Reading and London

---

7 Bean read the text of her interview in 'Effing the Ineffable: She Perceiving Her', unpublished lecture at *Unlimited Action: Limits of Performance*, organised by the author, Whitechapel Gallery, 28 May 2016. Extemporising, Bean added the statement by Sun Ra (Burks 1969: 18).

from the early 1970s) and casual disregard for bourgeois values, such as posterity, orthodoxy, administrative care or being preserved or revered as a 'seminal' artist. Her sensibility retains an ambivalent relation to mourning (hence her email's self-critical, parenthetical addendum).

This is the conceptual terrain Michel Foucault orbits in his famous excusatory prelude in *The Archaeology of Knowledge*, where he claims an author's permission to write 'in order to have no face', perhaps to stage this as the kernel of liberation in writing or in being an artist more broadly. 'Do not ask who I am and do not ask me to remain the same', Foucault pleads; 'leave it to our bureaucrats and our police to see that our papers are in order. At least spare us their morality when we write' (2003: 19). He asks to distance a work from the subjectivity of the author and at the same time asks to preserve in a text all the excess, inadequacy, discontinuity and contradiction that typifies a life. Nevertheless, Bean's perversity or humility – in wanting expressly to remain a well-kept secret – is, to some, no doubt, potently baffling in the present culture of self-promotion and the popular aspiration to total, networked presence.

A week after the 'I mourn not', I received a further email from Bean, containing a number of scanned sketches she made that had been retained by her partner and collaborator Paul Burwell, whose posthumous papers she keeps. One of Bean's sketches, made in the late 1970s, consists of a provocative written manifesto:

Art is the concept by
Which we measure our pain
I don't believe in Duchamp
I don't believe in Beuys
I don't believe in Warhol
I don't believe in Cage
I don't believe in Rothko
I don't believe in Klein
I don't believe in Ono
I don't believe in Rauschenberg
I don't believe in Hesse
I don't believe in the
Not me
That's reality

I believe in nothing but
MIRACLES

The manifesto is a stark statement of refusal, an active negation of – or suspension of belief in – primary figures in progressive art after modernism, many of whom privileged performance in their critical practices of art and were still active at the time of her writing. Bean's dissidence extends to everything outside her, negating the existence (or importance) of that which seems, cumulatively, to constitute external reality: 'I don't believe in the / Not me / That's reality'. Beyond her Oedipal figures (and, strictly, in some cases, peers) – from Beuys to Ono, Andy Warhol to Eva Hesse – whose authority is indexed yet bluntly refused in the list, Bean stakes her belief in that which exceeds rational belief: 'I believe in nothing but / MIRACLES.'

The search for the miraculous may be an impossibly counterintuitive 'thing' in which to invest, exclusively, the entirety of one's capacity to believe – but there, she suggests, lay the magic of the exercise. Perhaps she writes the manifesto as an exorcism of sorts or a determining sigil, as if to act out and thus to manifest her heretical relation to art history. The totemic function of the writing works to strike through the limitations of external reality, to underwrite both her historical exceptionality and an occult fantasy of herself as a miracle-maker who seeks to congeal into reality a series of impossible fictions.

Bean writes that the sketches – sheets with collaged photos, watercolour washes and pencilled aphorisms – were 'crumpled up, possibly pulled out of bins by him [Burwell] (he had a duality about ephemerality but essentially had a deep collector's urge)' (Bean, email to the author, 2 July 2015). Beyond the aforementioned works, Bean also gestures to an additional cache of letters to Burwell that contain drawings and ideas. She gestured to her own hesitation in sharing these, noting:

> [T]he private/public domain and all its blurriness haunts me often . . . on one hand I feel a seamlessness, on the other I am aware of impinging on certain consciousnesses and a certain breach of trust . . . I suppose this is an old dilemma in searching for what we posit as truth. (*Ibid.*, ellipses in original)

The helpful latter missive from Bean was less an act of contrition than a wilfully contradictory gesture, a winking refusal that her belief in her own essential dissidence – of being beyond intellectual capture – must not be allowed to settle into a new orthodoxy (she wouldn't keep an archive, which is not to say she may not retain archival materials). The letter also describes the vitalist aspect of archives: her letters are live things, artefacts that may speak in unruly ways, on behalf of the living, the non-living or the dead.

Bean's anxiety about becoming orthodox and her philosophical and aesthetic need to define and claim pastures new, is typical of her, across some five decades and counting. She has stated that her project since the 1960s has consisted of an attempt to become an 'a-artist' (as in a-theist) – a person who commits oneself to aisthesis without believing in the situation of art as a discrete phenomenon or in the artist as a stable identity. As an a-artist (or an anartist), Bean overhauls the Beuysian democratic standard: rather than advocating for the utopian ideal in which *every human being is an artist*, she holds out for a future horizon of consciousness in which 'no-one is an artist', for 'the "art" space is implicitly part of living' (La Frenais 2016: 4). The imaginative effects of her reinvention of art and life on a vital continuum include the actualisation or 'self-re-membering' of oneself as a distinctive personality, a non-entity of distinction, beyond or even against one's identity as an artist; and the invocation of things as sprightly (or spritely) activated entities. Whether that of a magus, witch or fool, hers is a continuum made strange, actualised and enchanting, even if such enchantments are the effects – not of concrete manifestations, but – of acts of sympathetic magic. If her practice seems impossible, illogical, unthinkable, its fullness rests upon this condition. You can't force a story that doesn't want to be told.

5

The art of sabotage

Before fatigue brings boxers to the boiler room of the damned, they live at a height of consciousness and with a sense of detail they encounter nowhere else. In no other place is their intelligence so full, nor their sense of time able to contain so much of itself as in the long internal effort of the ring. (Norman Mailer, *The Fight*)

I do not refute ideals; all I do is draw on my gloves in their presence. (Friedrich Nietzsche, *Ecce Homo*)

Box they may, in the boiler room of the damned, but the Kipper Kids are not your average boxers. The performances of the Kipper Kids – Harry Kipper and Harry Kipper (aka Brian Routh and Martin von Haselberg) – entailed variations on a composed yet strategically chaotic series of actions or 'ceremonies'. They were prolific in the 1970s and then performed only sporadically from the mid-1980s until their last public performance in 2003. Often staged within a jerry-rigged boxing ring of wooden posts and creosote ropes, their skits included the 'food ceremony', a methodical, excessive, ritual food fight, inspired by their early interactions with Hermann Nitsch, the Vienna Actionist; a 'tea ceremony', which picked apart the social niceties of tea-drinking rituals, including disfigured English and Japanese versions; 'Westside Story', in which they circled each other, sliced polythene sacs of chocolate syrup attached to each other's jockstraps (using razor blades) and rubbed the faecal liquid into each other's buttocks, all the while singing *Diarrhea*, their rendition of *Maria* from the ceremony's namesake; the 'wank ceremony', in which they wore truck-sized inner tubes round their waists, individually buttered each other's thumbs and fingers with a knife, then mimicked mutual masturbation while leafing through a phone book; and a 'balloon ceremony', where they wore paint-filled balloons under their T-shirts and stabbed each other with broken Blue Nun bottles, glazing themselves in splatters of neon paint and cheap wine, held six more balloons between their splayed fingers and blew into them to activate toy squeakers with flatulent expulsions of air.

Their performances involved serial improvisations on the same array of rituals and shticks – a variation without singularity, comparable in principle to their friend Anne Bean's commitment to a continuum across works. As a rule, the performances were untitled and therefore resisted isolation from each other as distinct works (when pressed, the Kipper Kids used a variety of placeholder titles, including *Silly Ceremonies, Up Yer Bum with a Bengal Lancer* or *Your Turn to Roll It*, followed by an arbitrary number). Each event was a rehearsal of their signature anti-aesthetic sensibility, signalled by kooky costuming, barely sublimated violence, liberal dousings in food or paint and other imminent dangers for themselves and bystanders. Often, the opening skit would inaugurate the threat of risk as an emotional ground tone for the ensuing performance: one Kipper Kid would place an egg into a length of doubled elastic affixed to an overturned table, creating a treacherously powerful catapult that stretched over the heads of the screeching audience. After shouting 'All clear!' he would fire the egg across the space, with a large, comical explosion that splattered the audience, as well as the other Kipper Kid holding the table. Extensive photographs from the period document their consistent yet cumulative aesthetic, especially as it evolved in terms of their costumes, props and the content of their actions.

The 'food ceremony' was perhaps the central event of their performances (**Figure 5.1**). In what amounts to a closely paced, choreographed and chaotic food fight, the Kippers begin by wearing boards on cords around their necks, each to which a 12–pack of eggs is attached. In a final reprisal at the National Review of Live Art, Glasgow in 2003, they slapped eggs onto each other's swimming-cap-clad heads, while singing non sequiturs in a campy music hall vein: 'Nice people, with nice manners, who've got no money at all, *ee-oh-ee-oh, prrrp!*' Messy actions follow in quick succession, both men wittering cute nonsense. Huge bags of flour are dumped over each other's slimy heads, followed by lashings of India ink that drip down their chests and backs. Pulling aside their own jockstraps, they colour their ballsacks blue with spray paint. They cover each other with industrial-sized cans of tinned spaghetti and tomato sauce, mushy peas and dustbins full of cranberry jelly, followed by four buckets of paint that create fluorescent deluges. They fill each other's jockstraps with dried herbs and cover each other's wet bodies with Bombay mix, spray-paint their own armpits as though using deodorants and coat each other with glitter. Throughout, they sing Flanagan and Allen's *Home Town* (1945) in an interpretation frothy with sibilants and breathy intonations. Finally, their make a cone of shaving cream on each other's heads, insert firecrackers, then light them, creating foamy explosions of surprising intensity.[1]

In the 1970s, particularly, the Kipper Kids became notorious for their extremity – that is, for the sprawling danger, drunkenness, unpredictability and baffled hilarity of their performances. From 1972 until the beginning of the 1980s, these performances

---

1 The Kipper Kids, *Your Turn to Roll It #54*, documentation of performance (38 mins), *National Review of Live Art*, 2003. A001255 National Review of Live Art Video Archive, Theatre Collection, University of Bristol.

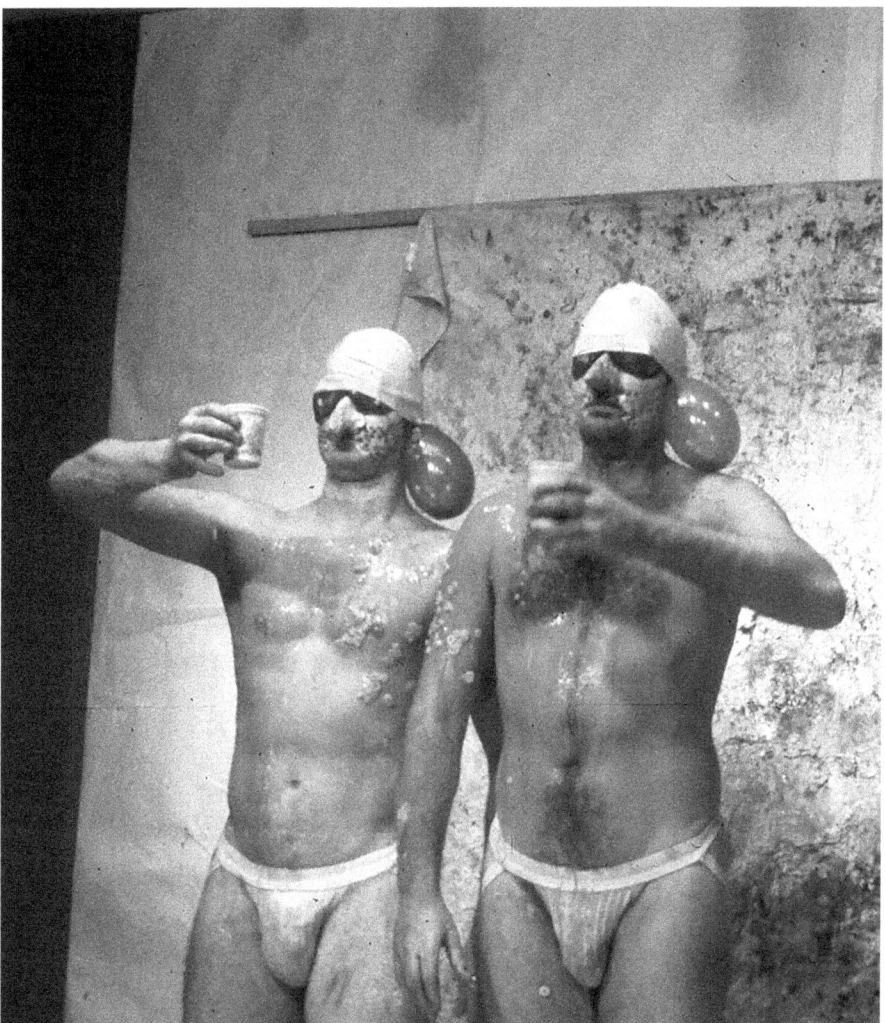

5.1 The Kipper Kids, untitled performance, Vanguard Gallery, Los Angeles, 1978

concluded more or less consistently with the aesthetic spectacle of the 'boxing ceremony'. The ceremony was never faked but, rather, involved a visceral and sustained event of self-boxing and inevitable bleeding from the pulverised nose of Harry Kipper (usually Routh). Routh remembers the action as a 'masochistic ritual' and always a kind of purgation, 'as if I had confessed and gotten something off my chest after I beat myself up', he recalled to Linda Montano (2000: 433).

A series of punches to the face may be a dreadful, painful sight to behold (in some settings, it may also or instead be thrilling). In the moment human meat connects heavily with itself, the puncher and the punched – and in a different manner, the viewing body – are suddenly, violently intimate with what the novelist and boxing connoisseur Norman Mailer calls 'the aesthetic juice of the punches', a libidinal 'juice' extracted from the raw material of the human form under duress (2000: 8) – even if or especially when the fight is mounted in the space of performance. For Amelia Jones, the material reality of the boxer in performance art provokes a sympathetic corporeal relation in the audience: 'We identify with the laboring body, experiencing the fatigue in our own bodies as well: the standing, the listening, the projective co-embodiment are exhausting' (Jones 2015b: 19). As boxers, the Kipper Kids are exhausted, exhaustive and – perhaps distinctively among artist-boxers – wilfully ridiculous. The apparent violence performed by either Kipper Kid is fundamentally self-directed (even when directed to his partner, who is a mirror of himself), returning us to the persistent fact of their attraction to sabotage, as a theme of their performances and an illimitable truth of their working lives.

In the boxing ceremony, Harry Kipper always fights himself (**Figure 5.2**). The other Harry Kipper officiates in the match: he eggs his doppelgänger on to greater feats of slapstick violence and at the same time protects him, as a lunatic referee-cum-coach. The fighting Kipper fights the good fight, subject to the rules of boxing (sort of) and to Mailer's higher 'cosmic laws of violence', to which all human animals are seemingly subjected (2000: 26). A fragment of video from an untitled performance-for-camera by the Kipper Kids (staged in Paris in 1973 without an audience and recorded by Jack Moore's Videoheads) shows a formidable act of self-boxing. The performance arena consists of a ramshackle boxing ring in the centre of the space, constructed from a large raised rostrum bound by creosote-soaked ropes strung around four posts at the corners. The ropes and floor are festooned with discarded clothing, indistinguishable scraps and 'end rolls' of unprinted newspaper, each used in earlier ceremonies. By this late point in the drunken proceedings, after an hour of mangled songs, drumming interludes, five-finger exercises, sausage-eating contests and beer sculling, their makeup is nearly rubbed off and their food-slathered, piss-drenched Boy Scout uniforms are lost in the debris.

The energy is nervous, escalated and explosive. The potential is violent. Harry Kipper (von Haselberg) officiates, entirely nude except for space-age-looking sunglasses, bovver boots and a cloth bonnet. In the 'pink corner', Harry Kipper (Routh) shadowboxes, wearing a robe and small, old-fashioned leather boxing gloves. Harry Kipper proceeds to punch himself solidly and repetitively in the chest, stomach, face and neck, in combinations of two punches, three – each landing squarely and noisily upon his own robust flesh, prompting little bursts of air to exit his body in clearly audible grunts and groans. He skips to his own beat, keeping the energy pumping. After a minute or so, Harry is down. The count begins. Harry is up at the count of eight. Circular jabs, crosses and lobs recommence. The other Harry Kipper (von Haselberg) rings out the beginnings and ends of rounds on a tin bell and massages and waters his pugilist friend. They pause for a quick bottle of beer each and exchange sweetly brutish words of encouragement and consolation. They return to their roles, as loutish brawler and senseless, harrying adjudicator. Exhaustion and bleeding ensue. When the end is nigh, eight minutes into the fight, the fighter falls forward for the final time, faceplanting into the copious rolls of paper. The makeshift bell peals and Harry Kipper holds up the arm of Harry Kipper, as he would henceforth, again and again, in

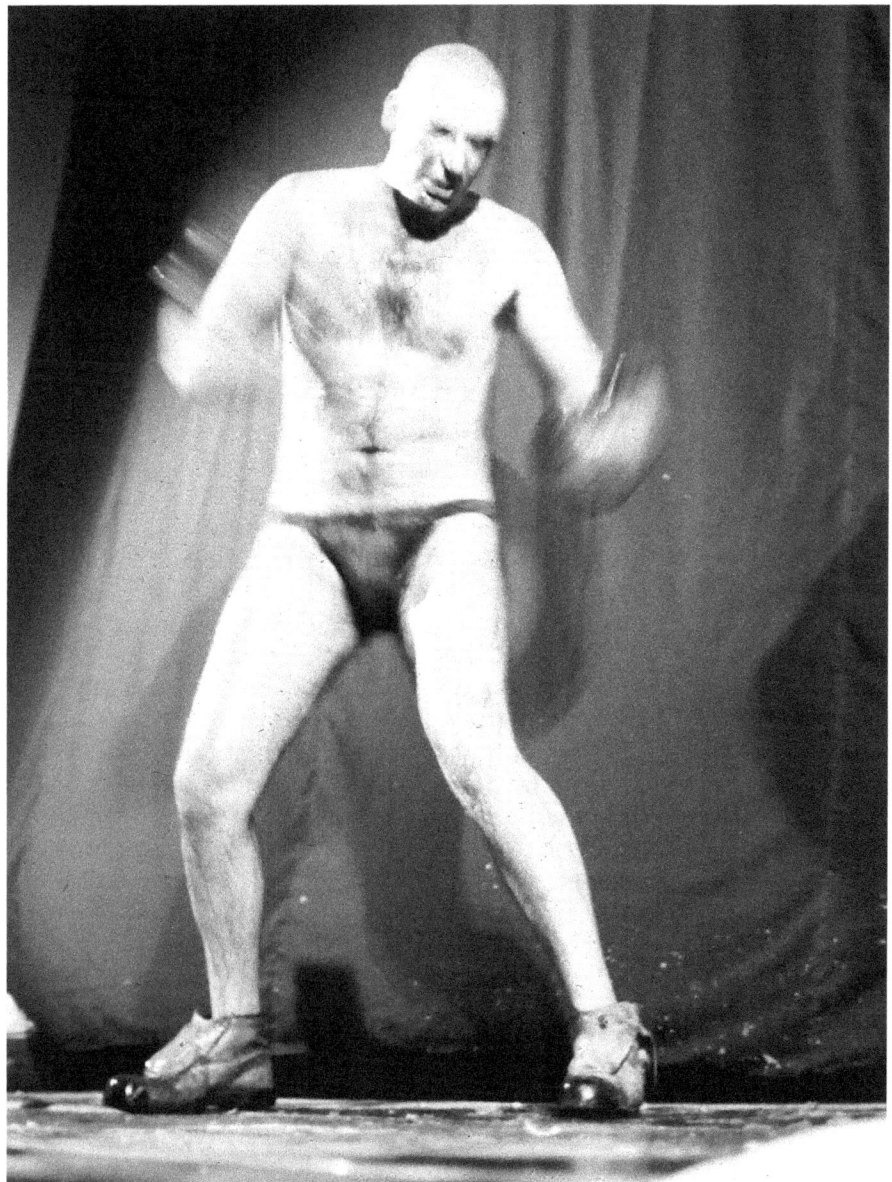

5.2 The Kipper Kids, untitled performance, Saletta Gramsci, Pistoia, Italy, 1980

violent, intimate, thrilling, baffling performances, almost the world over, for a decade to come. We have a winner, a new champion of insane extremity. Bloodied and dazed, it's Harry Kipper. The audience is inflamed. The performance is complete.

Tonight, in Paris, like every night, Harry Kipper has won and Harry Kipper has defeated himself. In its extremity and in their endurance, the culmination to the performance depicts a subject 'at a height of consciousness' – as becomes the boxer in Mailer's account of the 'internal effort' of a knockout fight – and as, too, it befits his idealised imagining of the artist at work. Yet such heights here are pathological, perverse, ecstatic and masochistic, submerged in what Mark Fisher describes as sport's 'purgatorial rhythms' (2014: 86). It is a pyrrhic victory, the kind of victory one can hardly bear to repeat. It is an act of sabotage.

Sabotage

Sabotage is a crucial element in the performances of the Kipper Kids. It also plays out in their pursuit of careers as artists. That is to say, in performance, especially in their physical relationships to audiences and outside of performance, including in its aftermaths or in dealings with curators, critics and others, the Kipper Kids were infamous, unpredictable and wild. They garnered infamy for the aggression, excessiveness and vigour with which they pursued their artistic goals and thus made their own situation more difficult, derailing their performances and their livelihoods through drunkenness, violence or other techniques of abandon (**Figure 5.3**). For example, touring with Anne Bean and the Kipper Kids in 1972, Cosey Fanni Tutti recalls the 'insanely wonderful' Kipper Kids arriving fully costumed at the ferry that would transport them to Belgium for a festival. She narrates that the duo proceeded to create drunken 'mayhem' throughout the journey, prompting a 'momentous ferry ride of wet-knickers laughter' – that is, their antics commenced well before and far outside the limits of any scheduled performance (2017: 127). Regardless of their apparent desires or aspirations – including to pull off a good show and, even, to *make it* as artists – as Routh phrased it, 'Harry Kipper would come along and just completely trash everything' (Johnson 2015: 74). Cases in point include their famously overzealous interactions with a museum audience in Basel in 1973, where, faced with well-turned-out gala punters dressed in suits and fine furs, the Kipper Kids altered their usual 'food ceremony', in which they flung bags of flour, fluorescent paint, sloppy foodstuffs and indelible ink over each other; in the heat of the moment, they pelted their upper crust audience with these noxious substances.

Such mishaps were regular occurrences. 'One time in Los Angeles' (at Los Angeles Contemporary Exhibitions in 1980), von Haselberg tells me, 'we threw ink into the audience, and I got sued by seven different people.' As a result of their excesses, he adds, '[w]ith each performance our potential options for venues was always shrinking' (Johnson 2015: 87). Other anecdotes tell of the pair punching a curator, disgracing themselves in another's home, throwing drinks or food on museum benefactors and terrorising a nonplussed William S. Burroughs for misjudged laughs; all such excitable drunken fiascos existed beyond or outside their performance work, yet were inextricably linked to their performances' internal condition of mayhem and to their reputations as artists. Sabotaging their own work, they often tended to sabotage their career prospects, as though their pursuit of an

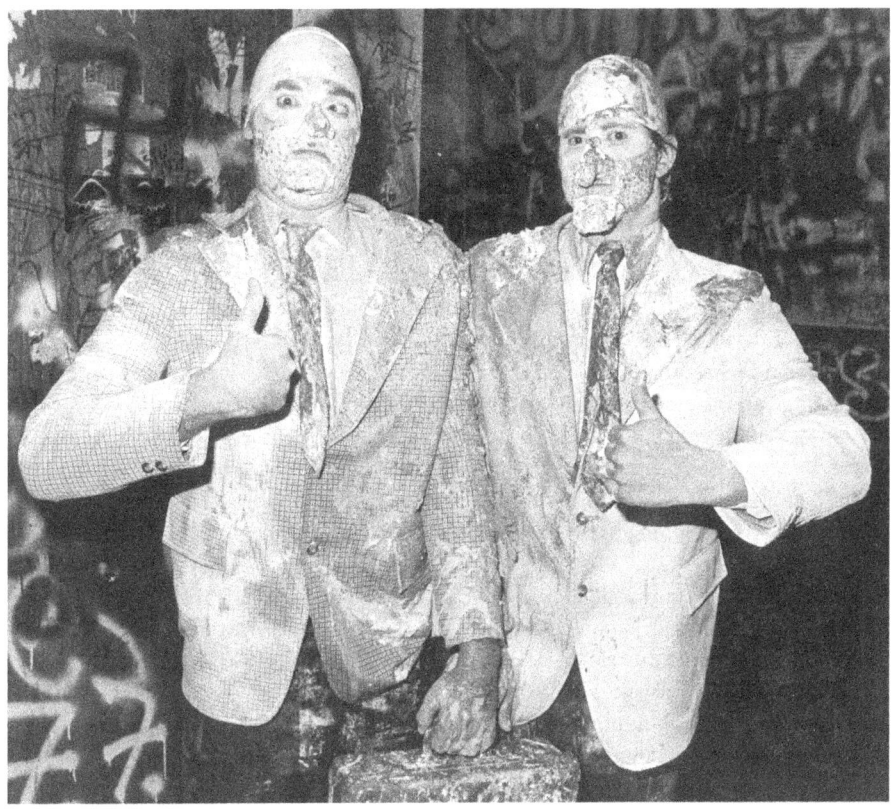

5.3 The Kipper Kids, untitled performance, Whisky a Go Go, Los Angeles, 1978

alternative aesthetics – the *anti-aesthetic* sensibility – also required or provoked a kind of drawn-out professional suicide that extended well beyond the performances proper, to their shared persona's sprawling function in their raucous lives. The long-term effects of such incorrigibility are tangible for the Kipper Kids: both retreated from performance art, had tortured relations to the market and museum culture and tended to be estranged personally from one another until shortly before Routh's untimely death from cancer in August 2018.

In the influential book *Images of Deviance*, sociologists Laurie Taylor and Paul Walton define sabotage as 'that rule-breaking which takes the form of conscious action or inaction directed towards the mutilation or destruction of [a particular] environment' (1971: 219). Concerned specifically with industrial sabotage as a form of social deviance, their essay recounts documented instances of the wilful impairment of the work environment: a shop assistant who jams her till to save a few minutes of rest from ringing up items (apparent 'breakdowns' as desperate 'break-times') or a sweet factory worker who retools the machinery in order to create Blackpool rock with the words 'Fuck Off' running through it; they study these and other ploys not for the criminal status of the workers' *perruques* and incitements but for 'the *meanings* or *motives* which lie behind such actions' (1971: 219–21, emphasis in original). Taylor and Walton set aside the *nature* of the interruptive action or inaction to theorise the way acts of sabotage take up a semiotic function: acts of sabotage are not merely irrational, malicious or a symptom of rage but plausible 'attempts to reduce tension and frustration', 'eas[e] the work process' or 'assert control' (1971: 220). Sabotage may thus be 'the contemporary example of neglected "grassroots" action' in causing the powers-that-be temporarily to lose face and hence 'a legitimate weapon [for] class struggle' (1971: 222, 238).

Outside the sociology of deviance, sabotage is a principle for a further range of popular and academic areas of thought, from self-help books that seek to resolve the problem of psychic self-sabotage to political theory and military history. For example, the political technique of the filibusterer follows the letter if not the spirit of the law, to sabotage an opponent's ability to produce a particular result, suggesting that sabotage may sometimes be formally conventional, even an elite strategy. Yet, in times of war, sabotage takes place as popular or guerrilla resistance (though such activity may also be engineered by military strategists to fuel insurgent activities behind enemy lines). The word *sabotage* evokes etymologically the *guerrillismo*, 'grassroots' aspect identified by Taylor and Walton. Its root resembles (but may not derive from) the French word *sabot*, a wooden shoe or clog: apocryphally, in the nineteenth century, disgruntled factory workers would fling their wooden clogs into working machinery, as a literal form of industrial action, to stymie the operation of their own collective labour. In the internet age, sabotage takes new forms that are both diffuse and epic, including hacktivism, adbusting and culture-jamming, all of which seek to deploy technology, on- or off-line, to disrupt, recast and *détourne* – indeed, to *clog* – a larger, often corporate strategy.

However, or in addition, Taylor and Walton note that sabotage is not exclusively a sober or hostile endeavour: '[m]any acts which are informed by a desire to reduce frustration in a situation where the saboteur is relatively powerless', they argue, 'are also devised to produce . . . a general chaos, often accompanied by merriment' – that is, sabotage can be 'fun', a 'gleeful release of tension' (1971: 230–1). While they caution against reading acts outside the workplace as sabotage – as they may more likely resemble vandalism (1971: 238) – the sociological account usefully sets up the project of sabotage in the work of the Kipper Kids. *Work* here is an operative term, reminding us that the practice of art – however madcap, uncontained and unproductive – is a form of affective, immaterial and frequently under-recompensed labour. As the Kipper Kids' anecdotes indicate, the labour of artistic production is frequently undertaken or presented in institutions structured by imbalances of agency or self-determination and of economic, social and cultural capital. The act of artistic sabotage is therefore freighted with particularly salient motives and meanings. Taylor and Walton note that the meaningfulness of sabotage had been ignored by earlier sociologists, because the acts were dismissed as irrational or misguided, or the saboteur's motives were explained away as the uncontrolled effects of being 'drunk', 'overcome' by feeling or 'temporarily incapacitated' by madness, hate or rage (1971: 224). Similarly, it would be convenient to disregard the Kipper Kids' disposition towards self-sabotage not as active and productive but as mere short-sightedness, the upshot of youthful mischief, punk rock radicalism, drink, personality disorders or poor career management. While some of these characteristics are in arguable operation, I follow Taylor and Walton's definition and approach to maintain that the Kipper Kids' early performances and films use sabotage as an elaboration of the anti-aesthetic sensibility – a strategic rethinking (even if partly unconscious) of the form and function of art and performance.

The creative signs of sabotage have occurred in the previous chapters – latently or with too much licence – as in, perhaps: Kerry Trengove's concerted attack on the sustaining institution of art; Ulay's literal invasion of, and criminal action against, the spectre of his own national identity; COUM Transmissions' relishing of their own incorrigibility and unacceptability as artists, come what may, and the legal repercussions; or, perhaps, Anne Bean's refusal to document, disseminate or iconicise her actions, so as to become a person without station, a non-person of distinction. By thinking critically about the performance art of the Kipper Kids, I attempt to sustain the importance of sabotage – as the strategic refusal or repudiation of traditional aesthetics, as well as a subterranean aesthetic in its own right – in the performance of extremity in the 1970s. At the same time, as a historian of excessive or transgressive acts, I hope to remain sensitised to whether (or not) by celebrating marginality, we confer it upon or claim it for our objects of study, particularly or additionally when summoning a theme as tendentious as (self-) sabotage. By celebrating artists or works of art as minor, resistant, self-destructive or irrevocably different, perhaps we keep them at bay, secure and inviolate in their cultural unavailability. If so, the latter is a tacit project of camouflaging a practice of art within the thickets of language, perhaps turning the forgotten, the dead, the impoverished or the strange into totems with which we do our theoretical or political bidding.

Sabotage – and specifically self-sabotage – is a marginal or covert theme for critical thinking about art and performance. The artist Jeff Nuttall mentions the term in a pioneering diagnosis of the breadth of performance art typologies in Britain in the 1970s. Writing in 1973, he states that two of the categories – 'other crusaders' of the 'blow-your-bone underground', such as Genesis P-Orridge, Carlyle Reedy, David Medalla or Stuart Brisley; or the wacky or wild 'comedy-trad-band' artists, such as Bruce Lacey, the Bonzo Dog Doo-Dah Band and Nuttall himself – are deliberately 'not pure artists' and 'not theatre at all', but rather 'seek to use the collective situation as a means to cultural sabotage' (Nuttall 2012: 177). The Kipper Kids would fit, cumbersome but happy, across these comic-anarchic categories, suggesting a context for their emergence and a means to consider their inheritances, lateral resonances and legacies. Moreover, the function of sabotage is secured as a contingent strategy for artists who found peers with whom to associate or collaborate, but who, nevertheless, could not make themselves fit into a designated form, field or sector.

Sabotage as an artistic strategy has been more robustly analysed in literary theory. The experimental writer Alain Robbe-Grillet discusses creative sabotage in a short essay of 1954 in his classic treatise *For a New Novel*, during a discussion of the writer Robert Pinget, who sought to write a book that was deliberately (in Pinget's words) 'spoiled in its broad outlines' (Robbe-Grillet 1970: 127). Robbe-Grillet notes that this takes shape though 'contradictions, variants, and dangerous leaps resulting

. . . in fantastic reversals – at least the *movement* which, if it is sometimes difficult to grasp amid this permanent sabotage, is never, ultimately, either foolhardy or conventional' (1970: 127–8, emphasis in original). Other characteristics of 'permanent sabotage' are telling. Deliberate spoliations of one's own art resemble or create 'confused' and 'ineffable impressions'; they are ciphers of 'a process without purpose' (1970: 128). The work 'can only turn in circles, unless it stops short, unashamedly turning back on itself; still elsewhere it branches off, divides into two or more parallel series which immediately react on each other, destroy each other, or unite in an unexpected synthesis' (*ibid.*), suggesting images of splitting and merging, combat and combination, which are particularly redolent for the serial, compulsively repetitive, strategically inept and recklessly auto-destructive performances of the Kipper Kids.

Self-sabotage is the turning of sabotage's directionality of effects against one's own person as a condition of one's personal, professional, creative or relational spheres of influence. It has a Romantic allure about its suggestion of an extreme wantonness of spirit and symbolises a kind of reckless enthusiasm typified by the potlatch. As William Burroughs describes it, the historical Native American practice of potlatch incurred 'a competitive destruction of [one's own] property carried out until one contestant was ruined and frequently died of shame on the spot'; for the Beat novelist this represents a 'magical' function to which the avant-garde sought to return (Burroughs 1993: 62–3). Indeed, the risks of creative sabotage are ambivalent, Robbe-Grillet writes, as they can be celebrated as those of 'a scrupulous experimenter in his laboratory' or, less sympathetically, as the aberrations of 'a visionary abusing his drugs' (Robbe-Grillet 1970: 130). The Marquis de Sade, one such visionary and an explorer of extreme human depths, also expounded a literary urge to self-sabotage, not as a theoretical mission but as a project of historical self-erasure: 'Once covered over, [my] grave will be sown with acorns so that eventually', he writes, 'the traces of my tomb will disappear from the face of the earth, and I flatter myself that my memory will be erased from the minds of men' (de Beauvoir 2012: 44). De Sade's dream of his material erasure after death (though, for such an exhibitionist, however cynical) follows suit from actively self-soiling his own character and respectability, as a writer of the most unregenerate depths of depravity. Sabotage is particularly tuned to the needs and actions of the marginal subject. Writing from prison, Antonio Gramsci explained the necessarily self-defeating practices of the subaltern classes via the 'fable of the beaver', an analogy for pyrrhic strategies against the oppressive power of state force and engineered consent: 'The beaver, pursued by trappers who want his testicles from which medicinal drugs can be extracted, to save his life tears off his own testicles' (Gramsci 2012: 223). As Burroughs, de Sade or Gramsci variously suggest, sabotage may produce operative effects but it does not always secure happy subjectivities, healthy bodies or polite social relations.

As an artistic technique, form or effect, sabotage may be counterintuitive as well as insurrectionary. It can be active or passive, violent or obscurely subdued. In a provocative example of a profoundly self-sabotaging conceptual art work, in which an artist directs harm towards their own person – or profile – through a kind of radical passive resistance, Lee Lozano undertook an endurance art action known as *Dropout*

Piece (1970), which she continued until her death in 1999. While the Kipper Kids' works retain and fetishise a sense of the silly, the joke, the prank or lark, epitomising the 'gleeful' dimension of some practices of industrial sabotage, Lozano's late pieces leave little space for fun: they are deadly serious, decidedly drastic. In *Dropout Piece*, a relentlessly transparent act of (industrial) sabotage, Lozano dropped out of the art world, discontinuing professional relationships, gallery representation, friendships and related communications, recasting the cumulative procedure as a work of art. Noting the political force of Lozano's project, Sarah Lehrer-Graiwer calls the piece a 'declaration of willed marginality' and 'critical defection', though one with disastrous results in terms of her social existence and any prospective professional security (Lehrer-Graiwer 2014: 13). Its partner action, *Boycott Piece* (1971) was just as extreme and no doubt more psychically self-lacerating: Lozano boycotted her own gender, refusing to converse or interact with other women for an unspecified period (though likely until her death). Lehrer-Graiwer tracks the development of Lozano's increasing frustration with the art world, her disinterest in accruing a profile or fame and her refusal to make saleable work 'for an anonymous, abstract art world' (2014: 75). *Dropout Piece* and *Boycott Piece* enabled Lozano to apply a form to life and to remake performance as (after Anne Bean) a Life Art enterprise – with dizzying, depressing or terrifying effects on the life of the artist.

As practices of withdrawal, Lozano's actions are exemplary acts of sabotage, interrupting and violating the sustaining institutions and agents of art, paradoxically both *as* and *against* art or performance. Her performances constitute a move that is profoundly against art and artists, against visual culture and thus against dominant conceptions of the aesthetic, providing a redolent context for the very different assaults orchestrated by the Kipper Kids. Thomas Crow describes this crisis in meaning as 'a drama of lives driven onto treacherous emotional shoals', adding (with reference to Bas Jan Ader and Christopher D'Arcangelo) that '[t]his move carries some risk in a postmodern intellectual culture imbued with suspicion of all reference, especially to themes of self-sacrifice in biographies of artists' (Crow 1996: 238). In Lozano's limit-work – and, in different ways, the Kipper Kids' – the anti-aesthetic artist examines formally what happens when performance overwhelms the life from whence it springs – as potlatch, sacrifice or sabotage.

What, then, are the stakes of creative sabotage? How does it disclose a peculiar kind of extremity, precisely as a counterintuitive or self-defeating form of agency? In terms of its negative effect on posterity, sabotage adds nuance to the presumption of malign intent or ineptitude on the part of academics and curators, as the sole factor in securing an artist's acceptance or marginality. How might the saboteur (here, an artist rather than a novelist, guerrilla or beaver) make a claim upon the position she or he takes up in relation to history, institutions, archives, art or life? To consider these questions, I look to the performances of the Kipper Kids, both live and for video, to explore and theorise the specific sensibility they espouse in their on- and off-stage antics, supported by interviews with the artists and a critical engagement with the politics of extremity, of violence and of sabotage. In this chapter's close, the film *K. O. Kippers* (1988) narrates and metaphorises a provocative and uncontainable development of the anti-aesthetic in their signature performances of the 1970s – in their case, a highly idiosyncratic exploration of negative or déclassé affects and styles, including silliness, ugliness, masochism, narcissism, absurdity, futility and stupidity. At the same time, the film capitulates in formal terms to market incentives, as if the urge towards self-sabotage could be tamed by looking to bigger production values, larger networks of dissemination and greater audiences. The effect is irreconcilable and incorrigible. (May the light of burning bridges lead the way.)

Rise and fall

The Kipper Kids formed in 1971 after meeting the previous year at East 15 Acting School, a progressive theatre conservatoire in East London whose curriculum was based on Joan Littlewood's Theatre Workshop. The names Harry Kipper and Alf Kipper originally designated distinct variations on a character type they invented during an acid trip at Frankfurt railway station in 1970 (a technique far beyond the bounds of conservatoire teaching, even in Littlewood's dynamic shadow). They recall no sensible rationales for the adoption of the surname 'Kipper' – the word is a dated one, seemingly specific in both historical and national terms (it is a strong-smelling smoked herring, enjoyed in Britain since Victorian times and relished as the breakfast food of the war generation). It's a funny word, 'kipper': terribly ordinary for a *nom de guerre*, yet strangely obscure, deliberately uncool and altogether unglamorous. The Kipper Kids quickly dropped 'Alf'. In their frequently inebriated states, neither could remember who was who; they further synchronised their behaviours and mutually inhabited the extreme, shared persona of Harry Kipper (Johnson 2015: 66–7).

A shared 'look' – a closely crafted and sustained visual style of makeup, dress and comportment struck by an artist as the substance or supplement of one's practice – is essential to the Kipper Kids' aesthetic. Their signature costumes included Scouts uniforms and leather boots, boxing outfits or, luridly, jockstraps paired with over-sized white T-shirts stuffed at the front with four balloons stapled to a concealed board (giving a joke-store impression of two or more rows of breasts); and a range of headwear, including swimming caps, tin helmets, party hats and the aforementioned pyramids of shaving foam loaded with fireworks. In a profile for *Rolling Stone*, their look was described as that of 'a debauched Tweedledum and Tweedledee' immersed in a 'ritualistic gross-out' (McKenna 1981: 54); while a further critic embellished their appearance in lovingly accurate terms as 'stocky British louts of yore hired by the gentry to cudgel errant country taxpayers', with 'concave faces' resembling 'twin images of men on the moon' or 'safecrackers with three-day stubble on their stalk-like chins' (Christon 1988). Their facial features, naturally striking, are accentuated to cartoonlike proportions, with greasepaint makeup and homemade prosthetic noses and chins fashioned from latex, papier-mâché or mouldable metal. Routh's nose, slightly pointed in life, becomes a prosthetically pronounced spike; more rounded, von Haselberg's is transformed into a bulbous hook. The difference in prosthetic nose-shapes – a rare departure in their mutual styling – seems to compound the psychotic similarity of their actions, their method and their volatility. They would accent their grossly accentuated chins and noses with heavily painted, cartoonish features: purple-black eyes, broad-spotted stubble daubed on in dots and sometimes little Chaplin-esque toothbrush moustaches.[2]

The makeup was more or less consistent across their performances, though accentuated in anomalous ways in some instances; for example, in one extraordinary action, at University Art Museum, Berkeley in 1979, the Kipper Kids presented their usual sequence, yet inverted the colour scheme to present a kind of Kippers-in-the-negative: grey-black paint covered their faces and the fronts of their bodies, giving stylised counterpoint to their moulded metal noses and chins and metallic-painted eyebrows and stubble.[3] One was stippled and extended in gold, the other in silver; their faces afforded the impression of fearsome gilded ceremonial masks. The visual effect of their makeup stressed the effect of their shared persona, even when the typical shape of their 'look' was altered, exaggerated or inverted. In a review of the performance in Berkeley, published in *Artforum*, Mary Stofflet noted the productive confusions prompted by the eccentric chemistry of their look, language, props and actions: the Kipper Kids 'proceeded plotlessly, to transform themselves . . . and various objects', she writes, 'into agents and implements for simple deeds performed in the most unnecessarily convoluted manner imaginable', with an effect of reading and meaning that was centrally 'uneasy' for the reviewer (Stofflet 1980: 103).

Across the Kipper Kids' repertoire, their shared demeanour involves a lumbering, dumbfounded physicality, from their ambling movement – what they call 'walking the wire' – to pointed gestures of the face and fingers. Dazed-looking and cross-eyed, with a gurning facial expression and jutting, prognathous jaw, they present as at once both baffled and mischievous. Their vocal style is comedic and aphasic, part Monty Python, part *Goon Show* – their singing often resembles the oddities of voice and content in the Goons' garbled, nonsensical *Ying Tong Song* (1956), for example. Harry Kipper speaks in a peculiar, self-invented idiolect, which is at times incomprehensible or otherwise consists of one-liners and inane chatter, interrupted by guffaws, squeaks, fart sounds, grunts, burps and parps and other phonetic oddities. Their speech suggests an autistic lingua – the language of children raised (not by wolves, but) by kippers.

From 1971 to 1974, the Kipper Kids presented performances in Britain (where they were based) and in Europe, appearing at universities, arts centres and theatres – and, disturbingly, as part of the cultural events programmed at the Summer Olympics in Munich in 1972, the occasion of the Munich massacre where 11 athletes and a policeman were assassinated by the terrorist organisation Black September.

---

2 Routh remembers the shared 'look' emerging from his own cartoons (Johnson 2015: 69). Von Haselberg challenges this account: 'Brian claims the character was based on cartoons he had been drawing. That may be true for him, but not for me. It wasn't until quite some time after we started doing the Kipper Kids, that I ever saw him draw cartoons and those were based on both of us, he with the straight nose, me with the hook' (email to the author, 20 October 2015).

3 A video of the performance (cut with a post-show interview conducted in the showers) was produced by David A. Ross for the series *New California Video* (1978); see Pacific Film Archive Audio Recordings, University of California, Berkeley: https://archive.org/details/cbpf_000045 (accessed 19 April 2016).

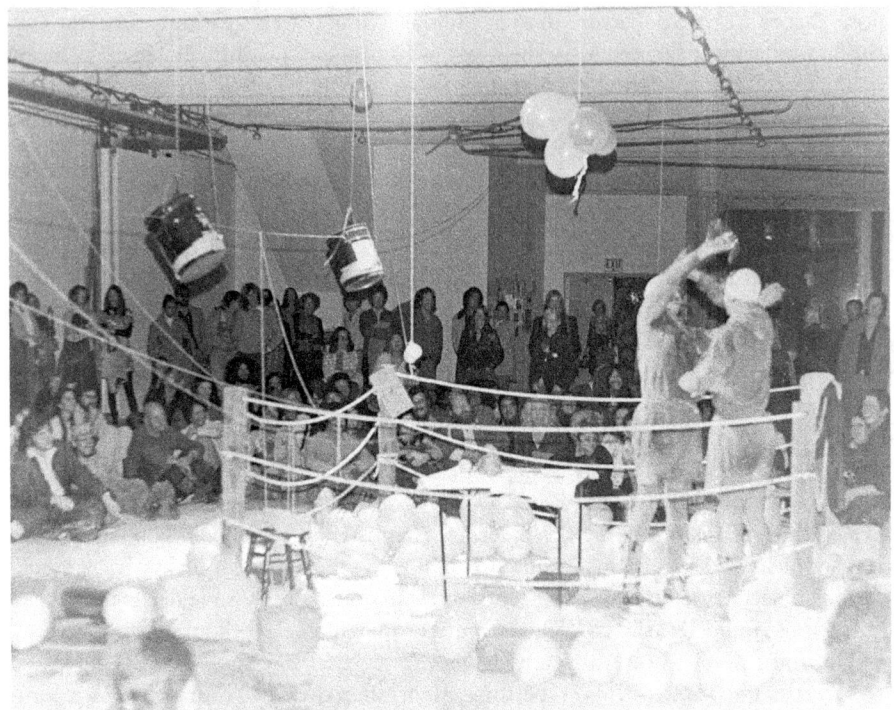

5.4 The Kipper Kids, untitled performance, Los Angeles Institute of Contemporary Art (LAICA), Los Angeles, 1974

The Kipper Kids emigrated to Los Angeles in 1974, on the casual advice of museum curator David A. Ross, who saw their performance at the Rudolf Zwirner Gallery in Cologne in 1973 and organised a number of events for the duo in California, beginning with a performance at Los Angeles Institute of Contemporary Art (LAICA) on 15 December 1974 (**Figure 5.4**). Their idiosyncratic performances – particularly in the 1970s – made a powerful impression on art-gallery visitors, as well as more diverse audiences drawn from punk and other subcultural milieus (for example as a warm-up for the Sex Pistols, Public Image Ltd and Henry Rollins), both in Europe and the USA.

For all their visceral excess, apparent puerility and jeering nonsensicality, the Kipper Kids were disarmingly savvy in their critical gestures. They understand violence, its degrees and intensities and how it can erupt from nowhere, from fun or from overexcitement, as men and children well know. In their ceremonies, the Kipper Kids pantomime the way civility is often performed grudgingly to avoid but also to sublimate interpersonal hostility, aggression, desire and hate. At other times they are simply sweet, but in a way that is cloying and which often flips into a relation that seems weird, toxic or scary. For art critic Peter Clothier, their work suggests a critically 'lunatic' refusal of normative social relations, emotional displays and aesthetic conventions. Of the performance at LAICA in 1974, he writes:

Each [ceremony] . . . is a ritual which becomes the occasion for fetishism, obscenity, and a series of sounds and gestures ranging from the low- to the clearly sub-human: burping, gobbling, squealing and squawking, poking, pulling, pinching, goosing, and so on. In short, a Freudian nightmare-comedy of oral and anal obsession. (1980: 165)

Curator Jay Sanders confirms this latter sentiment in gendered terms, arguing that in a performance by the Kipper Kids, 'the psycho-dramatic character of the hysterical male impulse was given free rein to wreak havoc on the proceedings, as the "comedy duo" form plunged off the deep end' (Sanders 2013: 32).

Von Haselberg reflects on their early intensity as a kind of 'synthesis' of being, bordering on the frightening intensity of feeling 'possessed' by Harry Kipper.[4] Their mutual character or shared persona was not simply an affectation devised for the stage, but, rather, became all-encompassing, both in their increasingly raucous performances and, by extension, in their shared daily lives. Of their linguistic and charismatic evolution, Routh remembers, prior to the first performances, '[w]e would be Kipper Kids in the street, in the pub and at parties. *We couldn't turn it off.* We tried to get away from one another . . . but as the Kipper Kids we were enmeshed. After that, we started thinking about putting it in some sort of theatrical context' (Johnson 2015: 67, emphasis in original).

As art doppelgängers, Gilbert and George's first live performance at the Nigel Greenwood Gallery in London in 1970 was particularly inspiring (Routh and von Haselberg were in attendance). The performance, *Underneath the Arches/Singing Sculptures* (1970) consists of the two artists dressed alike in suits, with metallic painted faces, singing a music hall song (by Flanagan and Allen) in a stylised manner. Notably, Gilbert and George are a significant example of a pair of artists who share an identity as a facet of their artistic practice and may have provided the Kipper Kids with an incentive to appropriate daily or pedestrian activities as the substance of performance. By co-creating artistic identities as the substance of their work, Andrew Wilson writes, 'the distance between creator and created was not just reduced but destroyed', a reading true to Gilbert and George as much as to the Kipper Kids (1993: 21). Moreover, as Charles Green writes of Gilbert and George, the doppelgänger suggests a deconditioned 'free subject' that is enabled 'precisely because of the teams' escape as individual "artists" from their personal bodies into the realm of uncanny phantoms', suggesting that the Kipper Kids may also be seen to enact a 'flight outside the prison-house of language' (Green 2000: 45). In what might function as a joke at the expense of Gilbert and George – perhaps prompted by a rebuff by the latter (Johnson 2015: 84) – the Kipper Kids would often sing their own versions of Flanagan and Allen tunes, including *Home Town* and – significantly – *Underneath the Arches*. Trolling the older artists, the Kipper Kids would sign the visitor books of exhibitions at the Acme Gallery as 'Gilbert and George' (the books are held in Acme's archives).

---

4 Anne Bean, the Kipper Kids and Nikki Milican, 'Meet the Artists', unpublished presentation, *National Review of Live Art*, 2003. A002555 National Review of Live Art Video Archive, Theatre Collection, University of Bristol.

Animal House for the intelligentsia

Critical responses to the Kipper Kids published in the 1970s provide detailed insights into their conflicted appeal for audiences and the latter's attempts to find a critical vantage point from which to size up the aesthetic effects of the work, which tended to leave them baffled, surprised or provoked. For example, a flurry of criticism was published in newspapers in response to a performance of the Kipper Kids' *Your Turn to Roll It, #56* at Los Angeles Contemporary Exhibitions (LACE) (4 October 1980), as part of *Public Spirit: Live Art LA* (introduced in Chapter 4). For example, Kristine McKenna's sympathetic review – accompanied by a photograph of the Kipper Kids by John Duncan – lauded the Kipper Kids' performance as '[t]he blockbuster event of [*Public Spirit's*] third quarter' (McKenna 1980: 142). Another critic, Tricia Crane described the performance in some detail: they began, she writes, 'by blasting their way through the windows of the downtown gallery, providing a jagged entrance from the fire escape over Broadway to the gallery-theater' (1980: 143). Describing their subsequent antics, including a number of songs – for example, their insanely unsexy version of *California Girls* (1965) by the Beach Boys – McKenna notes, '[i]t's basically *Animal House* for the intelligentsia' – referring to National Lampoon's anarchic gross-out frat-house farce *Animal House* (dir. by John Landis, 1978), a highly popular movie of the 1970s – 'and it was smirkful to see that well-heeled horde get a bit more than it bargained for' (*ibid.*). Of the material effects of their intensity, she notes, '[t]he Kipper Kids' shtick hasn't really changed much in five years, so the 550 fans who turned out (at five bucks a head) knew things were apt to get a bit messy. However, they did not expect to be thoroughly doused in flour and indelible ink' (*ibid.*).

If the Kipper Kids themselves avoid explaining the specific objects of their aggression – be they institutions of art, other artists or the art market – the art world and its audiences are, McKenna suggests, at least tacit targets of their saboteurial ire. At LACE, the Kipper Kids' messy antics included the creation of noxious clouds of chilli powder and flinging cans of SpaghettiOs, paper cups of paint and India ink and bags of flour onto each other, as well as into the audience (some of whom wisely wore protective raincoats). Of those who were ill prepared for such an onslaught, she reports,

> LACE subsequently was inundated with angry phone calls and cleaning bills, causing Harry Kipper [von Haselberg] to comment: 'People who know anything about us should have come a bit more prepared. Still, I think their anger is entirely justified. I thought it was a horrible thing for us to do. Whenever we throw things on the audience, I always feel a bit badly about it afterwards, but in the heat of the moment it always seems like the right thing to do.' Contrary to the complaints, one gets the feeling that the Kipper Kids' audience, like children in a funhouse, would feel cheated if they weren't somehow violated by these art-world bogeymen. (*ibid.*)

McKenna concludes that the Kipper Kids typified the *Public Spirit* programme's '"run-it-up-the-flagpole-and-see-if-anyone-salutes" spirit of surprise', which she deems charming and of 'vital brilliance'. Yet she also notes the hoodwinking potential of this sensibility, namely the generic risk of performance art as a holdout or haven for 'unfunny comedians, unskilled musicians and actors lacking any knowledge of theatre all copping the "I-don't-really-need-to-be-able-to-play-drums – this-isn't-music-it's-performance-art" escape clause' (*ibid.*). She thus puts the proverbial cat among the pigeons in terms of the possibility of failure and disappointment – and the threat of charlatanism or pretension – which may attend the vicarious thrill of artistic de-skilling, avant-garde disruption and aesthetic extremity.

Another critic, Hunter Drohojowska enacted this latter suspicion more emphatically and less self-reflexively, as if to stage a perceived silliness or pointlessness at the heart of the performance of extremity itself. In the *LA Weekly*, she claims the 'shocking' nature of performance art *tout court*, presenting an overview of the history of the form, beginning with Dada, followed by attempts to demonstrate the excesses of performance at *Public Spirit*, via epigrammatic descriptions of specific works by Terry Wolverton, Rachel Rosenthal, Chris Burden, the Kipper Kids and others. She writes, '[a]fter tossing bunches of uncooked wienies [miniature frankfurters] at the audience, Johanna Went threw herself in a pool of blood on the floor, howling' (Drohojowska 1980: 144). The overriding impression of performance art given in her article is one of ostentation as well as vacuity: 'Barbara Smith spent the evening in a coffin' (*ibid.*) and '[Richard] Newton was sitting on a bed of peanut butter sandwiches. He was drinking Pernod' (1980: 146). Of course, by removing details about the setting or the performed interactions, perhaps any performance can be made to sound pretentious or precocious through distilled images given in this style.

Drohojowska describes the Kipper Kids' *Your Turn to Roll It #56* as 'performance art as vaudeville', but seems to mean this ungenerously, as she concludes, '[i]t's not that they're bad artists, it's just that, personally, I'd rather stay home to watch the Three Stooges' (1980: 146). The gesture is candid and inoffensive, but her opinion stages an interesting category problem in the perception of the Kipper Kids, namely their intersectional relation to performance art (with which they do not fully identify), as well as with comedy, music, vaudeville or music hall, prompted arguably by the unprecedented interplay between madcap antics and pointless violence. More recently von Haselberg explained, 'I do think we liked the idea of being more entertaining than other performance artists, especially those we subsequently saw, whose work we didn't tend to find entertaining at all. We certainly didn't want to be *cerebral*' (Johnson 2015: 79, emphasis in original). The combination of entertainment and shock as functional values in the development of their performances is doubly disquieting for traditional aesthetics, laying a particular seed for the political efficacy and affective pungency of their anti-aesthetic. The latter is dialectical in nature, rooted in the historical and cultural situations of its emergence; more robustly, the refusal of aesthetic convention is tied up with a practical embrace, of or muddling with, déclassé cultural traditions and histories, especially those of song, music hall and comedy.

Here, as elsewhere in the style of their 'ceremonies' and their conflations of kookiness and violence, it is difficult to separate out the form and content of the Kipper Kids' performances from those of then-contemporary or near-historical traditions of comedy: music hall speciality acts, like the bottom-of-the-bill vaudevillian who plays

Ride of the Valkyries on his teeth with a toffee hammer (the image is Ian Breakwell's, in his film *Variety* [2001]); the slapstick violence of Buster Keaton or the Three Stooges, falling off, running into or being assaulted by other people or things; or zany assaults on sense and language by Spike Milligan, Frank Randle, Kenneth Williams, the Alberts, Stanley Unwin or Tommy Cooper, through magic, storytelling, word-mangling, buffoonery or song. Indeed, as Routh states, 'I think what I do is closer to vaudeville than to "art". I ended up as a performance artist not really by choice' (Juno and Vale 1987: 222). Each comic precedent suggests a kind of violence – against bodies or sense or language – in various and dissimilar ways.

Yet the prank or the joke is not antithetical to art. For example, the amusing, madcap or stunt-like aspects of Richard Newton's performances – a peer of the Kipper Kids in Los Angeles and a fellow exhibiting artist in *Public Spirit* – are self-evident in his works, beginning with their titles, from the eponymous pointlessness of *I Take You to a Room in Brawley and We Smell Onions* (1975) to *Touch a Penis with the Former Miss Barstow* (1979), in which Newton's penis was visible through a hole cut in a sheet and viewers were invited to poke or stroke it under the supervision of a former beauty queen (Lacy and Sternad 2012: 71). The tacit reliance of the Kipper Kids, as artists, on the joke, sustained by their references to beloved comedic antecedents like Keaton or Milligan and so on (and readable in Drohojowska's comparison to the Three Stooges or McKenna's invocation of *Animal House*), muddles the strategies with which we may validate certain practices as serious objects of aesthetic consideration (and therefore as art) and dismiss others as frivolous or compromised (and therefore as commercial entertainment). From one perspective, the Kipper Kids' debts to 'low' culture – to music hall, vaudeville or stand-up comedy – render them anything but extreme; from another, shuttling or trafficking such practices into the rarefied spaces of art might look like a barbaric intrusion, breaking a path for later practical joker-artists. Moreover, the sense of a previous time, one wrenched from its own sense of suitability to the present form – of old-fashioned comic performance intruding with a kind of madcap violence into the scene of performance art – works as a kind of semiotic pause: not so much a break but *crackle*. As Mark Fisher writes of contemporary music, the sound of crackle 'makes us aware that we are listening to a time that is out of joint; it won't allow us to fall into the illusion of presence' (2014: 21). A performance by the Kipper Kids is rich with this kind of meaningful disruption, this productive crackle in the texture of the image or the action.

For Drohojowska, their apparent inadequacy as comedians does not disqualify the Kipper Kids as artists, even as 'good' artists, but her statement of preference – she simply prefers other comedians – installs a set of standards or qualities against which the artists are measured, even if noncommittally. The effect is to tacitly demean their work's effectiveness and value as art, as well as to poke fun at their categorical slippage into other culturally retrograde anti-traditions. She sustains McKenna's suspicion by suggesting that performance art is a holdout for 'unfunny comedians' and other cultural failures. Of the range of critical demands made of *Public Spirit*, co-curator (and participating artist) Barbara T. Smith noted the contradictions that often characterise performance art criticism in the mainstream press, noting a preponderance of implied demands in terms of quality, affect and efficacy – namely, '1. that it have more polish, 2. that it not be boring, [and] 3. that it merge political and spiritual activism', adding, incisively: 'It is ironic that pop art was criticized because it was too facile and commercial, while performance is criticized because it is too raw and esoteric' (1980: 152). In the work of the Kipper Kids, this rawness and esotericism is typified by the spectacle of the boxing match. Describing their finale, Drohojowska writes, 'one Kipper, wearing boxing gloves, beat himself about the head and face until his nose began to copiously bleed. The other Kipper cleaned him up with mopfuls of filthy water and beer' (1980: 146). Placed among these other concerns, the description begins to chime with the earlier distillations of apparent silliness in the work of Smith, Went or Newton, for example, such that the act of self-boxing – which I take, otherwise, to be provocative and critically effective – settles in Drohojowska's account as one more instance in a series of random acts of senseless weirdness.

The fight

In taking up the figure of the boxer in their performances and enacting its science as a technology of self-destruction, the Kipper Kids might be seen to delve into the peculiar pathology of boxing, as well as that of art itself. The use of boxing both enacts and metaphorises the function of sabotage in their work, in tandem with their noted investments in comedy and vaudeville and their playful critique of language, gender and social relations. Boxing is a canny figure in this regard, as it has been theorised as a cipher for the irrationality and pathology of art. Norman Mailer notes the mutual psychopathy of boxers and artists when he writes (specifically, in relation to Muhammad Ali – whom Routh, for one, admired):

> Like artists, it is hard for [boxers] not to see the finished professional as a separate creature from the child that created him. The child (now grown up) still accompanies the great athlete [or artist] and is wholly in love with him, an immature love, be it said. (Mailer 2000: 57)

Mailer's equation of the pathology of art and the desublimated auto-aggression of boxing depends upon and recasts a series of Romantic clichés about art and artists: the artist is a masochistic, narcissistic subject, a horribly split one at that, both psychically mutilated and spiritually elevated by their calling. A self-creation and a product of their own childish fantasies of superiority, impregnability and invincibility, Mailer's (implicitly male) artist is a divided subject in the grip of the struggle towards *auto-poiesis*: the act of inventing oneself anew.

As a special category of men, boxers, too, like artists – and (other?) psychotics – fantasise about their own invulnerability and internalise the myth of their own radical singularity, Mailer suggests, in an irresolvable dream of subjective and physical exceptionality. He makes the parallel between boxing and mental illness painfully clear: 'Not many psychotics could endure the disciplines of professional boxing. Still, [a boxer] must live *in a world where proportions are gone*. He is conceivably the most frightening unarmed killer alive' (Mailer 2000: 46; emphasis added). Now aligned with the figures of the artist and the psychotic, as well as with the threat of subjective crisis germane to figurations of masculinity of distorted proportions, the boxer is the ultimate metaphor for the Kipper Kids. The paralleling of archetypes explains their incessant and contradictory stagings of infantilism, narcissism, crypto-autistic self-sufficiency, messianic masculinity, subjective confusion (their mirroring and sharing of identities) and their violence.

Their boxing is perhaps an alibi for a shared attraction to aesthetic violence, directed both towards each other and towards themselves (one may well be a surrogate for the other: in Routh's and von Haselberg's forced self-resemblance, such vectors of violence can be difficult to map). For Lynda Nead, an art historian and boxing trainer, boxing 'civilizes a form of fundamental human action – violent combat'. Its rules and regulations provide a structure that 'formalizes actions that would otherwise be considered immoral and illegal' – that is, acts of grievous or actual bodily harm or sadomasochism. Consensual by nature, she continues, boxing 'exists outside the moral values of victim and aggressor. It is theatrical and spectacular and its photographic images of physical aggression may enable a different scrutiny of the affects and aesthetics of violence and representation' (Nead 2011: 310). Von Haselberg pre-empts Nead, perhaps, when he tells a journalist that a Kipper Kids performance 'may be about our own lurking, festering violent impulses, and perhaps shows [audiences], in a magnified way, what may lurk beneath their own calm exteriors' – though he is quick to defuse any grandiose implications about ethics, aesthetics or politics: 'there's no intended message in our work', he continues. 'We say whatever you think we say' (McKenna 1981: 55).

Von Haselberg's caveats notwithstanding, Nead's reading prompts an analysis of images of professional boxing (her particular theme), but also, perhaps, a consideration of the surprisingly frequent appropriation of boxing in and as the performance of extremity, including in the work of the Kipper Kids. Moreover, the latter belongs to an expansive context: Ushio Shinohara's *Boxing Paintings* series (1960–61) in which he produced abstract paintings by punching canvases with paint-smeared gloves, as recorded in a series of photographs by William Klein; Joseph Beuys' *Boxing Match for Direct Democracy* (*documenta* 5, 1972), where he fought sculptor Abraham David Christian as the culminating action of 100 days of rigorous debate; Ion Grigorescu's suggestion of self-boxing using double-exposure in his film *Boxing* (1977); and more recent works by Johanna Went, Cassils, Jennifer Locke or Franko B. Indeed, boxing – and its correlate, athletic fighting, such as Yves Klein's appropriations of judo or George Mathieu's invocation of karate – recur as a frequent apparatus or style in performance art actions of the 1970s. In Nancy Buchanan's *Please Sing Along* (1974), for example, performed at the historic Woman's Building, Los Angeles, two men danced gracefully in the nude, creating shadows against the wall; then Buchanan and Barbara T. Smith (both clothed in white judo gear) engaged in an unsimulated fight, while a man read aloud dense, dry passages of art theory assembled by Buchanan into an unintelligible polemic.

Buchanan and Smith fought until they were too injured or exhausted to continue, then hugged, kissed and left the gallery, both parodying and intervening in the highly gendered nature of styles of physical and pedagogical aggression and submission in their social and artistic milieu (in teaching, critiquing, theorising and making art). In appropriations of boxing, judo or staged fighting, the gendered nature of the interaction speaks directly to what Nead calls the affects and aesthetics of violence and representation.

Other artists in the 1970s practised explicitly the semiotics of boxing as a sport and also directed more emphatically its styles and forces towards their own bodies in performance. Perhaps the best-known comparator for the Kipper Kids' spectacle of self-boxing in the period is Paul McCarthy's later video-performance, *Rocky* (1976). In *Rocky*, McCarthy wears boxing shorts, leather gloves and a rubber mask whose battered features, goggle-like strap across the eyes and flat cap suggest the visage of a cartoon burglar. Burlesquing Sylvester Stallone's machismo, McCarthy punches himself in his chest, stomach and masked face and slathers himself in ketchup to signify with schlocky artifice the messy irrigation of a boxer's body in blood, parodying the myth of an invulnerable masculinity monumentalised in the original *Rocky* (dir. by Stallone, 1974). Art historian Cary Levine writes that McCarthy's *Rocky* 'employs an inflated and autodestructive manliness to mock the macho persona of the Hollywood hunk', by undercutting the conventional 'priapic power' of such representations (Levine 2013: 95), as if to turn Hollywood film violence in upon itself. Interrupting the action with gestures towards masturbation, McCarthy's pantomime de-sublimates the anxiety that underwrites men's pedestrian performances of masculine bravado, our pretend imperviousness to emotional hurt and the barely latent erotics that condition investments in the spectacle of organised violence, such as that which characterises boxing, brawling, rioting, pranks or action movies. Levine acknowledges the similarities between McCarthy and the Kipper Kids, though he claims McCarthy was 'less slapsticky, and more truly grotesque than the Kipper Kids' infantile outbursts', perhaps undermining the richness and extremity of the Kipper Kids' work and the factual precedence of their enactment of self-boxing in and as performance (2013: 33–4).

As in McCarthy's onanistic spectacle, the precise nature of the sexual body is anomalous in the performances of the Kipper Kids. That is, the violence the latter will dole out during various 'ceremonies' is often coloured with eroticism, specifically a kind of jocular, puerile sexuality. When asked if he thinks there was an erotic dimension to their performances, von Haselberg acknowledged it as 'mostly fake eroticism': 'Real eroticism was there', he continues, 'but only potentially. If there was eroticism, it was always made fun of' (Johnson 2015: 86). The sexual nature of their theatrical violence – as a partly comedic intensification of masculine hijinks or bravado – contributes to the enduring difficulty of their work. The preponderance of the performance of gender in their works is conspicuous: jokes about wieners (in one skit, each ties a cold sausage to his penis); spray-painting their scrotums blue ('blueballing', as in to withdraw climax from a male sexual partner); or extended gags about the spaces and styles of conventional machismo, including uses of jockstraps and Scout uniforms, which conjure for me the homoerotic rituals of male recreational seclusion (of, say, the locker room or summer camp); and the frequency of toilet humour through fart sounds or visual evocations of leaky colostomy bags and shitty-looking chocolate smears. In one arresting instance from 1982, in collaboration with the popular comedian Bette Midler, these motifs come together in a performance in a public latrine to desublimate theatrically the litany of homosocial and scatological jokes: Midler hides shrieking and mugging in a toilet cubicle and feigns bafflement and horror at the semi-private horseplay that unfolds before her, namely that of the 'food ceremony', which the Kipper Kids stage with ritual abundance beside the communal sinks and mirrors.[5]

The erotic tone of the Kipper Kids' antics is typically suppressed, violent, hyper-masculine and uncouth – yet at the same time jocular, touchy-feely, zany. The know-ingness with which they perform eroticism lends a critical edge to what may be read as a pantomime of heterosexual machismo – a vaudeville of the sexuality of schoolyards, locker rooms and stag parties. Theirs is a world of sweetness and psychopathy in action, a dominion of violence and camaraderie *where proportions are gone*. As such the psychosexual worlds they construct seemingly recall Mailer's uneasy conflation of art, boxing, masculinity and psychosis, perhaps inflected by Robbe-Grillet's description of sabotage as a narrative space of 'contradictions, variants, and dangerous leaps resulting . . . in fantastic reversals' (1970: 127–8). Even the Kippers' shared persona suggests a kind of derangement of the self: a synthesis of being with another (a social relation) is unbuckled from its safety by the scary intensity of being *possessed* (as a psychological or paranormal phenomenon). This shattering of proportion – their annihilation of psychic co-ordinates from which to navigate a way out of performance and into a subjective space outside of art (what we confusingly call a life) – might climax in boxing, but it is also fuelled by drink. 'By the end of the show, by the boxing match', Routh tells me, 'I was always completely drunk. I couldn't really feel how hard I was hitting myself, and I was always getting black eyes.' Since in recovery, he reflects on the excesses of the 1970s:

> Partly, our act was very abusive. There was a lot of self-abuse – but also abuse directed towards each other, and to the audience. That's probably why we stopped doing it after a while. It was just too much – the physical violence, but also the drinking. I'm sure it did us a lot of harm. (Johnson 2015: 70)

Their pyrrhic, self-injurious, blackout-intoxicated tone – and the sometimes uncontrolled nature of their hijinks in and beyond performance – suggests the Kipper Kids' perverse willingness to unsettle their own claims to mastery, posterity and historical remembering. The latter suggests a further sexual politics to their actions. Unlike formally similar artists of the 1970s – McCarthy in his disorganised yet museum-friendly aesthetics or Gilbert and George in their shared (but tweedy) persona – the Kipper Kids followed through on their anti-aesthetic promise, never to allow themselves the privilege and safety of an institutional embrace.

---

5 The performance was for *The Mondo Beyondo Show* (dir. by Thomas Schlamme, 1982), a one-hour performance art special for HBO. Von Haselberg was the executive producer; he is married to Midler.

The anti-aesthetic

Turning in on itself – and in its self-direction with great violence against the person of the artist – art in the grasp of the Kipper Kids refers us back to the definition of the anti-aesthetic introduced in the discussion of Ulay's masochistic performative photography (see Chapter 2), where, as Hal Foster writes, the anti-aesthetic sensibility discloses a 'negation of art . . . in the anarchic hope of an "emancipatory effect"', while reaffirming a radical new version of art as 'a space beyond representation' (1983: xv). An anti-aesthetic sensibility, then, signals a historically contingent critical attitude, which is turned actively against the assumptions and conventions of modern philosophical aesthetics. As it pulled away from post-Kantian standards in the nineteenth century, the remit of aesthetics was retooled towards a network of styles, habits, aesthetics and forms that may refuse and rethink the visual and other constitutions of a politically effective artistic practice. Therefore, the anti-aesthetic sensibility frequently assumes that beauty – the past fulcrum of aesthetic convention – precludes or neutralises the critical efficacy of art. It is therefore anti-beauty, inasmuch as it is against aesthetics.

Arthur C. Danto uses the term 'kalliphobia' to explain the hatred or fear of beauty that typifies the anti-aesthetic, adding that this attitude has been 'epidemic' in avant-garde art since the beginning of the twentieth century. Danto argues that the anti-aesthetic derived from a political conviction that the standards of an unfair, corrupt and murderous society – particularly, in the early twentieth century, one that could sanction a newly industrialised and mechanised genus of war – could not be meekly accepted or licensed, such that beauty, as the prized value of a bankrupt culture, must be sacrificed (Danto 2004: 25). Finding a kalliphobic apotheosis in Dada, Danto sees it predicted in a prototypical avant-garde statement in Arthur Rimbaud's *A Season in Hell* (1873): 'One day I sat Beauty on my knees, and I found her bitter, and I abused her' (cited in Danto 2004: 25). The avant-garde 'abuse' of Beauty – characterised here in phallic, misogynistic terms – stages the political imperative to hold one's culture hostage to its own greatest cruelties, as an act of symbolic retribution. With the refusal or debasement of beauty came too the defamiliarisation of other dearly held values of modern aesthetics, including, most explicitly, that of disinterested critical judgement and the requirement of art's determining lack of utility, political or otherwise.

For post-war avant-garde artists, the continued institutional acceptance of modern aesthetic theory's conventional assumptions posed a series of challenges: to embrace an aesthetic of ugliness over beauty; to value efficacy and usefulness over mere purposiveness; to embody surprising or disconcerting intensities of pleasure and sexual desire; and to shatter the presumption of critical distance as a feasible position from which to engage with art. The emergence of a prototype of performance art in Dada, Surrealism, Futurism and Bauhaus – as fundamental variations on avant-gardism in the early twentieth century – is no accident (see Goldberg 1979). Performance art would continue to function as a crucible for the radicalisation of an anti-aesthetic sensibility, in tandem with a variety of fine art practices and forms, including naïve painting, the art of the insane, abject sculpture, experimental film and dissident collage. Shock, disgust, paranoia, dejection and outrage were crucially embraced, as affects that were optimal in their agreed negativity.

In the course of seeking to *épater la bourgeoisie* (the avant-garde mission to disquiet or confound the learned masses), controversy was not simply a nuisance or passive side effect, but an instrumental technique for the elaboration of new aesthetic strategies and the production of engaged audiences for the cultural transgressions they encountered. New genealogies of art after the advent of the historical avant-garde continued to resist the consolations of the supreme value of beauty, the refinement of taste, critical distance and the legislation of which objects and actions are 'proper' to aesthetic judgement. The use of unfamiliar materials, qualities and actions would be significant to these projects, especially in the mid-1950s and into the 1960s in, for example: the messy, anxious performances of the Gutai group in Japan, especially those of Kazuo Shiraga, who wrestled his way through a grey, post-apocalyptic-looking swamp in *Challenging Mud* (1955) and subsequently painted with violent kicks of his feet, suspended from a strop; or through the formally obscene, bloody and politically penetrating actions of the Vienna Actionists in continental Europe; or in the ecstatic, improvised and sexually liberated performances of Carolee Schneemann, beginning with her game-changing performance *Meat Joy* (1963). Each in their own way exploited performance art as an opportunity to recast aesthetics as the space of ugliness, excess, disgust, mess, unease and filth, as well as other differently demeaned effects, including drabness, silliness or ritual.

Emerging at the turn of the 1970s, the Kipper Kids were ideal and energetic inheritors of the anti-aesthetic sensibility, as road-tested by the aforementioned fore-bears. In their search for a new aesthetic, by way of a refusal of aesthetic conventions and the politics that attends them, the Kipper Kids enact what Georges Bataille has explained as a *low* aesthetic register. Bataille gives an account of his aesthetic theory in an essay of 1929 on a 'base', excremental feature of the human body, the big toe, which he depicts as a cultural surrogate for a range of artefacts or experiences that inspire disgust or enmity (1985: 22–3). His is a mythic anatomy of the human form, in which the head signifies transcendence – 'a head raised to the heavens and heavenly things' – and the toe is rooted in low materials, in muck and filth; Bataille's excremental philosophy enacts a ruinous inversion of a 'bias' in the traditional order of things 'in favor of that which elevates itself from the "subterranean hell"' (1985: 20). His counterintuitive reinstatement of the beatitude of the 'low' enables an anti-aesthetic theory in the form of a series of philosophically marginal economies of mood, from culturally elevated experiences to low or subterranean events.

Bataille's methodology, which he terms 'base materialism', is less a broadened continuum between the high and the low than a corruption of the conventional ordering of human cultural and social experience. He understands the elevated quotient – of soul, sentience, conceptuality and morality – in a disruptively dualistic fashion, namely, as inconsolably connected to, dependent upon and contaminated by its grounding in base matter, just as clarity of mind and intellectual transcendence are supported in the body by a foot whose mobile sole is stamped in dirt. 'Human life entails', Bataille writes, 'the rage of seeing oneself as a back and forth movement from refuse to the ideal, and from the ideal to refuse', such that this rage is directed at objects or artefacts (even those that constitute a part of oneself, for example the phalanges of the foot) that might seem to signify descent into the mire (1985: 20–1). Bataille enables a theoretical approach to the critical means and cultural effects through which one is 'seduced in a base manner' before an object or scene that inspires revulsion, shame, ambivalence, guilt or fear, so as to suggest an upheaval of the cultural hierarchy between high and low (1985: 23). One's undignified cultural descent involves a specific action – Bataille's mythic example is the desire to touch the queen's foot – or a cultural orientation. 'Here one submits to a seduction radically opposed to that caused by light and ideal beauty', he writes; 'the two orders of seduction are often confused because a person constantly moves from one to the other'. Ominously, he adds, 'seduction is all the more acute when the movement is more brutal' (ibid.).

In its pursuit of a dark or base seduction, in the sense suggested by Bataille, the anti-aesthetic may always involve or approximate a form of (self-)sabotage. It is self-defeating, in and of itself, because an anti-aesthetic sensibility attempts to unbind the conventions of the aesthetic, including its apparently naturalised ambition towards 'light and ideal beauty' and other mystifications, from within the structures of the aesthetic. The anti-aesthetic engages the problem of a limit, but cannot necessarily explode or neutralise it, for to some extent the anti-aesthetic is always a legitimising operation, through its contradictory framing in terms of that which it seeks to overcome (and after mid-century, by the institutional recuperation and containment of the historical avant-garde, whose scandal is neutered or tamed, as commodity, icon or treasure).

As aesthetics becomes detached from the production of discrete, saleable cosmetic objects and evolves into a practice of life and as art approaches the paradoxical situation of 'anti-art', performance art emerged as the linchpin of these transformations – not at the centre of culture, but at (or as) its vital margins. For literary theorist Terry Eagleton, aesthetics is itself characterised by contradiction or antinomy: as a dialectical concept, aesthetics tends to miss – or be actively undone by – its object (1990: 2–3). He argues that this provoked the emergence of 'anti-art', as 'an art which is not appropriable by the ruling order because – the final cunning – it isn't art at all'. This proposes an antinomy for art, which curtails its potential efficacy, for 'what cannot be appropriated and institutionalized because it refuses to distance itself from social practice in the first place may by the same token abolish all critical point of purchase upon social life' (1990: 371). The scope of the aesthetic has been broadened – but never, surely, destroyed – by the aggressions, contradictions and complications posed against it, in order to accommodate the anti-aesthetic as relevant to its reach.

Up Yer Bum with a Bengal Lancer (1976) is a unique work in the Kipper Kids' oeuvre – a video piece in which the two artists perform for the camera and explore the formal conditions of the moving image.[6] It stages and thus prompts a theory of the art of sabotage. Moreover, it provides a characteristic record of the efforts the Kipper Kids staged towards realising the promise of the performance of extremity

---

6 Collected in the Long Beach Museum of Art Video Archive (1970–2000), Getty Research Institute. Special collections, Accessions no. 2006.M.7.

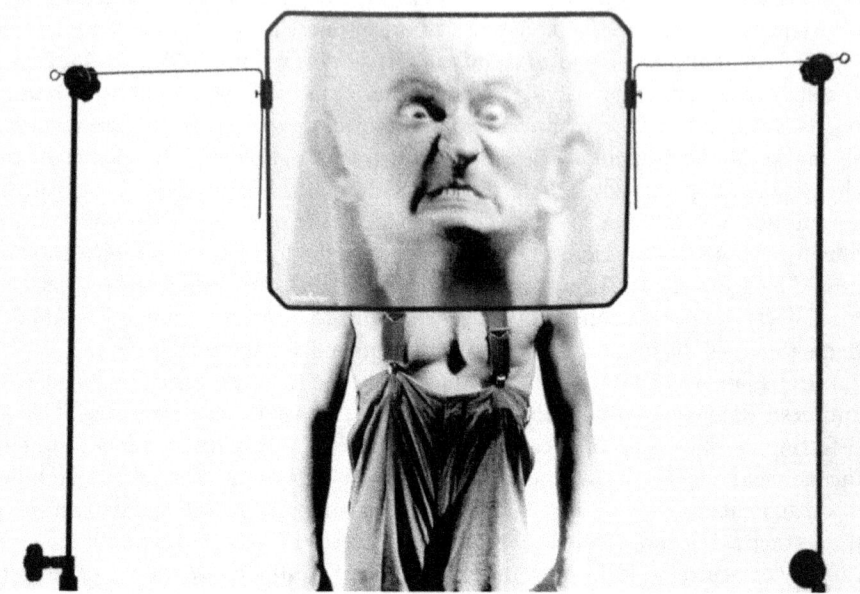

5.5 The Kipper Kids, *Up Yer Bum With a Bengal Lancer* (1976), production photograph
for video-performance

as a manifestation of the anti-aesthetic sensibility, as predicted by Bataille and complicated further by Eagleton, among others. Whereas other videos by the Kipper
Kids more straightforwardly document live performances, von Haselberg organised
the production of *Up Yer Bum* as a stand-alone video art piece for the Long Beach
Museum of Art (LBMA). Facilitated by David Ross, who spearheaded the museum's
pioneering video programme, von Haselberg commissioned John Baker and Dan
Zimbaldi as videographers and set up a studio in which to record the improvised
skits on Betacam SP. The resulting video, running to 25 minutes, is made up mostly
of solo performances to camera by von Haselberg, with an extended interlude in the
middle section performed with Routh.[7] The title is a malapropism or a (weak?) dirty
joke: a 'lancer' is a breed of soldier and 'Bengal Lancer' refers to a regiment of imperial
cavalry in India (as in *The Lives of a Bengal Lancer*, a book of 1930 and film of 1935
with Gary Cooper); a lancer's sword is a 'lance'. Either the sword is misnamed or the
gag is that one might be taken up the bum by a 'lancer' – by a soldier (or Gary Cooper)
or a part thereof. An explicit weapon such as a lance will not appear in the video, but
sexual innuendo and violent actions – the threat of a lance up the bum – ghosts its
constitutive performances.

In the opening scene of *Up Yer Bum with a Bengal Lancer*, von Haselberg appears
without makeup, facing the screen through a Fresnel lens (**Figure 5.5**) – a large,

---

7 The Kipper Kids are credited in the video as creators and copyright holders; however, it was shown at
  documenta 6 (1977) under Harry Kipper's name alone – in this case, as a solo work by von Haselberg.

rectangular magnifying glass used to focus lights – held in place upon a scaffold. He mugs, postures, turns his head to pull back his chin, smirks, gurns and grimaces. He starts to make noises, garbled squawks, guffaws and raspberries. He makes himself boss-eyed and pulls out his ears to the side. The Fresnel, which suggests both a mirror and a screen, distorts his face, neck and hands in a comical, funhouse fashion. Already buffoon-like, he now resembles a pinhead with the distended neck of a cartoon bruiser. After around two minutes, he whistles an enthusiastic, unrecognisable tune, interrupting it with fart sounds to complete the ditty. The song is a prelude to a series of comments and questions, delivered in a baffled, comic-cockney voice: 'Oi, oi! What's going on, eh? Oi? Wotcha playin' at? Cam on! Wot yer playin' at, eh?' He introduces a second voice, in a similarly cartoonlike Geordie accent, suppressing his mild German-Argentinian accent to borrow Routh's native Gateshead lilt. *'I can see you.* You can, can ya? *Ah certainly can!'* Cue more mugging.

Von Haselberg lifts the thick straps of his elasticated suspenders up and onto his head, creating a blunt V-shape across his face. He manoeuvres his neck and head to peek through the gap between the straps, passing one strap across his face so that his nose flattens out like a boxer's under the pressure. Later, von Haselberg will reprise the gesture with a rubber band, wrapping it across the lower portion of his nose to flatten it once again. The effect makes his voice sound adenoidal, complementing his inane, lisping vocalisations: 'My name is Billy, all my friends think I'm silly.' The use of the straps, as with much of the video, has a clear feel of improvisation. *Up Yer Bum* tests the formal qualities of video as a medium: for example, the cameraman zooms in close and the Fresnel causes the resulting image to flip vertically, showing the crown of von Haselberg's shaved head upside down at the top of the screen. It also tests the extent of the performer's ability to negotiate and respond to new materials and situations, through voice, expression and pose.

In the next scene, von Haselberg and Routh wear pale blazers over casual shirts. They share a rubber band across their faces and heads, which lifts up their noses into compressed, pig-like snouts. The action references the earlier use of the suspender-strap and the Kippers' frequent use of rubber bands in a similar fashion in various performances, including those subsequently adapted (in schoolgirl pinafores, painted freckles and pigtails) for the cult movie *Forbidden Zone* (dir. by Richard Elfman, 1980). Bound together and rendered even more farcical than usual in their appearance, they giggle together (likely facing a mirror) and engage in a pidgin conversation of trademark jibber-jabbering. After various playful gestures, improvisations and five-finger exercises, a telephone rings in the background. 'That'll show you', one says. 'That'll show you', the other replies. They repeat the exchange, ad nauseam, as the telephone continues to ring. 'Eh, do you think it might be for me?' The phone rings off. They mug still. Their exchange resembles a séance gone awry, a call-and-response of matched groans, intonations, word salad and vocal flourishes:

Hippopotamus.
Fatty.
Bertie likes his bacon.
Charlie likes his chips.

Wouldn't mind beef jerky.
Wouldn't mind a fuck.
Wouldn't mind a sausage.
Wouldn't mind a six-pack.

Their exchange of non-sequiturs makes a dizzying, blank, benign poem of sorts. They start corpsing, groaning. They're practically yodelling.

This is a game, innit!
Certainly is.
Can't complain.
Straight up.

Their communications are comprehensible, but arbitrary, disjointed and vacuous. The chosen words are practically without content – reiterations of found language, the odd cliché heard, remembered, then borrowed or smuggled into the appropriated text of the video. 'Let's go down to the Naafi and get drunk.' 'Let's get really pissed, eh?' The skit goes on, ending with von Haselberg slapping Routh on the head and face. Very suddenly, they break out of the charade and out of character and ask the cameramen a series of practical questions, straight-faced, with clear, articulate accents, as though to emphasise the former stylings and silliness as a put-on.

In the subsequent scene, the camera focuses on their lower legs, from just above their bare knees, down to their pulled up socks and black leather boots. To samba drums, the camera pans up to reveal their cocks and balls, each grasping the other's hand; higher in the pan, one holds a hammer and the other a saw. The instruments are weighted with a kind of latent violence, perhaps as surrogates for the 'lancer' of the title. As the camera continues to pan, we see their dumbfounded faces. Naked, holding their implements – though only the hammer is visible – the Kippers sing their peculiar rendition of *The Sheik of Araby*: a stuck-in-a-loop repetition of the title of a Tin Pan Alley song of 1921, coupled with the pre-verbal non sequitur *'ee-oh-ee-oh, fffrrrt*, a'right!' Still naked, but stripped of their weapons and framed in full, they shake their bodies in a St Vitus' dance of paroxysmal jives. They jerk, jolt and shudder violently and scream out garbled, rabid sounds. The shakes turn into a poking competition, enunciating each poke to the face, body, genitals or bum – *prrrp!* – with raspberries. The effect is demented, anxious and unnerving. They are on the brink of violence. They quickly dress and give a thumbs-up to the camera. The scene changes to a shot framed low across the middles of their bodies. They pull away their blazer flaps, unzip their flies and expose their penises – the shot frames their cheap blazers, smart pants and flopping meat. Harry Kipper on the right holds a large glass jar and both bring their penises close together, above the rim of the jar. They piss into it. We see the crossed streams of urine enter the rising level of liquid.

After returning to the mounted Fresnel, the shot zooms out. Von Haselberg is shirtless and wears baggy trousers held up by suspenders. The effect of the Fresnel, around a metre wide and a good distance forward from his body, creates an illusion of a massive, flattened expanse of face, propped atop his cartoonlike frame. Like a caricature copper with a cockney accent, he says, 'I say, I say, I say. How come your body's so small and your 'ead's so big, eh?' He moves backwards, until the Fresnel magnifies his face into a featureless expanse of grey and he falls down, collapsing vertically out of the shot. More mugging and he repeats the action. Nearby objects and furniture resound with the full weight of his fall.

Up Yer Bum with a Bengal Lancer is a document of individual and interpersonal interactions characterised throughout by a palpable economy of violence. Its violence is both patent – physical acts of aggression by one Kipper Kid against his own or his partner's body – as well as latent, in the sense that their interactions or their presentations to the intended audience take advantage of, or otherwise call into question, the agency, dignity or security of another person. As a collection of performances, it physicalises Bataille's base materialism, as a programme of visual and linguistic play upon a scaffold of perverse, destitute gestures and styles. The low quality of their repertoire is clear: their raw materials here are piss, genitals, sexual horseplay, the inane chatter of children or simpletons, violence. It is an unravelling, a sabotaging of the aesthetic from within its fortifications, recalling Robbe-Grillet's irrational mandate for the saboteur, namely the pursuit of a 'pathological proliferation', creating something lower than art, namely 'a secretion – one could say the *waste product . . .* of their delirium' (Robbe-Grillet 1970: 128, emphasis in original).

Celluloid Kippers

The Kipper Kids' marginality to the art world – as staged or perhaps parodied in the contents of their museum piece, *Up Yer Bum with a Bengal Lancer* – was perhaps compounded by their attempts at mainstream assimilation in the 1980s, particularly via cinema and television. Individually, they tend not to remember these projects kindly, with the exception of *K. O. Kippers*, a movie commissioned by Cinemax for its 'Comedy Experiments' series and shown on cable television in August 1988 (initially for six nights), as well as in public screenings around the same time (**Figure 5.6**). Routh recalls that their movies – such as their contributions to Richard Elfman's *The Forbidden Zone* (starring alongside Oingo Boingo, Viva, Susan Tyrrell and Hervé Villechaize) or their own shelved movie for HBO, *Mum's Magic Mulch* (dir. by Routh and von Haselberg, 1990) – might each be considered a 'sell out'; of *K. O. Kippers*, he recalls, however, 'I was actually proud of that movie. It holds up as a piece of work' (Johnson 2015: 75). Nevertheless, some critics were cautious in their praise for what appeared to be the willing containment or co-optation of maverick artists by the mainstream. For example, the cultural journalist C. Carr wrote in the *Village Voice* in 1988 that the news of their contract with Cinemax made her 'feel a twinge of anxiety – or loss', explaining this affect as 'the anxiety you experience when the boundary breaks'. Describing the process of containment, she argues that by entering the television and movie market, the authentically 'outrageous' and 'beyondo' Kipper Kids risked losing their edge: '[w]hat was once center floats to the

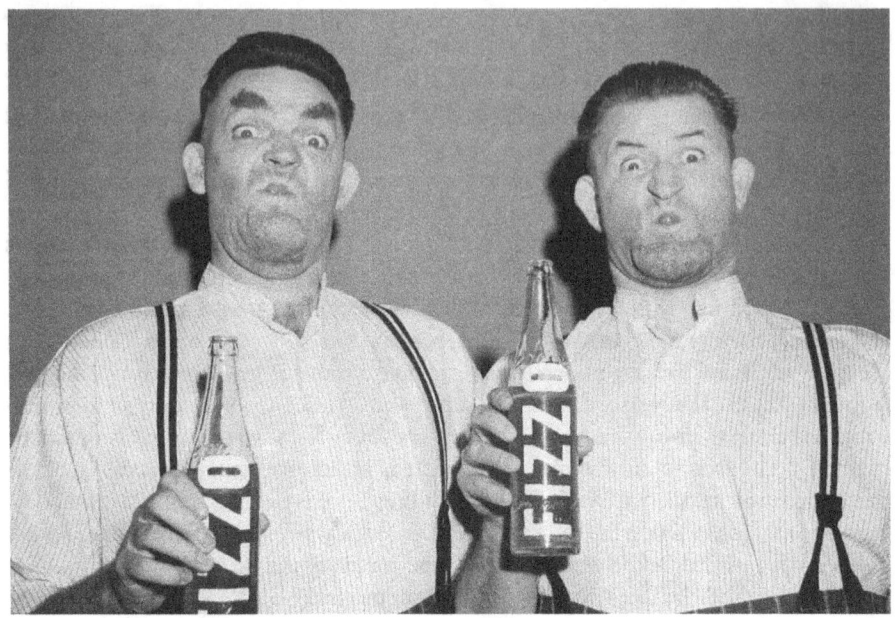

5.6 The Kipper Kids, *K. O. Kippers* (1988), dir. by Miroslav Janek, Cinemax, production photograph on set

edge, and vice versa. Everything flattens. And the freaks aren't happy in the sideshow anymore' (Carr 2008: 153).

Written by the Kipper Kids and directed by Czech filmmaker Miroslav Janek, *K. O. Kippers* runs to around 30 minutes. The plot involves a ruthless American scam-artist called Tony LaRosa (Joe Spinell, a co-star from *The Forbidden Zone*), hell-bent on exploiting two twin idiot-savant boxers, namely, the Kipper Kids. Early in the film, the bumpkin boxers make plain a proviso for their participation, namely, 'we refuse to ever fight each other – that's a promise we made our dearly departed mother on her deathbed, may she rest in peace'. The refusal of each to face his twin in the boiler room of the damned is the enabling condition of the plot, which provokes the inevitable climax of the film.

As in their live performances, Harry Kipper and Harry Kipper appear as dop-pelgängers. They share symmetrically harsh, Iron Mike hair fades, matching high-waisted trousers, work shirts and suspenders and their characteristic, ridiculously pronounced chins and stylised grey-blue five-o'clock shadows. Here, while their profiles are obscenely, goofily accentuated, the quality of the materials and technical support afford the Kipper Kids a kind of prosthetic realism entirely absent from their live performances. Indeed, in the latter, the prostheses tended to have a life or mind of their own. At one point in the action at the National Review of Live Art in 2003, for example, von Haselberg's chin falls off. Routh follows suit and pulls off his own. They face each other mugging and pull their jaws back to feign chinless faces with weak jawlines. They laugh with each other and the audience laughs along. They continue the act and eventually their noses fall off too.[8] Their laughter – and ours – is consistent in the Kipper Kids' performances, as a functional sign of their refusal to be serious, despite (or to exaggerate) their iconoclasm. In performances, the homemade stuck-on prosthetics play into this same candidness. Yet these elements of risk, play, surprise, improvisation and provocation are lost when the aesthetic is cleaned up to the extent we see in their movies.

The comic effect of *K. O. Kippers* relies less on the narrative content or dialogue, but rather on the surrealistic visual comedy of the Kipper Kids' inhabitations of the scenes; for example, in a farmyard in Mexico, the Kipper Kids use suspended, plucked chickens as punching bags and train by throwing roundhouses at eggs pelted at the pair by giggling *abuelas*; later, they play a ukulele by a campfire, accompanied by a heavily stylised version of Sir Harry Lauder's music-hall ditty, *Roamin' in the Gloamin'* of 1911: 'When the sun has gone to rest, that's the time that we like best, / Oh it's lovely roamin' in the gloamin'!' Lauder's quaint song of romantic wanderings in the antediluvian twilight is rendered perverse or plain bizarre in the Kipper Kids' quickened and lovingly mangled interpretation, sung with fart sounds, whistles, ono-matopoeic sing-alongs and erratic, expressionistic movements of the eyes and eye-brows. At the end of the song, its chorus is spoken in slow diminishing echoes, with ukulele accompaniments and cryptic pauses, until it is finally inaudible.

After suffering a series of indignities at the hand of their shady manager, like sleep-ing in a chicken coop for a bedroom and having a pissoir for a dressing room, on fight night their scheduled opponents are discommoded by drinking crates of Fizzo, the event sponsor's unpalatable soda. The Kippers are forced to fight each other, a pros-pect that would require them to betray their maternal pledge. As the crowd outside gets ugly, the Kippers huddle across their toilet cubicles and remonstrate through a combination of simultaneous chatter, curious gurnings and raspberry blowing and seemingly resolve to fight. In the ring, the two boxers are introduced in Spanish: the emphatic announcements accent the ridiculousness of their shared name. The two boxers throw a flurry of feinting blows into the air and dance their fancy footwork on the canvas. The referee instructs them to touch their leather gloves together; they retreat to the corners and rush towards each other. They parry each other without touching the other's bodies or gloves and the crowd begins to boo loudly. Tony rubs his face with anxious presentiment of catastrophe. One Kipper urges the other back onto the ropes and Harry Kipper harries, pushing his brother to the centre and further back to the opposite ropes. They bump chests and repeat the frenzied choreography, squeaking and burping their way across the ring, shadowboxing all the while. The booing grows urgent in its disdain.

The bell rings and the Kippers sit on their respective stools, looking beleaguered. The fat *abuelas* wash the fighters down with wet mops – lolling moist grey fibres over their faces and groins – and pop hard-boiled eggs into surprised mouths. Round two begins and the contestants punch *themselves* as opposed to each other. Each throws broadcasted hooks into his own face, punches to the midsection, jab-cross barrages,

---

8 The Kipper Kids, *Your Turn to Roll It #54*, documentation of performance, A001255 National Review of Live Art Video Archive.

left-right-right, one-two, busy combinations, uppercuts to the chin. (If Routh was an amateur boxer in his youth and his great-grandfather a bare-knuckle prizefighter, perhaps it shows in his gusto.) Each fighter works away at solitary assaults upon his own person. One fighter is remonstrated for grappling with his own head. The other traps his gloved hand inside the armpit of his own opposing arm. The crowd now laughs wildly. Shady Tony sits incredulous in the bleachers.

Round three. Each Kipper Kid ups the ante, treating his own body like a speed bag, battering himself with the panicked éclat of a drummer. The crowd's laughter subsides into shocked transfixion. The motion slows and we see Harry Kipper dealing himself a series of calculated deathblows, one-two, one-two, a jarring blow to the stomach, a sledgehammer in the chest, a hook blasting the jaw, a cross to the front of the face. The self-directed punches reverberate with echoing gunshot sounds. Punch drunk Harry goes boss-eyed, gaga. The other echoes his movements and punches. The fighters fall in slow-motion unison, collapsing to the ground with their heads next to each other in the frame. The sounds of gunshots turn to twittering birds. The referee counts in Spanish . . . *Ocho! Nueve! Diez!* It's a double K. O. for the Kippers. The shot cuts to them dancing around the ring with the referee holding up their arms in equitable jubilation. A mariachi band plays *Roamin' in the Gloamin'* and the crowd storms the ring.

The film reprised a theme of the Kipper Kids' previous commercial projects: notably, their performances in the midnight movie *Forbidden Zone* – much loved by cult audiences, but, for Routh and von Haselberg, now something of an embarrassment – also involved the spectacle of self-boxing. In the latter, they stand in a boxing ring, framed by a set painted (by Routh) with Kipper Kids cartoons and they punch themselves rhythmically while singing a glossolalic rendition of *Bim Bam Bum* after the song of 1941 by Machito and his Afro-Cuban Orchestra. In *K. O. Kippers*, however, self-boxing is also a parable of sorts for the incipient dissolution of their collaborative practice in performance, as they began to succumb to means and media beyond or outside the precise terms of the anti-aesthetic sensibility they had orchestrated since the early 1970s. In interview, Routh mentions the making of the film in the course of explaining the Kipper Kids' self-induced downfall:

> I remember lying in the trailer with Martin, on location in Mexico, wearing our makeup and costumes, and we were like, 'yeah, we're going to make this movie, and we'll be rich!' But we never could, partly because we would always sabotage ourselves. It wasn't a strategy – we just couldn't help it. (Johnson 2015: 74)

Von Haselberg agrees in spirit, noting: 'In terms of a career – a potentially successful career in the art world – yes, we were constantly sabotaging ourselves' (Johnson 2015: 79). *K. O. Kippers* also takes as its main subject the very spectacle of self-sabotage, namely the choreographing of each artist/persona staging an assault upon his own person, to save himself from betraying a higher principle (the mother's promise), as well as to rumble the objectives of a higher power (the sleazy manager's project of exploitation). Beyond the symbolic function of the closing scene, the film at large, more profoundly, can be read as a kind of sabotage – career suicide for the most *avant* of artists – as the film will have likely alienated both their own self-selecting audiences and (in their indelible weirdness) the potential new mainstream audiences they pandered to.

The moral of *K. O. Kippers* may be a masochistic one: in the grip of a peculiar, savant code, securing one's own principles – whether they be moral, ethical, political or aesthetic – warrants or triggers a performance of self-sabotage, fabulated by the image of self-boxing. Yet the principle itself, defined in terms of the uncontainable spirit of the anti-aesthetic, comes a dreadful cropper when the Kipper Kids capitulate to the values of mainstream representation, typified in the forced narrative of the film as a structural whole and by various smaller effects, such as the cinematic distillation and popularisation of their signature look – as formal misadventures that never quite work. In the content of their live works and in their overarching approach to being career artists, the Kipper Kids interrupt their own futures, yet secure their own eccentric, contradictory success, by way of a kind of violence against sense or logic – 'drawing on their gloves' (recalling Nietzsche's phrase) in the presence of formal or cosmetic ideals or in the face of cerebral limitations placed on their own vivid potential (Nietzsche 2004: 3). The cosmic laws of violence are rerouted, here, away from each other and towards themselves; elsewhere, such violence is channelled from the ether and directed towards audiences, institutions and their own self-image.

Yet the Kipper Kids were never quite co-opted. Today, they reserve the right to their own invisibility, incomprehensibility, foolhardiness and playfully terroristic company. In the summer of 2014, I sit sedate with von Haselberg in his studio. I ask him, 'Where is Harry Kipper now?' 'Well, he's here', he replies, gently but firmly, 'he's here' (Johnson 2015: 90). I feel a frisson of excitement and dread for the phantasm. Suddenly goofy, crazed, yelling, he cries, '*It could be any moment! I feel it now. I could jump out of my seat and go berserk!*'

Conclusion: Reckless people

In all their varied forms, the practices of performance that occur in the scenes privileged by this counterhistory belong to a superlative economy: a distribution of values characterised by being more than what is expected, necessary or conformingly desired. In the purlieu of the performance of extremity, even when facing it with only the most slight or recondite of historical records – a memory, gossipy remainder, photograph, rush of film, note or other archival trace – I am wide-eyed, gripped by laughter or alarm. The primary affect in the live event can be akin to being slapped in the face, grabbed by the scruff of the neck, lost for words, punched in the gut – or another corporeal analogy of dazzlement or transfixion. It is not only instantiated by the visceral excess of an image (of bleeding, wounding, duress, crime, fear or other sensate representations that seem to instantiate a thrill or crisis), but by all manner of images and ideas that provoke a vacillation in one's understanding of art, bodies and the world.

Over the course of the preceding case studies and the cumulative anomaly of their actions, the works of Kerry Trengove, Ulay, COUM Transmissions, Anne Bean and the Kipper Kids (and a constellation of other artists in comparative brief) have implied a number of common emergent themes beyond those set out in this book's introduction. These themes include indifference or wilful opposition to claiming the status of art for the actions, interventions or processes that constitute various artists' performances of extremity. Moreover and variously, the artists in question have disregarded, troubled, endangered or destroyed their own archives, towards a politics of ephemerality, instantaneity or historical disappearance; and have celebrated the diminution or dissolution of the (often conservative) promise of posterity. A further two themes – *recklessness* and *impossibility* – haunt the content and form of their performances of extremity. They are operative themes in a range of acts: from the pursuit of criminal acts without paying heed to the consequences of such actions, to the systematic disassembly of the autonomy of art or of life, to individual activities of self-injury, crisis, irrationality, unimaginable endurance, sabotage, incrimination or self-erasure. This conclusion takes two related issues – the reckless and the impossible – as the subject of its inquiry, hopefully to tease out some implications of these states of being and non-being. I do so by introducing a final case study, in relative brief, namely the work of Stephen Cripps, whose dangerous and risk-prone pyrotechnic performances and interactive sculptures were significant to the development of performance art – and the incipient cultural logic of the performance of extremity – in the 1970s, especially in his native England. I discuss his performance actions, which a contemporary reviewer described as demonstrating a 'lunatic fearlessness on the part of the artist', alongside references to a number of peers, to examine the spirit and effects of recklessness as a hidden cultural logic (Hill 1978: 55). I turn to his archive to explore his unknown 'impossible projects', namely a series of performances that remained conjectural or potential at the time of his death in 1982.

Cripps used explosions, fires, fireworks and dangerous contraptions in his performances, in part to explore the percussive potential of his materials as vectors for sound and to animate the sculptural, auto-destructive effects of his objects and activities (**Figure 6.1**). The works were volatile, unwieldy, foolhardy, dangerous and thrilling. Curator Jeni Walwyn describes them as 'at once intimate and dramatic, gentle and alarming, sonically tender and visually potent' and notes the artist's 'resistance

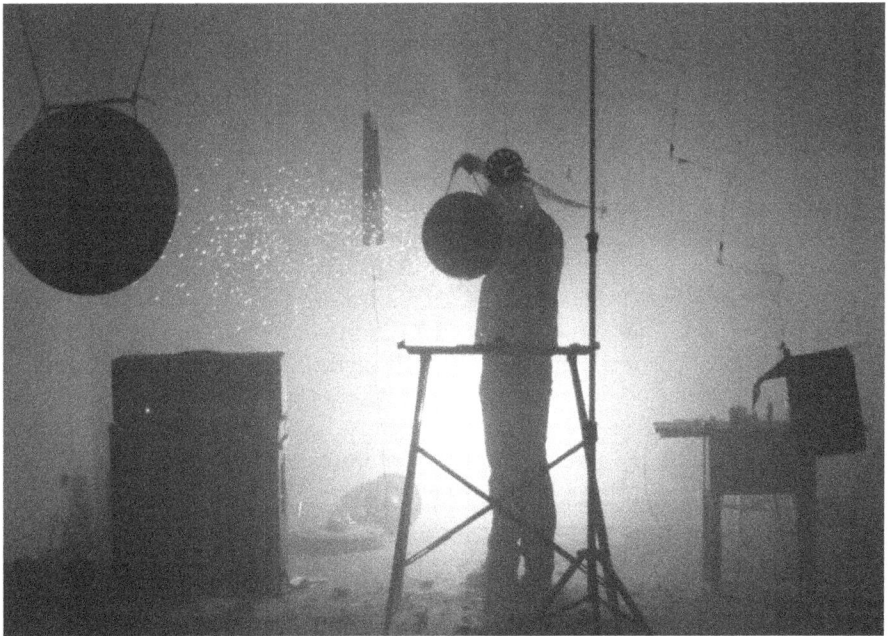

6.1 Stephen Cripps, *Cripps at the Acme: Drawings & Performances*, photograph of Stephen Cripps performing, 9–17 May 1980

to history and theory' (2013: 149). Indeed, Cripps himself notes the tension between alarm and consolation: 'There is an instinctive paranoia about explosives ... for all the dire things they can be used for', yet, he adds, '[s]ome very gentle things can come out of explosions'.[1]

In Cripps' use of fireworks in his realised works and in the explosions and uncontrollable conflagrations proposed in the 'impossible' works, the centrality of fire is profoundly suggestive. As the elemental philosopher Gaston Bachelard writes,

> A psychology of the experience of fire must devote itself to the study of the whole spectrum of human experience ... The most important lesson to be learnt from this psychology of the experience of fire is the importance of opening ourselves to a psychology of pure intensity, of the intensity of being. (1990: xii)

The 'intensity of being' is a productive phrase for the contents of this book: a paraphrase of sorts for the anomalous general ambition or affect of all the preceding case studies – and, too, for Cripps. Cripps' unfinished works of fire and disaster were suspended in their fantastical animation on account of the prematurity of his passing, as well as by the impossibly excessive – or extreme – nature of their imagining. Not least, this extremity involved insurmountable costs: in a drawing for the unrealised *Machine Carrying Hot-Air Balloon*, designed in the late 1970s, his handwritten notes explain that the aerial contraption would be powered by electricity and wind, which would prompt the movement of 'Heli-spirals – Conveyor belts, Ejectors, Percussion machines' and 'Screaming "bombs"'. In a jokey addendum, he adds, 'Wanted – One hot air balloon, generator, + £1,000,000,000.'[2]

Like other artists inhabiting this book's horizon of relevance, Cripps was influential in his day, yet is now less well remembered despite his earlier exemplarity. In *Flash Art*, art critic John Sharkey described Stephen Cripps as 'one of the most dynamic artists in Britain' (Sharkey 1980: 48); and Cripps' peer and collaborator David Toop remembers him fondly as also having 'let loose many informal, small-scale eruptions and conflagrations for the amusements of his friends and the consternation of his neighbours' (Toop 1992: 9) (**Figure 6.2**). His works spanned performance art, kinetic sculpture, painting and theatre design – he designed and built the sets for playwright Stephen Berkoff's *Agamemnon* (Greenwich Theatre, London, July 1976, with music by Paul Burwell and David Toop), for example – and his formal promiscuity resembles that of other uncontainable and relatively elusive artists of his artistic milieu, such as the deliberately incomprehensible poet Bob Cobbing, the auto-destructive sculptors Gustav Metzger, John Latham and Bruce Lacey or the conceptual artist-activists Monica Ross and Hannah O'Shea, all of whom forwent a signature style and experimented with surprising materials and practices, to such an extent that their

---

1 Stephen Cripps, untitled note, Acme Archive, Acme, London, Box: 'Cripps at the Acme and Publication No. 1', 'Stephen Cripps' file.
2 Stephen Cripps, drawing for *Machine Carrying Hot-Air Balloon*, Stephen Cripps Drawings Collection, Henry Moore Institute, Leeds, 2013.90/A/2/1/6: 'Unrealized Projects'. Cripps's papers were partly catalogued at the time of writing. Sandra Reimann prepared a Box List, and part of the collection has been individually filed and labelled. The titles and classifications of groups of drawings are Reimann's.

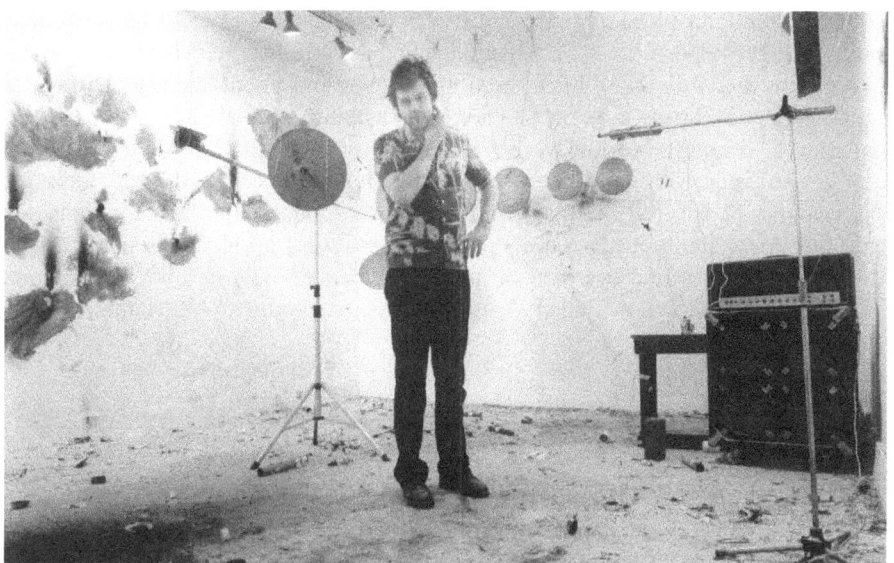

6.2 Stephen Cripps, *Cripps at the Acme: Performances*, photograph of Stephen Cripps after a performance, 1–5 June 1981

contributions are variously obscured in histories of art of the 1970s. In the specialised field of pyrotechnic performance art, Cripps's works compare to his contemporaries, Survival Research Laboratories, whose robotic pyrotechnics under Mark Pauline's designs have been terrifying in their extremity since 1979 (indeed, Pauline lost a hand to one in 1982). More recently, since 1990 the Chinese artist Cai Guo-Qiang has used gunpowder to trace the outlines of buildings and monuments and to create automatic, highly saleable paintings and drawings.

Written records from the 1970s and early 1980s demonstrate Cripps's innovative practice at the limits of performance. For example, Cripps's third and final residency at the Acme Gallery in 1981 garnered detailed commentaries, including a review by performance artist Roger Ely in *Performance Magazine*: when Cripps let off fireworks in the gallery or lit explosives behind suspended gongs, the performance was 'painful to the ear and disturbing', he writes, adding it was 'sinister' to experience 'plaster and debris from the ceiling striking my face' and to 'find your hands cringeing [*sic*] just below your earlobes', on account of the intensity of the blasts (Ely 1981: 28–9). Nevertheless, for Ely, 'Cripps is a player of the nervous system', able to manipulate his viewers into feeling like one is 'sitting out an attack – defenceless and unable to escape – waiting for the nuclear dust to settle' (1981: 29).

In *Artscribe*, critic Andrea Hill attempted a formal reading, stating that 'Cripps emphasises that his work is entirely non-associational and in no way represents a point of view about machinery or technology', perhaps displacing Ely's apocalyptic account of the way the works make meaning (Hill 1978: 55). She follows Cripps's lead by reading an exhibition and accompanying events in his *Machines and Performances* exhibition (Acme Gallery, 1978) as a *Gesamtkunstwerk*: 'it was a total experience [of] sound, vision, and physical sensation; it was unpredictable in effect and definitely on the dangerous side; and it was completely involving for the viewer'; Hill argues that Cripps therefore asks ethical and political questions about 'the degree to which an artwork can impose itself on the viewer's sensibility' and 'about the status of the gallery as a "container" for the work' (*ibid.*).

While his drawings and notes suggest unfathomably reckless adventures in the performance of extremity, Cripps did not live long enough to put his best plans into practice. These ambitious, wantonly heedless plans went up in smoke when Cripps died from an accidental overdose of prescribed methadone – in a botched attempt to kick a heroin addiction – aged 29, at his girlfriend's home in West London, on 18 June 1982.

Recklessness

Recklessness as a theme returns us to the central theme of the limits of art or performance, as explored throughout the preceding chapters. How does recklessness – an excess of action matched by a dearth of care or a deformity of volition – reiterate, complement or extend the earlier claims made for extremity by way of performance art? Recklessness is an unmarked logic of psychic, social or cultural life. For the *Oxford English Dictionary*, to be reckless is to be '[h]eedless of or indifferent to the consequences of one's actions; lacking in prudence or caution; willing or liable to take risks; rash, foolhardy; irresponsible' ('reckless, adj. and adv.' *OED Online*, March 2016). Now obscurely, to be reckless is to be unable to *reck*: a verb, 'to reck' means to devote one's care, thoughtfulness or alarm towards something or someone. The *OED* gives a wonderful example from the Jesuit poet Gerard Manley Hopkins: 'Little I reck ho! lacklevel in, if all had bread: / What!' ('reck, v.' *OED Online*, March 2016). Hopkins's poem, *Tom's Garland: Upon the Unemployed* (1887) proclaims how reckless its speaker is – specifically, in the context of his consumption with regards to the ethical fact of (the garlanded pauper Tom's) unequal rights to survival – suggesting that even in its root form, to reck is best suited to demonstrations of reck's lacklevelness, its absence or liberation from duty or (social) responsibility. Neither an affect nor an emotion, recklessness is a sensibility, then, an inverse disposition or active orientation to the world and to others.

While recklessness in those in authority (in a president, perhaps) is cause for grave concern, in the hands of artists – with little to lose in the grand scheme of things – having little to reck takes on salutary potential. For example, in the performance actions of Marcia Farquhar, a British performance artist who began making works in the 1970s, recklessness manifests in her uses of space, time and content – as well as in her resistance to documentation and posterity. A key early work of Farquhar's is known only anecdotally. In 1979, Farquhar took up a seat in a carriage on the Circle Line on the London Underground, armed with a case of fireworks and her signature ability to remember and recount stories (in recent performances she has spoken for up to 30 hours). At each of the 27 stations on the line, as the train stopped, Farquhar began a new story and released a different firework, setting up a network of impromptu relations between a memory, specific type of indoor firework (sparkler, ice fountain, black snake and so on), a specific station and a story. The performance took around 70 minutes and was witnessed by an incidental audience: by whoever happened to board the train and Farquhar's carriage at a particular station and for the duration of the number of stops they travelled for. The performance was not documented and did not have a title (if it did, the title has been lost – even to Farquhar). The performance stages an extreme commitment to the moment and disavows many of the conventions of performance by disabling the logic of a committed, sustained audience and by refusing to secure a future through the discrete terms given by a title and by documentation. If known at all to those who do not know Farquhar personally, it is by her legend. This is the case for much of Farquhar's work, which continues to be fleeting, incidental, resistant to archival impulses and incorrigible in its durations and settings.

A further performance of extremity of the 1970s, John Duncan's *Scare* (1976) stages the inflammatory nature of reckless performance as both explosive and inflammatory. A written statement by the artist (exhibited as part of the work) reads: 'Wearing a full-head mask, Duncan knocks on the front doors of two people he knows well. The moment each man answers, Duncan points a gun loaded with blanks point-blank at his face, fires once and runs.' Duncan's visual documentation consists of a single image of the artist wearing a fearsome skull mask under a black woollen cap and a metallic bomber jacket over black clothes. Provoking what must have been terrifying experiences for the two unprepared audience-participants (artists and collaborators Paul McCarthy and Tom Recchion), over two consecutive nights in Los Angeles, the artist's action is reckless in its lack of care towards its recipients, and terroristic in its shape and effects.

Duncan is known (and vilified by some) for the unmanageability and extremity of his performances in the 1970s, which culminated, infamously, in his performance *Blind Date* of 1980, in which he had himself vasectomised after ejaculating his final seed in the cadaver of a woman of colour acquired illegally in Tijuana, Mexico; presented as an audio recording of the sex act and an accompanying photograph of his genital surgery, *Blind Date* is widely condemned for its racial and sexual politics. Across such work, Karen Gonzalez Rice has sought to recuperate his work, arguing that Duncan 'displayed and critiqued American assumptions [about] masculinity', to enable him as 'prophetic witness to the dehumanizing, destructive impact of patriarchy on men, women, and children' – even if his chosen form was repugnant to his audiences (Gonzalez Rice 2016: 101). In the earlier *Scare*, he created a performance action that rendered in vivid terms the horror of masculinity, the function of male guilt and the haphazardness and hostility with which it manifests socially (problems, too, at the sordid heart of *Blind Date*).

Duncan's works of the long 1970s often appear reckless by taking the form of a trap, locking an audience into a social relation that would be frightening, seemingly inescapable, dangerous to one's person, ethically dubious and sometimes cruel – traits that sound like deficiencies, but which may suggest his work's emotional power and fascination. A student of Allan Kaprow at CalArts, Duncan's performances are an extreme example of Happenings and related forms that push art into estranged territories – in his example, gruesome, upsetting and demoralised ones – that otherwise seem alien to art's prior tactics, conventions and histories. *Scare* was prompted, Duncan writes (in the same statement exhibited as part of the work), as a 'response to meaningless attack from complete strangers' and contextualised by the social unrest and unpredictable urban violence of Los Angeles in the 1970s. As such, *Scare* appropriates the form of violent assault – an arbitrary and uncontainable burst of rage and hate – and directs it towards known (but unknowing) targets at the precipice of their hopeful safety, namely, at their own front doors.

For Gonzalez Rice, perhaps controversially, the fact of the artist's violent personal history provides a key to his work: 'Duncan's risk-taking actions coincided with his posttraumatic subjectivity', she writes, providing him with therapeutic opportunities to resolve or abolish 'the male self that continued to experience the pain of [his] childhood victimization' (2016: 114, 122). Performance scholars are frequently attracted to the fiction that a particular work may declare – or be solved by locating – the cracks and sutures in a maker's individual, subjective coherence. Yet performances neither make manifest nor require a detailed knowledge of an artist's psychobiography: the facts of the latter might provide a seductive anchor (or alibi or apologia) for explaining her or his actions, but biographical information about an artist cannot provide the 'truth' of an individual performance of extremity. Performance art will always deny or overwhelm the dream of its hermeneutic closure.

While reckless, Duncan's extremity was neither desperate nor arbitrary. He tells me: '*Scare* was effective because the participants clearly understood what had happened and why, without having to have it explained to them. Our friendships lasted for decades afterward, or still continue today' (Duncan, email correspondence with the author, 22 March 2016). Yet even though the shock may have settled into recognition to enable studied reflection by its *target* audience, such is the potential shape of even the most heinous of traumatic experiences more broadly. That is, *Scare* may echo the artist's personal experience (as Gonzales Rice is keen to confirm), but it enters more concretely into the experience of others as a traumatic event that will likely have left a new psychological mark, not as meaning but as structure: for McCarthy and Recchion, especially – and, in adulterated intensities, for us as more fully mediated recipients – the effect of *Scare* will have had an injurious significance that art (or theatre, film or literature) rarely has recourse to. For Duncan, this is fundamental to his practice: 'The driving force behind my work has always been to examine existential issues as deeply as possible, suspending social judgments that get in the way of making discoveries and accepting responsibility for the risks involved' (*ibid.*). As art, the mediation in *Scare* seems so slight – partly on account of the speed and intensity with which gunshots are performed and received – that it seems finally to prove the aspiration of performance art to immediate (or unmediated) experience. If the performance is transmuted from art into another species of event or gesture – as insult, attack, prank or crime – Duncan is suggestive about the proper form or shape he sought the action to attain: 'I found out much later from a lawyer that what I'd done in *Scare* was felony assault, but I looked at it more as a gift' (Gonzalez Rice 2016: 111).

The phenomenon of a gift that feels more like an assault (and vice versa) is redolent in all instances of the performance of extremity as narrated in this book.

In *Moffitt Building Piece* (1973) – the opening scene conjured in this book, in which blood and gore poured from under an Iowa City apartment door – Ana Mendieta strategically obscured the perpetrator and victim of an apparent trauma in the home. Duncan's contemporaneous *Scare* affords these identities a brutal clarity (even if the face of the attacker remains camouflaged). Indeed, comparing Mendieta and Duncan may be inflammatory to some: where Mendieta elegised victims of domestic and sexual violence, Duncan appropriated an act of violence in *Scare* (and monstrously in *Blind Date*) as a tactic in the creation of performance art. In *Scare*, there is little space for ineffability in the experience or reception: in their formal recklessness, Duncan's actions do not fetishise semiotic nuance or allow spectatorial disinterest.

Might *reckless artists* demand a reckless kind of history, a stunt-like mode of theory or critical thought? What would this history look like? How could thinking or writing make itself illicit, mercurial or helter-skelter? In scholarship, recklessness is an obscure, promiscuous critical term. Recklessness and its variants occur in an itinerant range of usages, for example as a term to describe personal attributes or as a diagnosis of legal, economic or political failures. In a biography, Marlon Brando is remembered for his 'reckless life': from his youthful love of pranks and 'gung-ho' personality to his precocious propensity for 'reckless self-indulgence' as an actor on set (Kanfer 2011: 22, 176). More gravely, in legal theory, recklessness is a criminal category akin to negligence and involves heedlessly endangering another's property, person or life. Capitalism is deemed reckless in economic accounts, suggesting the correlation between reckless corporate decision-making in pursuit of profit and, say, the risk of catastrophic effects, including health crises, mass death and environmental disaster. For Edmund White, art and desire are the last available territories for the reckless abandonment of moral, practical or ethical limits: the photographs of Robert Mapplethorpe, in his fetishistic embrace of black bodies, bodily appendages, penetrations and ornamentations, instruct White that 'passion, like art, is always irresponsible, useless' and 'regulated by its own impulses and nothing else' (White 1994: 84–5). The practices of art and of desiring attraction are 'the two supremely irresponsible modes of experience', White writes, enabling a practitioner (of sex and/or art) unprecedented licence in her or his treatment of the *idées reçus* of one's social environment (*ibid.*). For scholars of reckless or irresponsible practices and people, however, one's own scholarship does not quite descend into the untamed methodological wilds of recklessness.

Reckless action pre-empts or forecloses in the reckless person more studied or cerebral attitudes and practices of mind: reticence, doubt, consideration, diffidence or critical disinterestedness. One who acts recklessly – one who recks not – acts deliberately or passively without concern for the effects of one's decisions, lack of decisions, enactments and concomitant effects. As an anomalous or unmarked term, recklessness functions as the object of analysis in the preceding pages in its proximate or analogous forms: permissiveness, irresponsibility, libertinage, sabotage, potlatch, chaos or anarchy. Recklessness belongs to an obscure family of similarly incorrigible

sensibilities: irresponsibility, wildness or rowdiness, carelessness, mischief and diso-
bedience. These variations suggest a lack of control, danger and risk, social ineptitude,
a wilful refusal of laws social or seemingly natural; at times recklessness might be an
alibi for masochism, narcissism or self-destruction. Reckless people can be a liability
in life – reckless friends endanger one's safety or comfort, friendship itself, love, one's
possessions and other accoutrements of living. One can be reckless in a multitude of
directions or orientations. Perhaps you are reckless in bed, in love and hate; or in your
spending, jokes, dancing, drug taking, BASE-jumping or jaywalking. Each of your
excesses would be its own model of recklessness, the rule of your character or the
exception to its generality; your recklessness is a blemish or a trophy, to which may be
attached differing levels and styles of risk and consequence, from foible to inconvenience, to crisis, to your eventual death. Recklessness in others can be thrilling, baffling,
pitiful, annoying. Recklessness in oneself can be a hard won triumph over an intuitive
conservatism of spirit or, conversely, a drive that one might be desperate to learn to
overcome – in order, precisely, to survive oneself.

Reckless *artists* are liable towards risk or naive to its potential. They are prone to
stunts, heedless of dangers physical or psychic. Your clothes might get permanently
marked or destroyed in the presence of their performances: sometimes this may feel
like the outward presentation of your internal spattering or scarring by the artist or
by her, his or their event. Perhaps such artists are constitutionally irreverent. They
are all the more brilliant for this fearlessness, this freedom that can look maniacal,
stupid or feral. In portraits of the performance of extremity, perhaps the task of the
preceding pages has consisted of a tacit anatomy of recklessness. We see a model of
reckless subjectivity in Kerry Trengove's submission to a seemingly insurmountable
responsibility, without recourse for calling quits on its labour and duration; or in
Ulay's venturesome subjectivity, which calls forth or necessitates grand larceny (and
elsewhere, gratuitous surgery), as an urgency, an emergency of sorts for the artist,
without obvious rationale or potential for gain: 'I succeeded in doing it', he recalls,
'and that was all that mattered to me' (Johnson 2015: 22).

Recklessness emerges, too, as an ontological duty in Genesis P-Orridge's illicit
compulsion towards art without concern for prosecution; and in P-Orridge and Cosey
Fanni Tutti's courting of scandal or controversy without care for its personal consequences (which, to reiterate, were dire). Recklessness is critical, too, to the shape and
style of Anne Bean's continuum between art and life: from incidental performance
actions like risking drowning in the wake of a boat while swimming in the Thames
or thrusting her head through a plate glass window to ask a question about war; or
dropping a machete through the ceiling towards the barely protected body of Paul
Burwell (**Figure 6.3**); to the generalised recklessness of risking the very coherence of
a life when it is pushed to dis-integrity under the pressure of a total submission to art,
as a compulsion to 'transmit [consciousness] into life, quite powerfully – almost *too
powerfully*', as she describes it (Johnson 2015: 57, emphasis in original). This psychic
recklessness of de-structuring life and art extends to the ambition towards (or inability to avoid) sabotage, subterfuge and self-destruction in the wayward performances
and splintered careers of the Kipper Kids. Together they stage an exemplary, cumulative recklessness, where the shrine assembled to reckless freedom seems to require an

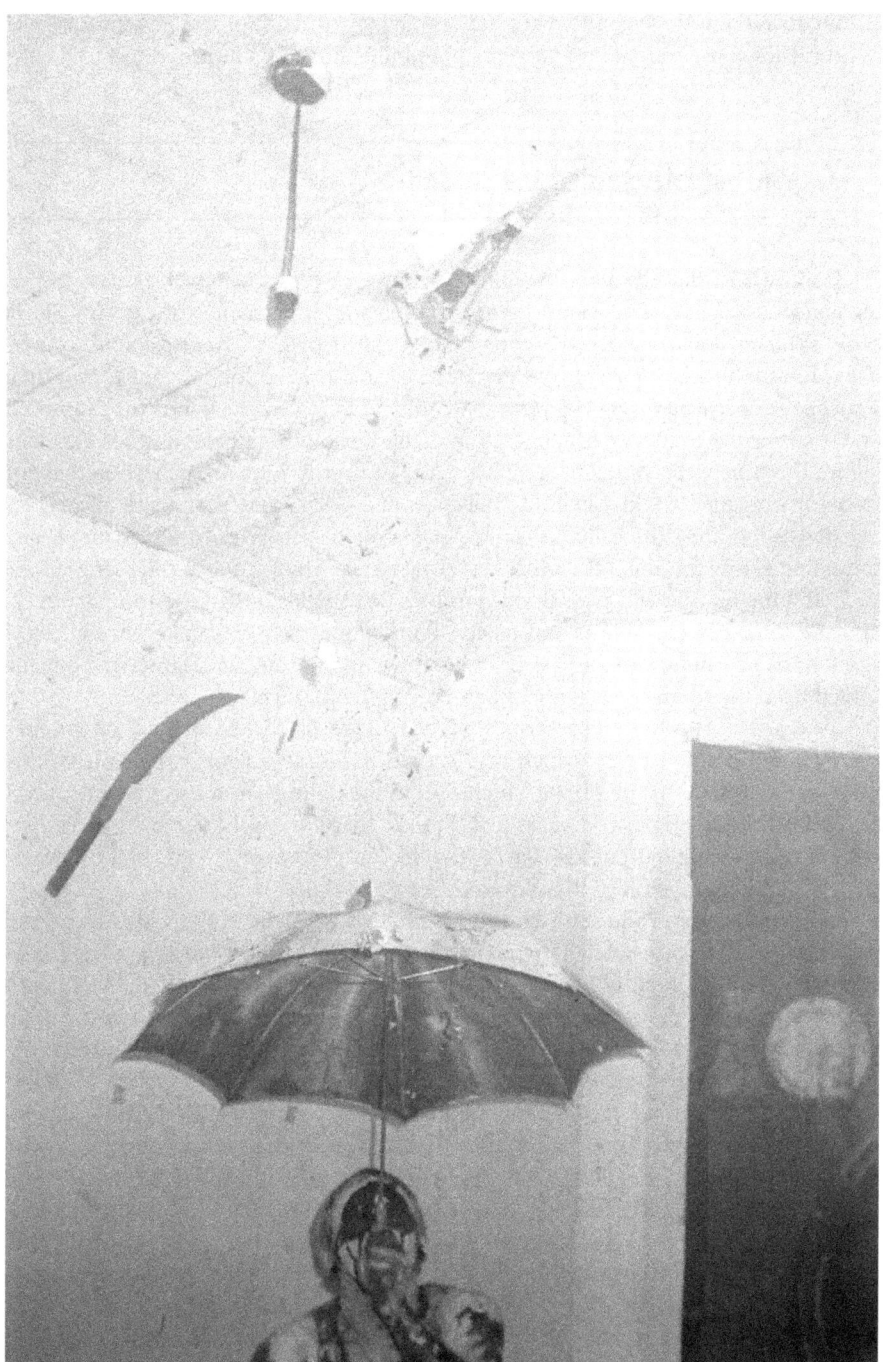

6.3 Anne Bean, Paul Burwell and Paul McCarthy, *Two Ps and a Bean* (1983), Bow, London.
Photograph by Linda Frye Burnham

all-out assault on the self and on aesthetics, leaving wreckage or wretchedness, as well as promising, obscurely, something like possibility, hope or a future.

Combustible sculpture in action

How and with what effects did Stephen Cripps seek or achieve recklessness in performance and what more might it tell us about the performance of extremity? The artist William Raban recorded a performance by Cripps in a remarkable document using 16 mm film, in the Acme Gallery, during the solo exhibition *Cripps at the Acme, Machines & Performances* (1–5 June 1981). Behind the camera stands the filmmaker and a cowering, excitedly endangered audience. The film is profound for the calm before the storm, the subsequent vivacity and excess of Cripps's orchestrated explosions of fireworks packed behind wall-mounted gongs and the visual effects that register in the film. The celluloid suffers materially as it strives to record the events unfolding before the lens – the white-out effects caused by the dense, billowing smoke, the red, blue or yellow screen-burns produced by explosions in the room's opacity and the sonic crackles, blasts and fizzles. Photographs at Acme, taken in the street, show smoke curling from the first-floor windows and the audience clustering outside, forced from the room by the unbreathable air of the performance space.

The artist Ally Raftery describes a formally similar performance, *Magnesium Flare* (Acme Gallery, 1978), which involved an immense indoors explosion, a 'large mushroom cloud of white smoke which shot to the ceiling and rolled down the walls' (1978: 14). She notes performances by Cripps in the same series that were incendiary but less life-threatening, such as *The Exploding Chocolate Cake* (1978), which 'covered the walls in a hieroglyph of disaster' and *The Burning Xerox Machine* (1978), a photocopier that 'mass-produced itself into extinction' by incinerating leaves of printed paper as quickly as it expelled them (*ibid.*). Yet at the apex of the series, the mushroom cloud of *Magnesium Flare*, a brigade of six fire engines was called, blocking off the one-way road to Shelton Street (the location of the Acme Gallery – and the site of Kerry Trengove's *Eight Day Passage* in 1977). 'This is trouble, this is', the fire chief is quoted as saying. Raftery recalls the firemen were heard 'muttering about inconvenience, public money, ventilation, explosives in public places and padlocked fire exits', before 'disappear[ing] into smoke' (*ibid.*). In a further performance, *Exploding Train Set* (aka *Werewolf Rampant Among Three Trains*) (1978), Paul Burwell and music scholar David Toop made loud and violent percussive sounds, using gongs, pipes and bells, while Cripps detonated the central carriage of a toy train with gunpowder – over-enthusiastically so – leaving himself a 'blackened smouldering figure, with blisters, singed hair, and no whiskers' (Raftery 1978: 15). Burwell concurs that the explosive powder ignited in Cripps's face, burning his skin and hair; in the course of the performance, Burwell 'scooped up some water in a shallow drum and threw it over him, to reduce the burns, and gave him some more so he could clear out his eyes', attesting to the limits to which Cripps might ordinarily go to achieve a profound effect upon his audiences, as well as to the necessary risks in his pyrotechnic approach (Burwell 1980: 29).

As evidenced in Burwell's deadpan retelling, Cripps's performances in the 1970s (like Farquhar's stealth performance in a train carriage) signal a mode of institutional performance on the cusp of health and safety or risk management, two models of an operative (and often inhibitive) approach to curating that safeguards audiences from dangerous activities – and may sometimes seem to safeguard artists from themselves. Art critic Linda Talbot notes corporeal endangerments in an exhibition by Cripps in 1977: '[s]ome children . . . had a narrow escape . . . as they dodged the machine spinning at high speeds' in their encounter with a sculpture constructed from parts of a crashed helicopter (Reimann 2017: 8). Raftery notes others still: at Acme, 'one lady's dress was drawn into the mouth of an air blower, and more often [the audience was] repulsed by blinding light, smoke and fumes. They are often forced to their knees and frequently driven out crawling after an experience close to that on the battle field or in a burning house' (Raffery, 1978: 15). The idea of a pro-grammed performance that, in Toop's account, constituted 'a violent world of sensa-tion which could, at an extreme, main or kill' is unthinkable in the present context of institutional curation, reminding us once again, perhaps, of our historical distance from the 1970s (Toop 1992: 11).

Despite the risk and mess associated with his actions, Cripps was frequently invited to present his work in museums. A photograph (by Michael Heindorff) from May 1979 shows Cripps and his collaborator Paul Burwell burning fireworks, flares and a flaming horn in the Museum of Modern Art, Oxford (**Figure 6.4**). Around the serial conflagrations and smoky emissions, we see – somewhat alarmingly – at least 16 framed paintings by Jackson Pollock, each of which must have shuddered or been besmirched by what Cripps remembered as a series of 'explosions' in the room, ferocious 'detonations' and a sonic blast caused by burning a pile of magnesium into which a microphone had been embedded (Harvey 1992: 54). Such artistic and curato-rial disregard for historical artworks – the victimised Pollocks on the walls – might seem wanton or unthinkable from a contemporary perspective. From another view, dispassion towards the safety of art, artists and audiences might disrupt the ideologi-cal necessity that art be fit for a child-safe world, which – with its precautions, restric-tions and disclaimers – has replaced the freedom to choose and the opportunity to be upset or affronted, which once might have represented a test of agency for adult consumers of culture. The inherent resistance of fire to control, inhibition or mastery is a vibrant symbol for a practice of performance (and of thought) that struggles against – or is demonstrably suppressed by – institutional practices of preventative risk management.

Yet Cripps was not entirely reckless. In an attempt to enable greater feats of pyro-technic excess (and perhaps to ensure safety in the light of the more ambitious feats he was scheming to achieve), Cripps trained as a fireman, graduating successfully from the London Fire Brigade Training Centre, Southwark, London, in August 1979 (he became part of Squad 54). Curator Rob La Frenais explains that Cripps was able to learn more fully to control the force and extent of his explosions – and also, perhaps unwittingly, broached a new strategy for performance, namely that of artists learning

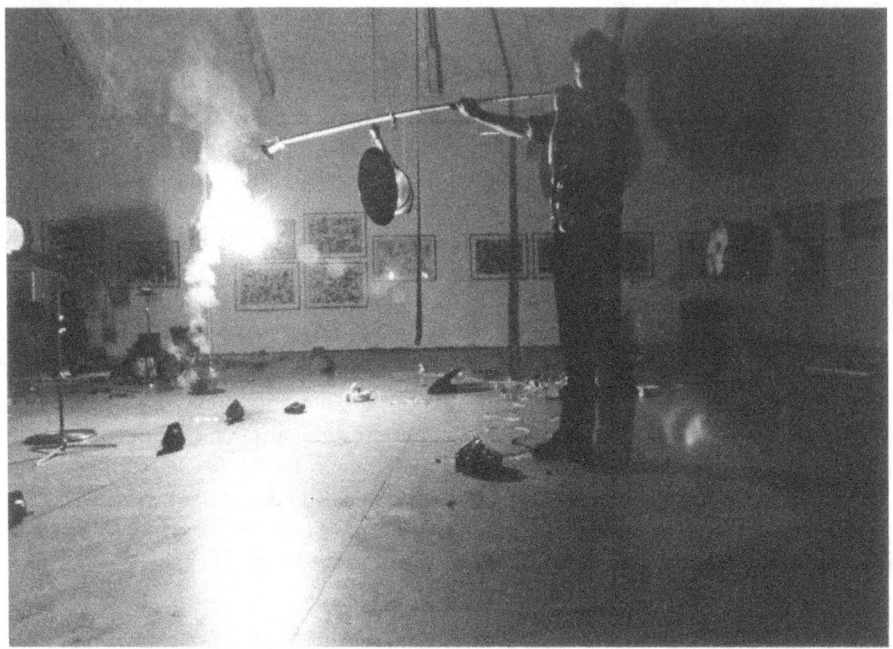

6.4 Stephen Cripps, untitled action with Paul Burwell, Museum of Modern Art Oxford, 1979

new trades, then basing the substance of their new work on that extra-artistic experience or vocation (La Frenais 1980: 15).

Impossible pyrotechnics

Cripps's performances were reckless, brilliant, coruscating exemplars of extremity. Yet his most provocative ideas – sometimes unruly beyond one's wildest measure – were those he imagined and designed but never realised. While sometimes curtailed by material conditions, Cripps's designs for unrealised works were typically irreverent in their grandiosity. Representative examples of his operatic extremity include his unrealised plans for *Portable Crematorium*, a flying funeral chamber whose mobility (and pipe organs) would be powered by heat rising from the combustion of a human corpse.[3] A further quick sketch shows the rudimentary process at work: 'Stiffs' are introduced into a machine on wheels and 'ashes' come out of the other end, accompanied by bellowing music.[4] In his friend Anne Bean's recollection, 'the gases from your

3 Stephen Cripps, drawing for *Portable Crematorium*, Stephen Cripps Drawings Collection, 2013.90/A/2/2/1: 'Unrealized Projects'.
4 Drawing for *Portable Crematorium*, Stephen Cripps Drawings Collection, 2013.90/A/2/2/3: 'Unrealized Projects'.

body would play your own death' (Wood 2017: 178). Set to involve choreographed flight paths and the release of armed bombs and missiles, *A Dance for Jets and Helicopters* was particularly closely planned (**Figure 6.5**). He would map a 'dance' for six Hawker Siddeley Harrier jump jets and eight Westland Wessex helicopters. Cripps's choreography for the 14 airborne 'principal dancers' was designed around a massive screen, curtain and runway; an extant short film by Cripps edits together footage of aircraft (filmed from a television screen) into a draft choreography. All correspondences between the control tower and aircraft would be audible to the audience over PA systems. This sound would be layered over the screaming of the jets, 'distress calls' and sonic effects designed for the 'dispersal of flocks' (of birds) in flight paths. The movements made use of the jump jet's capacity for vertical take-off and landing (a novelty in the 1970s, after the introduction of the technique in 1969); and conceived a *pas de deux* involving synchronised manoeuvres by the aircraft and the release of live 'rockets and bombs'.[5]

Many of Cripps's unrealised works are ambitious, dangerous and auto-destructive, like the subaquatic *Swimming Pool Machine: Balloon Exploder*, in which a large balloon would inflate at the bottom of a pool and burst at the point of over-extension to release a massive bubble of air that explodes up and out of the water.[6] Others are frankly macabre, like *Weighing Device: Fertility Weighing God*, a dangerous-looking 'woman and child weighing machine'; a drawing shows it uses a Ferris Wheel, Meccano motors, magnetic paint, electric kettle, 'shooting gallery' and 'Hair preener'; it also suggests what seems to be the possibility of a collaboration (a 'callibration') with the performance artist Stuart Brisley ('Bisley'). Here as elsewhere, Cripps demonstrates his tendency to recreate or intervene in familiar venues or events while imbuing them with something dangerous, weird or creepy. This found its apotheosis in the life-endangering, half-mad idea for *(Missile) Organ*. Drawn and collaged onto the salvaged sleeve of a tailor's sloper pattern, it suggests an ambitious and auto-destructive plan for a performance machine that would launch forty live ground missiles to create a massive and devastating pipe organ (**Figure 6.6**). It is perhaps Cripps's most outrageously reckless performance design.

Unlimited Action begins with a claim that no action exists beyond all limits – that is, that actions are subjected to material limitations, including legal, economic and social ones. Yet the logic of any unrealised project is both fundamentally limited (it is unfinished, artificially truncated and limited by the finitude that came too early) and at the same time remains categorically beyond all limits, for in being freed from its own future manifestation or curtailment (its inhibition, censure, ridicule, stigmatisation, exhaustion, misfire or failure), perhaps it cannot be contained. The unfinished work carries with it an emotional, even sentimental density. 'The work of the past is now in the past', Paul Burwell writes in a moving obituary for Cripps; refusing to write about his friend's past achievements, he adds, 'I can't help thinking about the events that were yet to come, and . . . the developments that would have followed. I was really

5 A drawing and untitled film collage for *Dance for Jets and Helicopters* are held in the Stephen Cripps Drawings Collection (2013.90); neither has been catalogued.
6 The three projects in this paragraph are all suggested in drawings that are presently uncatalogued.

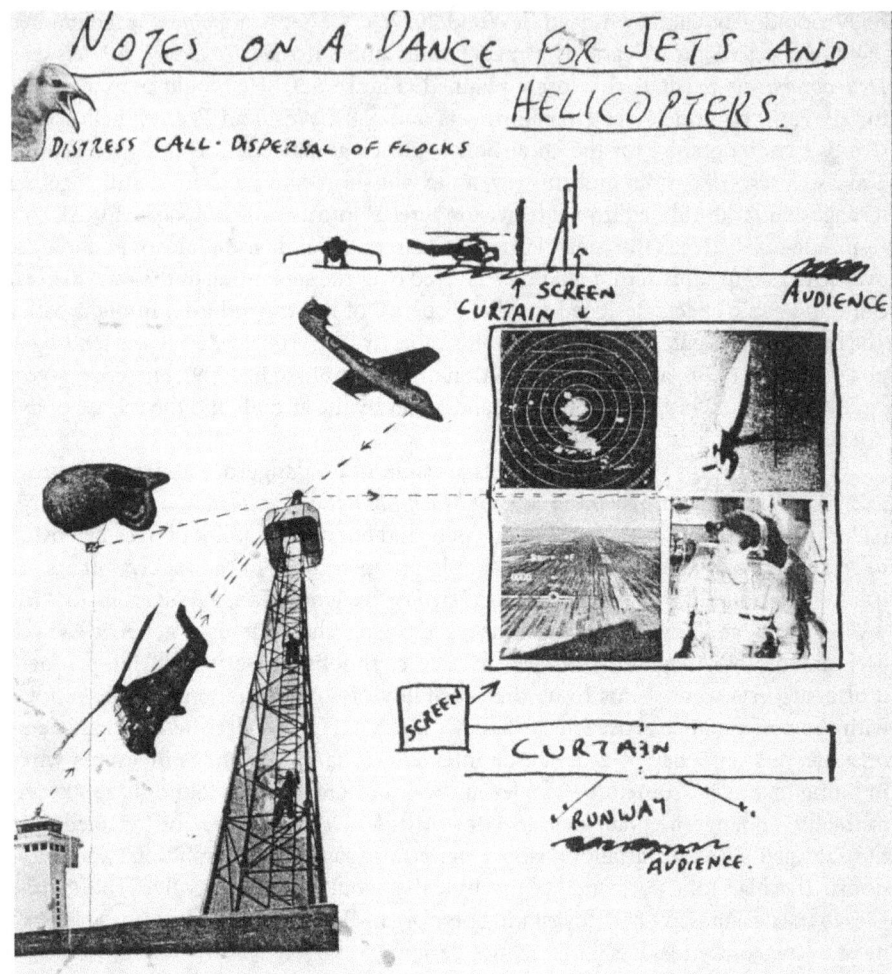

6.5 Stephen Cripps, *Notes on a Dance for Jets and Helicopters* (*c*.1978–82), ink drawing
on paper with collaged elements

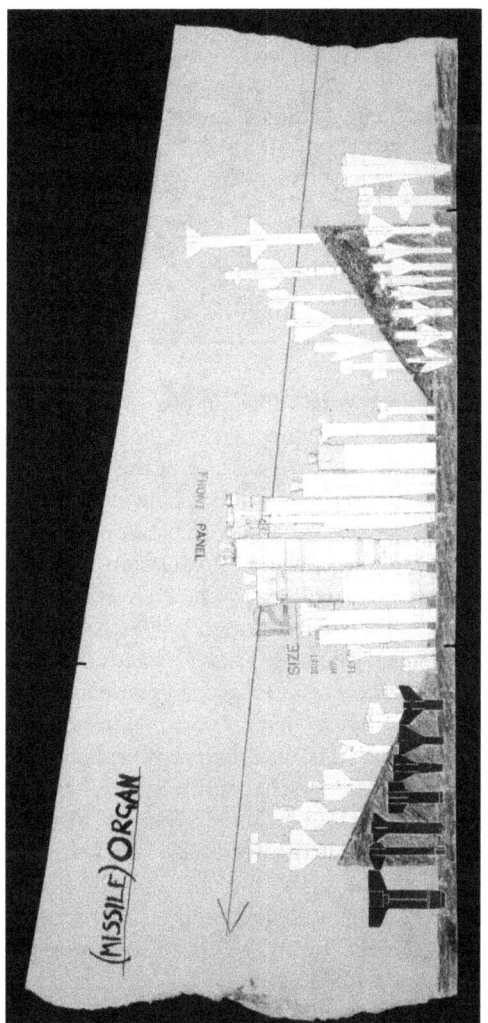

6.6 Stephen Cripps (*Missile*) *Organ* (*c.*1978–82), ink drawing with collaged elements on card

looking forward to the work of the future' (Burwell 1982: 33). Cripps's unfinished works resisted or were negated by their own impossible futures – for practicality, for lack of funds or lack of time (he died too soon). These works are potentialities, even if outlandish in design: they have become categorically impossible because he can never now enact them. Yet the unrealised works have a power unto themselves that is not denied but, rather, strangely accented by a lack of existence beyond their truncated lives in the drawings and annotations that survive the artist. That is to say, the performance of extremity lives in his designs rather that in their impossible realisation, as a potentiality that cannot be diminished. The animacy or vitality of these works resides in the way they fizz and pop as images and ideas, at the edges of possibility and as the sparks for outlandish imaginings unhindered by the terrible threat of their actual and catastrophic instigation. Cripps promises pyrotechnics not of the machine, ground or air, but of the mind. Such is the promise, in a sense, of all the performances of extremity accounted for in the preceding chapters, for none exists in the present but only may breathe in our capacity to think them, buoyed and harried as we are by the archival traces that outline these ephemeral and incorrigible actions.

A pyrotechnics of the mind

The performance of extremity is a style or genus of action that returns the most drastic of ideas, the most demanding of feelings, to the practices of performance art. The brain crackles with its intensity and the surface of the body breaks into a sweat. Of what might consist a pyrotechnics of the mind? How does it manifest itself in art or in performance and with what effects on the production and foreclosure of meaning? The author of three books on the subject of fire, Gaston Bachelard was transfixed by it as a sustaining but secret problem for psychoanalysis, philosophy and aesthetics. In posthumously published fragments, written around 1958, the philosopher of fire writes: 'Expression in inflamed discourse always exceeds thought, and to analyse it is to work out a psychology of excess . . . Images of fire are dynamic in their effect, and dynamic imagination contributes its dynamism to the psyche' (Bachelard 1990: 11). Bachelard's flame is humanising; it is 'ultra-living', yet ephemeral (Bachelard 1987: 7); it is the life force, yet a material fiction (like spirit, a flame has power, but no apparent materiality). Why fire? Why conclude with it? What can be made of its profuse sug-gestibility, its promiscuity as an element or image? Bachelard speculates in another book of fire, *The Flame of a Candle* (first published in 1961): 'Of all the objects in the world that invoke reverie, a flame calls forth images more readily than any other. It compels us to imagine; when one dreams before a flame, what is perceived is nothing compared to what is imagined' (1988: 1).

The flame, here, is that of a candle, a magnesium flare, the pilot light of a portable crematorium or the becoming-death of a missile organ. In its resistance to visual and intellectual capture, the figure of the flame is a neat metaphor for the ephemerality of performance – including that of the performance of extremity, however vivid in its lifetime or its ideation – and its resistance to full representation and total cognition. Documents of fire in performance, as with any performance, necessarily eclipse the sensory vitality of the event – its smells, sounds, sociality, climate, individual fears and collectively experienced eruptions. Neither can it be captured intellectually, for the searing physical extremity of a pyrotechnic performance, like the fullness of the flame itself that is its metonym, threatens to exceed the bounds of photography, film, memory or critical attention. What could be harder to hold on to, to document or to fix in reliquaries than the immediate and uncontainable spectacle of fire?

Art's inflammation of the senses, of ontology or of rational thought – this economy of sensory or intellectual overkill – is central to its own promise. This is particularly the case in Bachelard's philosophy: 'A poetic image only really speaks to me', he writes, 'once it has been accepted as a psychologically privileged moment of exaltation, as a *transformation of one's being through Language*' (1990: 12, emphasis in original), as epitomised in the wildness of flames. The profound excessiveness of fire – its all-consuming, devastating, consummately negating aspect, at the very limit of visibility and presence – is a feasible (if romantic) analogy for the same excesses of the performance of extremity. Fire, here, is a cipher for that which cannot be sustained, by way of a livid transformation of the senses and the subject. Bachelard continues, 'in poetic imagery there burns an excess of life, an excess of language', spurred in its burn by 'the heat of language – that great hearth of undisciplined expression in which, afire with existence, in the almost mad ambition to spark some existence beyond, something beyond existence comes into being' (1990: 13).

There is pleasure in identifying a limit, in a text or an identity or a world, if it is one that can facilitate – and ideally yield – to the creative challenges placed upon it. The limits of a text (or a work) will not be necessarily apparent to its own creators or to the casual reader. Yet all texts contain a limit – a break, gap, struggle or tension through which a text makes and forecloses meaning. Searching for such a gap produces its own satisfaction, particularly when its fault or its grain is furtive, half-covered or disavowed. A peculiarly intimate pleasure is afforded the writer by seeking out a limit in a text, as well as in oneself (do I flinch, cry, laugh or sigh?) and by embodying the scene where the limits of textual and bodily experience coincide (it is too much, I crumble – or else *I am afire with existence*). The scene of witness allows a viewer to seek out, spy-like, a rupture, a slippage or fault in the foundations of a text, upon which a whole world has been created. The intensity of bodies, the swelter of language and the spark of mad ambition are prime values, as I see it, for the performance of extremity. Its actions are reckless, impossible, incorrigible, unlimited. The limits of performance are not a check placed on art's radical potential, but a sustaining problem inside the work, a tangle of significations that enables a sensibility and inflames the production of meaning.

In elaborating a limit and engaging its threat, in performance art as in other practices of living, one does not simply overcome it. One finds oneself in the vicinity of that which is in excess: you become vulnerable to the exigencies of the power that makes it so.

REFERENCES

Published documents including online sources and clippings reproduced in archives are included below. Multiple entries by the same author are ordered by date of publication. Details of unpublished archival documents (including writings and audio-visual recordings) are provided solely in footnotes.

The abbreviation 'PR77' denotes that a clipping is reproduced without page numbers in 'Press Reviews 1976/77', part of an unpublished series titled 'Supporting Artists: Acme's First Decade, 1972–1982', Acme Gallery Archive, London.

Adderley, Suzy (1977). 'Five Days in July Performance at Acme and at AFD: Review', *Artscribe* 8 (September), 51–2.

Alonso, Carmen (2010). 'Joseph Beuys 1968–1972' in *Joseph Beuys: Parallel Processes* (Düsseldorf: Shirmer/ Mosel), pp. 190–1.

Amore, Anthony M. and Tom Mashberg (2011). *Stealing Rembrandts: The Untold Stories of Notorious Art Heists* (New York: Palgrave Macmillan).

Anawalt, K., 'Why Not L.A.' (1980). *High Performance* 11–12, 3.3–4 (Fall/Winter), 132–5.

Archer, Michael (1985). 'Over-Riding Imperatives' in *Kerry Trengove: Points of Defence* (Londonderry: Orchard Gallery). Unpaginated.

—— (1991). 'Obituaries: Kerry Trengove 1946–1991', *Art Monthly* 150 (October), 25–6.

Bachelard, Gaston (1987). *The Psychoanalysis of Fire*, trans. by Alan Ross (1964 rpt. London: Quartet).

—— (1988). *The Flame of a Candle*, trans. by Joni Caldwell (Dallas: Dallas Institute of Humanities and Culture).

—— (1990). *Fragments of a Poetics of Fire*, ed. by Suzanne Bachelard, trans. by Kenneth Haltman (Dallas: Dallas Institute of Humanities and Culture).

Bataille, Georges (1985). 'The Big Toe' in *Visions of Excess: Selected Writings, 1927–1939*, trans. by Allan Stoekl (Minneapolis: University of Minnesota Press), pp. 20–3.

—— (1986). *Erotism: Death and Sensuality*, trans. by Mary Dalwood (1964 rpt. San Francisco: City Lights Books).

Bazley, Thomas D. (2010). *Crimes of the Art World* (Santa Barbara: Praeger).

Bean, Anne (1980). 'Low Flying Aircraft', *High Performance* 11–12, 3.3–4 (Fall/Winter), 120–1.

—— (2005). Untitled statement, *Kinship International Strategy on Surveillance and Suppression*, www.kisss. org.uk/KISSS/launch.html (accessed 14 December 2015. URL no longer active).

—— (2016). 'Arc Live', *Anne Bean*, annebeanarchive.com/arc-live (accessed 28 July 2017).

Benn, Tony (1979). *Arguments for Socialism*, ed. by Chris Mullin (Harmondsworth: Penguin).

Bennett, Andy (2009). *When the Lights Went Out: Britain in the Seventies* (London: Faber & Faber).

Bennett, Jane (2010). *Vibrant Matter: A Political Ecology of Things* (Durham: Duke University Press).

Beuys, Joseph (1990). 'Interview with Willoughby Sharp' in *Energy Plan for the Western Man: Joseph Beuys in America*, ed. by Carin Kuoni (New York: Four Walls Eight Windows), pp. 77–92.

Boal, Augusto (2000). *Theatre of the Oppressed*, trans. by Charles A. and Maria-Odilia Leal McBridge and Emily Fryer (London: Pluto Press).

Bojan, Maria Rus and Alessandro Cassin (2014). *Whispers: Ulay on Ulay* (Amsterdam: Valiz Foundation).

Bourriaud, Nicolas (2002). *Relational Aesthetics*, trans. by Simon Pleasance, Fronza Woods and Mathieu Copeland (Dijon: Les presses du réel).

Bracewell, Michael (2007). *Re-Make/Re-Model: Art, Pop, Fashion and the Making of Roxy Music, 1953–1972* (London: Faber & Faber).

Brecht, Bertolt (1987). 'On the Critical Attitude', *Poems, 1913–1956*, ed. by John Willett and Ralph Mannheim with Erich Fried (New York: Routledge), pp. 308–9.

—— (2014). 'First Appendix to *Buying Brass* Theory' in *Brecht on Performance: Messingkauf and Modelbooks*, ed. by Tom Kuhn, Steve Giles and Marc Silberman (London: Bloomsbury Methuen), pp. 121–2.

Brett, Guy (2006). 'Within Living Memory' in Anne Bean, *Autobituary: Shadow Deeds* (London: Matt's Gallery), pp. 5–27.

—— (2008). 'Tissues of Thought: Performance and Some Other Works in London 1970–1985', *Third Text* 22.2 (March), 237–56.

—— (2013). *Rose Finn-Kelcey* (London: Ridinghouse).

BREYER P-ORRIDGE, Genesis (2006). 'Letters: Coum On', *Art Monthly* 295 (April), 15.

Bryan-Wilson, Julia (2014). 'Against the Body: Interpreting Ana Mendieta' in *Ana Mendieta: Traces*, ed. by Stephanie Rosenthal (London: Hayward Gallery of Art), pp. 27–37.

Burks, John (1969). 'Sun Ra', *Rolling Stone* 31 (19 April), 16–18.

Burroughs, William S. (1993). 'The Fall of Art' in *The Adding Machine: Selected Essays* (New York: Arcade), pp. 60–9.

Burton, Scott (2012). 'From Literature to Performances' in *Collected Writings on Art and Performances 1965–1975*, ed. by David Getsy (Chicago: Soberscove Press), pp. 222–4.

Burwell, Paul (1980). 'Letter to the Editor', *Performance Magazine* 7 (July–August), 28–9.

—— (1982). 'Stephen Cripps', *Performance Magazine* 18 (August–September), 33.

—— (1984). 'Whirled Burning Wire Wool Spark Wheels', *Theatrephile* 2.5 (Winter), 54–5.

Buskirk, Martha (2005). *The Contingent Object of Contemporary Art* (Cambridge and London: MIT Press).

Butcher, Peter (1982). 'The Animal Within' in *Zoos: Gilles Aillaud, Duncan Smith, John Stalin, Kerry Trengove*, ed. by John Barzdo (London: Institute of Contemporary Arts), p. 58.

Campbell, Duncan (1976). '"Dirty" Porridge', *Time Out* 318 (16–22 April), 8–9.

Carr, C. (2008). 'The Kipper Kids in Middle Age' in *On Edge: Performance at the End of the Twentieth Century*, revised edition (Middletown: Wesleyan University Press), pp. 148–53.

Christon, Lawrence (1988). 'Kipper Kids Seek a K. O. on Cinemax', *Los Angeles Times* (31 July), articles. latimes.com/1988-07-31/entertainment/ca-10775_1_kipper-kids (accessed 26 January 2015).

Cleave, Maureen (1976). 'Londoner's Diary: Art and Mr Orridge', *Evening Standard* (22 October 1976), 19.

Clothier, Peter (1980). 'The Kipper Kids: An Endless Ritual' in *Performance Anthology: Source Book for a Decade of California Performance Art*, ed. by Carl E. Loeffler with Darlene Tong (San Francisco: Contemporary Arts Press), p. 165.

Cohen, Stanley (2002). *Folk Devils and Moral Panics: The Creation of Mods and Rockers* (1972 rpt. London and New York: Routledge).

Coogan, Amanda (2015). 'Dublin and Performance Art, Twenty Years of Action, 1970–1990' in *Performance Art in Ireland: A History*, ed. by Áine Phillips (London and Bristol: Live Art Development Agency and Intellect), pp. 107–21.

Cork, Richard (1976). 'The Message in a Brick', *Evening Standard* (30 December), 11.

—— (2003). *Everything Seemed Possible: Art in the 1970s* (New Haven: Yale University Press).

Cosey Fanni Tutti (2017). *Art Sex Music* (London: Faber & Faber).

Crane, Tricia (1980). 'Pies in the Face, Person on the Cross – All as Signs of Times', *Valley News*. Reprinted in *High Performance* 11–12, 3.3–4 (Fall/Winter), 143.

Crow, Thomas (1996). *Modern Art in the Common Culture* (New Haven and London: Yale University Press).

Danto, Arthur C. (2004). 'Kalliphobia in Contemporary Art', *Art Journal* 63.2 (Summer), 25–35.

Darling, Michael (2009). 'Target Practice: Painting Under Attack 1949–78' in *Target Practice: Painting Under Attack 1949–78*, ed. by Darling (Seattle: Seattle Art Museum), pp. 14–86.

De Beauvoir, Simone (2012). 'Must We Burn Sade?' in *Political Writings*, ed. by Margaret A. Simons and Marybeth Timmerman (Urbana and Springfield: University of Illinois Press), pp. 44–101.

Derrida, Jacques (1982). *Margins of Philosophy*, trans. by Alan Bass (1974 rpt. Brighton: Harvester Press).

—— (1986). *Glas*, trans. by John P. Leavey, Jr. and Richard Rand (Lincoln: University of Nebraska).

Deves, Keith (1976). 'MP Tears Strip off the Porny Art Show', *The Sun* (19 October), 3.

Dewey, John (1934). *Art as Experience* (London: George Allen & Unwin).

Dovkants, Keith (1976). 'Sex Show Report for DPP', *Evening Standard* (22 October), 1.

Doyle, Jennifer (2013). *Hold It Against Me: Difficulty and Emotion in Contemporary Art* (Durham: Duke University Press).

—— (2016). 'Distance Relation: On Being with Adrian' in *It's All Allowed: The Performances of Adrian Howells*, ed. by Deirdre Heddon and Dominic Johnson (London and Bristol: Intellect and Live Art Development Agency), pp. 305–19.

Drohojowska, Hunter (1980). 'Art on Stage', *LA Weekly*. Reprinted in *High Performance* 11–12, 3.3–4 (Fall/Winter), 144–6.

Dumbadze, Alexander (2013). *Bas Jan Ader: Death is Elsewhere* (Chicago: University of Chicago).

Eagleton, Terry (1990). *The Ideology of the Aesthetic* (Oxford: Basil Blackwell).

Editorial (1976). 'The Sun Says: Prostituting Britain', *Sun* (21 October), 2.

—— (1977a). 'Art is . . . Bricking Yourself in a Cell', *Western Mail* (26 October). PR77.

—— (1977b). 'Bricked Up Alive for Sake of Art', *Yorkshire Post* (26 October). PR77.

—— (1977c). 'Cheers as Human Mole Surfaces', *Yorkshire Post* (2 November). PR77.

—— (1977d). 'Dig this Art . . . It's his Only Way Out', *Royal Cornwall Gazette* (27 October). PR77.

—— (1977e). 'Human Mole Surfaces', *Eastern Daily Press* (2 November). PR77.

—— (1977f). 'Kerry Comes to the Surface', *West London Observer* (10 November). PR77.

—— (1977g). 'Kerry Trengove, Passage, The Acme Gallery', *Miss London* (24 October 1977). PR77.

—— (1977h). 'Robbie Programme (Art) Transmission: 15 August 1977, 20.30–21.00 BBC1', *Art Monthly* 11 (October), 4–9.

—— (1977i). 'The Wilder Shores of Art', *Observer* (18 December). PR77.

—— (1977j). 'Tunnel is his Work of Art', *Western Morning News* (26 October). PR77.

Ely, Roger (1981). 'Stephen Cripps Acme Gallery', *Performance Magazine* 12 (July–August), 28–9.

English, Darby (2007). *How to See a Work of Art in Total Darkness* (Cambridge and London: MIT Press).

Farnell, Ross (1999). 'In Dialogue with "Posthuman" Bodies: Interview with Stelarc', *Body & Society*, 5.2–3, 129–47.

Fend, Mechthild (2009). 'Emblems of Durability: Tattoos, Preserves and Photographs', *Performance Research* 14.4, 45–52.

Fischer-Lichte, Erika (2008). *The Transformative Power of Performance*, trans. by Saskya Iris Jain (London and New York: Routledge).

Fisher, Mark (2009). *Capitalist Realism: Is There No Alternative?* (Winchester and Washington: Zero Books).

—— (2014). *Ghosts of My Life: Writings on Depression, Hauntology and Lost Futures* (Winchester and Washington: Zero Books).

Ford, Simon (1999). *The Wreckers of Civilisation: The Story of COUM Transmissions and Throbbing Gristle* (London: Black Dog).

Foster, Hal (1983). 'Postmodernism: A Preface' in *The Anti-Aesthetic: Essays on Postmodern Culture*, ed. by Foster (Port Townsend: Bay Press), pp. ix–xvi.

Foucault, Michel (1991). *Discipline and Punish: The Birth of the Prison*, trans. by Alan Sheridan (1975 rpt. London and New York: Penguin).

—— (2003). *The Archaeology of Knowledge*, trans. by A. M. Sheridan Smith (1969 rpt. London: Routledge).

Freire, Paulo (1996). *Pedagogy of the Oppressed*, trans. by Myra Bergman Ramos (1970 rpt. London: Penguin).

Gamboni, Dario (1997). *The Destruction of Art: Iconoclasm and Vandalism Since the French Revolution* (London: Reaktion).

Garrard, Rose (2010). 'Kerry Marshall Trengove: A Memoir', *Art Cornwall* (September), www.artcornwall. org/features/Kerry_Trengove_by_Rose_Garrard.htm (accessed 28 July 2017).

Genet, Jean (1969). *Funeral Rites*, trans. by Bernard Frechtman (New York: Grove Press).

Ginsberg, Allen (2001). 'Howl' in *Selected Poems 1947–1995* (London and New York: Penguin).

Goldberg, RoseLee (1979). *Performance: Live Art 1909 to the Present* (New York: Harry N. Abrams).

Gonzalez Rice, Karen (2016). *Long Suffering: American Endurance Art as Prophetic Witness* (Ann Arbor: University of Michigan Press).

Gramsci, Antonio (2012). *Selections from the Prison Notebooks*, ed. and trans. by Quintin Hoare and Geoffrey Nowell Smith (New York: International Publishers).

Green, Charles (2000). 'Doppelgangers and the Third Force: The Artistic Collaborations of Gilbert & George and Marina Abramović/Ulay', *Art Journal* 59.2 (Summer), 36–45.

Gurdjieff, G. I. (1992). *Beelzebub's Tales to his Grandson: An Objectively Impartial Criticism of the Life of Man*, trans. by Jeanne de Salzmann (1950 rpt. New York and London: Viking Arkana).

Hagen, Rosemarie and Rainer Hagen (2000). *What Great Paintings Say: Old Masters in Detail* (Cologne: Taschen).

Harman, Graham (2005). *Guerrilla Metaphysics: Phenomenology and the Carpentry of Things* (Chicago and La Salle: Open Court).

Harvey, Jonathan (1992). *Stephen Cripps: Pyrotechnic Sculptor – A Monograph* (London: Acme and the Stephen Cripps Trust).

Heathfield, Adrian (2009). *Out of Now: The Lifeworks of Tehching Hsieh* (Cambridge and London: MIT Press and Live Art Development Agency).

Held, Jr., John (1991). *Mail Art: An Annotated Bibliography* (Metuchen and London: Scarecrow Press).

Hill, Andrea (1978). 'Reviews: Stephen Cripps at Acme, Maedée Duprès at the Battersea Arts Centre, William Henderson at AIR', *Artscribe* 12, 54–5.

Hill, Charles Christopher (1979). 'Anne Bean has a Short Conversation with . . .', *High Performance* 5, 2.1 (March), 20–3.

Hobsbawm, Eric (1995). *The Age of Extremes: The Short Twentieth Century, 1914–1991* (London: Abacus).

Hunter, John E. (1983). 'Standards for the Design, Installation, Testing, and Maintenance of Interior Intrusion Detection/Alarm Systems' in *Museum, Archive, and Library Security*, ed. by Lawrence J. Fennelly (Boston: Butterworths), pp. 373–426.

Iles, Chrissie (1988). 'Taking a Line for a Walk: Interview with Ulay and Marina Abramović', *Performance Magazine* 53 (April–May), 11–19.

Indiana, Gary (2014). *A Significant Loss of Human Life* (Los Angeles: Semiotext(e)).

Jackson, Shannon (2011). *Social Works: Performing Art, Supporting Publics* (Abingdon and New York: Routledge).

Jelinek, Robert and Sašo Kalan (2016). *Ulay: Don't Read This* (Vienna: Der Konterfei).

Johnson, Dominic (2015). *The Art of Living: An Oral History of Performance Art* (Basingstoke and New York: Palgrave Macmillan).

Johnston, Jill (1984). 'Hardship Art', *Art in America* 72 (September), 176–9.

Jones, Amelia (1994). 'Dis/playing the Phallus: Male Artists Perform their Masculinities', *Art History* 17.4 (December), 546–84.

—— (1998). *Body Art/Performing the Subject* (Minneapolis: University of Minnesota Press).

—— (2010). 'Notes on a (Impossible/Eternal) Return' in *Notes on a Return*, ed. by Sophia Yadong Hao and Matthew Hearn (Sunderland: Sunderland Art Gallery), pp. 7–12.

—— (2015a). 'Individual Mythologist: Vulnerability, Generosity and Relationality in Ulay's Self-Imaging', *Stedelijk Studies* 3 (Fall), 1–16.

—— (2015b). 'Material Traces: Performativity, Artistic "Work," and New Concepts of Agency', *TDR: The Drama Review* 59.4, T228 (Winter), 18–35.

Jones, Jonathan (2013). 'The 10 Most Shocking Performance Artworks Ever', *Guardian* (11 November), www.theguardian.com/artanddesign/2013/nov/11/scrotum-top-10-shocking-performance-art (accessed 28 July 2017).

Juno, Andrea and V. Vale (1987). *Pranks!* (San Francisco: Re/Search Publications).

Kanfer, Stefan (2011). *Somebody: The Reckless Life and Remarkable Career of Marlon Brando* (New York: Faber & Faber).

Kelley, Jeff (1993). 'Introduction' in *Allan Kaprow: Essays on the Blurring of Art and Life*, ed. by Jeff Kelley (Berkeley: University of California Press).

Kent, Sarah (1977). 'Exhibitions', *Time Out* (20 October). PR77.

Knischewski, Gerd (2008). 'An Awkward Sense of Grief: German War Remembrance and the Role of the *Volksbund Deutsche Kriegsgräberfursorge*' in *The Lasting War: Society and Identity in Britain, France and Germany after 1945*, ed. by Monica Riera and Gavin Schaffer (Houndmills and New York: Palgrave Macmillan), pp. 100–19.

Krauss, Rosalind E. (2013). 'The Mind/Body Problem: Robert Morris in Series' in *Robert Morris*, ed. by Julia Bryan-Wilson (Cambridge and London: MIT Press).

Kuspit, Donald (1988). 'Chris Burden: The Feel of Power' in *Chris Burden: A Twenty-Year Survey*, ed. by Sue Henger and Peter Kosenko (Newport: Newport Harbor Museum of Art), pp. 37–43.

La Frenais, Rob (1980). 'After the Fire: Cripps Goes Back to his Ordinary Job as a Performance Artist', *Performance Magazine* 6 (April–May), 14–6.

—— (2016). 'What's in a Name? Anne Bean Interviewed', *Art Monthly* 398 (July–August), 1–5.

Lacy, Suzanne and Jennifer Flores Sternad (2012). 'Voices, Variations, and Deviations: From the LACE Archive of Southern California Performance Art' in *Live Art in LA: Performance in Southern California, 1970-1983*, ed. by Peggy Phelan (Abingdon and New York: Routledge), pp. 61–114.

Langdon Down, Grania (1980). 'Blast It! He's Creating Again', *Mercury* (23 May). Reproduced without page numbers in Stephen Cripps Drawings Collection (uncatalogued, Box 15), Henry Moore Institute.

Leary, Timothy (1973). *Starseed: Transmission from Folsom Prison* (San Francisco: Level Press).

Lee, Pamela M. (2012). *Forgetting the Art World* (Cambridge and London: MIT Press).

Lehrer-Graiwer, Sarah (2014). *Lee Lozano: Dropout Piece* (London: Afterall Books).

Levine, Cary (2013). *Pay For Your Pleasures: Mike Kelley, Paul McCarthy, Raymond Pettibon* (Chicago: University of Chicago Press).

Lingis, Alphonso (2011). *Violence and Splendor* (Evanston: Northwestern University Press).

Lippard, Lucy R. (1972). 'Catalysis: An Interview with Adrian Piper', *TDR: The Drama Review*, 16.1 (March), 76–8.

—— (1997). *Six Years: The Dematerialization of the Art Object from 1966 to 1972* (1972 rpt. Berkeley: University of California Press).

Lydiate, Henry (1978). 'Self-Expression and the Law', *Art Monthly* 13 (December–January), 37–8.

Madden, Moss (1991). 'Letter to the Editor', *Independent* (16 September), 12.

Mailer, Norman (2000). *The Fight* (1975 rpt. London: Penguin).

Mandelkau, Jamie (1977). 'Tunnelling for Art (Can You Dig it?), *NME: New Musical Express* (October). PR77.

Manning, Keith (1977). 'Artist Tunnels Out of Cell', *Morning Telegraph* (2 November). PR77.

Mather, Ian (1976). 'The Mischievous Art of Genesis P-Orridge', *Observer* (11 April 1976), 2.

McEvilley, Thomas (2005). *The Triumph of Anti-Art: Conceptual and Performance Art in the Formation of Postmodernism* (New York: Documentext/McPherson & Company).

—— (2010). *Art, Love, Friendship: Marina Abramović and Ulay – Together and Apart* (New York: Documentext/McPherson and Company).

McEwen, John (1978). 'Barbara M. Reise, 1940–1978: A Footnote', *Art Monthly* 15 (March), 2–3.

McKenna, Kristine (1980). 'Performance Art in its Infancy', *Los Angeles Times*. Reprinted in *High Performance* 11–12, 3.3–4 (Fall/Winter), 142–3.

—— (1981). 'The Kipper Kids' Ritualistic Gross-out', *Rolling Stone* 340 (2 April), 54–5.

Miles, Barry (2010). *London Calling: A Countercultural History of London Since 1945* (London: Atlantic).

Millar, Chris (1983). 'Profile: Anne Bean – A Portentous Event in Earshot of Braying Donkeys', *Performance Magazine* 20–1 (December–January), 4–8.

Milne, Seumas (2014). *The Enemy Within: The Secret War Against the Miners*, fourth edition (London and New York: Verso).

Minsky, Helen (1977a). 'Cheerio . . . I'll See You All in Eight Days', *Evening News* (25 October). PR77.

—— (1977b). 'Mole Man is Seven Feet from Freedom', *Evening News* (31 October 1977). PR77.

Mitchell, W. J. T. (2005). *What do Pictures Want? The Lives and Loves of Images* (Chicago and London: University of Chicago Press).

Molesworth, Helen (2003). 'Work Ethic' in *Work Ethic*, ed. by Molesworth, exh. cat. Baltimore Museum of Art (University Park: Pennsylvania State University Press), pp. 25–51.

Montano, Linda M. (2000). *Performance Artists Talking in the Eighties* (Berkeley: University of California Press).

Mulholland, Neil (1998). 'Why is There Only One Monopolies Commission?: British Art and its Critics in the Late 1970s', unpublished PhD thesis, University of Glasgow.

—— (2003). *The Cultural Devolution: Art in Britain in the Late Twentieth Century* (Burlington: Ashgate).

Mullen, Brendan (2003). 'Cease to Exist', *LA Weekly* (17 April), www.laweekly.com/music/cease-to-exist-2136273 (accessed 28 July 2017).

Myles, Eileen (2015). *Chelsea Girls: A Novel* (1994 rpt. New York: Ecco/HarperCollins).

Nairne, Sandy (2011). *Art Theft and the Case of the Stolen Turners* (London: Reaktion).

Naylor, Colin (1976). 'London', *Art and Artists* 11.2, 122 (May). Reproduced without page numbers in Genesis P-Orridge Papers (uncatalogued, Tate Archive, London: 'G.P.O. v G.P.-O. (Trial Documents) file'.

Naylor, Colin and Genesis P-Orridge (1977). *Contemporary Artists* (London and New York: St. James Press).

Nead, Lynda (2011). 'Stilling the Punch: Boxing, Violence and the Photographic Image', *Journal of Visual Culture* 10.3 (December), 305–23.

Nicolson, Annabel (1977). *Escaping Notice* (London: self-published). Unpaginated.

Nietzsche, Friedrich (2004). *Ecce Homo: How One Becomes What One Is*, trans. by Anthony M. Ludovici (1888 rpt. Mineola: Dover).

—— (2008). *On the Genealogy of Morals: A Polemic*, trans. by Douglas Smith (1887 rpt. Oxford: Oxford University Press).

Nixon, Mignon (2006). 'Eva Hesse: A Note on Milieu' in *Sculpture and Psychoanalysis*, ed. by Brandon Taylor (Aldershot and Burlington: Ashgate), pp. 161–76.

Norman, Geraldine (1987). *Biedermeier Painting 1815–1848: Reality Observed in Genre, Portrait and Landscape* (London: Thames & Hudson).

Nuttall, Jeff (2012). 'The Situation Regarding Performance Art, 1973', *Contemporary Theatre Review* 22.1, Live Art in the UK (March), 175–7.

O'Dell, Kathy (1998). *Contract with the Skin: Masochism, Performance Art, and the 1970s* (Minneapolis: University of Minnesota Press).

Ono, Yoko (1996). 'To the Wesleyan People (1966)' in *Theories and Documents of Contemporary Art: A Sourcebook of Artists' Writings*, ed. by Kristine Stiles and Peter Selz (Berkeley and Los Angeles: University of California Press), pp. 736–9.

Orage, A. R. (1985). *Commentaries on G. I. Gurdjieff's All and Everything: Beelzebub's Tales to his Grandson*, ed. by C. S. Nott (Aurora: Two Rivers Press).

Ouspensky, P. D. (1950). *In Search of the Miraculous: Fragments of an Unknown Teaching* (London: Routledge/Kegan Paul).

P-Orridge, Genesis (2000). 'Statement: Thee Ulterior Removal Van ov COUM (Excerpt)' in *Live in your Head: Concept and Experiment in Britain 1965–75*, ed. by Judith Nesbitt (London: Whitechapel Art Gallery), p. 65.

—— (2002a). *G.P.O. v G.P.-O.: A Chronicle of Mail Art on Trial* (1976 rpt. Toronto: Art Metropole). Unpaginated.

—— (2002b). *Painful but Fabulous: The Lives and Art of Genesis P-Orridge* (New York: Soft Skull).

P-Orridge, Genesis and Peter Christopherson (1976). 'Annihilating Reality', *Studio International* 192, 982 (July–August), 44–8.

—— (1979). 'COUM Transmissions: Annihilating Reality' in *Performance by Artists*, ed. by A. A. Bronson and Peggy Gale (Toronto: Art Metropole), pp. 65–71.

Phelan, Peggy (1993). *Unmarked: The Politics of Performance* (London: Routledge).

Phillips, Adam (2001). *Houdini's Box: On the Arts of Escape* (London: Faber & Faber).

Piotrowski, Piotr (2012). *Art and Democracy in Post-Communist Europe* (London: Reaktion).

Pollock, Griselda (2013). *After-Affects/After-Images: Trauma and Aesthetic Transformation in the Virtual Feminist Museum* (Manchester and New York: Manchester University Press).

Pooley, Leana (1977). 'Artist "Buried Alive" for 8 Days', *Evening Standard* (24 October). PR77.

Post Office Act 1953 s. 11(1): 'Prohibition on sending by post of certain articles.' The National Archives, www.legislation.gov.uk/ukpga/Eliz2/1–2/36/section/11/enacted?view=plain (accessed 28 July 2017).

Raftery, Ally (1978). 'Magnesium Flare: Cripps at the Acme', *Ramp* 2 (June), 14–15.

Rancière, Jacques (2013a). *Aisthesis: Scenes from the Aesthetic Regime of Art*, trans. by Zakir Paul (London and New York: Verso).

—— (2013b). *The Politics of Aesthetics: The Distribution of the Sensible*, trans. Gabriel Rockhill (London: Bloomsbury).

Rankine, Claudia (2015). *Citizen: An American Lyric* (London: Penguin Books).

Reich, Wilhelm (1948). *The Discovery of the Orgone*, trans. by T. P. Wolfe (New York: Orgone Institute Press).

Reimann, Sandra Beate (2017). 'Stephen Cripps' Performing Machines' in *Stephen Cripps: Performance Machines*, ed. by Reimann, exh. cat., Museum Tinguely, Basel (Vienna: Verlag für Moderne Kunst).

Ricoeur, Paul (1977). *The Rule of Metaphor: Multi-Disciplinary Studies of the Creation of Meaning in Language*, trans. by Robert Czerny with Kathleen McLaughlin and John Costello (Toronto: University of Toronto Press).

Robbe-Grillet, Alain (1970). 'A Novel that Invents Itself' in *For a New Novel: Essays on Fiction*, trans. by Richard Howard (New York: Grove Press), pp. 127–32.

Roberts, John (1980). 'Dog Ways', *Artscribe* 21 (January), 40–1.

—— (1982). 'Kerry Trengove: From Discipline to Discovery' in *Zoos: Gilles Aillaud, Duncan Smith, John Stalin, Kerry Trengove*, ed. by John Barzdo (London: Institute of Contemporary Arts), pp. 59–64.

—— (1991). 'Kerry Trengove: Obituary', *Independent* (9 September), p. 24.

—— (1992). *Kerry Trengove (1946–1991)* (London: Chisenhale Gallery). Unpaginated.

—— (2015). *Revolutionary Time and the Avant-Garde* (London and New York: Verso, 2015).

Robertson, Geoffrey (1979). *Obscenity: An Account of Censorship Laws and their Enforcement in England and Wales* (London: Weidenfeld & Nicolson)

Rosenberg, Harold (1966). 'Mobile, Theatrical, Active' in *The Anxious Object* (Chicago: University of Chicago Press), pp. 259–72.

Sanders, Jay (2013). 'Love is an Object' in Sanders with J. Hoberman, *Rituals of Rented Island: Object Theater, Loft Performance, and the New Psychodrama – Manhattan, 1970–1980*, exh. cat., Whitney Museum of American Art, New York (New Haven: Yale University Press), pp. 27–39.

Sartre, Jean-Paul (1963). *Saint Genet: Actor and Martyr*, trans. by Bernard Frechtman (London: Heinemann).

Scheer, Edward (2010). '"What if Somebody in New Zealand Wants to See it?" Performance Art's Cover Versions' in *After the Event: New Perspectives on Art History*, ed. by Charles Merewether and John Potts (Manchester and New York: Manchester University Press), pp. 218–26.

Schimmel, Paul (1998). 'Leap into the Void: Performance and the Object' in *Out of Actions: Between Performance and the Object, 1949–1979*, exh. cat., Los Angeles Museum of Contemporary Art (New York and London: Thames and Hudson), pp. 17–119.

Sereny, Gitta (1995). *Into That Darkness: From Mercy Killing to Mass Murder* (1972 rpt. London: Pimlico).

Sharkey, John (1980). 'Performance Art in Britain', *Flash Art* 94–5 (January–February), 46–9.

Shaviro, Steven (2014). *The Universe of Things: On Speculative Realism* (Minnesota: University of Minnesota Press).

Smith, Barbara T. (1980). 'Public Spirit, Performance Possibilities', *Artweek*. Reprinted in *High Performance* 11–12, 3.3–4 (Fall/Winter), 152.

Smith, Patti (2015). *M Train* (New York and Toronto: Alfred A. Knopf).

Söntgen, Beate (2016). '"I Suffer, Therefore I am": Self-Inflicted Pain as a Last Resort in Political Art' in *Ulay: Life-Sized*, ed. by Matthias Ulrich, exh. cat., Shirn Kunsthalle Frankfurt (Leipzig: Spector), pp. 115–17.

Speer, Albert (1970). *Inside the Third Reich: Memoirs* (New York: Simon & Schuster).

Stauble, Claudia (2013). *The Paintings that Revolutionized Art* (Munich: Prestel).

Steedman, Carolyn (2001). *Dust: The Archive and Cultural History* (Manchester and New York: University of Manchester Press).

Steiner, Wendy (1995). *The Scandal of Pleasure: Art in an Age of Fundamentalism* (Chicago and London: University of Chicago Press).

Stofflet, Mary (1980). 'Review: The Kipper Kids, University Art Museum, Berkeley' *Artforum* 18.6 (February), 103.

Storr, Athony (1996). *Feet of Clay: A Study of Gurus* (London: HarperCollins).

Sutherland, John (1982). *Offensive Literature: Decensorship in Britain, 1960–1982* (London: Junction Books).

Tagg, John (1987). 'Should Art Historians Know Their Place?', *New Formations* 1.1 (Spring), 95–101.

Taylor, Laurie and Paul Walton (1971). 'Industrial Sabotage: Motives and Meanings' in *Images of Deviance*, ed. by Stanley Cohen (Middlesex: Penguin), pp. 219–45.

Taussig, Michael (1993). *Mimesis and Alterity: A Particular History of the Senses* (New York and London: Routledge).

Thacker, Eugene (2011). *In the Dust of this Planet: Horror of Philosophy, Vol. 1* (Winchester and Washington: Zero Books).

Tickner, Lisa (1980). 'One for Sorrow, Two for Mirth: The Performance Work of Rose Finn-Kelcey', *Oxford Art Journal* 3.1 (April), 58–71.

Tisdall, Caroline (1977). 'Acme Gallery: Kerry Trengove', source unknown (31 October). PR77.

Tillotson, Robert G. (1977). *Museum Security* (Paris: International Council of Museums).

Toop, David (1992). 'Aftershock' in *Stephen Cripps: Pyrotechnic Sculpture*, ed. by Jonathan Harvey (London: Acme and Stephen Cripps Trust), pp. 9–20.

—— (2013). 'The Woman Seen Sweeping the Sea: Annabel Nicolson Escaping Notice', *A Sinister Resonance* (5 February), davidtoopblog.com/2013/02/05/the-woman-seen-sweeping-the-sea-annabel-nicolson-escaping-notice/ (accessed 23 May 2016).

Trengove, Kerry (1985). 'Notes from the Project' in *Kerry Trengove: Points of Defence* (Londonderry: Orchard Gallery). Unpaginated.

Turner, Alwyn (2008). *Crisis? What Crisis? Britain in the 1970s* (London: Aurum Press).

Ulay (2016). '*Korrespondenz zum Verhältnis*' in *Ulay: I Other*, ed. by Alenka Gregorič and Tevž Logar (Ljubljana: City Art Gallery), 210–11.

Wagner, Anne (2016). 'At Tate Britain', *London Review of Books* 38.4 (14 July), 20–1.

Walker, John A. (1999). *Art and Outrage: Provocation, Controversy and the Visual Arts* (London: Pluto Press).

Walwyn, Jeni (2013). 'Volatile Materials in Image Making: The Appeal of Fire and Explosives in the 20th and 21st Century, using the Work of Stephen Cripps as a Point of Articulation', *Performance Research* 18.1 (Spring), 149–57.

Ward, Frazer (2012). *No Innocent Bystanders: Performance Art and Audience* (Hanover: Dartmouth College Press).

Wescott, James (2010). *When Marina Abramović Dies: A Biography* (Cambridge and London: MIT Press).

Wesley, Brian (1976). 'Show Shocks Even a Stripper', *The Sun* (20 October), 20.

White, Edmund (1994). 'The Irresponsible Art of Robert Mapplethorpe' in *The Burning Library: Writings on Art, Politics and Sexuality 1969-1993*, ed. by David Bergman (London: Picador), pp. 82–5.

Whitehouse, Mary (1982). *A Most Dangerous Woman?* (Tring: Lion).

Wichmann, Siegfried (1985). *Spitzweg: Zeichnungen und Skizzen* (Munich: Bruckmann).

Widrich, Mechtild (2014). *Performative Monuments: The Rematerialisation of Public Art* (Manchester and New York: Manchester University Press).

Wildeblood, Peter (1957). *Against the Law* (Harmondsworth: Penguin).

Wilson, Andrew (1993). 'Art for Life's Sake', *Art Monthly* 168 (July–August), 19–22.

Wilson, Leigh (2013). *Modernism and Magic: Experiments with Spiritualism, Theosophy and the Occult* (Edinburgh: Edinburgh University Press).

Wilson, Siona (2015). *Art Labor, Sex Politics: Feminist Effects in 1970s British Art and Performance* (Minneapolis: University of Minnesota Press).

Wolff, Janet (1993). *Aesthetics and the Sociology of Art*, second edition (1983 rpt. Houndmills: Macmillan).

Wood, Catherine (2016). 'What is Performance Art Now?', *Tate Etc.* 38 (Autumn), 54–9.

Wood, Jon (2017). 'Cripps at Corsham: A Gallery Discussion' in *Stephen Cripps: Performance Machines*, ed. by Sandra Beate Reimann (Basel and Leeds: Museum Tinguely and Henry Moore Institute), pp. 175–80.

INDEX

Note: 'n.' after a page reference indicates the number of a footnote on that page.

Abramović, Marina 8, 10, 19–20, 21, 26, 64, 66, 84, 149
Acconci, Vito 8, 13, 26, 45, 128
Acme Gallery 31, 35, 39, 43, 44, 54, 58, 60–1, 169, 191, 198, 199
action (definition of) 8–10
Ader, Bas Jan 12, 21, 165
Adolf Hitler Fan Club *see* Smith, Pauline
aesthetics 5, 7–9, 11–12, 15–16, 21, 23, 26, 29, 33, 45–56, 64, 71–3, 89, 96–9, 105–6, 110, 118, 139, 145–7, 171–5
see also aisthesis; anti-aesthetic
affect 9–10, 10–11, 14, 24, 28–9, 80, 122–3, 174–5, 177–8, 183–4, 188, 190
aisthesis 73, 132–3, 145, 146–8, 151–2, 154
animals 1–3, 28, 58–60, 73
anthropocentrism 148–50
anti-aesthetic 5, 8–9, 54–5, 88–9, 97, 165–6, 177–9, 183, 186–7
appropriation 17–18, 54–6, 71–5, 86, 88, 89, 95, 99–102, 105, 107–20, 174–5
Araeen, Rasheed 45
archive 22–3, 25, 35, 60, 152–4, 165, 188
Arsem, Marilyn 55
art and life 4, 9–10, 12–13, 15, 28–9, 32–3, 46–50, 54–6, 73, 94, 96–9, 104–6, 124–6, 129–31, 134–5, 139–40, 145–6, 196

avant-garde 3, 6, 96–9, 104, 110, 120, 146, 164, 177–9

bad theory 143–4
Baker, Bobby 54
Baldessari, John 97
Bataille, Georges 15–18, 178–9, 183
Bean, Anne 124–54, 160, 165, 196, 200–1
being-partkdolgduty 142–6
see also Gurdjieff, G. I.
Berkoff, Stephen 190
Bernsteins 129, 141–2
Beuys, Joseph 26, 146, 153, 154, 174
blood 1–3, 10, 19, 20, 21, 29, 77, 84–9, 93–4, 97, 114, 133, 139–40, 147, 149, 158–9, 171, 173, 175, 178, 188
body modification 7, 21, 29, 63, 86–9, 113
Bonzo Dog Doo-Dah Band 163
Bow Gamelan Ensemble 134
boxing 155, 157–60, 173–6, 185–6, 187
Breakwell, Ian 108, 111, 172
Brecht, Bertolt 33, 60
Brener, Alexander 77
BREYER P-ORRIDGE, Genesis 90n.1, 91, 97, 105
see also P-Orridge, Genesis
Brisley, Stuart 13, 45, 55, 128, 163, 201

Buchanan, Nancy 174–5
Burden, Chris 6–8, 45–6, 97, 171
Burroughs, William S. 17, 94, 110, 135, 160, 164
Burwell, Paul 134–6, 136n.6, 151–2, 153–4, 190, 196, 198–9, 201–3

Cazazza, Monte 113
censorship 16, 90–1, 100, 107, 110
charlatanry 40, 142–3, 170–1
Christopherson, Peter (aka Sleazy) 90, 90n.2, 91n.4, 112, 116
class 50–3, 56–7, 68–70, 72, 76, 161–2, 164
cliché 45, 80, 122, 143, 173
Cobbing, Bob 190
collaboration 49–50, 54–5, 58–60, 82, 103–4, 120, 129–30, 130n.5, 140, 151, 164
comedy 163, 167, 169, 171–2, 175–6
commodification 9, 33, 46–7, 55–6, 76–7, 98–9, 179
containment 5, 47–8, 57, 73, 77, 91–2, 136–8, 162, 165–6, 179, 183–4, 187, 190–1, 194, 200–5
contingency 2–3, 10, 17, 74–5, 98, 132–3
Cosey Fanni Tutti 90, 92–4, 97, 100, 106–7, 108, 112, 115–22, 160, 196
    see also COUM Transmissions
COUM Transmissions 40–1, 90–123, 163
counterhistory 5–6, 18–19, 188
crime 6, 7, 62, 64–73, 75–7, 88–9, 92, 99–104, 106, 111–13, 115, 121–2
Cripps, Stephen 134, 135, 136n.6, 189–204
Crowley, Aleister 113, 140, 141
culture war 23, 96

danger 5–7, 9–10, 13–14, 21, 42, 48, 66–7, 128, 130, 133, 138, 156–60, 189–90, 192–6, 198–200
D'Arcangelo, Christopher 70–1, 165
Ddart Performance Group 40, 41, 95
Death Factory 92, 100, 115
De Beauvoir, Simone 90–1, 121–2
decoloniality 23, 50–1
dematerialisation 49, 56, 98–9
    see also ephemerality
De Sade, Marquis 121–2, 164
De Saint Phalle, Niki 72
Dewey, John 47–9, 97–8, 146
dialogical aesthetics 33, 43, 49–50, 53–4, 58–60, 77
Donagh, Rita 129, 139

doppelgängers 158, 166, 169, 184
drunkenness 156–7, 160–1, 162–3, 176, 182
Duchamp, Marcel 74, 102, 105, 120, 153
Duncan, John 136, 170, 193–5

Ely, Roger 135, 191
endurance 4, 6, 9, 10, 12, 31–2, 44–6, 55–6
English, Rose 45
enigma 124–8, 132–3
ephemerality 99, 132–3, 153–4
escapology 42, 72
ethics 3–4, 10, 11, 19–20, 34–5, 46–7, 54–6, 89, 98, 122, 144, 174, 192–5
excess 4–7, 12, 16, 28–9, 44–6, 55, 73, 160–1, 171, 192–6, 204–5
experience 8, 19–20, 28, 46–54, 73, 97–8, 105, 122, 135, 140, 146, 190, 193
EXPORT, VALIE 19–20, 21, 86, 149
extremity (definition of) 4–8, 10–14, 15–18, 26, 28–9

Farquhar, Marcia 192–3, 199
Finn-Kelcey, Rose 45, 74
fire 189–93, 198–200, 204–5
fireworks *see* pyrotechnics
Fluxus 146
Freire, Paulo 33, 50–4, 56–7, 60
funding 14, 40, 41, 54, 95–6, 119, 190

Garrard, Rose 34, 35
gender 23, 44–6, 52, 84, 86, 90n.1, 101, 118, 120–1, 130, 165, 169, 173–6, 193
Genet, Jean 63–4
Gilbert and George 130n.5, 169, 176
Ginsberg, Allen 142–3
Glass, Ted 102–4
Grigorescu, Ion 175
guerrilla curating 73–4, 89
Gurdjieff, G. I. 129, 141–9, 150–1
Gysin, Brion 17

Happenings 5, 9, 48, 98, 146, 194
hardship art 9, 20
Haselden, Ron 54
health and safety 199
Hsieh, Tehching 12, 20

iconicity 26, 80–1, 124–5, 128–30, 131–3, 139, 163
iconoclasm 71–5, 76, 185
imagination 16, 57
impossibility 125–6, 132–3, 154, 200–4
indecency 95–6, 99–101, 108–12, 115, 122

injury 10–11, 18–21, 73, 84–6, 89, 92–4, 147,
        188–9
    see also blood
institutionalisation of art 26, 77, 97
    see also commodification

Jones, Kim 32
journalism 26n.1, 39, 40–4, 94, 95–6, 107,
        108, 111, 118–19, 121, 170–3
    see also media wall

Kaprow, Allan 48, 146, 149, 194
Kelly, Mary 95–6
Kipper, Harry *see* Kipper Kids
Kipper Kids 113, 129–30, 142, 155–87
Klassnik, Robin 92, 99
Klein, Yves 73–4, 153

labour 9, 25, 34, 46–8, 54–8
Lacey, Bruce 107, 108, 163, 190
Latham, John 190
laughter 95, 129, 143, 184–5, 188, 205
    see also comedy
Law of Similarity 138–40
Law of Reversal 140
Leary, Timothy 143, 148
limits 5, 10–18, 28–9, 34, 53, 63, 89, 122–3,
        147
    limit-acts 12, 51, 57, 58, 60
    limit-experiences 15–16, 57, 73
    limit-situations 51
    see also excess; extremity (definition of)
Little, Ted 111, 119
Lozano, Lee 164–5
Luthi, Ürs 113

MacLennan, Alastair 13, 55
magical thinking 72, 73, 128, 130–1, 138–40,
        164
    see also occult
mail art 98–105, 106–11, 121
Manson, Charles 24, 107, 113
Mapplethorpe, Robert 195
Marioni, Tom 11–12, 21, 32
masculinity *see* gender
McCarthy, Paul 128, 136, 151–2, 175–6,
        193–4
McLean, Bruce 55, 130n.5, 149
Medalla, David 43–4, 45, 163
media wall 38, 116, 121
Mendieta, Ana 1–3, 195
metaphor 42, 50–3, 57, 76, 174, 204
Metzger, Gustav 190

Millar, Chris 129, 138, 141
Mishima, Yukio 7
modernism 5, 45, 126, 153
Montano, Linda 13, 20, 32, 157
Moody and the Menstruators 130n.5

naming 63, 72, 92, 166
narcissism 44, 150, 173–4, 196
nation 62–3, 72–83, 101–2, 138
Nauman, Bruce 26
Nazism 72, 81, 88, 113
new materialisms 28–9, 148–50
Newton, Richard 171, 172, 173
Nicolson, Annabel 132, 145
Nuttall, Jeff 163

obscenity 91, 96, 100, 108, 112
    see also indecency
occult 72, 126, 129, 141, 142–3, 146–8, 150,
        154
    see also bad theory
Oiticica, Hélio 75
Ono, Yoko 71–2, 128, 146, 149
ordeal art 9, 20–1
O'Shea, Hannah 190
Ouspensky, P. D. 129, 141, 143–4

pain 4, 7, 13–14, 19–21, 45, 57, 84–6, 98, 139,
        147, 153, 157, 194
    see also injury
Pane, Gina 20, 21, 26, 113
parliamentary questions 40, 95, 119
pathology 4, 11, 14, 41, 97, 173, 183
photography 65, 100–1, 102, 174, 188, 195,
        204
    documentation of performance 6, 35, 116,
        120–1, 124–5, 126–7, 130
    performative photography 83–9,
        116–18
Pinoncelli, Pierre 70
Piper, Adrian 11–12, 21
Poor Poet, The (painting)
    readings of 78–83
    theft of 64–70, 73–4, 83
Pope.L, William 10, 32, 52–3, 149
P-Orridge, Genesis 90–123, 135, 163
    see also COUM Transmissions
pornography 7, 94, 97–8, 100–6, 108, 110–11,
        114–22
    see also indecency
potlatch 164
poverty 16, 32, 69–70, 78–80, 82–3, 97
press coverage *see* journalism

punk 96, 135, 141–2, 162–3, 168
pyrotechnics 136n.6, 166, 189–91,
    198–200

Queen, the (representations of) 100–2,
    122

Raban, William 198
recklessness 164, 192–200
Red Army Faction 66–7
Reedy, Carlyle 164
Reise, Barbara 108, 111, 119
risk *see* danger
Rolfe, Nigel 55
Ross, Monica 139, 190
Routh, Brian *see* Kipper Kids

sabotage 115, 160–6, 173–4, 176, 179, 183–7,
    195–6
sacrilege 16
Schneemann, Carolee 10, 128, 178
sensationalism 7–8, 27, 41–2, 44, 130n.5
Shafrazi, Tony 76–7
Shinohara, Ushio 176
Shiraga, Kazuo 178
Smith, Barbara T. 136, 171, 172–3, 174–5
Smith, Jack 149
Smith, Pauline 104, 108
Spitzweg, Carl 64, 72, 77–80
    see also Poor Poet, The (painting)
sport 7, 34, 41, 47–8, 57, 160
    see also boxing
stealth performance 1–3, 6, 16, 64–71, 76–7,
    106–11, 116–21
Stelarc 20, 22
Sun Ra 152

surgery 7, 28, 86–9, 90n.1, 93, 149, 196
Survival Research Laboratories 191

'Tate Bricks' controversy 95–6, 114
tattooing 29, 86–9, 113, 149
theft 75–6
theosophy *see* Gurdjieff, G. I.
Throbbing Gristle 105, 116, 119
Toop, David 190, 198
Trengove, Kerry 30–61, 70, 121, 128, 143,
    163, 196, 198
trial 11–12, 63, 106–11
    see also crime
Tutti, Cosey Fanni *see* Cosey Fanni Tutti

Ukeles, Mierle Laderman 56
Ulay 10, 16–17, 62–89, 99, 129, 149, 163, 196

vandalism 32, 71, 75–7, 125, 162–3
    see also iconoclasm; theft
Vautier, Ben 73
Vienna Actionism 72–3, 113
violence 1, 7, 11, 13–16, 24, 70, 71–2, 76, 83,
    139–40, 147, 157–60, 168, 171–6, 182–3,
    187, 193–5, 199
    see also boxing; sabotage; vandalism
vitalism *see* new materialisms
von Haselberg, Martin *see* Kipper Kids

war 13, 20, 24, 34, 76–7, 81–2, 86–8, 133,
    139–40, 147
Warhol, Andy 153
Went, Johanna 171, 173, 174
Whitehouse, Mary 108
Wilke, Hannah 149
working *see* labour

EU authorised representative for GPSR:
Easy Access System Europe, Mustamäe tee 50,
10621 Tallinn, Estonia
gpsr.requests@easproject.com